The Pictorial World of the Child

In this lavishly illustrated book, Maureen Cox gives a comprehensive and scholarly account of children's understanding and appreciation of art and their developing ability to produce their own pictures. She discusses the main influences on children's picture-making, including the popular media, adults' examples and other children's pictures, as well as children's own inventiveness and level of cognitive development. She considers the intriguing question, does children's art follow the same pattern of development as the history of art? Although much of the book traces the artistic development of typically developing children, it also includes a discussion of children with intellectual disabilities as well as those with a talent for art, some of whom are children with autism. We tend to think of pictures as a strictly visual medium, but the section on blind children's ability to recognise pictures challenges this assumption. Maureen Cox evaluates the way that various professional groups use children's pictures – to assess their level of intellectual development, to help diagnose and overcome emotional problems, and to aid recall of past events. Finally, she concentrates on children's art in the educational context, discussing the art curricula in different countries and different educational philosophies and suggesting ways in which these different approaches could be evaluated.

MAUREEN COX is Reader in Psychology at the University of York, UK. She has published eight books, including *Visual Order: the nature and development of pictorial presentation* (edited with N. H. Freeman, Cambridge, 1985), *The Child's Point of View: the development of cognition and language* (2nd edition, 1991), *Children's Drawings* (1992) and *Teaching Young Children to Draw* (with G. Cooke and D. Griffin, 1998).

The Pictorial World of the Child

MAUREEN COX
University of York, UK

CAMBRIDGE
UNIVERSITY PRESS

CAMBRIDGE UNIVERSITY PRESS

Cambridge, New York, Melbourne, Madrid, Cape Town, Singapore, São Paulo

CAMBRIDGE UNIVERSITY PRESS

The Edinburgh Building, Cambridge CB2 2RU, UK

Published in the United States of America by Cambridge University Press, New York

www.cambridge.org
Information on this title: www.cambridge.org/9780521531986

First published 2005

Printed in the United Kingdom at the University Press, Cambridge

A catalogue record for this book is available from the British Library

ISBN-13 978-0-521-82500-9 hardback
ISBN-10 0-521-82500-8 hardback
ISBN-13 978-0-521-53198-6 paperback
ISBN-10 0-521-53198-5 paperback

To Tony

Contents

Plates

Figures

Every effort has been made to contact copyright holders for their permission to reprint the figures in this book. The publishers would be grateful to hear from any copyright holder who is not here acknowledged and will undertake to rectify any errors or omissions in future editions of this book.

Tables

Acknowledgements

I would like to thank friends, colleagues and publishers who have given me permission to reprint pictures and figures already published elsewhere. I am grateful to various libraries, archives, museums and galleries for their permission to reproduce works of art and for supplying photographs or electronic copies for this purpose. I also thank my undergraduate and postgraduate students for the use of the drawings they have collected. Finally, but by no means least, I thank my partner, Tony Wootton, for his support during the writing of this book, our useful discussions regarding its content, and his careful and critical reading of the manuscript.

1 Introduction

Most children start to draw or paint when they are about 2 years old, and they take great pleasure in scribbling or daubing paint on the page. By the age of 4 or 5 years they are able to produce recognisable figures (see figure 1.1) and they continue to create interesting and charming pictures for a number of years. From the age of about 10 or 11, however, children's interest and confidence in art-making often declines; although their pictures may be more detailed, they seem to lack the boldness of those completed in their earlier years. Indeed, by adulthood most of us feel that we have not mastered the ability to draw and give up altogether, perhaps believing that we must have a special aptitude or gift to be able to produce a tolerably good picture. Yet this attitude has not always been so prevalent. In the nineteenth century sketching and painting in water-colours were a part of a young lady's education and, although not all girls would have had an aptitude for them, it was thought possible that these skills could be learned. In the latter part of that century and up until the 1940s formal tuition in drawing and painting were included as part of the standard curriculum in schools. Like many other skills, picture-making is a demanding activity and does not come easily to everyone, but it can, nonetheless, be improved with tuition and practice.

Pictures are becoming increasingly important in our modern world. We see visual images all around us – as illustrations or advertisements in books, newspapers and magazines and on billboards, on the television,

Figure 1.1 The king, *by the author at the age of 4 years.*

in the cinema and on our computer screens. Written instructions or explanations often come to us accompanied by illustrations, and sometimes instructions may even be presented entirely in pictorial form. Pictures are also produced as 'art'. Usually we tend to think of art as an activity carried out by trained or amateur artists who deliberately set out to produce an artwork that will evoke some kind of response in the viewer. The communication of an idea is inherent in this process, although its interpretation may be as much on the side of the viewer as on that of the artist. Whether children are capable of engaging in the production of art is debatable. In fact, the notion of the *child artist* is relatively modern. In the eighteenth century Rousseau (1762/1964) would not have described the child in this way, even though he advocated the activity of drawing for children. By the late nineteenth century, however, reference was being made to the child as artist (e.g., Parker 1894) and the term *child art* may have been coined by Franz Cizek (see Viola 1936), who became a progressive art teacher in Vienna.

This change in the status of children's scribbles and unsophisticated drawings came about, in part, because of a change in thinking about children themselves. Instead of thinking of them as potentially wayward beings in need of correction and firm guidance, some philosophers and educators believed them to be 'innocents', untainted by culture and civilisation and closer to a natural and noble state. This attitude was particularly related to children's picture-making. Artists such as Kandinsky, Klee, Miró and Picasso have strived to capture an uncontaminated childlike purity of expression. To this day, many people continue to hold this rather romantic notion about children's artwork, even though it seems to ignore the fact that children are brought up within a social setting and cannot help but be influenced by the culture that envelops them, and this includes the visual images they see. Increasingly the boundaries of what is and is not art are being expanded. Interestingly, a *drawing* was hardly considered to be art in the earlier part of the eighteenth century, but more the *preparation* for producing a work of art, such as a finely worked painting in oils. Nowadays almost any materials and subject matter are acceptable, although not necessarily without attracting plenty of public debate and, often, derision. For some people, art may also encompass children's pictures. Although I do not agree that children's pictures are always 'art' I shall, nonetheless, use the terms *art* and *artwork* in this book in relation to both children's and adults' production of pictures.

The study of children's pictures began in the nineteenth century. One of the earliest enthusiasts was Töpffer (1848), who included two chapters on children's drawings in a posthumously published book. His ideas were taken up by Gautier (1856) and then, later in the nineteenth century, a more scientific exploration of children's pictures came in with, for example, the inclusion of drawings in Darwin's (1877) study of his son's development, the publication of Cooke's (1886) article 'Our teaching and child nature', Ricci's *L'Arte dei Bambini* (1887) and Barnes' (1893) 'A study of children's drawings'. Over the years there has been a variety of approaches to the study of children's pictures; researchers have investigated different aspects and processes and professionals have used children's pictures for different purposes. For example, in the late nineteenth century psychologists became interested in how drawings could help reveal something about their cognitive processes, such as the formation of mental representations and memory. This approach burgeoned with the 'cognitive revolution' in the 1960s and has remained an important way of studying children's pictures. Other approaches and concerns have included the aesthetic and emotional dimensions of children's artwork, and the use of their pictures as indicators of their intelligence and emotional stability. Interest has also continued in children's understanding and appreciation of pictures as well as their own ability to produce them. Not least has been the concern of art educators regarding the purposes of art and the methods of teaching it. Although some of these approaches and interests go in and out of fashion, an interest in children's pictures continues to this day, as evidenced by a steady output of books and journal articles from researchers around the world.

The continuing accumulation of research findings is testament to the enduring popularity of this area of research. However, the large number of publications necessitates selectivity in a new book and this one is no exception. As I did not intend to write an all-inclusive compendium of known research, I have been deliberately selective, giving more coverage to some topics and less to others, such as the development of children's depiction of the human figure, which has been covered extensively in previous publications (e.g., Cox 1993, 1997). I have also been selective by sometimes choosing only a limited number of research studies on any one topic or issue. Again, it seems unnecessary to make an exhaustive inventory of studies when a point can be made with just a few examples of supporting evidence. I am well aware that not all authors would have made the same choices.

As the title of the book suggests, I shall be concerned primarily with pictures rather than other forms of artwork, such as three-dimensional modelling. And, although painting will be mentioned, I shall in fact concentrate on drawing since most research studies on children's pictures actually concern their drawings. This probably reflects the fact that children engage most in the activity of drawing, mainly because paper and pencils are more readily available and are less messy than paint. Celebrated for his draughtsmanship, David Hockney (Hockney & Joyce 1999) believes in the importance of drawing. He is also well known for his opinion that the image is crucial to art and also for his promotion of figural artworks as a vital genre. In fact, most of this book will be about figural or representational pictures, as opposed to non-figural or abstract ones, since most children's artwork is figural.

I begin, in chapter 2, by addressing the following issues. What do children think counts as a picture and what does not? Do they need tuition in order to recognise the objects in pictures or is this an innate ability? Do they confuse the depicted object with the real object that it 'stands for'? How does children's understanding of the representational nature of pictures develop? Although I refer to various theories of visual perception and the perception of pictures, both in this chapter and from time to time in the rest of the book I felt that too much coverage of them could detract from my central focus, namely children's understanding and production of pictures. Consequently, I have included brief outlines of these theories in an appendix and have referred the reader to it where appropriate throughout the text.

In chapter 3 I pursue the issue of children's understanding of pictures, but with respect to their appreciation of them. What are their preferences regarding abstract or realistic pictures? Do they appreciate the emotional mood of a picture as well as its overt subject matter? Can they understand metaphorical expressions of emotion as well as literal ones? What do they understand about the intention of the artist and the role of the viewer in the interpretation of a picture? Since the pictured objects are not the same as the real ones, there is scope for misunderstanding or different interpretations of a picture (Freeman & Parsons 2001).

In chapter 4 I move on to discussing young children's first attempts at picture-making. Are their scribbles really 'purposeless pencillings', as Burt (1933, p. 319) thought? I examine the developments found within the scribbling period and consider the claim that children sometimes intend their scribbles to be representational. I also consider whether the scribbling period is actually necessary for later drawing development. Do children stumble on representational drawing by accident or are they actively involved in trying to make their pictures recognisable? Although children learn to draw more recognisable figures as they get older, their pictures may still look peculiar to adult eyes. For example, they often include objects and scenes drawn from an impossible viewpoint or from mixed perspectives. In chapter 5 I discuss the way that children select lines and shapes to 'stand for' real objects. It has been argued (e.g., by Luquet 1927/2001) that in creating their pictures children are focussing on what they know about the structure of the objects rather than on the way they happen to look from one particular viewpoint – a distinction known as intellectual versus visual realism. I review the evidence for this claim and consider the extent to which these two kinds of realism are linked to different stages in development. Finally in this chapter, I discuss the older child's desire to draw in a more visually realistic way and what factors might be influencing this change in emphasis.

It is rare for very young children to organise their figures in a systematic way on the page. Indeed, the figures are not presented as part of a scene and may not even be aligned with the edges of the page. The way that children learn to construct their pictures in a more coherent way is discussed in chapter 6. A further, important problem in picture-making is how to suggest the third, or depth, dimension, given that the picture surface has only two spatial dimensions. I discuss children's developing ability to use a number of pictorial devices for this purpose, such as occlusion, size and height on the page, and the depth lines of linear convergence perspective. As well as their ability to use pictorial depth cues, children also develop a sensitivity to aesthetic composition, although this may be overshadowed by their desire to master the representation of spatial structure. Moving on to chapter 7, I discuss children's ability to depict the expression of emotion. This includes both the literal expression of emotion (e.g., a happy face or a sad face) and also non-literal or metaphorical ways of suggesting emotional mood (e.g., bright colours and a blooming tree for happiness and dark colours and a withered tree for sadness). Does this ability occur later than the ability to *understand* the emotional mood of a picture and, in their own pictures, do children use literal means of expressing emotion earlier than they use the non-literal? Is it true that the pictures produced by very young children are highly expressive but that this quality declines as children become more concerned with visual realism?

Some authors (e.g., Luquet 1927/2001; Eng 1954; Kellogg & O'Dell 1967) have claimed to find similarities between children's pictures and those produced in prehistoric or preliterate societies. The implication is that the changes that occur in a child's artistic development parallel those in the history of art, both of which are moving towards a natural or predetermined goal – the 'ontogeny recapitulates phylogeny' argument (Haeckel 1906). Other authors (e.g., Hagen 1985) reject this view entirely even claiming that there is no development in art. In chapter 8 I discuss the beginnings of art in prehistoric times and go on to trace changes over the historical period, assessing the extent to which we can see similarities to or differences from the artistic developments taking place within the child. With regard to both the history of art and the child's artistic development, I consider whether changes can be regarded as systematic and orderly and also discuss the reasons that changes come about.

Up to this point in the book I have discussed artistic development in typically developing children. In chapter 9 I consider artistic development in those who might be regarded as special. I have included a number of different groups: children with a non-specific intellectual disability, those with Down's syndrome, talented artists, some of whom have autism, and blind children. Is the artistic development of those children who have some kind of disability the same but slower than that of typically developing children, or do these special children develop in a different way? I outline the skills that talented artists seem to share, including those with autism, and consider some biological and environmental influences that might have been responsible for their talent. The inclusion of blind children in a book about art might seem an odd choice. Surely, art is a visual medium. So, how can blind people understand pictures or even produce them themselves? In fact, with a special raised-line kit, blind people can recognise and produce pictures. Indeed, the study of blind children's use of raised-line pictures has been very important in furthering our understanding of artistic development. That it is not confined to sighted individuals raises interesting questions about what psychological processes are actually involved in art-making.

Since most research studies have been conducted not only on typically developing children but also on those living in western countries, we may have a biased view of the pattern of artistic development. In chapter 10 I review a number of cross-cultural studies and those that have tested children in various non-western cultures. Is the ability to understand and appreciate pictures universal? Do adults or children in non-pictorial cultures need tuition in order to understand pictures or is this ability innate? I describe some of the differences in the style of children's pictures around the world and speculate about the way these styles might be transmitted from one generation of children to the next. But, as well as identifying differences, I also consider what aspects of children's picture-making activity can be regarded as universal.

In chapter 11 I discuss the use of children's drawings by various groups of professionals, such as educational psychologists, clinicians and therapists. In particular, I discuss the evidence for the use of children's drawings as indicators of intelligence or emotional stability. How reliable and valid are the tests based on children's drawings? In addition, I review some of the studies that show that drawings can be useful as memory aids, particularly applicable when children are interviewed by social workers or police investigators and when their eye-witness testimony may be used in court proceedings. If drawings are useful aids to memory then they should also have a role in children's education. In chapter 12 I discuss children's art and education. First of all I outline the view that there should be freedom of expression in art and that adults should refrain from influencing what children produce, for fear of stifling their creativity. I argue that, in fact, children's art does not proceed in a vacuum and that 'outside' influences are an inevitable part of the process. I outline the kinds of art curricula devised at different times and in different countries and discuss comparative studies that have documented the differences in children's artwork associated with different educational approaches. I outline the core activities included in modern school curricula for art, including observational drawing and appreciation of adults' art, and review studies that have tried to evaluate the efficacy of particular approaches to art teaching. In chapter 13 I highlight some of the issues arising from my review of the literature on the various topics covered in this book.

Like adult artists, children produce pictures for a number of reasons – to express and communicate their ideas and feelings, to exercise control over the pictorial domain and, not least, to engage in a very pleasurable activity. It is well over a hundred years since children's pictures became the focus of research, and children's artwork continues to fascinate parents, teachers and a variety of others working with or interested in children. My aim in this book is to help further that interest and appreciation.

2 Children's understanding of the representational nature of pictures

In our modern-day culture we are surrounded by visual images. We see them on television, in the cinema and on our computer screens, in books, newspapers and magazines, on advertising boards, stamps, greetings cards and T-shirts, as information in schools and museums and as art in galleries as well as in our own homes. No other creatures apart from human beings have habitually produced or made use of pictures for communication or indeed for any other purpose (Cabe 1980; Gibson 1980) and there has probably never been a time in history when visual imagery has been so prolific and ubiquitous.

What is a picture?

It is difficult to define a picture. It can be as simple as a few marks or a wash of colour on paper or canvas; it can be a photograph or a computer-aided image; it can be a decorative pattern or a representation of real or imagined objects; it can appear to be 'flat' or have the quality of depth, even to the extent that we feel we are looking into a real three-dimensional space; it may or may not have meaning beyond its materials; it may be regarded as 'art' or may have a more functional purpose such as an illustration or a diagram. As Gibson (1979) says, 'No one seems to know what a picture *is*' (p. 270). One thing we can say, I think, is that a picture is a surface that may have been painted or marked in some way for the purpose of evoking some kind of response (in terms of sensation, thought, interpretation or emotion) from the viewer. Usually, pictures are deliberately produced although, as Deręgowski (2000) has pointed out, they can sometimes occur unintentionally – for example, when we recognise a particular object in an accidental ink blot or stain; but even accidentally produced pictures may then be *chosen* by the artist to be shown as artworks.

Very many pictures are representational in that they present the viewer with a realistic and life-like image of people and objects. In addition, the artist may be trying to capture an incident in an historical or religious story or the emotion or psychological truth in a particular situation or encounter. Different genres such as historical painting and religious painting, portraiture, still-life and landscape have different subject matter and different purposes. As with the development of landscape painting in Europe in the seventeenth century, pictures may challenge what can count as suitable subject matter.[1] They can also challenge conventional ways of depicting subjects, as when, for example, Max Ernst's *The Virgin Spanking the Christ Child before Three Witnesses* presented an unusual and perhaps shocking alternative to conventional images of the virgin and child. Others, such as Chris Ofili's *Afrodizzia*, in which elephant dung was incorporated into the picture, not only allude to an African context but also challenge our assumptions about what kinds of materials can be used in a picture.

Not all pictures are representational. Indeed, many are what we call 'abstract' and may have no further meaning than the pattern they present to us or the materials they are made of. Some artists, adopting a minimalist approach, have completely rejected the notion that a picture should represent something else or have any meaning other than itself. As Frank Stella declared about his striped and geometric paintings, there is nothing 'besides the paint and the canvas' and 'what you see is what you see' (Glaser 1968, pp. 157–8). Whether or not pictures are representational, it is not necessarily the case that the job of the artist is to convey some meaning or message that we, the viewers, must try to discover; an alternative approach to our thinking about pictures is that the meaning is 'something that is to be constructed and then imposed' by the critic or observer (Wollheim 1993, p. 134). For example, the image of *Myra* by Marcus Harvey is not shocking in itself – it is simply a portrait of a woman – but rather is transformed by our knowledge that Myra Hindley was one of the 'Moors murderers' who tortured and killed a number of children in the 1960s. The poignancy and horror we might feel is then compounded by the way the image has been constructed – from children's handprints. So, the business of making and looking at pictures is not unidirectional – one of 'giver and receiver' – but an interaction of the intention, ideas and skill of the artist *and* the level of knowledge and personal and social references that the viewer brings to the enterprise of engaging with a work of art.

What do children think a picture is?

Thomas, Nye, Rowley and Robinson (2001, study 1) gave children a variety of objects, models and pictures and asked them to point to

[1] With a few exceptions, such as a landscape by Altdorfer painted in 1532, most landscapes were included either as the backdrop to portraits or historical or religious paintings or provided a context in which events took place. Dutch painters in the seventeenth century focussed on the naturalistic landscape as a topic in its own right.

the ones that are 'just pictures'. Three- and 4-year-olds judged that real objects such as a packet of crisps or a candy-bar are not pictures. They also did not accept clay or pottery models of animals as pictures. Nonetheless, what they did regard as pictures is quite wide – colour photographs of real objects, line drawings of recognisable objects as well as nonsense objects, drawings of an abstract irregular shape, a drawing of a circle bisected by a wavy line, complex abstract forms and repeated patterns. At age 6 to 8 years children made exactly the same judgements except that a few had doubts about the patterns and were not inclined to accept them as pictures. By age 9 to 10 years there was a distinct change in children's judgements: with regard to the drawings, nearly all of them regarded the realistic drawings of objects as pictures; however, rather few accepted the abstract pictures, the patterns or the drawings of nonsense objects.

In further studies these researchers found that whereas 3- to 4-year-olds accepted script and numbers (study 2) and also plain cards (study 3) as pictures, older children rejected them. That younger children include writing in their category of a picture is not surprising, since both writing and drawing can be done with the same materials and the first letters that children produce are often those included in their drawings (Kellogg 1969). Historically, early writing systems were based on pictographs (see chapter 8) and even today writing or printed text is acceptable as a picture to (some) adults (e.g., Fiona Banner's *The Desert*, a huge picture containing a transcription, in the artist's own words, of the events of the film *Lawrence of Arabia*). The youngest of Thomas and colleagues' (2001) children accepted images on paper or card as pictures but were less likely to accept images on the surface of a block or on a mug (study 3). The findings were the same whether the children were asked to identify 'pictures' or 'drawings' (study 4).

It seems, then, that the younger child's notions of what a picture is are quite wide, although they seem to be restricted to two-dimensional surfaces. But by the ages of 9 or 10 years children have become more rigid in what they think. In particular, they seem to have adopted the criterion of visual realism as the main yardstick by which to make their judgement. Even though the pictures of nonsense objects in Thomas and colleagues' study were composed of visually realistic parts, these children still rejected them. This greater emphasis on representation and visual realism by older children has also been reported by Gardner, Winner and Kircher (1975), Freeman (1980) and Parsons (1987).

Babies' responses to objects and pictures

Pictures can engage our thoughts, imagination and emotions but they are, nonetheless, primarily visual things. So, when do we first engage with our visual world? The baby's world was once described as a 'blooming, buzzing confusion' (James 1890, p. 488) and it was considered that it would take some time for the senses to become organised. We know now that the baby's world is far from confused. Although their eyesight is not as clear as adults', newborns can still see well enough to perceive faces and other objects (Courage & Adams 1990). They prefer to look at complex rather than simple patterns and they also prefer the human face (Fantz 1963; Dayton et al. 1964). At an average of only 9 minutes old they will look more closely at a moving schematic face than at a blank head or a head with scrambled features (Goren, Sarty & Wu 1975). At only a few hours after birth they prefer to look at their mothers' faces rather than at a stranger's face (Bushnell 2001), and will do so even if the images are videotaped and presented on a computer screen (Walton, Bower & Bower 1992). Since babies have not seen faces before they were born they obviously learn to do this very rapidly indeed. It has even been claimed that newborns can learn to identify a face in eight-tenths of a second (Walton, Armstrong & Bower 1998).

There are a number of studies that demonstrate babies' ability to discriminate between a real object and its picture. For example, Fantz (1961), using non-social stimuli, found that babies from 1 to 6 months of age looked more at a sphere than at a two-dimensional circle; Pipp and Haith (1977) found that 1-month-olds looked at a recessed L-shaped stimulus more than at its two-dimensional equivalent, and Cook, Field and Griffiths (1978) showed that by the age of 12 weeks babies can discriminate a photograph of a cube from a real cube. Even younger babies – ranging from only 5 hours old to 9 days old – were tested by Slater, Rose and Morison (1984). Each baby saw a specially made black object (with either a cross-like or a circular construction) placed against a well-lit white background and also a photograph of that object, presented side by side. All the babies spent more time looking at the object itself (over 80 per cent of the looking time) rather than at the photograph. Even when they had one eye occluded (to exclude binocular cues), they still spent longer looking at the real object (69 per cent of the looking time). So, even for these very young babies, objects in a picture are not treated in exactly the same way as their real-world equivalents.

This body of research tells us that very young babies are more interested in the moving images of a face than in still images, and seem to prefer real objects to their pictures. In fact, as Butterworth (1989) has claimed, 'Perception in the baby is not pre-adapted for comprehending pictures' (p. 82). By the age of 5 months, however, babies treat a real, familiar face and a photographic slide of that face in the same way (Dirks & Gibson 1977) and perceive the similarity between a real object, such as a doll, and colour or black and white photographs of it (DeLoache, Strauss & Maynard 1979). But how will they treat a less realistic representation?

Lewis (1969) investigated babies' responses to a photograph of a face, a line drawing of a face and a line drawing of scrambled facial features. He tested babies aged 3, 6, 9 and 13 months. The youngest babies looked longest at the photograph compared with the other faces, but the 6-month-old babies looked at the drawing of the face almost as much as they looked at the photograph. Other researchers (e.g., DeLoache, Strauss & Maynard 1979) have also found that 5-month-olds perceive the similarity between photographs and line drawings of faces and that babies of 6 months can recognise familiar people from line drawings if the drawings accentuate the individual's distinctive features (Tyrrell et al. 1987).

Piaget (1954) claimed that the newborn does not perceive depth in the environment and that it is only through handling objects that the baby gradually discovers their various properties, including their three-dimensionality. As pointed out above, very young babies respond differently to real three-dimensional objects and to their pictures, so they are already perceiving some information about depth. Babies at only 2 days old are also capable of size constancy (Slater, Mattock & Brown 1990). Size constancy refers to the fact that we perceive an object as being the same size even though its projected size diminishes as it moves away from us. Babies are also capable of shape constancy, our tendency to perceive an object as remaining the same object even though its projected shape changes as it moves and as we view it from different angles. Bower (1966) reported shape constancy in 2-month-old babies and Slater and Morison (1985) have reported it in newborns. Babies seem to be using dynamic information in their perception of objects and their spatial layout in the environment (Butterworth 1989). In contrast to Piaget's view, other researchers, such as Gibson (1987) and Spelke (1991), claim that babies are 'prewired' to pick up information about objects in their spatial world at a very early age (see appendix). There are, however, some cues to depth – such as seeing depth in a picture – that do not seem to be present early on and may take a number of months to develop (Slater 1989).

In order to discover whether babies can perceive depth in pictures, Yonas, Cleaves and Pettersen (1978) used a very large photograph of a window with six panes, taken at a 45-degree angle so that the window-panes on one side appeared to be nearer to the viewer than those on the other side. At least, this is how an adult would interpret the scene. But would babies see it in the same way? The researchers placed the babies in front of the photograph (see figure 2.1) and observed whether they had a preference for reaching towards some parts of the window rather than others. The babies wore an eye patch in order to remove binocular information. At age 5 months there was no preference for any particular part of the window, but at age 7 months they reached out more to the 'nearer' side of the window than to the middle or to the 'more distant' side. By the age of 7 months, then, babies will respond spatially to the depth

Figure 2.1 *An infant seated in front of a 'perspective' photograph of a rectangular window.*

information provided in a two-dimensional image. In this particular case the image provided information about relative size of the nearer and farther parts of the window as well as linear perspective and angle perspective information.

A potential problem with this kind of study is that it depends on a baby's ability to reach. In fact, a large number of babies – especially the younger ones – had to be eliminated from this study because they did not reach at all. Reaching is itself something that improves with development (see Harris & Butterworth 2002). However, although Yonas and his colleagues acknowledge that reaching continues to improve after the age of 5 months, they maintain that it is sufficiently mature and precise at this young age to be used as a valid measure of babies' responses to depth in pictures. The reaching technique has been used to investigate a variety of other pictorial cues to depth, demonstrating that 7-month-old babies are sensitive to relative size, partial occlusion, shading and texture gradients, as well as the ability to perceive an enclosed outline drawing as a tangible surface (Yonas, Arterberry & Granrud 1987). These studies *consistently* show that at age 7 months babies perceive depth in pictures, but that at 5 months they do not. Thus, sensitivity to pictorial depth cues seems to occur somewhere between the ages of 5 and 7 months.

Do naïve observers understand pictures?

Most of us have grown up in societies in which we have experienced pictures from a very early age, probably from the day we were born. Some aspects of pictures, like those of real objects, seem to be understood very early and appear not to require special explanation or tuition. But what if one were a naïve observer – someone born into a non-pictorial culture or born into our own culture but prevented from seeing pictures? On encountering pictures for the first time, would we recognise what they depict?

For some theorists – the constructivists, for example (see appendix) – the artist and the observer must have a shared understanding of the style and techniques used in a picture, and we have to learn whatever is current in our particular culture. If this is so, then we might expect to see differences among cultures in the way that pictures are understood. Furthermore, a naïve observer would not spontaneously recognise the objects in pictures, but would have to learn to 'read' them (Goodman 1968; Wartofsky 1972). This view presumes that we need experience, if not tuition, of pictures and, presumably, of the depicted objects too, although it is unclear whether we would need to experience pictures and objects concurrently. In Gibson's ecological theory (see appendix), in contrast, since the basic process of perceiving objects in pictures requires no special skill or knowledge, then recognising the objects and their layout in a picture should not depend solely on our knowledge of the cultural conventions of picture-making and should not pose a particular problem for people in different cultures; similarly, young children should not have a problem understanding the content of pictures.

With the spread of mass communication and global travel, societies that have no experience of pictures are now very rare. In order to find out whether pictorially naïve people could recognise the objects in pictures we may have to rely on quite old and often anecdotal evidence. In fact, the early reports of adults' first encounters with pictures are very mixed. For example, Livingstone (1857), Thompson (1885), Lloyd (1904) and Fraser (1923), all travelling in Africa, related that local people seemed to be frightened and reacted as if the pictures were real. In all these cases, however, the pictures or photographs were projected onto a screen and were therefore very large. In addition, the content was sometimes dramatic (e.g., Abraham about to sacrifice his son, Isaac, with a knife) and the slide shows were held at night-time. That the viewers were frightened by these images does not necessarily mean that they thought they were real. Even though we are very familiar with lurid and dramatic imagery and know it is not real, we are still capable of being frightened by it – in still pictures, on television or at the cinema.

There are other early reports of people in non-pictorial cultures *unable* to understand the nature of pictures at all, or at least not when they first encountered them. Deręgowski, Muldrow and Muldrow (1972) found that members of a remote group in Ethiopia, who were unfamiliar with pictorial art, seemed to ignore the animal pictures on a piece of paper and, instead, sniffed the paper, tasted it and crumpled it, listening to the noise. When some aspects of a picture were then pointed out (e.g., 'Look at the horn of the ox, and there is his tail'), they came to see its resemblance to the real object. This realisation seems to be quicker and easier for younger rather than older people (Beach 1901; Kidd 1905).

The evidence on naïve adults' reactions to pictures from more recent and better-designed studies will be discussed in chapter 10. For now, suffice it to say that these studies indicate that people who have had no or very little experience with pictures are able to recognise familiar objects in pictures. It may be, however, that they need at least some minimal explanation of what a picture is in order to be able to do this. As regards their understanding of the depicted spatial arrangement of objects, it seems that naïve people will perceive depth in a picture if it has been constructed according to accurate perspective principles. Although perspective is not the only means of representation, nor necessarily the most aesthetically pleasing, it appears to be the most successful way of specifying spatial layout (Jones & Hagen 1980). When a picture diverges from this system, then there is more variation in the way it is interpreted by people in different cultural groups.

It is difficult in most modern societies to find children who have had no experience of pictures. However, a study which tried to restrict a child's access to pictures, or at least to restrict direct picture-naming experiences, was carried out by Hochberg and Brooks (1962). As far as possible this child was brought up without pictures and was never told what pictures represented or allowed to overhear pictures named or their meaning explained. The testing procedure began when the boy was 19 months of age because, by that time, he had started to seek out pictures himself. A set of pictures (including a car, a shoe, a doll, a key, etc.) was prepared and shown to the child, one at a time. A line drawing of each object was always shown before a photograph of that object.

After this initial testing the boy was given a large number of picture-books and had monitored access to still pictures, although not to moving pictures (e.g., television). Adults still did not engage in picture-naming with him, although they did engage with him in naming games involving solid objects. After one month the boy was tested again in the same way as before; some of the same drawings and photographs were used a second time, but some were new. Both this session and the previous one were audio-recorded.

The real objects, whose pictures had been presented in the testing sessions, were then presented to the boy to be named, so that two judges could experience the child's pronunciation of each item. The judges heard the recordings and were asked, independently, to decide which objects were being named. Both judges and the parents agreed on the child's correct recognition of seven out of eight line drawings presented in the first testing session and six out of ten in the second session (72 per cent success rate); there was some disagreement about the child's naming of five drawings. It should be pointed out that the authors reported a considerable amount of 'chatter' on the tapes as well as interruptions; in fact, these problems particularly affected four of the photograph trials. When these are eliminated from the analysis we find that there was unanimous agreement on twelve out of eighteen photographs (67 per cent success rate). In both line drawings and photographs, then, this child was able to name the majority of the pictures.

It is worth reiterating that the child was not brought up in an environment *completely* free of pictures; although pictures were kept to a minimum, the important point is that he was shielded as far as possible from the naming or interpretation of them. It would have been interesting to have compared his test performance with that of 'normal' children, to see if they would have performed any better. Nevertheless, Hochberg and Brooks regarded the boy's performance sufficiently highly in order to claim that at least one child is capable of recognising pictures of objects without specific training or instruction.

The evidence suggests that pictures – even simple line drawings – of familiar objects are easily recognised by children and adults who have had very little or no prior experience of pictures. They can recognise the content of a picture with perhaps only a short explanation of what a picture is, but without the need for extensive training or tuition. The ease with which naïve observers perceive what pictures depict provides evidence against the existence of separate processes of picture perception and supports the view that perceiving pictures is basically the same as, or at least as easy as, perceiving the ordinary environment (Jones & Hagen 1980). We should be cautious, however: even if we accept that the recognition of pictures is relatively easy and universal, this does not necessarily mean that the ability is innate. As Haber (1980) has pointed out, it may be that the recognition of real three-dimensional objects is learned. If the recognition of objects in pictures and the recognition of real objects share the same kind of process, then it follows that the recognition of objects in pictures may also be learned or, at least, is based on processes that were originally learned.

The dual nature of pictures

Perhaps the majority of what we call 'pictures' contain images that we recognise and, in general, we have no difficulty in 'reading' them. Yet, it is an extraordinary feat of the imagination to make something out of simple materials – such as pencil or water-based pigment on paper – which can stand for or evoke the idea of something else, such as a reclining nude, a bowl of fruit or a rainy day. Although the actual materials of a picture are usually rather mundane, we have the ability to 'see beyond them' to the object, scene, mood or emotions to which the picture refers.

If we take a close-up view of paintings such as those by van Gogh, the pattern of the brush-marks can dominate what we see. This is also the case for some of the pictures by Rembrandt or the late work of Monet, as well as Seurat's paintings, in which the figures are composed of tiny dots. The obvious way in which the paint has been applied to the canvas makes the craft of the picture more explicit. In contrast, we are less aware of the materials of the picture in the work of, say, Campin or Ingres, as the introduction of oil paint enabled painters to achieve a glossy finish free of brush-marks. The materials are even less obvious in *trompe l'œil* pictures, which are deliberately intended to fool us or at least to allow us to marvel at the artist's ability to give the impression of a real three-dimensional scene. In this case, we see the scene and not the craftsmanship; it is the fact that the craftsmanship is *not* explicit that makes the picture so compelling and so fascinating.

In general, though, we know that we are looking at a picture and, except in very special circumstances, we do not mistake the picture for the real thing and neither did the artist intend us to. Indeed, some artists have made us explicitly aware of the *dual* nature of pictures. In his *The Treachery of Images* (*Ceci n'est pas une pipe*), for example, Magritte is reminding us that although we are looking at a pipe, it is not a real pipe but only a picture of one (see figure 2.2). Whether the materials and the craftsmanship of a picture are clearly evident or not, we as adults and experienced observers of pictures accept the duality of pictures – they are objects in themselves and yet at the same time they can represent or refer to objects, sensations or emotions beyond themselves. Gregory (1970) noted that pictures 'are seen both as themselves and as some other thing' (p. 32), and Gibson (1979) also pointed out that 'a picture is both a surface in its own right and a display of information about something else' (p. 282). It is because of this dual nature that picture perception 'always requires two kinds of apprehension that go on at the same time'

Figure 2.2 *In* The Treachery of Images (Ceci n'est pas une pipe) *René Magritte reminds us that his painting is not a real pipe, only a picture of one.*

(Gibson 1979, p. 283). Michotte (1962) recommended a simple test to demonstrate that adults do not normally confuse a depicted object and a real object. One simply asks them to pick up a pictured object. They will say it cannot be done and probably also think we are insane for asking!

Do children understand the duality of pictures?

We know that adults understand the dual nature of pictures, but what do we know of children's abilities in this respect? Babies' interest in pictures and their ability to perceive the objects and depth information in them is very impressive. However, it is difficult to know whether they understand that the pictured object is a *representation* of the object or whether they think it is the *same* as the object or at least another version or type of it. The potential confusion of picture and object is an issue raised by Fagot, Martin-Malivel and Dépy (2000) in their review of research on non-human animals' ability to recognise objects in pictures. They argue that in most studies where the animals (mostly chimpanzees but also pigeons) behaved towards a picture in the same way as to the real object, we cannot discount the possibility that these creatures may simply have confused the picture and the object or at least were treating the picture as a simplified or degenerate version of the object. In other words, they may not have understood the dual nature of pictures. And this argument may also apply to young children.

Piaget (1929) had no doubt that young children do not fully understand that a picture is not the same as the object it represents and that it generally does not possess all the properties of the object it depicts. He said that children tend to confuse the 'sign' and the thing 'signified' and characterised the child below the age of about 6 or 7 years as a 'realist'. Similarly, Bühler (1930) claimed that children pass through a stage during which they treat 'pictures of objects just like the objects themselves' (p. 77), a view shared by Kennedy (1974), Haber (1979) and Gibson (1980). There are various examples in the literature of young children appearing to confuse the picture with the real object: Church (1961) reported children apparently attempting to pick up the patterns on a playpen or stains on woodwork and to stroke the pets in a picture-book, and Perner (1991) gives the example of a 16-month-old who tried to 'put on' a picture of a shoe. Children ranging in age from 9 to 24 months have been reported, by Murphy (1978), to hit the pictures and scratch at the pages as if to lift up the pictures, and Ninio and Bruner (1978) reported similar behaviour in one particular child, tested from age 8 to 18 months, as well as his attempts to look behind the pages as if seeking the back of the depicted objects. Callaghan, Rochat, MacGillivray and MacLellan (2004) also found that their infants, aged 6 to 18 months, tended to grasp at the depicted objects of toys in photographs in the same way that they did when given the real toys. However, this tendency occurred more when the photographs were held down on the table by the researcher. When the infants were allowed to explore the photographs freely they started, at about the age of 9 months, to look at the pictures rather than manually explore them. Although DeLoache and colleagues (1998) also reported that 9-month-old infants will manipulate pictures and try to pick up a pictured object, they found that this tendency faded by 19 months of age. The degree of realism may be an important factor, as it seems that less realistic pictures, such as black and white photographs and line drawings, are less likely to be manipulated than are colour photographs (Pierroutsakos & DeLoache 1997).

One explanation for this 'realist' behaviour in children is that they may simply lack *experience* with pictures and that by manipulating them they are trying to understand their nature. DeLoache and colleagues (1998) ruled out the possibility that their children could not distinguish between pictures and real objects and also reported that the children did not appear to be surprised or upset when they could not pick up a pictured object. So, rather than being confused about the picture and the real object it depicts, it may be that in touching and manipulating the pictures children are simply trying to find out more about them as objects in themselves. They know that they are *different* from real objects but they still find them puzzling and need to investigate them. Beilin and Pearlman (1991) consider that the experience of objects in the real world cannot help children learn about the properties of pictures *as objects*, and that they can obtain this information only from experience with the actual picture materials. Liben (1999) describes the child's sometimes puzzling behaviour as a 'struggle to confirm and test the boundaries between representation and referent' (p. 309).

Another possible explanation for children's apparent confusion is that they may be treating a picture as *analogous* to the real object, as if they were saying 'I know this is only a picture of a shoe but this is what you would do with it if it were a real shoe.' If they do not show surprise or distress, then it could be that they are displaying a precocious form of pretend play (Bower 2002). In a sense, a picture of a shoe *is* a pretend shoe and it would not be inappropriate to pretend to put it on. It is possible that the child who did this may even have been making a joke!

A source of confusion regarding pictures and their referents might be the *language* in which pictures are discussed. When we look at picture-books with children we do not normally ask, for example, 'Where is the *picture* of a baby?' or 'Where is the *picture* of a cat?', rather, we simply ask 'Where's the baby?' or 'Where's the cat?' We do not normally make this picture–object distinction explicit; indeed, we do not normally make it explicit for ourselves. In their investigation of the way that parents read picture-books with their children, Liben and Szechter (2000) found that parents almost never made comments about the production of the pictures themselves or their aesthetic nature. So, even though children can discriminate between pictures and the objects they depict they might, nonetheless, treat pictures as a variety of the real objects, and perhaps as a substandard version of them (Woolley & Wellman 1990; Perner 1991).

Although the language we use to discuss pictures might lead to confusion it is possible, nonetheless, that young children might use words to help them link a picture with a particular object. In Callaghan's (2000a) study children were shown a picture of an object which would 'tell them' which of a set of objects they should put in a box. Children aged 2 years 6 months were very poor at this task; 3-year-olds' performance was also poor when simple line drawings were used but better with colour paintings and perspective drawings. In a second study, the children were asked to name the object in the picture before making the picture–object match, and this verbal activity led to an improvement in their performance. Callaghan suggests that at age 2 years 6 months children may be reliant on words when processing pictures and that it is not until their third year that they develop a more independent understanding that pictures can be used to stand for particular objects in the world (see also DeLoache 1991, 1995b; DeLoache et al. 1998).

According to DeLoache and her colleagues (e.g., DeLoache & Burns 1994; DeLoache, Pierroutsakos & Troseth 1997; DeLoache et al. 1998) the young child's acquisition of the concept of 'picture' includes his or her understanding that the depicted object is two-dimensional, non-tangible and non-real; she or he also has some idea of the contexts in which pictures typically occur as well as the uses to which they can be put. When the child encounters a picture a dual mental representation supposedly occurs: a picture of object X is represented as 'picture of' as well as 'object X'. Some or all of the child's existing representations of object X will be activated just as if she or he were seeing the real object, but the 'picture of' tag tells her/him that this is not the real object but a picture of it. This means that some of the features of the real object do not apply – specifically, those relating to its three-dimensionality. In fact, the 'picture of' tag inhibits the child from physical action towards the object in the picture. Callaghan (1999) suggests that this acquisition of the picture concept stretches over three phases: until sometime in their second year children respond to a picture as if it were the object itself; towards the end of the second year they respond to the picture as an interesting object in its own right; around the middle of the third year children begin to grasp the relationship between the picture and the object it represents.[2] This picture concept is necessary for the child to develop pictorial competence, although even children well into the primary school years may continue to show some confusion between objects and their depictions.

By the age of 3 to 4 years children make few errors if asked to select an item from a mixed set of real objects and their pictures, if the context makes it clear which sort of item is required. In one study (Thomas, Nye & Robinson 1994, experiment 2) the experimenter asked children in the 'real things' condition to help her by fetching specific items for a range of jobs she had to do (e.g., jobs requiring a pencil, mug, comb, etc.). Overwhelmingly, the children brought real objects rather than pictures; on some trials they even reported that no appropriate real object was available rather than bring the picture instead. Children in the 'pictures' condition were asked to fetch items to fill in the gaps in a scrapbook story, and most brought pictures rather than the real objects.

In a further study (Thomas et al. 1994, experiment 3) the experimenter asked 3- to 4-year-olds to sort mixed sets of pictures and real objects into appropriate categories. She asked each child to name two real objects (e.g., banana, apple, plant or a biscuit), two trick objects (plastic versions

---

[2] This understanding that one thing can represent or stand for another begins to develop in most children towards the end of their second year and is evident in pretend play when, for example, they might use a banana as a telephone (Piaget 1952; Fein 1981).

of the objects) and two colour photographs of the real objects. After each item had been named correctly the child was allowed to handle it while the experimenter pointed out various properties. For example, she said: 'It's just a trick/picture. Feel it, it doesn't feel like a ___. You couldn't eat it (or grow it in the ground), could you?' In the case of the real objects, the experimenter said that the item *could* be eaten (or grown in the ground). The item was then placed in front of the child and two questions were asked: 'Does it *look* like a ___?' and 'Is it *really* a ___?' (The order of these two questions was counterbalanced across all the children.) There was no significant difference between the correct answers to trick objects and to the pictures, but both of these elicited fewer correct answers than did the real objects. The kind of error that children made was when, for example, they judged that a plastic apple or a picture of an apple both looked like an apple and really was an apple. The experiment was repeated (experiment 4), but this time real objects, colour photographs and colour drawings of the objects were compared; two forms of questioning were also used in order to compare those of the authors themselves and those of Woolley and Wellman (1990), who had previously found better perform-ance with pictures than with trick objects. In fact, although the children's performance for real items was higher than before, there were no signifi-cant differences due to the two types of pictures nor to the two types of questioning.

Beilin and Pearlman (1991) investigated the extent of children's confu-sion of certain properties of pictures (colour and black and white photo-graphs) and the real objects they depict. They asked children questions about the functions of the depicted objects (e.g., 'Can you eat this picture of an ice-cream?') and about their physical properties (e.g., 'If you touched this picture of an ice-cream would it feel cold?') as well as about the real objects. They found that 5-year-olds almost never confused the functional properties of pictures and objects although, very occasionally, they confused their physical properties. Most 3-year-olds made some errors and, like the older children, had more problems with the physical properties than with the functional ones. The researchers concluded that there is some evidence that children confuse properties of the object with properties of the picture but that, even by age 3 years, the tendency is relatively weak.

There are, however, some problems with this study. To begin with, it could be that 3-year-olds are actually more confused than the researchers found, since a quarter of their sample had already been screened out at a pretest. In fact, Beilin and Pearlman acknowledged this problem. In this kind of study there is also a potential problem regarding which particular physical features the researchers choose to target. For example, although the picture of an ice-cream might feel less cold than a real ice-cream, it is still likely to feel cold rather than hot. Thus, rather than a confused response, 'Yes' could be construed as a correct answer to the question 'If you touched this picture of an ice-cream would it feel cold?'

In summary, despite their ability to recognise objects in pictures and their ability to discriminate pictures from real objects there are still some ways in which children talk about or deal with pictures that suggest some confusion between them and their referents. Nye, Thomas and Robinson (1995) point out that such confusion may not be a unitary phenomenon and that there are a number of potential sources of confusion that might explain the kinds of errors noted above. It may be the case, as DeLoache and her colleagues have claimed, that children have not yet acquired a stable picture concept. Their manipulations of pictures may indicate a curiosity in actively trying to find out exactly what the nature of pictures is. The way we talk about pictures may be a help but it may also be a hindrance in separating the object from its depiction. Even if children do realise that the picture is not the same as the object they may, nonetheless, treat it analogously, especially if they are involved in pretend games. Indeed, much of children's normal experience with pictures probably has more to do with pretend games and relatively little to do with gathering accurate information about the pictures' referents. For example, when parents look at picture-books with their children they may encourage them to weave a story around the characters so that the activity is more concerned with fantasy than reality. If this is the case then it is not surprising that many children will be ill-prepared for research tasks that concentrate on picture–referent relationships (Nye, Thomas and Robinson 1995).

A developmental sequence in the understanding of pictorial representations

The age at which we believe that children understand a visual representation such as a picture depends to a large extent on what we mean by 'understanding'. Liben (1999) argues that simply being able to recognise an object in a picture – a cat, for example – is not enough; she prefers to credit children with true understanding only when they have acquired the ability to use pictures for new insights, a view she admits is somewhat conservative. She describes a sequence of levels, based on the body of research evidence to date, that characterises this development from early infancy through to adolescence.[3] Whereas some other researchers, such as DeLoache (1995a & b), have concentrated more on the child's developing understanding that a picture can stand for

---

[3] It should be pointed out that Liben's account is quite broad in that it relates to all sorts of 'external' representations, including three-dimensional models as well as pictures.

something in the real world, Liben also emphasises their developing understanding of the nature of the picture surface itself. This 'surface' side of the duality of pictures is given particular emphasis in her embedded model of the understanding of graphic representations.

At level 1 (*referential content*) babies recognise objects in pictures and are sensitive to pictorial depth information; they may, however, confuse the pictured object and its referent or may, at least, be exploring the difference between a picture and the real object it represents. At level 2 (*global differentiation*) young children differentiate the pictured object from its referent. However, surface features of the picture may sometimes intrude into the conceptualisation of the depicted object. For example, 4-year-olds sort toys by function more often when they are sorting the real toys than when they are sorting drawings of these same toys; furthermore, they sort line drawings by colour or size more often than by function (Melendez, Bales & Pick 1995). At this level, then, the 'stand for' relationship between the picture and its referent has not yet been fully understood.

It is not until level 3 (*representational insight*) that children understand that the pictured object can be used to stand for the real object and are able to use pictures as information about the nature and location of the real objects. DeLoache's (1989, 1995a) research shows that this insight appears at about the age of 3 years. At level 4 (*attribute differentiation*) children still have to come to understand that whereas some of the features in a picture give information about the referent others do not, and, conversely, some features of the referent are shown in the picture but some are not. Thus, even when children are able to differentiate between pictures and their referents they may still confuse their features (see, e.g., Beilin & Pearlman 1991). When they have understood that there is not a perfect match between the representation in a picture and the object itself, children then have to understand how the correspondences for picture and object work for various *kinds* of representation. This is Liben's level 5 (*correspondence mastery*). A photograph, for example, is taken from one particular viewpoint, and objects at a certain distance will be in focus whereas others will be blurred; nonetheless, it is usually fairly realistic and recognisable. A map, however, is likely to be more abstract and have less physical similarity to the referent; it may also have an aerial perspective or even mixed perspectives. At level 6 (*meta-representation*) we come to realise that different rules and conventions are used in different media (e.g., maps versus graphs) and in different cultural traditions, and also that different purposes require different kinds of representations. This last level is unlikely to be achieved until adolescence.

This developmental sequence, Liben argues, is broadly age-related but should not be thought of in terms of a series of abrupt and discrete stages. It is unlikely that age, or age alone, is responsible for the progression. As well as being related to developmental changes in general, changes in representational understanding will also be linked to an increased understanding about real objects (i.e., the referents that pictures point to) and about the actual making of pictures themselves.

Summary

We might think that we know what a picture is, but what counts as a picture can be quite diverse – a photograph, a computer-aided image, a painting, a drawing – and may be representational or 'abstract'. Young children also have a wide definition of a picture, which may include script and numbers. By the age of about 9 or 10 years, however, their ideas have become more rigid, with more emphasis on representation and visual realism. Babies begin to engage with the visual world at birth and are particularly interested in objects that are moving rather than in still images; by 5 or 6 months, though, they can recognise faces in pictures, and by 7 months they are sensitive to pictorial depth cues. It is relatively easy for naïve observers (i.e., people in non-pictorial societies or a child brought up without pictures) to understand pictures, with only a minimal amount of explanation needed; depth in pictures is easily understood by naïve observers when the picture is drawn according to accurate perspective principles.

As adults we understand the duality of pictures, that is, that they are objects in their own right as well as, often, representations of something else. Whether children understand this duality has been the topic of a considerable amount of research. It seems that young children may know the difference between a picture and the real object it represents, but their behaviour is often confusing when, for example, they try to pick up a depicted object. This behaviour may reflect an attempt to understand the nature of pictures rather than some inherent confusion between picture and referent. Nonetheless, young children do make errors when asked to use pictures to convey information and may not understand, until their third year, that a picture can stand for a specific object. In fact, they may be reliant on language as a mediating factor in their development of this ability. Even later, children may still make errors regarding which properties are shared by a real object and its pictorial representation and which are not. We can trace a sequence of development in children's understanding of pictures as representations. In the next chapter I shall investigate children's understanding and appreciation of pictures as works of art.

3 Children's appreciation of pictures

The previous chapter was mainly concerned with children's developing understanding of pictures as representations of real objects. Although this is one purpose – indeed, possibly the main purpose – of most picture-making, it is not always simply about making depicted objects look recognisable and convincing. Many artists are not primarily concerned with visual representation per se, but with conveying a certain mood or emotion, and many philosophers agree that *expression* is one of the primary functions of art (e.g., Langer 1953). To this end, artists may deliberately distort an image in order to evoke a certain mood; a famous example is *The Scream* by Edvard Munch (see figure 3.1). Others may choose to convey mood solely through the use of, for example, line and colour, abandoning any attempt at visual representation. In some cases, artists may be unconcerned with the notion that something must be 'conveyed' between them and the viewer, believing that the interpretation of the picture largely depends on what it means to the viewer. And some artists eschew any form of representation and meaning beyond the materials themselves. It seems, then, that understanding and appreciating a picture, particularly a 'work of art', can be a tricky business. Tricky it may be but, arguably, 'understanding art is especially important today because of the increasingly important role of visual materials in our society' (Freeman & Parsons 2001, p. 80). But if we as adults sometimes find it difficult, how about children? How does their thinking about and appreciation of pictures develop?

Are there stages in children's thinking about pictures?

As discussed in chapter 2, children as young as 3 and 4 years have clear views about what constitutes a picture and what does not (Thomas, Nye, Rowley & Robinson 2001): basically, any pattern, abstract form or representation on a two-dimensional surface is acceptable, whereas three-dimensional objects are not. It is not until the age of 9 to 10 years that children become much more restrictive and overwhelmingly accept only realistic representations of objects as pictures. But what about their *preferences* among these various types of pictures? McGhee and Dziuban

Figure 3.1 The Scream *by Edvard Munch.*

(1993) showed 2- to 3-year-olds pairs of paintings (one realistic and one more 'abstract') and, for each pair, the children were asked to choose the one they 'would like to take home'. In fact, the children did not have a preference for the realistic or the abstract art and their choices were stable over a five-week period. At this very young age, then, children seem to be quite open to what a picture might be, a finding that is in line with that of Thomas and colleagues (2001), but by age 4–5 they prefer realistic rather than abstract paintings (Coffey 1968).

In order to find out how children's thinking about pictures proceeds, Parsons (1987) interviewed children and adults about various works of art by, for example, Chagall, Goya and Picasso.[1] He found that the participants were at different stages in their thinking. Children between 4 and 7 years (at stage 1) tended to react idiosyncratically: for example, a child might say she liked a picture because it had a dog in it and she had a dog,

[1] Taylor (1989) criticised Parsons' study on the grounds that it was based on a narrow range of pictures, mainly selected from about 1850 onwards.

or because it was predominantly blue and her favourite colour was blue. Children in stage 2, from about 7 to 10 years, were primarily concerned with the subject matter of the picture and with how realistically it had been depicted (see also Lark-Horovitz 1937; Machotka 1966; Taunton 1980).

At stage 3, from about 10 to 14 years, the individual begins to talk about a picture in terms of its expressiveness – the emotion it conveys – and is now aware of the subjectivity of aesthetic experience. At stage 4, the abstract properties of the picture – its style, the medium, colour and so on – become the focus of attention. At the highest level, stage 5, viewers not only judge a picture within a particular artistic tradition, but now also judge the tradition itself; furthermore, they understand that art can be a way of raising questions and not merely of conveying some fact or 'truth' about the world. There is not necessarily a steady progression through the later stages, particularly stages 4 and 5; rather, the stage where people end up is influenced very much by the experiences they have had engaging with artworks: 'To be twenty years old, or forty, does not guarantee being able to understand in a stage four or five way. To do that we must have had experience with art, experience in which we have worked at understanding a variety of paintings' (Parsons 1987, p. 12).

Although Parsons provided no quantitative data for his assertions, there are other studies (e.g., Gardner, Winner & Kircher 1975; D'Onofrio & Nodin 1990) that have, and, on the whole, their findings are consistent with the general pattern of his stage model. In addition, a study by Gillison (1995) has supported Parsons' stages 1–3, although it found little evidence for the kinds of reasoning Parsons described for stages 4 and 5, even among adults. And this, of course, is not inconsistent with Parsons' claims. Thus, although younger children tend to operate according to the earlier stages of the model, it seems that experience with pictures is very important, especially as regards progression through the later stages. Child (1965), for example, found that university students' aesthetic judgements correlated positively (.49) with the amount of formal art education and experience they had had in looking at pictures in galleries and elsewhere.

We can conclude from the existing studies that there is some support for the notion of a sequence of stages in our thinking about art, a sequence which appears to be, roughly, age-related. We should be cautious, however, in our use of the term *stage*, as the Piagetian notion of stage (Piaget 1970) assumes a discrete and invariant sequence. In the Piagetian sense the kind of reasoning at each stage is qualitatively different from that in the previous stage and the sequence is rigid, allowing no omissions nor variation in the order of the stages. Until it is clear whether children can omit a stage in their thinking about pictures, whether the stages can appear in a different order or whether different kinds of thinking associated with different stages can coexist in the same child, the claim of a stage-like development may be best avoided as its meaning may be misconstrued.

The relationship between a picture, its referent, the artist and the observer

Most research has concentrated on children's understanding and appreciation of a picture itself, that is, whether they can recognise the objects in a picture, whether a picture is a good representation, and what they think a picture 'is about'. This approach is in line with the 'modernist' view of aesthetics, which maintains that the meaning is there *in the picture* and that our understanding of it can be grasped directly through perceptual observation; our aesthetic appreciation does not depend on anything external to the picture itself. In contrast, the 'postmodern' or contemporary view, which developed in the last quarter of the twentieth century, has stressed the importance of the context in which the picture was created as well as the different experiences that observers bring to their engagement with the work.[2] It is not until a much later stage in an individual's aesthetic development that he or she is likely to consider the wider context in which a work of art has been produced. It was with this postmodern view in mind that Freeman (1995, 1996) conducted his inquiry.

In contrast to the tradition of asking children about their opinions of and reactions to particular pictures, Freeman engaged children in a more generalised discussion about the relationship between the picture and its referent (a real or an imagined object), the artist who made the picture and the observer who looks at it. When he asked children of primary school age 'What is a picture?', they mentioned a variety of things, such as: a picture is *of* an object or *about* some topic; pictures can be *special* or interesting; someone actually *made* the picture; and somebody *looks at* the picture. Freeman suggested the idea of a net of relationships to guide our thinking about some of these elements and how they are connected (see figure 3.2). At the centre of the net is the picture (P). Linked to it and to each other are the world (W), that is, the object(s) that the picture represents or refers to, the artist (A), and the observer or beholder (B). Because of the complexity of this net we should expect to find considerable unevenness in children's reasoning about pictures (Freeman & Parsons 2001).

Parsons (1987) had claimed that many children hold the view that whereas a beautiful thing can be the subject of a beautiful picture, an ugly thing cannot. This kind of reasoning is characteristic of his stage 2, and when Freeman (1995, 1996) asked 7-year-olds 'If something is really ugly could you get a good picture of it?', nearly all of them said you could not and that an ugly thing makes an ugly picture.[3] For 11-year-olds,

---

[2] See Parsons (1996) for a brief review of some of the issues in the modern/postmodern debate.

[3] Kindler, Darras & Kuo (2000), however, have reported cultural differences in response to this question. French and Asian children tended to deny that an ugly thing can be art whereas Canadian children (of European ancestry) agreed that it can. Also see chapter 10 on cultural differences in children's art.

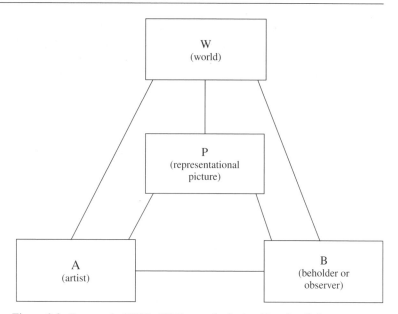

Figure 3.2 *Freeman's (1995, 1996) net of relationships that links a representational picture with the artist, the beholder (or observer) and the world.*

however, the issue was not so straightforward. They replied 'not necessarily' and that it depends on the skill of the artist. So there is a shift from considering a picture solely in terms of its representation of something in the real world (the W–P link in the net) to considering the artist's role in making this representation (the A–P link). When asked about the *artist's* feelings when producing a picture, the 7-year-olds said that if the artist is happy then the picture will be 'happy and good', but if the artist is sad the picture will not be 'good'. At this age, then, children appear to believe that the artist's mood will be directly transferred to the canvas. In contrast, the 11-year-olds thought that a sad artist might still be able to produce a good picture if he or she is skilful enough. The *observer* (or beholder) is not mentioned spontaneously at all as a potential 'ingredient' in this process of understanding pictures (the B–P link). In fact, when asked whether our *own* feelings will affect the way we see a picture, most of the 7-year-olds said that they will not because what matters is what is in the picture; in contrast, most of the 11-year-olds said that our own feelings do affect the way we look at the picture.

It seems, then, that earlier reasoning is based on a straightforward relationship between the subject matter of a picture and the real-world object it is supposed to represent. This 'realist' reasoning gives way, later, to include a consideration of the way a picture is produced by an artist and also of what an observer brings to the process of engaging with and interpreting a picture. In other words, children are beginning to talk in terms of the net of relationships involved. Their thinking is becoming more complex and more flexible. This change in pictorial reasoning that occurs in mid-childhood is, according to Freeman and Parsons (2001), nothing short of a 'conceptual revolution' (p. 74).

Children's sensitivity to the abstract properties of a picture

In earlier childhood there is a concern with realism and, according to Parsons (1987), little attention to the abstract properties of pictures – their colour, composition and so on. Some studies have investigated children's development in this regard and have focussed on particular kinds of abstract property. For example, several have demonstrated that young children are not sensitive to the quality of *line* in a picture (Carothers & Gardner 1979; Winner & Gardner 1981; Winner, Blank, Massey & Gardner 1983), nor to variation in *brightness or shading* (Carothers & Gardner 1979), nor to *compositional balance* (Winner & Gardner 1981). In contrast, O'Hare and Westwood (1984) have shown that 6-year-olds can correctly sort pictures produced by different artists according to the artists' use of line (its thickness or shading, for example), even though they cannot articulate the differences they perceive. With regard to *colour*, O'Hare and Cook (1983) investigated 5- to 11-year-olds' ability to recognise the colour-style in a series of pictures, and found that by 8 years of age children can detect style differences.

Callaghan and MacFarlane (1998) criticised some of these earlier studies and, using improved methodology, showed children aged 6 and 9 years and adults paintings by artists such as van Gogh, Gauguin and Magritte. On each trial the participant had to choose from a pair of pictures the one that 'looked like it was painted by the same artist that painted the one at the top (the target picture)'. When the subject matter was the same for all three pictures (e.g., all portraits or all landscapes) performance at all ages was well above chance. If the styles were also highly discriminable (e.g., Magritte versus van Gogh portraits), then the 6-year-olds performed just as well as the 9-year-olds and the adults; however, their performance was lower when the styles were of low discriminability. In contrast, when the subject matter varied across the three pictures *and* the style differences were low in discriminability, then the performance of all participants was very low (more or less at chance level); when style differences were highly discriminable, 9-year-olds and adults performed very well but the 6-year-olds did not.

These results confirm Steinberg and DeLoache's (1986) findings that when subject matter is controlled young children – at age 6 years – show a sensitivity to style. When the subject matter of the pictures varies it interferes with the task of focussing on style, and, interestingly, this is a problem not only for children but for adults too, especially when the differences in style are not easily discriminable. Callaghan and MacFarlane's participants were also shown sets of pictures in which the subject matter conflicted with style choices. There was some evidence that 6-year-olds performed above chance level in choosing a similar style of picture, even when a subject matter match was also possible. The importance of this study is that it shows that young children are sensitive to style and can focus on it while ignoring the variation of subject matter; furthermore, it shows that children's judgements about artistic style are influenced by the relative discriminabilities of the style and subject matter in the pictures.

Golomb (1992) and her students have carried out a number of studies designed to investigate children's preferences for pictures – usually pictures drawn by children or stylised pictures drawn by the researcher but based on children's drawings. Of particular interest are the children's judgements regarding colour, detail, proportion and depth (Manale 1982). Four- to 11-year-olds were shown pairs of drawings in which these stylistic features were pitted against each other. So, for example, a simple coloured drawing of a house might be paired with a more detailed outline drawing, or a 'flat' but coloured drawing of a cake might be paired with a three-dimensional-looking line drawing. The children were required to choose the best picture. On the whole, 4-year-olds were extremely inconsistent in their responses; however, those who were consistent preferred coloured pictures over detailed ones. This trend held for 5-year-olds but from 7 years onwards children preferred detailed pictures, even if they were uncoloured. Thus, an ordered age-related sequence of preferences emerged, with colour first and detail second; after that came proportion (i.e., realistic size differences among the objects within a scene) and, last of all, depth ('three-dimensional' rather than flat line drawings), although even at age 10–11 years many children's preferences were inconsistent on this variable.

Even though it can be demonstrated that young children are sensitive to style, this does not mean that they use the abstract properties of a picture in their spontaneous judgements or discussions of pictures. Indeed, it is generally acknowledged that they are sensitive to style only when the task demands have been simplified, such as when the subject matter has been held constant across pictures (e.g., Steinberg & DeLoache 1986); otherwise they prefer to judge art on the basis of subject matter (Gardner 1972; Steinberg & DeLoache 1986) and rarely refer to the abstract properties of pictures (Blank, Massey, Gardner & Winner 1984; Winner et al. 1983). Of course, if the pictures *are* 'abstract' then the abstract properties are more obvious and children are more likely to refer to them (Jolley & Thomas 1994).

Children's understanding of the literal expression of emotions in pictures

Whereas children up to about the age of 10 years are primarily concerned with subject matter and how realistically it is depicted, older children begin to appreciate the *emotion* expressed in a picture (Parsons 1987). An artist may express emotion in a literal way by, for example, painting a smiling or a crying figure. On the other hand, she may choose a non-literal way – symbols or metaphors, such as a bright sun to suggest happiness or a withered tree to suggest sadness. Another non-literal way of suggesting emotion is to vary the abstract properties of a picture, using bright colours and upward lines to suggest happiness and dull colours and downward or jagged lines to suggest sadness or anger. First of all, though, I will review some of the studies that have investigated children's developing sensitivity to the *literal* depiction of emotions.

It has been argued that for most emotions it is the *face* that provides the essential sensory feedback (Tomkins 1995). So important is the face and the emotions that it conveys that particular areas of the brain – notably the right parietal lobe – are involved in interpreting the facial expressions of emotion (Young et al. 1993). Although the right hemisphere seems to be especially important, the left hemisphere as well as other areas may be involved too: for example, the amygdala is involved since people with amygdala damage have difficulty in recognising the expressions of fear, anger and disgust but not happiness, sadness and surprise (Calder et al. 1996; Killcross 2000).

Darwin (1872) compiled a taxonomy of facial expressions of emotion and suggested that the expression and recognition of the basic emotions of happiness, sadness, fear, anger, surprise and disgust are both universal and innate. His evidence for these claims was that these expressions can be seen in adults in many different societies and also in very young children. There is, indeed, considerable evidence that the basic emotions are expressed in much the same way in all cultures (e.g., Ekman 1982; Ekman & Friesen 1986; Izard 1971, 1977, 1991). Nonetheless, there have been criticisms of these studies (e.g., Frijda 1969; Russell 1994; Russell & Fernández-Dols 1997; Fridlund 1994) leading to the conclusion that the claim for universality is weak and can best be described in terms of only 'minimal universality' (Russell & Fernández-Dols 1997, pp. 16–17).

As for the evidence regarding young children, we know that newborn babies are particularly responsive to faces (Fantz 1963; Johnson et al. 1991) and can even imitate facial expressions (Meltzoff & Moore 1983; Reissland 1988). Babies' own facial expressions are associated with particular basic emotions (Ganchrow, Steiner & Daher 1983) and the expressions of older babies (from 2.5 to 9 months old) are congruent with different kinds of mother–child interaction (Izard et al. 1995). By the age of 12 to 18 months infants will respond appropriately to their mothers' facial expressions: they will approach a novel toy if the mother smiles but not if she adopts a fearful expression (Klinnert 1984). These findings suggest that there is at least some support for the notion that facial expressions are innate.

For very young babies it is the *moving* face that elicits a response but by the age of 5 or 6 months babies will attend to photographs of faces and to line drawings, and can even recognise familiar people from line drawings (see chapter 2). The face in a picture is considered by some (e.g., Spiegel & Machotka 1974) to be 'the seat of emotional expression' (p. 168), even when it has only vague features. Gombrich (1960) observed that almost any lines inside an oval shape will give the impression of an intended facial expression. Brunswik (1956) has shown how subtle changes in the relationships among the different features of the face can significantly affect our judgement of its expression. Understanding these relationships as well as the ability to exaggerate them is the 'stock-in-trade' of cartoonists and caricaturists and, in fact, Gombrich (1972) has pointed out that a caricature can be a convincing image without being objectively realistic. Indeed, a caricature can be more instantly recognisable than a photograph of the same person.

In order to study *children's* ability to understand the emotions conveyed by facial expressions in pictures Russell and Bullock (1985, 1986) asked them to judge the facial expressions in a series of photographs. The expressions were posed by actors. These researchers reported that by age 4 to 5 years children's judgements of the facial expressions are similar to those of adults. One of my students (Skipper 2001) asked children aged 4 to 5 years and 6 to 7 years as well as a group of adults to identify the six basic emotions posed by a woman in a set of photographs (see figure 3.3). It can be seen from table 1 that the adults recognised them all equally well; the older children's performance was exceptionally high for happy, sad and angry and high for disgusted, frightened and surprised. The younger children's performance was lower but still quite high for most of the emotions. Russell and Bullock (1985, 1986) also studied even younger children – aged 2 years – and found that they can differentiate between positive and negative emotions (happy versus angry); however, they have more difficulty in differentiating between different kinds of negative emotion (angry versus sad, fear or disgust).

Whereas these studies asked children about the expressions in photographs, others have used cartoon faces (see figure 3.4). Schulenburg (1999), another student of mine, tested 2-, 3- and 4-year-olds. On average, the 3- and 4-year-olds were correct on four out of the six expressions but the 2-year-olds were only correct on two. The emotion most easily recognised was happy, closely followed by angry, and the most difficult were fear and

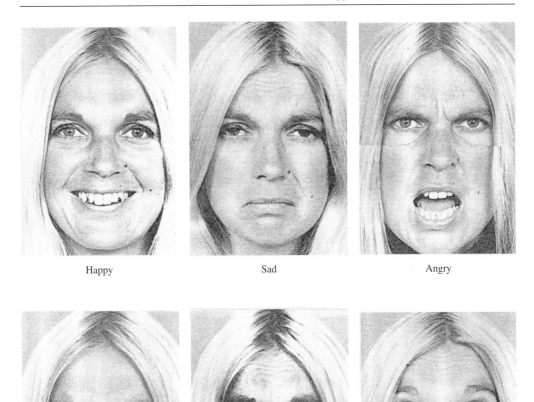

Happy	Sad	Angry

| Disgusted | Frightened | Surprised |

Figure 3.3 *Photographs of a woman modelling six different facial expressions of emotion (from Ekman & Friesen 1975).*

surprise, which were often transposed, echoing the pattern of results found when photographs were used as the stimuli. Sayil (1996) also found that happy cartoon faces were named most accurately by her 4- and 6-year-olds.

In fact, there is some evidence that children are better at recognising emotions in *drawings* rather than in photographs (MacDonald, Kirkpatrick & Sullivan 1996). One of my students (Marfleet 2002) showed each child (with an average age of 6 years 9 months) the cartoon faces (see figure 3.4) as well as photographs of the six basic facial expressions

Table 1 *Successful recognition of the six basic facial expressions of emotions by three age groups.*

(In percentages)

	4–5 years	6–7 years	Adults
Happy	90	95	100
Sad	80	95	100
Angry	65	95	100
Disgusted	60	70	100
Frightened	36	76	100
Surprised	32	68	100

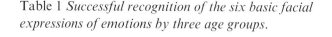

Figure 3.4 *Cartoon faces of six different emotional expressions.*

(see figure 3.3).[4] When the child saw each set of six faces she was asked to 'find the happy face', 'find the sad face' and so on. The order of emotions was randomised and the faces were reshuffled for each emotion. Happy and sad were the most easily recognised in both the photographs and the cartoons, but the other emotions (anger, disgust, fear and surprise) were better recognised in the cartoons. It should not surprise us that cartoons might be easier to recognise, as the artist is likely to include only the most relevant information in a drawing whereas much redundant information will be included in a photograph; in addition, the expressions in a drawing or caricature are likely to be exaggerated.

Whether photographs or cartoons are used, happy is the emotion that seems to be the most easily recognised. Happy and also sad and angry expressions may be easier to recognise because they are more likely to be simple emotions, whereas surprise, for example, tends to be a more complex emotion (Wellman 1990; Perner 1991). Baron-Cohen, Spitz and Cross (1993) suggest that simple emotions can be attributed to some straightforward situational cause, whereas our interpretation of a

---

[4] Twenty undergraduate students had already been given this task (Schulenburg 1999): seventeen were in total agreement about which face expressed each emotion; three more also agreed on four of the expressions but chose the 'fear' face for surprise and the 'surprised' face for fear.

complex emotion, such as surprise, depends on our understanding that someone's expectation has been thwarted. Indeed, in a pilot test, Profyt and Whissell (1991) found that young children have difficulty in understanding descriptions of the situations that might cause surprise. Thus a complex emotion such as surprise has a more 'cognitive' basis. Baron-Cohen and colleagues (1993) have also considered further explanations for the greater difficulty with surprise. One is that it may be a blend of happy and fear. Certainly, in Marfleet's study (2002) the most common errors made when asked to choose the surprised face were happy and fear. Another possible explanation is that whereas happy and sad can be largely understood from the shape of the mouth (upturned or downturned), surprise seems to involve both the mouth and the eyes. There is some evidence that children remember and evaluate information from the mouth region before that around the eyes (Cunningham & Odom 1986; see also chapter 7). Whatever the reasons for the relative ease or difficulty with which emotions are recognised from facial expressions in pictures, children as young as 2 years are beginning to recognise at least some of them.

Children's understanding of the non-literal expression of emotion in pictures

Many, if not most, works of art suggest emotion in *non-literal* or metaphorical ways as well as, or instead of, a literal way. So, rather than suggesting happiness by, for example, a smiling face (literal), the artist might choose to paint a picture of a sunny day or a blossoming tree. Not only can the subject matter reflect or suggest the emotional mood of the picture but so also can its abstract properties – the colour, the line, the composition and so on.

Since the metaphorical expression of emotion is less obvious than a literal depiction, we might reasonably assume that an understanding of the metaphorical will develop later. At what age, then, do children begin to grasp the non-literal dimension of art? Carothers and Gardner (1979), Jolley and Thomas (1995) and Jolley, Zhi and Thomas (1998) found that most children aged 7 years are *not* sensitive to visual metaphor and that this ability does not develop until about age 12; however, some studies claim to have found evidence of metaphorical understanding in 6-year-olds (Morra, Caloni & d'Amico 1994; Winston et al. 1995) and even among 4- to 5-year-olds (Winston et al. 1995).

Callaghan (1997, study 1) showed children a set of sixteen paintings, covering a range of styles, periods and artists. The emotional mood was conveyed by both the subject matter *and* the abstract properties of the pictures. Fifteen artists had rated the pictures on the degree to which they expressed four particular emotions (happy, sad, excited and calm) and there was a high level of agreement. Examples of the pictures are Picasso's *The Pigeons* (happy), van Gogh's *A Pair of Shoes* (sad), Matisse's *The Nightmare of the White Elephant* (excited) and O'Keefe's *Sky above Clouds* (calm). The children had to match each picture with a photograph of an actress portraying the appropriate emotion. Across the 5 to 11 age range there was an increase in the level of agreement between the children and the artists, but even the 5-year-olds performed above chance, indicating that quite young children are sensitive to the non-literal expression of emotion. The results were similar in a second study, in which all sixteen pictures were available at the same time and the children were required to pick the best and then the second best example of each emotion, as well as to provide a justification.

Whereas Callaghan's study used figural paintings, others have used *abstract* art as the stimuli, and in these cases, of course, it is the abstract properties of the pictures only that indicate the mood. Some authors (Blank et al. 1984) have reported that at age 5 years children respond better than chance to recognising the appropriate mood; others, however, have found that such an ability is not evident until much later – not until at least age 9 years (Winner et al. 1986). Since both these studies used very similar procedures it is difficult to know how the conclusions could be so different. Jolley and Thomas (1994), however, pointed out two potential methodological problems. First, the earlier studies asked children to choose from a pair of abstract paintings the one that matched the literally depicted mood in a portrait painting. The problem here is that the portrait is likely to have both literal and non-literal properties and children might use either as a basis for their choices, and this confounds the basis of the selection. A second problem concerns the paired presentation itself. Although children might actually be able to perceive the appropriate mood in the picture they choose, equally they might choose this picture simply because its mood is different from the non-selected picture.

In their own study, Jolley and Thomas tried to get around these problems by presenting children with one abstract painting at a time and asking them to name its emotional mood (happy, sad, angry or calm). Five-year-olds could recognise only the happy pictures better than chance. Sensitivity to happiness and anger developed quickly between the ages of 5 and 7 years, with sensitivity to calm and sadness developing more slowly. These findings support Parsons' claim (1987) that young children are more likely to read positive feelings than negative feelings into paintings. Overall, Jolley and Thomas' (1994) results suggest that sensitivity to metaphorical expression of mood in pictures is beginning to emerge around the age of 5 years, but that it then takes a considerable time to develop.

Two further problems have been indicated by Callaghan (1997). One is that language-based tasks may impede young children's performance, and the other is that since children prefer realist to abstract art (Winner 1982) they may perform less well with abstract pictures. In her own study, Callaghan (2000b) used representational pictures in a non-verbal matching task. She found that whereas her 5-year-olds performed above chance level, the 3-year-olds did not. However, when the children completed the task in the context of a game (the experimenter chose some paintings to match the emotion of a teddy bear) even the 3-year-olds were able to choose a further picture to match his emotion. This cultural 'scaffolding' helped the children to achieve something that they could not do on their own (see also chapter 12). On the whole, though, the results of this study and of others suggest that children are beginning to understand the metaphorical expression of emotion at about the age of 5 years, somewhat later than their understanding of literal expression.

As children's early preferences for pictures are often based on colour (Manale 1982), it is perhaps colour that is the most salient abstract property as far as they are concerned. Machotka (1966) and Rump and Southgate (1967) also found that colour was the most frequently mentioned reason given by 6- and 7-year-olds for liking a picture. One of my students (Platten 2003) asked 6- to 7-year-olds, 10- to 11-year-olds and some adults to select a face (from a set of six differently coloured faces). Participants had to select the most appropriately coloured face for happy, sad and angry. They also did the same thing for a set of six trees, also coloured differently. Yellow was the most popular choice for happy, in both the faces and the trees tasks. The choice of yellow increased with age (faces: 20%, 45%, 90%; trees: 30%, 60%, 75%). Dark colours tended to be chosen for sad (38% in the faces task and 68% in the trees task), although there were no significant differences among the three age groups. Red and black were popular choices for angry (faces: 45% red and 47% black; trees: 40% red and 40% black), and, again, there was no effect of age.

Another student (O'Neill 1997) asked ten adults to judge whether each of seven colours was happy or sad. Yellow and orange were judged to be happy by all ten participants and red, green and blue by nine of them. Black was judged to be sad by all ten, and brown by nine. A group of 4- to 5-year-olds and a group of 7- to 8-year-olds were also given the same task and responded in a similar way to the adults. The exception was green: whereas the adults and older children judged it to be a happy colour the younger children were evenly split between happy and sad. Although many of the research studies have found it is only at age 5 that children are beginning to be sensitive to metaphorical expression in pictures, this study indicates that even 4-year-olds can, at least in some circumstances, link colours with certain emotions and, on the whole, they do this in the same way that older children and adults do.

What do children know about the role of the artist in the making of a picture?

Pictures are objects that are usually made intentionally by an artist. What do children know about this relationship between the artist and the picture – the A–P link in terms of Freeman's net of relationships (see figure 3.2)? First of all, what do they know about the attributes of an artist – such as an artist's age and whether he or she is a real person rather than, say, a machine? Gardner and colleagues (1975) found that young children have a very poor understanding of these issues: many 4- and 7-year-olds had little conception of the skills required to make a picture and believed that works of art could be produced by anyone. Actually, this is perhaps not all that surprising, since adults routinely expect young children themselves to produce pictures, even though they are not works of art. Callaghan and Rochat (2003, study 1) asked 2- to 5-year-olds to make judgements about line drawings produced by a 'little brother' (aged 4 years), a 'big brother' (aged 10 years) and a 'grown-up Dad', and a further picture produced by a 'drawing machine' (i.e., a computer printer) (see figure 3.5).

On each trial the child was shown a photograph of one of the artists and was asked to find the pictures made by this particular artist. Eight pictures (including a lollipop, a tree, a bear, a cube and so on) drawn by the target artist were available, as well as eight pictures by one other non-target artist. Thus, on each trial the children were asked to discriminate between the work of two artists. In fact, the 2- and 3-year-olds did not perform significantly above chance on any of the pairings. The 4-year-olds were above chance when the pictures were drawn by real people (adult versus older child, adult versus younger child, and younger versus older child artists), but not for the person versus machine pairings. Five-year-olds were above chance for all pairings, although only at chance for the pictures produced by the adult and the machine – perhaps, the most difficult comparison.

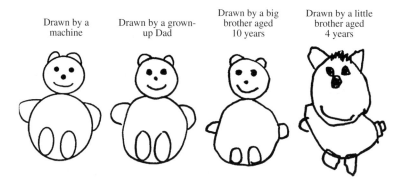

Figure 3.5 *A bear drawn by four different artists (Callaghan & Rochat 2003).*

These findings indicate that although 4-year-olds perform quite well if asked to select pictures according to the age of the artist, they cannot judge on sentience (whether the artist is a real person or not). By age 5, however, children are quite good at these discriminations, although it is perhaps not surprising that they still cannot easily tell the difference between an adult's drawing and a computer-printed one; some of the children commented that both these drawings were more precise than those drawn by children.

Some studies have restricted the subject matter of the drawings – using only pictures of the human figure – but have presented examples from a much wider age range of artists. Goodnow, Wilkins and Dawes (1986, study 1), for example, used a set of eight figures drawn by children aged 4 to 10 years. All possible pairs of these figures were then presented to children, themselves aged between 4 and 11 years. For each pair they were asked to select the figure drawn by the older artist. Only 25 per cent of the youngest children were correct on 75 per cent or more of their choices; this percentage rose to 44 per cent for kindergarten children (average age 5 years 4 months), to 88 per cent at age 7 and to 100 per cent for 9- to 11-year-olds. These results show that success is not really achieved until at least age 7 years. Fayol, Barrouillet and Chevrot (1995) used Goodnow and colleagues' drawings and followed their procedure with children ranging in age from 2 years 6 months to 11 years. In fact, their children were more successful than Goodnow's, with the 3- and 4-year-olds both achieving a success rate of 69 per cent. This may have resulted from the earlier attendance at preschool by most French children, who might then have been more likely to recognise differences between pictures made by younger and older drawers.

Not only are quite young children adept at telling which of two drawings is drawn by an older rather than a younger child, they are also successful at ordering a series of drawings according to the artists' increasing age. Trautner and colleagues (1989) asked children aged 5 to 10 years and some adults to rank a set of five figure drawings according to the age of the artists (5, 6, 7, 8 and 9 years). Even the youngest participants were able to order these drawings with an accuracy above chance level, and this skill then increased with age. Similar results were obtained by Tryphon and Montangero (1992).

The studies mentioned so far have all used copies of real children's drawings as their stimuli. Many aspects of these drawings change as the child artist gets older (see chapter 5) and it is difficult to know which features children are taking into account when they make their judgements. Using nine figures, Dye and Dowker (1996) investigated children's sensitivity to two particular features: the head–trunk ratio of the figure and its complexity. Five- and 7-year-olds were shown photographs of a 3-, 6- and 10-year-old child and an adult and asked which one had drawn

Figure 3.6 *Human figure drawings used by Cox and Hodsoll (2000) – upper set for boys and lower set for girls.*

each figure. Neither age group was sensitive to the head–trunk ratio. The 7-year-olds but not the 5-year-olds were sensitive to the complexity of the figure, allocating the simple figures to younger artists and the more complex ones to older artists.

In order to check if 5-year-olds might be sensitive to complexity if a greater range was presented, Cox and Hodsoll (2000) used Dye and Dowker's figures but, in addition, included a 'tadpole' figure (see figure 3.6). Since Dye and Dowker had found no effect of the head–trunk ratio, this variable was not manipulated; otherwise, the same procedure was followed. The performance of the 7-year-olds was good, just as Dye and Dowker had found, and also, not surprisingly, 85 per cent of them said that the tadpole figure had been drawn by a 3-year-old. The perform-ance of the 5-year-olds was also similar on the figures used by Dye and Dowker, that is, they were not sensitive to complexity. With regard to the tadpole figure, however, 58 per cent of the 5-year-olds said it had been drawn by a 3-year-old and a further 25 per cent said it had been drawn by a 6-year-old. So, although 5-year-olds are not sensitive to the *subtle* changes that older artists make to their figures, most of them do realise that the simple tadpole figure is likely to have been drawn by a very young child.

The idea of presenting more obviously discriminable figures was carried further by Jolley, Knox and Foster (2000, study 2). They presented sets of four drawings (such as those in figure 3.7) and asked their children to match each picture with a photograph of the artist (aged 2, 4, 6 or 10 years). Two older groups of children (8-year-olds and 12-year-olds)

Figure 3.7 *A set of human figure drawings used by Jolley, Knox and Foster (2000).*

performed very well on this task. A younger group, who were tadpole drawers, were quite good at allocating the scribbles to the 2-year-old and the appropriate figures to the 10-year-old, but less successful at correctly allocating the 4- and 6-year-olds' drawings. The youngest group, who were scribblers, were also quite successful at attributing the scribbles to the 2-year-old but less good at correctly allocating the other figures. The results indicate that children even as young as 2 years are beginning to be aware that the kinds of pictures children produce will alter as they get older, something Piaget (1969) has referred to as *diachronic thinking*.

Whereas some studies have investigated personal characteristics of the artist – such as age – and how these are related to the style of their pictures, others have focussed on the artist's intention or mood. For example, what do children understand about an artist's intention to draw a particular object and the actual drawing that emerges? In order to investigate this issue, Browne and Woolley (2001) put the intention of the artist in conflict with the resemblance of the picture (for example, the artist said he would draw a bear but the picture turned out like a rabbit). Four- and 7-year-olds as well as adults named the picture according to what it resembled (a rabbit) rather than the artist's intention. When the drawings were ambiguous (i.e., when half the participants said it looked like a bear but the other half said it looked like a rabbit) the 7-year-olds and the adults relied on the artist's intention when naming the pictures whereas the 4-year-olds did not. It would appear, then, that by age 7 children have some understanding of the artist's intention in making a picture.

Callaghan and Rochat (2003) investigated children's understanding of the effect an artist's mood might have on his or her artwork. As these researchers are concerned that interviewing children (as Parsons and Freeman did) may underestimate their understanding but that experimental tasks might overestimate it, they use a combination of methods in their own work (study 2). They showed children video clips of artists working in either an agitated way or a calm way, although the drawings themselves were not actually visible. The children were then shown two drawings and had to judge which artist drew each picture. Whereas 5-year-olds were quite good at the task, 3-year-olds did not perform above chance level. The task was easier, however, when the children were asked to identify a drawing made by a calm artist rather than an agitated artist.

In a subsequent study (study 3), 3-, 5- and 7-year-olds were shown photographs of two artists, one happy and one sad, and were asked to say which pictures were painted by which artist. Of twelve pictures presented, six had been judged, by fifteen artists, to be happy and six, sad. The 3-year-olds performed only at chance level. In contrast, the 5- and 7-year-olds were very successful and could match the mood of the artist to the mood of the paintings. These findings support those of Freeman that a happy artist will paint a happy picture and a sad artist will paint a sad picture, although Callaghan and Rochat have shown that this reasoning is prevalent among 5-year-olds as well as 7-year-olds.

The 5- and 7-year-olds were also specifically asked about the mental state of the artists and how this might influence their pictures. All 7-year-olds and most 5-year-olds felt that artists would make a painting that matched their mood, and this response confirmed their performance on the picture task. But when asked if artists *could* make a painting opposite to their mood, two-thirds of the 7-year-olds and half the 5-year-olds said that they could. However, when asked to name a happy or sad event in their own lives and then whether an artist could make a picture evoking an opposite feeling, only five 7-year-olds out of twelve and one 5-year-old out of twelve conceded that it was possible. Nonetheless, when asked if this was possible if the artist was *very skilled*, seven of the 7-year-olds and six of the 5-year-olds agreed that it was. These responses indicate that by age 7, and even at age 5, children are beginning to be able to think about the way that an artist's skill might enable her to produce a picture that does not directly mirror her own feelings.

Taken together, the evidence from these studies indicates that very young children, even as young as 2 years, have some idea that the age of the artist will have a bearing on the kind of picture she draws. It is not until a few years later, however, that children begin to understand the way that the artist's intention or mood might (or might not) affect her pictures. Existing studies indicate age 7 for intention and age 5 for mood. It is important to stress that children's understanding may only be beginning at these ages, and is certainly not considered to be 'fully-fledged'. Nonetheless, the findings indicate that both Parsons (1987) and Freeman (1995, 1996) may have underestimated the age at which children begin to understand the role of the artist in the making of a picture.

The role of the observer in interpreting a picture

People have different experiences and different kinds and amounts of knowledge that may affect the way they interpret or judge what they see. However, below about the age of 10 years children are thought not to take into account the role of the observer in interpreting a picture (Parsons 1987; Freeman 1995, 1996). So, when do children actually realise that people can have very different interpretations of the same thing?

A number of researchers (e.g., Chandler & Helm 1984; Taylor 1988) have investigated this issue by showing children a drawing and then covering it so that only a small part is visible through a cut-out window. The children are then asked what another child, who has only seen a small part of the picture, will expect the complete picture to look like. Four-year-olds attribute their own knowledge of the complete picture to the naïve observer, but by age 7 children realise that the naïve observer may not be able to identify the picture correctly. Pillow and Henrichon (1996) showed children covered pictures with an *ambiguous* feature (e.g., a pointed oval) displayed through a cut-out window. On two trials the same complete picture was then revealed (e.g., a cat with pointed ears). The children had to predict what picture would be revealed on the third trial. Not surprisingly, they predicted that it would be the same picture as before. In fact, it was a different one (e.g., a flower with pointed petals). They were then asked to say what a puppet would predict given the same sequence. In a series of experiments the authors found that 4- and 5-year-olds predicted that the puppet would say that the third picture was a flower. So, these children were assuming that the puppet would have the same knowledge as they themselves currently had; in other words, they were behaving in an egocentric manner. Children aged 6 years, however, realised that two people can have different interpretations of the same stimulus and were able to predict that the puppet would mistakenly guess that the third picture would be a cat (in line with the children's initial assumption), even though the children themselves knew that the third picture was actually different.

Whereas the studies mentioned above indicate that children may be able to take into account different people's knowledge by the age of 6 or 7 years, other studies (e.g., Ruffman, Olson & Astington 1991) have found that 4-year-olds perform quite well on this kind of task. We presume that these age differences are the result of differences in the tasks or procedures between research studies. All of these studies have focussed on the knowledge and expectations of different observers rather than on their feelings, as Freeman (1995, 1996) did. In fact, they have been carried out within the body of research that has investigated the development of a 'theory of mind' – the notion that other people's behaviour can be explained in terms of the beliefs they hold about a situation. In that field of research, some authors (such as Perner 1991) reckon that the acquisition of such a theory is absent in 3-year-olds but is developing from about the ages of 4 to 6 years. Other researchers (e.g., Chandler 1988) believe that children's understanding of other people's knowledge and beliefs starts earlier than age 4 but develops more gradually and is certainly not complete by age 6 or 7. Nonetheless, these studies demonstrate that children have some understanding that different observers, bringing different knowledge to the task, will interpret a picture in different ways. And, this understanding is occurring at an earlier age than that suggested by Freeman (1995, 1996).

At one time the modernist concern was with the fundamental truth or essence of a work of art – the notion that there is one 'correct' way to understand it. A more contemporary or postmodern view is that there may be many meaningful ways (Parsons 1996). The contexts in which the observers view an artwork can be equally relevant and will give rise to multiple interpretations of it. Indeed, critics do not necessarily agree about a particular work. That children as young as 4 to 6 years are beginning to understand that different observers may have a different understanding of a picture indicates that they are capable of engaging in such a discussion.

Summary

Preschool children's ideas of what constitutes a picture are quite varied and, furthermore, these children also seem to have no particular preference for abstract or realistic pictures. By the age of 7, however, children's main concern is with representational realism. There is then a shift in thinking, at around 10 or 11, when older children begin to take account of the emotional expression of a picture, its abstract properties (such as line, colour and so on) as well as the broader context of picture-making, including the roles of both the artist and the observer.

One line of research has pursued the question of whether young children are sensitive to the abstract properties of pictures. The evidence suggests that 6-year-olds do show such sensitivity if the subject matter is held constant. Even at age 4 years some children exhibit stable preferences for colour. A preference for detail emerges at age 7 and a preference for proportion and then depth much later still. Other research has investigated children's understanding of emotional mood in pictures. It is not surprising that the youngest children understand emotion in a literal way, through the expression of faces – especially happy faces. The understanding of non-literal or metaphorical expressions of emotion is a later development – only just beginning at about age 5 years. However, if we consider the studies on colour then even 4-year-olds link particular colours with certain emotions, just like adults do.

As well as the research studies that have concentrated on a child's understanding of the picture itself, others have investigated the role of the artist. Even 2-year-olds have some idea that the age of the artist will affect the kind of picture she draws. By age 5 children are starting to think about the way artists' moods might or might not affect their work, and by age 7 they understand that an artist's intention might be different from the way the picture turns out. By this age children are also able to consider the role of the observer in the interpretation of a picture, understanding, for example, that different observers may have different interpretations of the same picture.

Much of the evidence suggests that children's sensitivities and understanding are far in advance of what we have been led to expect. It is important to stress, however, that although a number of studies have revealed that children are sensitive to many aspects of pictures and picture-making at quite a young age, this does not mean that they normally think about and discuss pictures in such a sophisticated way. What it does suggest is that, potentially, they are capable of making aesthetic judgements about pictures and engaging in critical discussions about art. Although for many years the emphasis in art education was on self-expression, in more recent times there has been an increased emphasis on art appreciation and this is now included in the National Curriculum for Art and Design in the UK (see chapter 12).

4   Children's early mark-making

It is fairly easy to recognise the objects represented in a picture. People in non-pictorial cultures have little difficulty with pictures when they first encounter them (see chapters 2 and 10) and a child brought up with almost no experience of pictures and no explanation of them was able to identify the objects in line drawings when they were first presented to him at the age of 19 months (see chapter 2). Even though the objects in a picture may be easy to recognise, the meaning or interpretation of a picture, especially as a work of art, may be more difficult (see chapter 3). What counts as a good picture may depend on the artist's intentions and criteria and also the criteria that observers bring to the act of evaluating pictures. Pictures are also not necessarily easy to produce, and even the most sophisticated art lover and critic may not be able to produce a passably good one. In fact, most untrained adults find drawing difficult, and it would not be surprising if young children find it difficult also. As with many abilities, such as language, understanding often precedes performance (Dale 1976).

The first scribbles

Most young children in modern cultures scribble, and many of them begin at a very early age – from about 12 months onwards. They make marks with a pencil or crayon or, often, with their fingers – in mud, a spilt drink or on a steamed-up window pane. Many parents and most nursery schools encourage young children to draw and, despite the mess, to paint. There is rarely any pressure at this early age to conform to a particular way of drawing; usually any marks made by the child are greeted with enthusiasm and are often regarded as products of self-expression.[1] However, praise usually depends on whether the child paints or draws on appropriate surfaces rather than on walls, furniture or other

---

[1] The kinds of marks that children make will vary depending on the medium. Kellogg (1969), for example, found that with thick brushes and paint children produce thick round shapes and wide lines, whereas with fine-line markers they produce more detailed and controlled forms. Golomb (1974, 2002) also reported that children find different forms of representation depending on the medium they are working in.

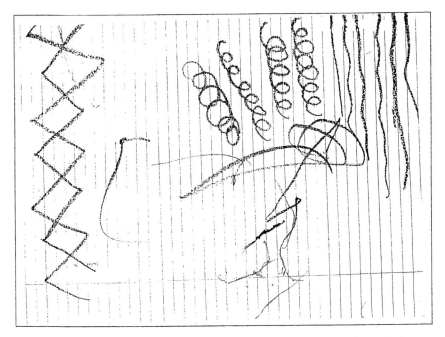

Figure 4.1 *Mother's zigzag (left), loopy (upper middle) and straight line (upper right) scribbles. Amy's responses (centre) at age 1 year 1 week. (Drawn on lined paper.)*

valuable objects. *Where* it is appropriate to make marks has to be learned as well as *how* to make them!

   The early marks that young children make are often thought of as meaningless scribbles or 'purposeless pencillings' (Burt 1933, p. 319). Several writers (e.g., Burt 1933; Bühler 1930) have discussed scribbling largely in terms of motor movements, and Burt and others (e.g., Bender 1938; Harris 1963) recognised that it is an enjoyable activity for young children, primarily because of the rhythmic movements of the arm. It is not only the motor activity itself, though, that interests children. They have usually witnessed their parents or older siblings writing, drawing or doodling on paper, and they delight in watching various forms appear on the page – a face, a cat, a house and so on. Between the ages of 12 and 15 months children will request their mothers to draw by looking at them and offering them the drawing materials, and by the age of 18 months children will explicitly suggest the topic of the drawing to their mothers (Yamagata 1997). Also, at about 18 months children make marks on particular parts of their mothers' drawings (see figure 4.1) and, by 22 months, can add recognisable parts to a shared drawing (e.g., adding eyes to a face). So, young children already have some idea that this activity involves making visible marks that can be made to resemble a real object. If they themselves are given a pencil-like implement that does not leave a mark they lose

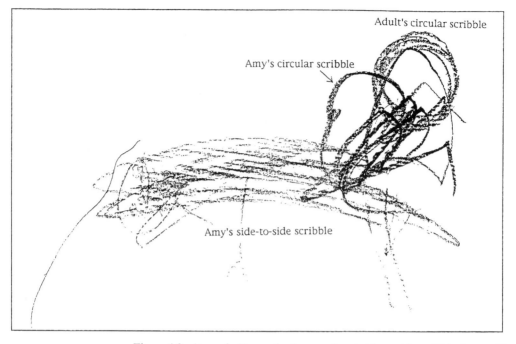

Figure 4.2 *At nearly 20 months Amy produced side-to-side scribbles but could also attempt to copy her mother's circular scribble.*

interest very quickly (Gibson & Yonas, cited in Gibson 1969). It seems, then, that children are very interested in the marks they produce and the visual feedback from their scribbling is extremely important, a point also made by Eng (1954).

Although early scribbles may be uncontrolled and formless, as well as non-representational, we can see them develop as children gain more experience and control over the pencil. Based on his observations of his own three children, Matthews (1983, 1984) reported a series of mark-making movements which he regards as the basis of later drawing activity. First of all, the child makes downward stabbing movements, which Matthews calls *vertical arc* movements. Sideways sweeping *horizontal arc* movements are made in relation to a horizontal surface, and the child also engages in *push–pull* movements with a pencil or brush: the pencil is pushed away and then pulled back again, producing visible marks on the paper. Later, at around the age of 18 months, the child gains more control over these marks and can separate push movements from pull movements as well as rotate the pencil or brush to produce spiral whirls (see figure 4.2). This rotational movement is gradually further controlled until the child can produce a closed shape. Essentially, these early marks are a record or trace of the child's body movements or gestures in space. As Matthews (1999) says, 'The infant's use of visual media is built upon

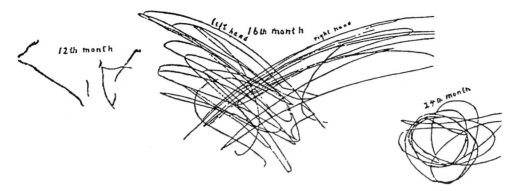

left hand 16th month right hand

12th month

14th month

Figure 4.3 *Major's (1906) son produced tentative scribbles at age 1 year, side-to-side scribbles at 16 months and circular scribbles at age 2 years.*

the expressive use of the body in early infancy' (p. 157), and Kindler and Darras (1998) also argue that 'the roots of pictorial representation can be traced back to first icons of gestures born out of the interaction of the sensory-motor activities and the activity of the central nervous system' (p. 166).

A similar sequence of marks was observed by Major (1906), who traced the development of scribbling in his son, 'R' (see figure 4.3). Around the time of his first birthday, R would strike the paper with a pencil, a spoon or some other implement, apparently in imitation of an adult's drawing or writing activity. R's earliest tentative marks at age 12 months gave way to freer and more rhythmic side-to-side movements at 16 months. This swinging motion became more purposive and under control by the time R was 18 months old. He added other movements to his repertoire: as well as horizontal lines, often returning upon themselves, he produced vertical and circular or spiral scribbles at age 2 years. As these circular scribbles became more controlled, R could produce an irregularly shaped figure roughly like a circle or an oval.

Other researchers (e.g., Eng 1954) have also reported this pattern of development, culminating in children's ability to curtail their looped scribbles to produce a closed form (Bender 1938; Piaget & Inhelder 1956). Although this early scribbling phase has often been dismissed or underestimated the child is, nonetheless, experimenting with mark-making, gaining greater control over the pencil or brush and enlarging the repertoire of marks he can produce. Matthews (1994) claims that these robust forms of behaviour are 'deep structures' that can be observed in different contexts and in different cultures; in other words, they may be universal. However, since he has observed the same kinds of mark-making movements in young children in only two different cultures – London and Singapore – we need more evidence to support his claim.

Gestural or action representations

Even though their first marks with pencil, crayon or paintbrush do not necessarily represent anything, this does not mean that children at around the age of 1 year are incapable of representation. For example, they can and will use the drawing materials themselves in representational ways. At the age of 12 to 14 months children have been observed to wrap a crayon inside the drawing paper and say 'bye bye' or 'hot dog' (Wolf & Perry 1988). Wolf and Perry call these behaviours *object-based representations*. From age 12 months children will also make representational gestures or actions that leave marks on the page. Wolf and Perry describe how one child 'hopped' a pen across the page, saying 'bunny', leaving a trail of marks, although it is unlikely that she had any idea that the marks might resemble footprints. The representation seems to be all in the gesture, and Wolf and Perry have called it a *gestural representation*, which echoes Vygotsky's (1978) observation that 'we are inclined to view children's first drawings and scribbles as gestures [rather] than as drawing in the true sense of the word' (p. 107).

Matthews (1984) has also drawn our attention to this kind of representation, although he calls it an *action representation*. From a video recording of his son's painting activities, Matthews describes the way that, with the rotational movement of the paintbrush on the page, Ben seemed to be mimicking the action of an imaginary car as it went round a corner and out of sight. That it is the *on-going* action which was important is supported by the fact that the child's comments were made during the process of the painting.[2] Matthews suggests that this is an 'early use of drawing to symbolise and monitor a movement in time and space' (p. 4). The overlapping spirals of paint were the public traces left over from that event. Interestingly, at the end of the child's commentary on this action he announced that the car had disappeared, and this seemed to coincide with the line becoming obscured by the build-up of paint. It is not clear whether this visual cue provoked the end of the event; if it did, then it suggests that the marks the child makes are not only by-products of an action but can guide the course of the action itself – in this case, bringing it to an end.

In cases of gestural or action representation, it seems that children do not intend to capture a visual likeness of the objects involved, but are more concerned with the action or event. Furthermore, it is the *process* of the drawing, not the product which is important, and children may not be at all interested in retaining the picture after it has been completed. As the marks

---

[2] Young children's vocalisations while they are drawing suggest that their pictures are in fact 'multi-media' productions (Kindler & Darras 1994; Kindler 1994a; Kindler & Darras 1998).

left on the page are unlikely to bear any visual likeness to a real object, it will be difficult if not impossible subsequently for anyone, including the children themselves, to make sense of them. Because of this shortcoming, Golomb (1992) has questioned whether these action representations can truly be regarded as examples of symbolic behaviour, and argues that 'Only when the child recognizes that his lines and shapes carry meaning that is independent of the motor action that produced the shape can one consider the drawing as a representational statement' (p. 15). Nonetheless, this activity that produces gestural or action pictures may be useful in laying a foundation for later and more visually representational forms (Wolf & Perry 1988).

Accidental and intentional representations

How does the child move from producing seemingly meaningless scribbles to drawing objects that are recognisable? One answer, proffered by Luquet[3] (1927/2001), is that this transition occurs accidentally. According to Luquet, a young child makes marks and shapes for the sheer joy of doing it; she does not believe that she herself can make them look like real objects, even though she knows that adults can. Then she begins to see in her scribbles a resemblance to objects in the real world (see figure 4.4). Luquet calls this *fortuitous realism*. Undoubtedly, children do see things in their scribbles and they will 'label' them verbally and talk

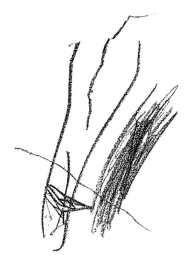

Figure 4.4 *Amy, aged 2 years 11 months, recognised a tree trunk and some apples in her scribble.*

---

[3] Originally Luquet (1913) published a longitudinal study based on his daughter's drawings, although later (Luquet 1927) he made a wider study and Costall's English translation of this later work (Luquet 1927/2001) has been invaluable in clarifying his claims.

Figure 4.5 *Amy, aged 2 years 10 months, recognised the shape of a bird in her scribble. Then she added an eye and some legs.*

Figure 4.6 *Joe, aged 3 years 6 months, was asked to draw a person.*

about them, an activity sometimes referred to as *romancing* (Golomb 1974); they will also attribute meaning to their scribbles if an adult questions them (Adi-Japha, Levin & Solomon 1998).

At first, according to Luquet, as the likeness between the drawing and the object was accidental, the child does not know how she did it; she may be unable to repeat it and may not even try. As she continues to recognise things in her scribbles she comes to realise that she herself can produce 'realistic' things. She may even be able to modify an accidental likeness. For example, my daughter, aged 2 years 10 months, added an eye and legs to an accidental shape that she had identified as a bird (Cox 1992) (see figure 4.5).

This realisation that figural representation is possible tempts the child to try, from the outset, to draw particular objects. In fact, from the age of about 20 months children often announce in advance what they are going to draw, indicating that they have an intention to draw that particular object (Duncum 1993). We can reasonably assume that this is indeed what they go on to draw, although children often change their minds mid-drawing; Major (1906) noticed that his son frequently changed his mind as to the thing he wanted to draw when the lines seemed to suggest a new object. When Joe, aged 3 years 6 months, was asked to draw a person (see figure 4.6) he said, 'I do Daddy.' As he observed the spiral that emerged on the page he said, 'It's going round. It's a train track. I can't do Daddy' (Cox & Parkin 1986, p. 364).

Luquet claims that when children deliberately attempt to draw a particular object this usually occurs just after they have drawn the same

Figure 4.7 *Sarah, aged 3 years 8 months, progressed from drawing an undifferentiated closed shape to a recognisable figure within a single drawing session (Golomb 1974).*

object accidentally. He gives the example of a boy aged 3 years 8 months who had drawn a curved line and then said that it was a croquet hoop; he immediately drew another croquet hoop on purpose. From this point on, says Luquet, the child will often announce beforehand what he is going to draw. Despite these claims, I have seen no evidence to suggest that children routinely try to repeat a figure that they have fortuitously produced (a criticism also made by Matthews 1999), nor that it is only children who have already 'seen' a figure in their scribbles who then go on to draw one intentionally. Some studies (e.g., Alland 1983; Harris 1971; Golomb 1993) have shown that children – and adults – who have not drawn before move fairly rapidly to drawing something realistic without having 'discovered' these forms accidentally in their scribbles (see figure 4.7). Golomb and Whitaker (Golomb 1981) also found that their 2- and 3-year-old scribblers could make a reasonable attempt at a representational drawing when they were requested to do so; again, there was no evidence that they had accidentally recognised these forms in their own scribbles.

It is more likely that children begin to draw in a representational way because they have an intention to do so. They already realise that their marks *could* be made to resemble a real object if only they could choose the appropriate marks and put them together in the right way. And this is the major task they are confronted with: to find ways to realise their intentions. But, there is no distinct shift in stage; Luquet (1927/2001) points out that children will still produce a likeness by accident and will also continue to make scribbles that have no meaning at all.

Identifying the components

In order to produce a recognisable representation children have to decide which components of an object to include and, also, how to draw them. There is evidence that they can 'extract' or identify the components of objects at quite an early age even though they cannot draw them themselves. Yamagata (2001) showed children some predrawn pictures – human and animal faces and some cars. The children, aged 1 year 6 months, 2 years, 2 years 6 months and 3 years, were asked to colour each picture. Other children from the same age ranges were given the outlines of a face and a car and were asked to finish them. After they had completed their first task all the children were asked to draw a picture of their mother. Not surprisingly, there was an increase in performance on each task with increasing age. Although the youngest children, at age 1 year 6 months, could not draw a picture of their mother's face nor add the features to an outline, some of them were able to make marks on the features of a predrawn face (see figure 4.8). The results show that, although they could not draw a face themselves, these children could at least mentally identify the components of a face. By age 2 years 6 months many of the children could draw the features inside a facial outline and 3-year-olds performed well on all of the tasks. In my own unpublished data, I have also found that nearly all of a sample of twenty 3-year-olds could draw the eyes, nose and mouth inside a facial outline and all of them were successful when an adult dictated the order for them.

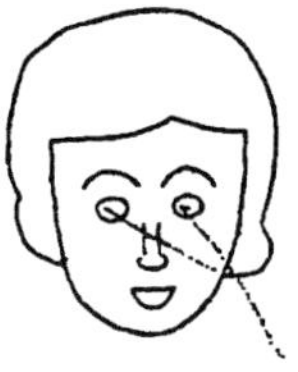

1 year 10 months

1 year 9 months

2 years 10 months

Figure 4.8 *Children's responses when they were asked to colour some outline drawings (from Yamagata 2001).*

For Yamagata, these findings indicate that the emergence of representational drawing depends on the mental extraction of the component parts
of the object to be drawn, and then on the actual drawing of these parts.
She argues that representational drawing does not always arise through
fortuitous realism and that children from a very early age are much more
intentional than Luquet gave them credit for.

Spatial correspondence between object and drawing

Young children have a good idea about where different parts
should be located in a drawing. For example, when I drew a figure –
a head and torso – for my daughter (aged 1 year 11 months) and then
asked her to add the arms and the legs she made some side-to-side
scribbles for the arms and some vertical scribbles for the legs; the curved
line to the left of and overlapping the face is a hat (see figure 4.9). These
marks were not randomly added but were targetted at the appropriate

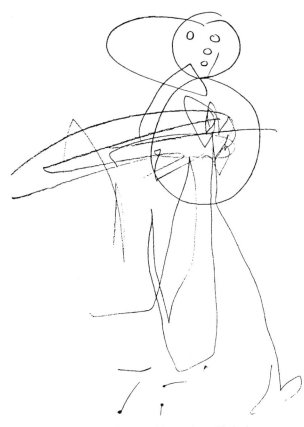

Figure 4.9 *Amy, aged 1 year 11 months, added a hat, some arms and some legs
to a predrawn head and body.*

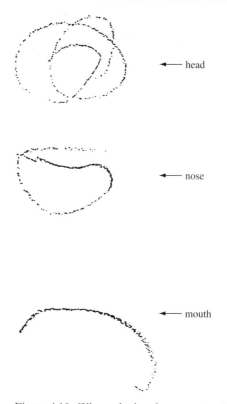

head

nose

mouth

Figure 4.10 *When asked to draw a person Kate, aged 3 years, drew a head, a nose and a mouth.*

parts of the figure. Similarly, when Kate, aged 3 years, was asked to draw a person she made a spatial 'list', starting with the head at the top, then the nose and finally the mouth (see figure 4.10). In cases such as these there seems to be a spatial correspondence between the items in the drawing and the spatial arrangement of the real items, even though the marks often do not look like their real-life counterparts at all.

Golomb (1974, 1981) also reported a similar effect when she dictated the body parts to young children who normally only produced scribbles. These children correctly ordered the items along the vertical axis of the figure (e.g., hair above the head, tummy below the head, legs below the tummy) even when the verbal order did not always match the spatial order of the figure. Wolf and Perry (1988) have reported these *point plot representations* in children from age 20 months and Matthews (1999) also notes young children's ability to mark the different elements in a drawn object even before they are able to make explicitly different shapes for them.

The search for equivalents

Long before they themselves can draw a recognisable object, young children have seen older children and adults draw them. They know, then, that producing a visual resemblance to a real object is, at least, one of the goals of drawing. The child's earliest deliberate representations may bear no resemblance to the real object at all, but may simply 'stand for' that object. When asked to draw a person, for example, the child may draw a squiggle or a closed shape (Cox & Parkin 1986; Cox 1993) (see figure 4.11). At this stage he may simply be making a mark – any mark – because that is what he has seen others do. But at least he has got the idea that a mark or shape is what you have to produce when you want to draw something.

At around the age of 2 or 3 years most children discover how to make a closed form – a roughly circular or oval shape. This is an important achievement. The shape is a *good form* in Gestalt terms and its importance, according to Arnheim (1974), is that it seems to suggest the contour of a figure against a background that gives the figure a solid-looking quality.[4] It is one of the simplest forms that can denote an object and can signify the 'thingness' of objects, that is, the solid property of three-dimensional things (Golomb 1992, p. 27). Piaget and Inhelder (1956) claimed that young children use an undifferentiated closed form to represent all sorts of differently shaped objects. Because these forms often have no obvious visual likeness to the real object they stand for, they may not endure as representations, that is, although we may regard them as representational at the time they are produced, the child herself will be unable to interpret them at a later date.

Although the child may have produced the closed form accidentally at first, it is particularly useful for representational purposes and seems to give impetus to the business of making the drawing have some visual resemblance to real objects (see chapter 8). It is ambiguous, though, if it fails to resemble the real object in terms of shape or detail. It may be this

Figure 4.11 *Simon's drawings of people at age 3 years (left: 'It's my Mummy') and 3 years 2 months (right: 'Mummy and Daddy').*

---

[4] See appendix for a brief overview of the Gestalt theory.

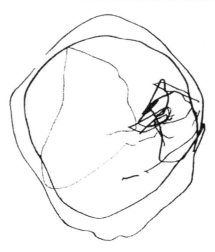

Figure 4.12 *Joel, aged 2 years 5 months, explains, 'There's a baby in here ... a baby in the water.' (Matthews 1984.)*

ambiguity that encourages the child to adapt it, making it more elaborate and complex and reflecting something of the visual appearance of the object it is supposed to stand for. Thus, the 'primordial circle' (Arnheim 1974, p. 175), which may be used indiscriminately at first to stand for any object, comes to represent only rounded objects when the child invents or learns other graphic forms, which can stand for differently shaped objects.

A closed contour not only encourages the child to look for a resemblance between it and objects in the real world, but also encourages her to make marks within its boundary. Matthews (1984) claims that with the development of the closed form the child has started to construct a pictorial space. He gives the example of his son's drawing of a circular closed shape with a small area of scribble inside it, drawn when Joel was aged nearly 2 years 6 months (see figure 4.12). The line represents a contour or edge – of a bath, perhaps. And, as Joel says, 'There's a baby in here ... a baby in the water' (p. 18). Thus, the closed form has an 'inside' that contains the baby in the water, and the line separates it from the 'outside'. This inside–outside is a *topological* distinction (Piaget & Inhelder 1956) and a property of many objects or scenes that the young child is interested in drawing.

According to Golomb (1981), the child's *intention* to draw a certain object includes a desire to capture some visual aspect of that object. Although Piaget and Inhelder (1969) regarded the activity of drawing as partly assimilation (a playful activity without regard to what the drawing looks like) they also considered it as accommodation (an attempt to capture some of the features of the real object). In order to achieve this visual correspondence we need to *re*present the object. The emphasis is on the *re* in 'representation', that is, we need to present the object again. However, we cannot represent it in the sense of 'cloning' or duplicating it since, in most cases, the object we want to depict will be three-dimensional and the picture surface has only two dimensions. By using lines and shapes we have to find ways of suggesting the object. This relationship is not arbitrary. As Arnheim (1997) has argued, 'the representation ... does not consist in copying or extracting or selecting from the observed facts but in creating equivalents of them in the given medium' (p. 11). Thus, for Arnheim the child is engaged in a search for or invention of 'equivalents' – graphic forms that can stand for and bear some resemblance to the objects they represent (see also Goodnow 1977). At first, these graphic equivalents are very simple lines or shapes that stand for a much more complex object; later, children find more elaborate ways to suggest this equivalence (see also Arnheim 1974; Golomb 2002). These equivalents are not replicas or reproductions but symbols, and as DeLoache (2002) says, 'A symbol represents, refers to, denotes something other than itself' (p. 207). Thus, representational picture-making is a symbolic activity.

In his (1993) study of two girls' drawings over the period from age 16 months to 3 years, Duncum found that at age 19 months for one child and at 2 years for the other they used graphic equivalents to stand for real objects (e.g., circles for eggs). In some of the examples already given (e.g., Amy's 'bird' in figure 4.5), different kinds of marks are used appropriately to denote different elements, for example, a dot for an eye and vertical lines for legs. In her figure completion (see figure 4.9), Amy used horizontal and vertical lines appropriately for the limbs and drew a curved line for the hat. She did not copy the circular shapes she had just seen me use for the head and the body of the figure, even though circular or spiral scribbles were in her repertoire. It is possible that she had deliberately selected appropriate marks to represent the differently shaped items she was adding. Kate made a spiral scribble for the head (see figure 4.10), a more controlled circular form for the nose and then an open curved line for the mouth. These could be the beginnings of *figural representation*, where the shape of the elements in the drawing bear some recognisable visual relationship to the real objects they stand for. Matthews (1984) gives the example of the first figural representation produced by his son, Ben. Having drawn a cross-shaped figure, made with push-pull and horizontal arc movements, Ben announced that it was an aeroplane (see figure 4.13). That in some cases these children's verbal declarations came after the drawings were finished suggests that they were responding to the *visual* similarity between the marks they had made and the objects they resembled. Matthews (1997) has observed that children as young as 2 years 6 months are able to modify their scribbles to show the difference between a sphere and a sausage-shaped object that they were asked to draw. He also found that some 3-year-olds will use a circle for the sphere and a rectangular shape for the sausage; some of the children who could not draw such clearly differentiated shapes could, nonetheless, produce

Figure 4.13 *Ben, aged 2 years 1 month, combines push-pull lines and horizontal arcs and announces, 'This is an aeroplane.' (Matthews 1984.)*

curved lines for the sphere and parallel lines for the longer object. These are clear examples of children's attempts to make their drawings match the shape of the objects they are meant to represent, an issue I shall pursue in chapter 5 with a discussion of Willats' (1981, 1985, 1987) account of the way that children develop denotation systems.

The aesthetic balance of children's early drawings

For some authors, notably Kellogg (1969), representation is not on the child's agenda at all; rather, the child is concerned with the *aesthetic* qualities of the marks she makes. From her enormous collection of children's spontaneous drawings, Kellogg proposed that children develop a considerable repertoire of scribbles. In fact, she claimed that there are

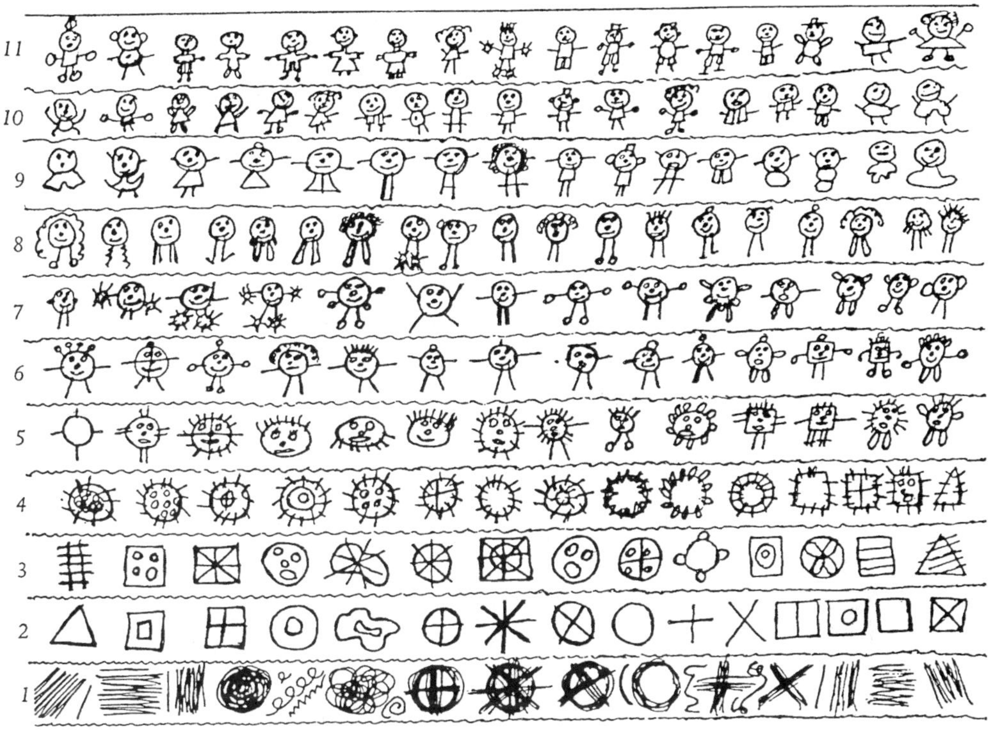

Figure 4.14 *Kellogg (1969) believed that children's basic scribbles are combined and recombined to produce increasingly more complex forms.*

twenty different basic scribbles that act as 'building blocks' (Kellogg & O'Dell 1967, p. 19) for children's drawings, although each child does not necessarily produce all types. These scribbles are practised and then combined and recombined to produce increasingly more complex forms. Kellogg calls a cross, made with two diagonal strokes, a *diagram*; framed inside a circle or a square it becomes a *combine*. A figure composed of three or more diagrams is an *aggregate*. The figures can be elaborated into *mandalas* (see level 3 of figure 4.14); then, at a later stage, *sun schemas* appear (see level 4 of figure 4.14). The *designs*, based on these graphic formulas, are used to create forms that have no representational intention, although they can be used, if necessary, to represent particular objects. Kellogg claims that it is adults rather than the children themselves who insist that the marks should represent objects. Although adults may be well meaning they are, in Kellogg's opinion, essentially misguided in trying to impose representational interpretations on what are essentially non-representational graphic forms.

Not only do the child's graphic configurations become more complex, but they also become more aesthetically balanced and the child monitors their placement on the page. Kellogg embraced the ideas of Jung (1964) and the Gestalt psychologists (e.g., Koffka 1935; see appendix) that there are basic and universal shapes and *good forms* that have aesthetic appeal, and, for Kellogg, the young child is concerned with the visually aesthetic balance of form rather than with the need to represent something. Later, when the child eventually does produce representational forms, she uses the units already in her repertoire. So, the child's earliest representational drawings will resemble these prior non-representational forms more than they do the visual characteristics of the real objects that she is trying to draw. For example, Kellogg sees evidence of *mandalas* and *sun schemas* in children's first attempts to draw the human figure. These radially symmetrical forms are, she argues, particularly well suited to stand for the human figure.

Although, undoubtedly, children do produce various kinds of scribbles (Major 1906; Matthews 1983, 1984), the evidence for Kellogg's very detailed claims is not very compelling. Golomb and Whitaker (Golomb 1981) asked adults to categorise the scribbles produced by the 2- to 4-year-old children in their study. They found that inter-rater reliability was very low when the judges were dealing with the finished drawings, although much better (70 per cent) when they watched the whole process of the children's scribbling. Nonetheless, the judges could only agree on two broad categories of scribble – those which were circular, loopy or included whirls and those which involved repeated and densely packed parallel lines. Although Kellogg's twenty different scribbles appear easily discriminable, in reality this has not proved to be the case.

In Kellogg's own data just over 9 per cent of children aged 2 years to 2 years 6 months drew mandalas and only about 4 per cent of children aged 4 years 1 month to 4 years 6 months drew sun schemas. Such low frequencies suggest that these forms are not very common. Alland (1983) has also questioned the supposed universality of these forms as, in a number of different cultures, he failed to find examples of circles or mandalas. Again in her own data, Kellogg reported that sun schemas and human figures appeared at the same age rather than in sequence; this casts doubt on the notion that representational drawings, such as human figures, are derived from these so-called earlier forms. Indeed, about 80 per cent of Golomb and Whitaker's 3-year-old scribblers and about 39 per cent of their 2-year-olds produced representational figures on request or in response to the dictation of body parts, even though they had not progressed through the steps proposed by Kellogg. We only have to observe children's early drawings of the human figure (the 'tadpole' figures) to see that, in contrast to Kellogg's claim, most are not in fact radially symmetrical; far more frequently, the legs are elongated and the arms of the figure are often completely missing (Cox 1993).

Another problem with Kellogg's account is her argument for the *lack* of certain forms in children's scribbles. For example, she notes that young children rarely produce diamond shapes, the reason being that they are not, as far as the child is concerned, aesthetically good forms. This argument is, however, circular (they are not good forms because children do not produce them) and also contradicts the fact that the diamond *is* a good form in terms of Gestalt principles (a point made by Bremner 1996). A more likely reason for the absence of diamond shapes in young children's pictures is simply that the diamond is difficult to produce – most children cannot copy a diamond accurately until at least the age of 7 years, and some adults find this task difficult too (Laszlo & Broderick 1985). Although Kellogg does not completely dismiss problems of production, they are certainly de-emphasised in favour of matters of aesthetic balance. The problem with her claim that children are concerned about the aesthetic balance of their shapes is the lack of any independent evidence: just because we observe that many children produce carefully drawn and symmetrical patterns does not mean that their main aim is an aesthetic one.

When children begin to ascribe meaning to their scribbles, they do so, according to Kellogg, because of pressure from adults. It is certainly the case that children sometimes show their scribbles to parents or caregivers and it may be that this is mainly for approval (Gardner 1980). This activity of sharing provides an opportunity for social interaction and may also involve the adult in communicating the idea of representation to the child. The child may make up a name for her drawing simply because she is expected to do so, as Kellogg claims. In Yamagata's (1997) study, suggestions from the mother frequently stimulated a more representational drawing from children from the age of 18 months. Again, this could be interpreted as influence, if not pressure, from the adult. There are many examples, however, of children spontaneously naming their scribbles when they suddenly see a likeness to some object in the real world. Children are also keen to name what they are about to draw, even if they change their minds in the process as the emerging shapes remind them of something else. Nonetheless, it may be, as Kellogg would probably argue, that the general idea that children's scribbles should 'be something' has been imposed on them by adults. It is difficult to discount the claim that pressure from adults is the main reason that children shift towards representational drawing; however, it is reasonable to hold the view that it is not the only cause.

Are there stages of scribbling?

Some authors, such as Matthews (1984) and Golomb (1992), have emphasised the representational intentions of young children's early mark-making activity, whereas others, such as Kellogg (1969), have focussed on children's interest in aesthetic balance and their disregard for

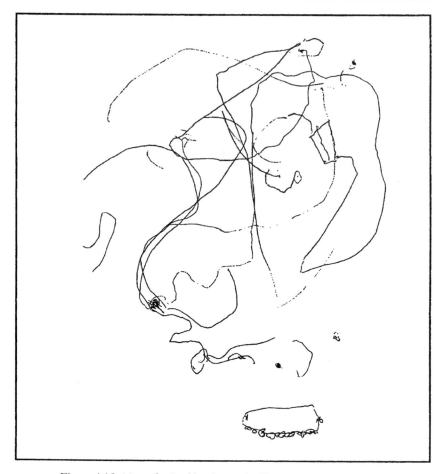

Figure 4.15 *'A car for Daddy who crashed his car' by Quentin, aged 2 years 10 months (Kindler & Darras 1997).*

representation. Nevertheless, all contend that there is some developmental change over this early period of drawing. Can we regard these changes as *stages*? Usually, the use of this term carries a Piagetian meaning (e.g., Piaget 1970; see also Smith 2002), that is, it implies that each stage is discrete and qualitatively different, that each new stage completely supersedes the previous one, and that each stage is necessary and cannot be missed out.

The different representational systems outlined by Wolf and Perry (1988) – object-based, gestural or action, point plot, and figural representations – may develop in a roughly sequential way, but these authors do not regard them as stages in the Piagetian sense. Rather, they form a gradually enlarging repertoire that the child, and the adult, can call upon as and when required. Kindler and Darras (1997) give an example of action *and* figural representations used in the same picture, 'A car for Daddy who crashed his car' (see figure 4.15). Quentin, aged 2 years

10 months, drew a large scribble of his father's car accident (which Quentin had witnessed) and then added a new car at the bottom of the page. Each of these systems of representation has its own uses and its own limitations, and the child's task is to develop them and to know when to use them.

Although Kellogg (1969) gave the impression of a fairly orderly progression through the steps outlined in her account of children's early drawing activity, she was careful to say that, based on her longitudinal data, not all children necessarily progress through all the steps. In fact, in both the representational account and in the aesthetic account of children's early drawings, although there may be changes taking place, they should not be regarded as rigid and discrete stages. In any case, the development from scribbling to representational drawing is not always smooth: there can be lulls when children are not interested in drawing at all, and other periods when they will prefer to scribble even though they have already demonstrated their ability to draw more complex forms or even representational figures (Eng 1954; Cox 1992). We assume that producing a drawing can be quite taxing for young children and, sometimes, they may simply want to lapse into a pleasurable and less-demanding activity such as scribbling.

Is scribbling necessary for later drawing development?

Although there is little evidence for the detailed steps or stages in scribbling advocated by Kellogg (1969) there is, nonetheless, some evidence for a shift from early uncontrolled scribbles, through more controlled and distinct lines and forms, to representational drawing (Major 1906; Matthews 1983, 1984; Cox & Parkin 1986). Just because a series of changes is related to increasing age does not mean, however, that each step is developmentally necessary. We know from a number of cross-cultural studies (e.g., Alland 1983; Harris 1971) that many children and adults, who have had no previous opportunities to draw, quickly progress to drawing representational figures without going through extended periods of scribbling activity. Nonetheless, even in these extreme cases there does seem to be at least a minimum of experimentation necessary before a recognisable representation is produced. For example, Harris shows how a 5-year-old boy in a remote area of South America, who had not drawn before, produced some squiggles and closed forms in his first attempt, before moving on to drawing tadpole and then conventional figures (see figure 4.16). Other researchers, such as Fortes (1940, 1981), Haas (1978) and Court (1981), who have collected drawings from children and adults with no previous experience of this activity, have also observed how people experiment with scribbles and patterns before quickly moving on to producing a recognisable figure. Although people in remote areas may

Figure 4.16 *The first drawings of an illiterate 5-year-old boy living in the South American Andes (Harris 1971): (a) the first scribbles, (b) a tadpole figure the next day, (c) tadpole figures a week later, (d–f) figures selected at weekly intervals although drawings were made daily, (g) figure drawn after six months with no practice, (h) figures drawn one week later.*

already have experienced mark-making by, for example, using sticks or stones to mark in the mud or sand or on a rock face, when confronted with a new medium they may scribble in order to explore the properties of this unfamiliar marker and its effect on the unfamiliar surface of the paper.

As well as the data from naïve drawers in isolated cultures, we also have evidence from blind children using a raised-line technique. Both Millar (1975, 1994) and Kennedy (1980, 1983, 2003) have demonstrated that some congenitally blind children are able to construct figures that are representational and also recognisable to sighted observers (see chapter 9). On the whole, however, it is older children (aged about 10 years) who produce recognisable figures, whereas younger children produce a more 'scribbled' form. Even so, the older children in Millar's study had already experienced the raised-line technique in a previous spatial experiment, so they had some idea of how lines could be produced intentionally. It seems, then, that a period of scribbling, however brief, may be necessary in the sense that it allows children to experiment with the medium in order to find out what its possibilities are and encourages their fine motor control over the pencil or crayon. Golomb (1992), also, has argued that scribbling can be a useful experience in allowing children to become acquainted with the drawing materials and how they can be used to produce shapes that can be linked meaningfully to objects and people in the real world. However, the shapes that scribblers produce when asked to draw particular items (such as a mother, a baby, a car, a house and so on) tend to be much more controlled, with the use of closed contours, compared with the more unruly scribbles of their 'free' drawings (Golomb 1981). Although it is possible that they could select from their repertoire of scribbles, it seems that 'request' drawings demand on-the-spot solutions – solutions that are not solely dependent on prior scribbles and patterns.

Summary

Most children's first attempts to draw occur at around the age of about 12 months. Although their early scribbling tends to be uncontrolled and formless it quickly becomes more disciplined and we can observe different kinds of arm and hand movements, which leave different sorts of marks on the page. These movements may in fact be universal, although we need more evidence to support this claim. Even though their scribbles are unrecognisable, children sometimes attribute meaning to them and there is also evidence that they may sometimes intend them to be representational from the start. It seems that children often represent the *movement* of objects with their gestures and that the marks they leave on the paper are the trace left behind from this transient representation. The notion of an entirely non-representational stage or period in children's drawing development is difficult to sustain; at least, it is not as clear-cut as some writers have claimed. Even so, some writers maintain that a drawing is not truly representational until it bears some visual resemblance to the object it represents and is able to sustain itself as a representation independent of the child's accompanying gestures or verbalisations.

Some writers, such as Luquet, have argued that children move towards producing recognisable images in their drawings by accident, when they suddenly 'see' that their marks bear some resemblance to real objects. Although there are many examples of this *fortuitous realism* in the literature, it is unlikely that this is the only or main way children shift towards realism in their drawings. There is a good deal of evidence that they already *intend* to make their scribbles and shapes stand for and resemble real objects, even if they cannot yet achieve this goal. They have some idea of how an object (such as a face) can be mentally divided into different components (e.g., eyes, nose, mouth) and are able to maintain the spatial correspondence of these components in their drawing, even though the marks themselves do not look like the components they are meant to stand for. The problem children are confronted with is how to make the lines and shapes in their drawings reflect the shapes of real objects.

Although many authors have concentrated on the representational nature of children's drawing, Kellogg has argued that the young child's primary aim is not with representation at all but with the aesthetic qualities of their picture-making. The evidence for many of the details of Kellogg's theory is not strong; however, the emphasis on aesthetic interests is one that is lacking in most other accounts of children's drawings, and Kellogg's contention that representation is mainly imposed on the child by adults is difficult to refute.

Neither the representational nor the aesthetic accounts claim that there are distinct stages in children's early drawing development, at least not in the Piagetian sense of 'stage'. A more accurate view is that although different representational forms may be acquired successively, these are retained as a repertoire that the child can call on as and when appropriate. Children seem to enjoy the activity of scribbling both in terms of motor movements and the marks they produce. A period of scribbling is useful in developing children's familiarity with the materials and the different kinds of marks and shapes that can be produced. However, an extended period of scribbling is probably not strictly necessary, as the evidence suggests that some children and adults who have had no previous experience with drawing are able to produce representational images with only very minimal experimentation.

5   Being realistic

Young children's scribbles may sometimes be representational even though we cannot recognise what they are meant to be. The drawings gradually become more recognisable, however, as children begin to use lines and shapes as graphic equivalents of the objects they want to draw. We see these pictures as charming, even though or, perhaps, because they exhibit a certain primitiveness and lack the visual realism that we, as adults, may feel a picture should have. Nonetheless, according to Luquet (1927/2001), children intend their drawings to be realistic, in the sense that they want to make a good likeness of the object. So, what kind of realism do they have in mind and how do they grapple with the problems involved in creating a realistic picture?

Intellectual and visual realism

Some of the things young children draw seem bizarre. The truncated forms we call 'tadpole' figures are notable examples (see figure 5.1). The torso seems to be missing, and the arms, if they are included, stick out from the sides of the head. Even when a drawing is more recognisable than this it may, nonetheless, be an impossible view of the object, for example, when a 'transparency' drawing shows parts of the object or scene that would not normally be visible at all (see figure 5.2). Some drawings depict more of an object or scene than one could see from any one position (e.g., 'folding out' drawings – see figure 5.3); indeed, pictures often appear to have been drawn from a jumble of different viewpoints (see figure 5.4).

Ricci (1887), one of the earliest writers on children's drawing, suggested that children are not attempting to show the actual appearance of objects but, rather, are expressing their knowledge about them. This idea was developed further by Kerschensteiner (1905), who claimed that children include those features in a drawing which are central to their concept of that class of objects, and the axiom 'children draw what they know rather than what they see' has been credited both to Kerschensteiner and to Luquet (1927).

Luquet called this mode of drawing *intellectual realism*,[1] the idea being that the basic details and structure of an object or scene are shown but not

[1] In fact, Luquet originally called it *logical* realism.

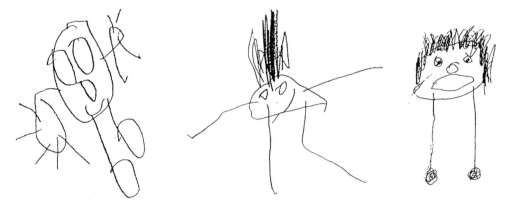

Figure 5.1 *'Tadpole' figures drawn by preschool children.*

Figure 5.2 *A 'transparency' drawing of a gorilla who has eaten his dinner (Arnheim 1974).*

from one particular viewpoint. The child's intention is to provide the 'most faithful and complete representation of the object' (Luquet 1927/ 2001, p. 122). Intellectual realism is contrasted with *visual realism*,[2] which more faithfully reflects how things look from one fixed viewpoint. In the visually realistic mode, transparency drawing gives way to occlusion, and folding out and mixed viewpoints are replaced by perspective. Intellectual and visual realism both have their advantages and disadvantages.

---

[2] Various other terms for these two modes of representation have been used in the literature, including object-centred versus viewer-centred (Marr 1982) and array-specific versus view-specific (Cox 1985).

Figure 5.3 *In this 'folding out' drawing of a cat, by Amy aged 4 years 5 months, we appear to see the underside of the body (note the belly button), all four legs and the tail. The face is drawn from the front.*

Intellectual realism can give us more information about the invariant structure (Gibson 1979; also see appendix) and features of an object or scene, but we may not be able to tell from which viewpoint it was drawn. In contrast, visual realism preserves the viewpoint and shows us how the object appears from it, but this may be at the cost of losing some of its invariant features and distorting its structure. Sometimes it is quite obvious that a depicted object or scene has not been drawn from a particular viewpoint and therefore can be classified as intellectually realistic. Quite frequently, however, it is difficult for us to decide, as intellectual and visual realism may coincide, as when, for example, a child is asked to draw a model placed in its typical or canonical orientation.[3] It is often only under experimental conditions that these two modes can be teased apart, when a model is presented for drawing in a non-canonical orientation.

By the mid-childhood years children pay more attention to visual realism and are more successful in drawing a model from a particular viewpoint. Support for this shift from intellectual realism to visual realism in a drawing task has been provided by a number of researchers, including

---

[3] The canonical orientation is the object's typical view and that which best displays its important structural or invariant features (Gibson 1979; Freeman 1980). In canonical orientation, human figures face the viewer whereas cars and horses are viewed from the side (Ives & Rovet 1982; Luquet 1927/2001). The canonical form may refer to the typical orientation of the whole object or to its constituent parts.

Figure 5.4 At the seaside *by Amy, aged 6 years 6 months. Note the frontal view of the people and the jelly fish, the side view of the dog, the donkey and the fish, and the aerial view of the picnic.*

Freeman and Janikoun (1972), who asked children aged between 5 and 9 years, first of all, to draw a cup from imagination. Nearly all the cups had a handle attached to the side but had no flower design on them. Next, the children were asked to draw a particular cup that was placed in front of them; the handle was turned out of sight but a flower design on the side of the cup was clearly visible. The younger children – aged 5, 6 and 7 – drew a handle on the cup in their pictures. This inclusion of the handle declined with age; few 8-year-olds and no 9-year-olds drew it. Very few 5-year-olds drew the flower but the numbers gradually increased until, at age 9, all the children included it, indicating that with increasing age the children paid attention to the model. These findings provide supporting evidence for Luquet's claim that there is a shift from intellectual to visual realism around the age of 7 to 8 years (see figure 5.5).

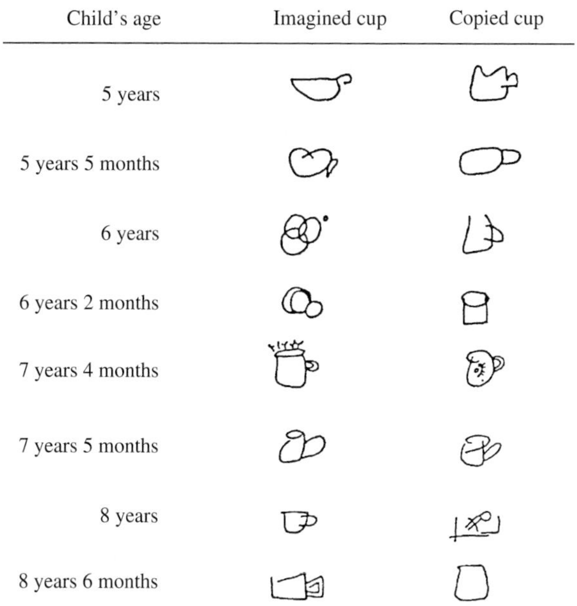

Child's age	Imagined cup	Copied cup
5 years		
5 years 5 months		
6 years		
6 years 2 months		
7 years 4 months		
7 years 5 months		
8 years		
8 years 6 months		

Figure 5.5 *All the imagined cups have a handle. The younger children continue to add the handle when drawing from a model; the older ones tend to omit the handle and include a flower design. (Freeman & Janikoun 1972.)*

The internal model

Young children rarely draw objects directly from observation, and even if we put an object in front of them and ask them to draw it they may not look at it very carefully. In any case, as writers such as Golomb (1993) have pointed out, a picture cannot be a copy of the object because of the intrinsic differences between the properties of the two-dimensional medium and the three-dimensional object. In fact, Luquet (1927/2001) argued that children actually draw from an *internal model*, whether or not a real model is available. The real model serves simply to activate the internal model. In forming this internal model children are not copying the object but are engaging in a creative mental act. Luquet described the model as a bit like a photograph in which certain details are in focus but others are not. So, although the internal model 'contains' the whole object, some parts of it are more focussed and important, and these parts may not be the same ones each time the child accesses or generates the model.

We can infer from the drawing itself which parts of the object are important to the child and which are less so. Important features are included and less important ones are minimised or omitted altogether.

The important features are generally decided on the basis of their role or function. A handle serves an important function on a cup – it is a *defining* or *primary feature* – whereas a design is merely an optional extra. If we consider children's spontaneous drawings of a cup, they almost always include a handle but rarely a decorative design.

Let's take another example – the young child's 'tadpole' drawing, a figure which seems to consist only of a head set upon two legs; the torso appears to have been omitted and the arms are often missing. Researchers have regarded the head as important because it contains our perceptual apparatus, and the legs, because they give us an upright stance and also suggest mobility (Barnes 1893; Ricci 1887). The torso is considered unimportant if we accept that it has been omitted from the drawing (Cox 1992, 1993) or, also, if we believe that it is present but undifferentiated, as in Arnheim's (1974) interpretation – that is, the torso is included either within the head contour or, implicitly, between the legs of the figure. Luquet (1927/2001) argued that young children have not failed to notice the torso but, since they are ignorant of the vital organs it contains, they 'do not see its point' (p. 61). The omission of the arms indicates, for some writers at least (e.g., Golomb 1988), that they are of peripheral importance. A problem with this reasoning is that it is in danger of becoming circular – something is important because it is included and it is included because it is important.

Despite the well-known axiom that children draw what they know rather than what they see, we can surmise from Luquet's photographic analogy that they will not necessarily draw *everything* they know about an object – only what is most important. We also have empirical evidence that young children know a lot more about the different parts of, for example, the human body than they include in their figure drawings: they can point out and name different parts of their own bodies and of predrawn figures (Golomb 1973, 1981; Brittain & Chien 1983; Cox 1992, 1993). If they know more than they include in their drawings then there is not necessarily a one-to-one direct mapping between children's knowledge and what they draw on the page.

Even though they may be drawing mainly from their internal model, young children are not necessarily responding in an *automatic* way. In Freeman and Janikoun's (1972) study some of the children, at all age levels, changed the shape of their cups – from a rounded shape for the imagined cup to a more square shape, in accord with the shape of the observed cup. It seems, then, that these children had noticed this aspect of the real model. In fact, just because children often do not draw what they see does not mean that they have not paid attention to the model, as Matthews (1999) has been at pains to point out. Some of Freeman and Janikoun's (1972) children indicated that they were aware of their own particular view of the cup and the fact that the handle could not be seen,

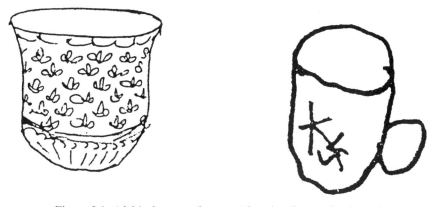

Figure 5.6 *Adult's drawing of a cup with its handle out of sight (left). Amy, aged 4 years 11 months, included the handle in her drawing (right).*

even though they had included it in the drawing. One child said that he had included a handle because 'if you turned it [the cup] round it would be there' (p. 1121). Another child expressed unease even though he had omitted the handle: 'Well, without the handle it looks like a pot. Shall I put it in to make it a cup?' (p. 1120). When my daughter was aged 4 years 11 months I asked her to draw a cup whose handle was turned out of sight. She drew the bowl of the cup first and then looked back and forth between the model and the drawing before adding a handle (see figure 5.6). She commented, 'I can't *see* the handle, but I'm going to draw it anyway. It makes it look better' (Cox 1992, p. 93). She seemed to be concerned that the depicted cup was not recognisable as a cup unless it had a handle.

These examples indicate that children are not necessarily forced to 'tip out' their internal model in an unthinking way. They are aware of what they can and cannot see from a particular viewpoint, but they are also concerned to make the object in their drawing recognisable (by including its defining features). When these concerns are in conflict it seems that young children tend to opt for intellectual realism rather than visual realism. Older children, on the other hand, appear to understand that the purpose of the task is visual realism and are more willing to draw only what they see.

The development of denotation systems

Although Luquet's (1927/2001) notion of the internal model may be useful in highlighting the salient features of the object, it is unclear how the child then proceeds to producing marks on the page. Even though he proposed that drawings are 'translations' from the internal model, Luquet did not give a detailed account of how this translation is brought about. One attempt at bridging this gap is Willats' (1981, 1985, 1987) account of denotation systems that map these internal mental representations, based on features of objects in the real *world* (*scene primitives*), onto corresponding elements in the picture (*picture primitives*). Willats' account does not tell us why children choose to include or omit certain parts of an object, such as the human figure for example, but seeks to explain children's ways of drawing the parts they do decide to include.

Willats assumes that young children are working from object-centred mental representations, based on invariant properties of the objects rather than on the way they happen to look from a particular viewpoint.[4] We can describe objects according to an extendedness principle: for example, a head is a bulky object that extends more or less equally in all three spatial dimensions; although a hand is also a three-dimensional object, we think of it as flat, extending mainly in two dimensions; arms and legs are also three-dimensional, but we tend to think of them as long things that extend mainly in one direction. Sometimes we wish to draw not three-dimensional objects but two-dimensional surfaces such as a finger-nail, the one-dimensional line of an eyelash or the virtually zero-dimensional point of the pupil of the eye. Willats' idea is that we select from our graphic repertoire of dots, lines and shapes those which will best capture the perceived dimensionality of these real objects. We are likely to choose a picture primitive with the highest possible dimensional index. So, for example, a closed round shape (or *region*) will best represent a bulky, three-dimensional volume such as a head.

The young child has only a limited number of picture primitives to choose from – basically, dots, lines and an enclosed region. Dots might be used appropriately to represent dot-like eyes and lines for various things that are linear-like in a real scene. However, when it comes to using a region, the young child is not able to vary its shape. Therefore, a roughly circular region will be used to represent a range of objects that in reality have different shapes. Thus, various objects, such as a head, a ball, a cube and a house, will look very similar in the young child's drawings. In figure 5.7a, a child has drawn circles when asked to copy both a circle and a triangle. Slightly later, *shape modifiers* will be added to represent particular shape properties of the object (Willats 1992a; see also Piaget & Inhelder 1956). For example, lines attached to a circular region indicate the edges or corners of a square or the point of a diamond (see figure 5.7b). Later still, by the age of about 4 years 6 months, when they can draw a square, children may use it to

---

[4] Willats' account owes much to Marr's (1982; Marr & Nishihara 1978; also see appendix) computational approach to visual perception, which details the mechanisms involved in detecting visual information at the retina (a viewer-centred representation) and the subsequent processing of an internal or object-centred representation of it, which in turn enables us to recognise objects even when they (or the viewer) are moving and presenting constantly changing views. Whereas Marr was concerned with internal representations, Willats is concerned with the mapping between internal representations and external representations, such as pictures.

Copy of a circle

Copy of a triangle

a

Copy of a square

Copy of a diamond

b

Copy of a circle

Copy of an ellipse

Copy of a square

Copy of a triangle

c

Figure 5.7 *At first, young children use a circle to depict many differently shaped forms (a); later, they add features to differentiate curved and angular forms (b); eventually, they are able to vary each shape (c).*

represent a variety of angular objects and reserve the circle for curved objects (see figure 5.7c). In this way, shapes become differentiated in their drawings. In contrast to the drawings based on object-centred representations, the drawings of older children tend to be based on viewer-centred representations, and the lines and shapes now represent the edges, contours and shapes of an object seen from a given viewpoint.

Willats seems to suggest that there are 'natural' ways to conceptualise certain objects. For example, the torso of the human figure is a bulky three-dimensional object that is generally longer than it is wide, and children in most modern societies tend to use a large region to represent it in their drawings. A problem with this account is that children, and indeed adults, in some other cultures use a vertical line for the torso (see chapter 10). We assume that they have attended to the length of the torso and have conceptualised it, like a limb, as extending in only one salient dimension. Thus, the shape of objects (particularly non-geometric forms such as the human figure) can be conceptualised in different ways, and some societies may favour one way over another. Indeed, these variations are also seen in some young children in modern cultures when they are trying out various possibilities and have not yet settled on the schemas most prevalent in their culture (see chapter 10). Thus, children's conceptualisations of objects may not be universal. And it follows that their choice of graphic equivalents for those objects will not be universal either.

Conservatism and flexibility

A child's drawings of a particular type of object often look remarkably similar, as if they have been drawn to a specific formula or schema. The reason is, according to Luquet, that the internal model tends to be *generic*, in the sense that it highlights the important features of a stereotypical member of its class. A house, for example, may be conceptualised as having four windows, a centrally placed door, a pitched roof and a chimney. A child's drawings of houses may look very similar, following this same schema, despite the fact that she herself may live in a semi-detached house, her friend in a terraced house and her grandmother in a bungalow (see figure 5.8). Similarly, the child's human figures often look as if they have all been drawn to a basic schema (see figures 5.9, 6.1 and 6.3). Luquet (1927/2001) called this phenomenon *conservation of the type* and saw it as evidence for the relative stability of the internal model, although, as I pointed out earlier, Luquet did not regard it as completely rigid and allowed the possibility that the child might focus on different aspects of an object at different times.

Like Luquet, van Sommers (1984) also argued that children may be constrained by their mental image or internal model of what they are trying to draw.[5] However, whereas Luquet argued that the internal model is based on a generic example of a particular class of objects, van Sommers believes that it is based on the actual schema that the child works out when she first begins to draw that object. Whereas for Luquet the internal model exists independently from the drawing, for van Sommers it is directly

---

[5] Van Sommers recorded 5- and 6-year-olds' attempts to draw from observation over several sessions and found that their successive drawings of the same object were very similar.

Granny's house

Amy's house

Val's house

Figure 5.8 *Amy, aged 5 years 5 months, uses the same basic schema for drawing houses.*

Figure 5.9 *Amy, aged 5 years 2 months, has used the same basic schema for drawing all her human figures.*

linked to the drawing activity; this schema acts as the visual goal towards which subsequent drawing attempts are directed, that is, having produced a satisfactory drawing the child then tries to replicate it. Thus, the child is guided by her visual memory of what the finished drawing should look like; it is the product rather than the process which accounts for the conservative outcome. The child does not necessarily follow a sequential order within the drawing but may vary the order and also the direction of the strokes from one drawing to another.

Once young children have devised a schema for a particular kind of object they may continue with it for a considerable length of time. A well-known example is the tadpole figure drawn by most children at some time between the ages of about 2 and 5 years. Although some children have been known to draw only one or two of these forms and then move on to drawing a more conventional figure,[6] there are others who continue to draw the tadpole for many weeks and even months (Cox & Parkin 1986). It can be quite difficult to persuade these children to alter their figure, as I have discovered in a series of tasks conducted with the help of various students (Cox 1992, 1993). One attempt to reduce the demands of the drawing task involved the experimenter in dictating the parts of the figure to the child (Stone 1989). The idea was to ensure that the child would draw all parts, including the torso, which is normally omitted, and that they would be drawn in the order that most conventional drawers follow. Although most of the tadpole drawers, with an average age of 3 years 2 months, did include the torso (as a dot or a squiggle), they did not draw it as a clearly defined and separate contour below the head; in addition, nearly all of the children attached the arms to the head of the figure. In other words, the children still produced their tadpole form. The tentative way in which they added the torso suggests that they were not sure how to draw it and, furthermore, that they were not sure where to place it.

I also carried out a copying task in which the children were asked to copy a conventional figure drawn by the experimenter. In one condition (the *whole figure* group) the children watched the experimenter draw the whole figure, naming each part as she went along. Just over half the children (55 per cent) drew a conventional figure when they copied this model. Another group (the *segment* group) drew each segment of the figure immediately after the experimenter had drawn hers and 68 per cent of them drew the conventional form. A third group (the *repeated segment* group) copied three of these segment-by-segment figures, and the percentage of children drawing the conventional form rose to 72 per cent. Control groups who were asked to draw either one figure or three figures

---

[6] The term *conventional* refers to a figure in which the torso is drawn below the contour of the head and with the arms of the figure attached to it.

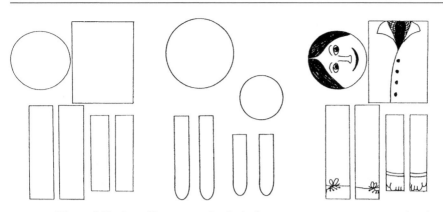

Figure 5.10 *Over 50 per cent of tadpole drawers can construct a conventional human figure with the pieces on the left; over 80 per cent are successful with those in the centre and all are successful with those on the right.*

all drew tadpole forms. Thus, simple repetition only led to more tadpole figures.

Although this study demonstrated that young children will copy a new form, I wanted to know if the effect would last. Two days later the children were asked to draw a human figure. Most children in the whole segment group reverted to their tadpole schema and only 23 per cent drew a conventional figure. The percentage of conventional figures in the segment group was 36 per cent and in the repeated segment group it was 61 per cent. We have to go to considerable lengths, then, to encourage children to change their usual way of drawing the figure and, although in this study the effect lasted for two days for some children, we do not know whether it would have continued for longer. Luquet (1927/2001) noted that suggestions from other people on the way the child draws may have a temporary effect but often do not lead to a lasting change. Accidental changes made by the child herself – even those that make the figure appear more realistic – may also be reversed in a later drawing.

I stated earlier that children know a lot about the human figure, including the fact that it has a torso with arms attached to it. So, the production of the tadpole form does not imply a lack of knowledge on the child's part. Nor is it a memory problem since a dictation task is not very successful in eliciting conventional figures. The problem seems to be that the tadpole drawer has not developed a schema for the torso of the figure. If we provide one, by including it among a selection of precut pieces of card in a construction task, then the child is able to produce a successful conventional figure, including the torso and attaching arms to it (Bassett 1977; Cox & Parkin 1986); Cox 1993; Cox & Mason 1998) (see figure 5.10).

In this construction task the tadpole drawer is able to reorganise the overall schema of the human figure to accommodate the inclusion of a torso, a manœuvre not possible in a drawing task once the legs have been added below the head of the figure. The difficulty then is in the drawing task, not with the child's conceptualisation of the figure. The problem in the drawing task, according to Karmiloff-Smith (1990), is that the child has practised a sequentially ordered set of movements and cannot modify it; the 'program' must be run in its entirety. She cannot rethink the schema and work out how it could be rearranged so as to include an extra segment (such as the torso). This procedurally encoded knowledge is followed by a slightly later period when some modification of the schema is possible but only at the beginning or end of the sequence. Greater flexibility in altering the schema occurs later still when modifications can be made *during* the drawing procedure.

Karmiloff-Smith asked children aged between 4 years 6 months and 10 years to draw a man and also another man 'who does not exist' (i.e., a fantasy figure); they were also asked to draw a real and a non-existent house and a real and a non-existent animal. All of the children drew adequate pictures of the real objects. Over 90 per cent at all ages succeeded in drawing 'non-existent' versions, although a few of the youngest children simply drew their schema again. If we examine the changes children made from their normal schema in the standard pictures to that in the 'non-existent' cases, the younger children mainly changed the shape, either the general shape of the object or particular parts of it; otherwise, the structure remained the same. Some children omitted certain features, but these were features normally drawn at the end of the drawing procedure. Very few of these younger children added an extra feature, but all of them who did so added it at the end of the drawing sequence. The older children made alterations to their normal schema in a variety of ways: they added and omitted particular features and altered the orientation of the figure; what is more, they made these modifications during the course of the drawing procedure. These findings indicate that the youngest children had more difficulty in adapting what seems to be a fixed procedure; they 'ran off' their drawings in a fairly automatic way. Older children were more flexible although still relatively constrained in the modifications they could make. The oldest children made the greatest number and type of modifications, the reason being, as Karmiloff-Smith has argued, that they redescribed the sequential list in terms of a spatial structure whose parts could then be worked on individually and in any order. Thus, this process involves making knowledge that was formerly implicit in the mind *explicitly available to the mind*. This explanation in terms of representational redescription is part of Karmiloff-Smith's (1992) more general model of cognitive development.

A serious problem with this explanation is that a young child ought to follow the same sequential order of strokes when drawing the same object on different occasions. But, as I mentioned earlier, van Sommers (1984) found that this is not the case; children vary the order over a series of drawings. Others studies (e.g., Spensley & Taylor 1999; Barlow 2003) have also found that their children, aged 4 years, do not produce the elements of a man in a strict sequential order each time. A further difficulty with Karmiloff-Smith's account is that some studies have failed to replicate her findings. For example, Spensley and Taylor (1999) repeated the man and non-existent man tasks and also asked the children to draw a man with a beard. In contrast to Karmiloff-Smith's children, their 4-year-olds were able to make alterations mid-procedure. Studies by Zhi, Thomas and Robinson (1997), Berti and Freeman (1997), Morse and Bremner (1998) and Picard and Vinter (1999) have also found that some children, as young as 5 and even 3 or 4 years, can adapt their usual drawing procedure in order to draw, for example, a man with two heads. We can conclude, then, that young children are not as procedurally rigid as Karmiloff-Smith has claimed.

Whereas the studies discussed above were based on children's drawing from imagination, some studies have demonstrated flexibility in young children's drawing from a model. Cox and Moore (1994), for example, asked 4-year-old tadpole drawers and 4-, 6- and 8-year-old conventional drawers to draw different views of a model man as well as one from imagination. Many of the children, even at age 4, were able to add items of clothing, omit items or alter the shape of the torso and the hair in accordance with what they could see. Most of the youngest children made only one alteration; even so, the results show that young children are able to modify their figures and, furthermore, that the modifications can be made within the process of the drawing rather than at the beginning or the end of the sequence (see figure 5.11). One of the features of this task that may have been particularly effective in eliciting variations in their figure drawings was the successive orientations of the same model, an issue to be discussed later in this chapter. According to Luquet (1927/2001), by the age of 6 years children recognise that the use of the same schema for different orientations of the model is not very satisfactory and this study indicates that this awareness is present in even younger children.

Taken together, these various studies show that young children are capable of altering a well-established drawing sequence (see also Smith 1993; Cox & Lambon Ralph 1996; Cox, Koyasu, Hiranuma & Perara 2001); it is unlikely, then, that their formulaic and conservative drawings are the result of an inflexible procedure that they are 'programmed' to follow. And, indeed, in the light of mounting evidence Karmiloff-Smith (e.g., 1999) reassessed her position, arguing that procedural rigidity may be weaker in the domain of drawing (as opposed to, for example, the domain of language) since the external trace (i.e., the mark on the page) shows the child where to continue after she has interrupted her schema to make a mid-procedure alteration. Nonetheless, this weaker version of procedural rigidity has been criticised by Barlow (2003), who found that children's rigidity in their normal figure drawing does not predict their ability to

Figure 5.11 *A figure drawn from imagination and the front, back and side views drawn from a model (Cox & Moore 1994).*

alter their schemas when requested; children could even change their schemas when they were not able to see what they were drawing (i.e., when the trace was invisible but was recorded by a computer 'art pad'). These findings throw doubt on Karmiloff-Smith's theory.

Although we see some conservatism in children's drawings, we also see flexibility. Although they develop certain schemas, such as the 'shorthand' tadpole figure that serves the purpose of a 'graphic equivalent' to the human figure (Golomb 1981), children do not necessarily draw it in a rigid sequence; however, because it is easily recognised and evokes the idea of a person many children carry on using it for some considerable time. Nonetheless, a number of studies has shown that, even at age 4, some children are capable of altering their schemas in order to add additional items or to show a different point of view.

Are there progressive stages of realism?

There has been a tendency in the literature for researchers to talk about a progression from intellectual to visual realism as though visual realism is a more advanced and mature stage of development. Although he used the term *stage*, it seems that Luquet did not use it in a Piagetian way, that is, in the sense that the stages are discrete, progressively ordered and invariant. I believe that this rather rigid view of stage has endured because Luquet's ideas and evidence were adopted by Piaget and Inhelder (1956), who then moulded them to their particular stage account[7] of the development of spatial concepts (stage 1 – synthetic incapacity;[8] stage 2 – intellectual realism; stage 3 – visual realism). According to this account, children do not even begin to develop the ability to take a particular point of view of a scene until about the age of 7 years.

Since Costall's translation of Luquet's work (Luquet 1927/2001) we have a better idea of what Luquet meant. It turns out that he saw intellectual and visual realism as conventions or choices that we can make. Intellectual realism is not a 'childish' convention, and an adult as well as a child may choose to make an intellectually realistic drawing in order to show more than can actually be seen from a certain viewpoint. In fact, as Luquet pointed out, many drawings by adults 'hardly differ from those of children around twelve years old' (p. 128). Many artists, both ancient and modern and those in different cultures, have chosen to include different viewpoints in the same picture (see figures 8.8, 8.9 and 8.10). Thus, intellectual realism may coexist with visual realism and is not necessarily replaced by it, and there is no abrupt transition from one form to the other. Furthermore, we should not see visual realism as the endpoint of artistic development and, as Golomb (1993) contends, it should not serve as the standard by which children's drawings are judged.

---

[7] It must be said, however, that Piaget himself may have intended the notion of stage to be more flexible than the way in which many writers have interpreted it (Flavell 1971; Lourenço & Machado 1996).

[8] *Synthetic incapacity* is a term used by both Luquet and Piaget and Inhelder and refers to the young child's inability to co-ordinate the spatial relationships and proportions between the different elements in a drawing.

Young children are not held back by some general cognitive constraint from attempting to draw from a particular viewpoint, and, in fact, as we have seen from some of the evidence I have outlined above, young children at least as young as 4 are capable of visual realism. Children may well be aware of perspective representations but choose not to attempt them themselves because of the limitations of that sort of picture. In fact, Luquet claimed that children, certainly as young as 6, are aware of the possible contradiction between how an object appears from a certain angle and what they actually know about it. Goodnow, Wilkins and Dawes (1986, study 3) found that children aged 6 and 7 years draw more conservatively when requested by an adult but more experimentally for their own purposes. This suggests that children make choices regarding the mode of representation they use.

Once they start to draw more often in a visually realistic way the habits of intellectual realism may continue and children may depict an object in a visually realistic way on one occasion and then, in a later drawing, change to an intellectually realistic way; they may also use both modes of representation in the same drawing. Although the two modes are sometimes very obvious, sometimes they are not. Matthews (1999) gives as an example the drawing of a cube, which many young children represent with a single square and which a number of writers believe represents the whole object and not just one face of it. Evidence for this interpretation comes from Moore (1986), who found that many young children included the colours of all the faces of a multicoloured cube inside this one contour; similarly, Willats (1992c) found that some children included all the spots of a dice within a single rectangular shape. Aside from the fact that Matthews has failed to replicate the findings of other researchers, he also criticises this assumption. It may be that the child changes from intellectual to visual realism from moment to moment within the same drawing. A child who draws one face of the cube may then decide to add the various patterns or colours he sees on each of its faces; he may feel it inappropriate to place these outside the square and so he places them one after another inside it. This child, according to Matthews, is thinking in an *episodic* way as he continually makes decisions as the drawing goes along, and the final picture may contain both intellectually and visually realistic kinds of information.

According to Luquet (1927/2001), most people renounce intellectual realism as a mode of graphic representation in favour of visual realism even though they may not be able to attain this goal fully. But this does not mean that visual realism is an 'advance', as there is nothing wrong or childish about intellectual realism. In order to create a single and unified visually realistic picture the child has to understand that the drawing surface represents a single moment in space and time – a snapshot of how the object looks from that particular angle at that particular moment.

However, we should remember that although the broad trend in the western artistic tradition since the Italian Renaissance has been towards visual realism, the trend may be different in other cultural traditions (Hagen 1985; Cox 1992; see also chapter 8).

Are research tasks biased towards intellectual realism?

Although there appears to be a bias towards intellectual realism among young children, it may also be the case that the research tasks themselves are biased towards this kind of representation. For example, Freeman and Janikoun (1972) asked their children to name a cup and also allowed them to inspect it before they settled down to draw it. It is possible that this attention towards the object focussed the children's efforts on making it recognisable as a cup, that is, swayed them towards producing a canonical view, even though the handle was not visible when the cup was placed in position for the drawing task.

Bremner and Moore (1984) tested this hypothesis in two separate experiments. In the first one, 5-, 6- and 7-year-olds were asked to draw a coffee mug, although it was never named as such. All the children who were asked to draw a mug with its handle in view included a handle in their drawings. Of the children who had the opportunity to inspect the mug both visually and manually before it was placed ready for drawing with the handle out of view, six out of ten 5-year-olds, six out of ten 6-year-olds and one out of ten 7-year-olds included the hidden handle. A further group of children were not able to see the handle of the mug before or during the drawing. Of these, only two (both of them 6-year-olds) included the handle; the vast majority omitted it. Thus, inspection of the mug increased the number of intellectually realistic drawings.

In their second experiment, Bremner and Moore presented 6-year-olds with a mug positioned so that the children never saw its handle at all. Some children were asked to draw the object, which was not named ('Can you draw it for me?'). Afterwards they were asked to name it in order to check that they knew what they were drawing: twelve of them named it successfully and two did not; of these twelve, eleven omitted the handle and one included it. Another group of children was asked to name the object before they drew it: eleven were successful and three were not; of these eleven, ten included the handle in their drawings and one omitted it. Thus, naming the mug before they drew it dramatically increased the number of children who included the hidden handle in their pictures. A study by Lewis, Russell and Berridge (1993) replicated these findings regarding the naming of the object.

The instructions given to children have also been shown to affect the kind of drawing they make. When more explicit instructions are given (e.g.,

'Please can you draw X for me exactly as you see it from where you're sitting?'), children are more likely to draw what they see compared with a more general instruction (e.g., 'Please can you draw X for me?'). Barrett and Bridson (1983) found that children aged 4 years 6 months drew a more visually realistic picture, and Lewis, Russell and Berridge (1993) also found this to be the case among 5-year-olds. Taken together, the results of these various experiments indicate that aspects of the task such as the opportunity to inspect and name the object and also the explicitness of the instructions influence the way that children choose to depict the object.

The causes of change

Despite the conservatism in young children's drawings, they increasingly search for more realistic ways of representing objects (Golomb 1981; Goodnow 1977; Luquet 1927/2001). What brings about this change, particularly the shift towards visual realism from about the age of 7 to 8 years? Piaget and Inhelder (1956) accounted for it in terms of the child's awareness of different viewpoints, his own included. In order to imagine or draw a particular view of an object the child must be consciously aware of the viewpoint and how the object will appear from that position. This projective concept of space develops around the age of about 7 years. There have been a number of critical reviews of Piaget and Inhelder's account (e.g., Cox 1980, 1991), but one of the most critical pieces of evidence comes from a study by Ives (1980), in which children were asked to describe a particular view of an object or to choose a picture to match that view. Whereas 89.5 per cent of 3-year-olds and 92.5 per cent of 5-year-olds could describe verbally which side of an object (its front, back or side) could be seen, only 38 per cent of 3-year-olds and 51 per cent of 5-year-olds could select an appropriate picture. In a more complex task (Ives 1983), used with 5-year-olds, this effect was still evident: 83 per cent were correct with the verbal mode of response but only 47 per cent with the pictorial mode. Another study, by Pillow and Flavell (1985), also showed that 3-year-olds who could describe a particular view of a scene nonetheless tended to rely on intellectual realism when representing it pictorially. Although the children were asked to *select* a picture rather than to draw one themselves, the findings suggest that children may understand how objects appear from a particular viewpoint before they can make a pictorial representation of that view. Although they may understand that objects in the scene are occluded, they nonetheless may prefer either to select or to make a picture that shows the 'best view' of the scene, that is, that shows the objects separately and non-occluded (Liben 1978; Liben & Belknap 1981; Light & Nix 1983). Despite these findings that children may prefer an intellectually realistic response, we also know that, at age

4 years, some children are able to alter their own drawings to take account of different views of an object (e.g., Cox & Moore 1994). It seems, then, that Piaget and Inhelder's explanation for the shift to visual realism in pictures is not tenable.

Despite the criticisms of Piaget and Inhelder's explanation for change, it seems to be the case that when children do try to draw in a visually realistic way, particularly from a real model, they have a different attentional strategy compared with those children who draw in an intellectually realistic way. Sutton and Rose (1998) made video recordings of 4-, 6- and 8-year-olds while they produced five drawings of coffee mugs, presented singly or in pairs, in various orientations and, in one scene, containing a spoon. As expected, the 8-year-olds produced more visually realistic drawings than did the younger children; these visually realistic drawers spent more time overall looking at the models and they also looked more often; furthermore, they looked during the task as well as at the beginning of it.

If this different 'looking' strategy enables the older children to produce a visually realistic picture, then it might be possible to persuade younger children to use it. In their second study, Sutton and Rose found that more explicit instructions, while increasing looking at all ages, increased the 4-year-olds' looking at the beginning of the task and the 6-year-olds' looking during the task. The instructions had a big effect on the 6-year-olds' drawings: 85 per cent of them drew visually realistic pictures with the explicit instructions as compared with 59 per cent for the standard instructions. There was no comparable effect for the 4-year-olds. As expected, most of the 8-year-olds drew visually realistic pictures irrespective of the detail in the instructions.

Some studies have asked children to state verbally or to point to the aspects of the scene that they can actually see. For example, Jolley (1991) presented children aged 4 to 9 years with models of a man in a boat and a man on horseback. Half the children were asked which parts of the man could be seen and which parts could not; half did not have this discussion. Whereas most of the 8- and 9-year-olds drew visually realistic pictures whether or not they had had the discussion, among the younger children it was those in the discussion group who attempted to draw what they could see (see figure 5.12). A study such as this (and also Cox 1986) has brought the children's attention to the model *before* they begin to draw; others have interrupted the child during the drawing process (e.g., Ingram 1983; Cox 1985) and have also been successful in producing more visually realistic drawings. An exception, however, was a study I carried out with Nieland (cited in Cox 1992) in which 5-year-olds were asked to draw a ball partly hidden by another ball placed in front of it. Neither the children who had a discussion of the scene before the drawing nor those who had it after the first ball had been drawn went on to draw a visually realistic scene; instead, they drew two separate circles, as did the children who had no discussion of

Figure 5.12 A man in a boat *and* A man on horseback *drawn by Royanna (right), aged 6 years 8 months, after a discussion about what parts of the models were visible. The same topics drawn by Gemma (left), aged 6 years 9 months, with no discussion of the models. (Jolley 1991.)*

the scene at all. It is not clear why discussion failed to be effective but it may be that this particular scene is especially problematic as it contains two separate and identical objects that young children may prefer to depict with separate contours on the page (Cox 1991). Despite this exceptional case, a number of studies have shown that it is possible to persuade young children, even as young as 4 years old, to focus on the way the scene looks and to draw only what they can see.

Whereas some researchers have engaged children in overt discussion about the way the scene looks from their point of view, others have brought their attention to the appearance of the scene in less explicit ways. Davis (1983, study 1), for example, demonstrated that when children aged 4 to 6 years are asked to draw two cups side by side, one in canonical orientation and the other with its handle turned away, they will omit the hidden handle (see figure 5.13). These children would normally include the handle if asked to draw a single cup with its handle turned out of sight. It seems that the contrast in orientation of the two cups is sufficient for the child to notice the way they look and that the only difference is that the handle is visible on one but not on the other. The salience of orientation was also demonstrated in a further study (Davis & Bentley 1984) but in this case 5- to 6-year-olds were asked to draw a single

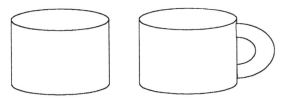

Figure 5.13 *Children are asked to draw two cups, one in canonical orientation and one with its handle turned out of sight.*

cup in one particular orientation and then a second cup, also presented on its own, in a different orientation.

Another example of an attempt to bring the child's attention to the way the scene looks is the cops and robbers task (Cox 1981, study 5) in which a policeman chases a robber who then hides behind a wall. Unfortunately for the robber the top of his head sticks up above the wall! The point of the task is that it emphasises what can be seen and what cannot from the policeman's perspective (which also coincides with the child's). Most children from age 6 onwards drew only the part of the robber they could see; they were not tempted to draw the whole of the figure. Although many of the 4-year-olds drew a whole robber, placing him either above or to the side of the wall, 44 per cent of them drew a more visually realistic picture (see figure 5.14).[9] Further investigation (Cox 1985) revealed that, for 6-year-olds at least, it is not necessary to present the task as a game nor to emphasise that the robber is hiding (a finding also reported by Light & Foot 1985). In fact, other pairs of objects will elicit the same effect: the majority of children will draw only what they can see as long as the two objects arranged one behind the other are dissimilar; in contrast, two same-shaped objects are more likely to elicit intellectually realistic draw-ings (Cox 1991). These findings hold good for children as young as 6 years, but they are less impressive for 4-year-olds, and it may be that younger children need to have their attention drawn to the appearance of the scene in a more overt way before they will produce a visually realistic representation. And, indeed, in a study by Arrowsmith, Cox and Eames (1994) 4- and 5-year-olds used visual realism when the notion of hiding was involved but not when the objects in the scene were merely dissimilar. Thus, stronger cues may be required if younger children are to inhibit their tendency to draw this scene in an intellectually realistic manner and to opt instead for visual realism.

Another explanation for change concerns children's memory capacity. According to Luquet, children usually draw from an internal model and, although he did not use these terms, we might suppose that the internal

---

[9] In a replication of this study, Su (1991) found that 69 per cent of 4-year-olds produced visually realistic pictures.

Figure 5.14 *Although some children drew the whole of the robber, placing him above or beside the wall, others drew only the part that they could see (Cox 1992).*

model is stored in long-term visual memory and then activated or accessed in short-term or working memory when the child (or, indeed, the adult) sets out on a drawing task. Whether or not the drawer can hold the complete image in her 'mind's eye' is debatable. Van Sommers (1995), for example, has argued that this is highly unlikely since our imagery processing tends to be both sequential and fragmentary. Furthermore, the information we bring to bear on the drawing task may not be all visual, but in other forms too, such as abstract knowledge, motor movements and so on (see chapter 9 for a discussion of drawing by blind people). Thus, even though we produce a single drawing it is not necessarily the case that this has resulted from a single intact image or even a single concept. As evidence for this argument, van Sommers cites a study by Brooks (1968), who asked adults to form a mental image of a capital letter and then to count its corners. Even those who could do this task successfully reported that they did not see the letter as a whole but 'moved around it', inspecting it section by section. If we attempt to draw while observing a real model in front of us we still need to use memory; from the moment we observe the part of the model we want to draw we must hold that image until we manage to put the marks on the page. Van Sommers (1995) gives an example of an elderly woman with brain impairment who developed difficulties with short-term visual memory; despite having been a commercial artist, her attempts to copy simple geometric forms produced some incomplete results.

These examples suggest that some models, either internal or external, may present a challenge to some drawers. In children, we might expect that a limited memory capacity will place constraints on what they can draw but that an increase in that capacity will enable them to plan and produce more complex drawings. Morra (1995) has proposed a neo-Piagetian account based on the ideas of, for example, Case (1985) and Pascual-Leone (1970). Basically, mental capacity (or *M capacity*) increases as the child develops, enabling her to manipulate increasingly complex information. The processes involved in drawing might include, for example, deciding to draw a particular object or scene, activating the relevant schemas and then making the drawing, which may also involve adapting the schemas. Increases in children's ability in these respects is related to an increase in M capacity rather than to chronological age itself (Morra & Perchinenna 1993; Morra, Moizo & Scopesi 1988).

Whereas Morra's approach assumes a *unitary* short-term or working memory for processing information, other accounts, such as that of Baddeley and Hitch (1974), have proposed a complex set of stores and systems and, in particular, a separate visuo-spatial memory system suitable for use in a drawing task. The limitation in young children's working memory capacity may be one of the reasons why they rely on well-practised schemas stored in long-term memory. As in Morra's account, so in this one too, developmental improvement in drawing is related to an increase in visuo-spatial capacity (although Gathercole 1998 has pointed out this could also be attributed to an increased 'central executive'). Berti and Freeman (1997), Spensley and Taylor (1999) and Picard and Vinter (1999) have also suggested that various information-processing factors, such as planning, monitoring and awareness as well as working memory, are implicated in the causes of representational change in drawing.

There is undoubtedly a relationship between complexity of drawing and an increase in mental or memory capacity, although this alone is unlikely to be responsible for changes in the way children draw. For example, it does not explain why children continue to draw tadpole figures in a dictation task when memory problems have been alleviated. It also does not explain the shift to visual realism, since, as I have outlined already, we have many examples of young children (presumably, with less memory capacity) attempting to draw what they see even if they are not very successful at it. Nonetheless, it may be that an increased memory capacity is needed for particularly complex drawings, such as those based on the system of linear convergence perspective (see chapter 6). So, although increased memory capacity may be necessary, it is unlikely to be sufficient in itself to promote effective change.

Other potential spurs to change are of various kinds. Some children adopt the style of other children or adults (Paget 1932). Presumably, something about these other schemas recommends them in preference to the children's usual styles. Similarly, children may become more aware of the style of drawings in the mass media – books, cartoons and so on – and begin to adopt that way of drawing for themselves (Wilson & Wilson 1977; see also chapter 10). According to Luquet (1927/2001), modifications may also come about by accident and even by lack of skill. Another cause of change may be that children are confronted with problems in their drawing tasks – either in their own spontaneous drawings or those posed in research studies – and they actively seek solutions to these problems. Sometimes they may find that their usual schema is inadequate if, for example, they want to depict a person from a radically different viewpoint (Cox & Moore 1994). In this case they may be dissatisfied with their usual front-facing static figure and be spurred on to experiment with solutions to this problem; in this way they change or extend their repertoire of graphic schemas. In another example, Willats (1992b) asked children aged 4 to 12 years to draw a model figure holding a plate. The

Figure 5.15 *A girl, aged 7 years 7 months, has foreshortened the arms of the figure holding a plate towards the viewer (left); the plate held aloft by the right-hand figure is foreshortened (Willats 1992b).*

arms of the figure were either pointing directly at the viewer or were held above the head of the figure; thus, they were either foreshortened or non-foreshortened. The plate was seen by the viewer either as a disc (non-foreshortened) or as an edge (foreshortened). Very few of the 4-year-olds changed the shape of the arms or the plate to represent foreshortening; typically, the arms were drawn as 'sticks' and the plate as a circle. About two-thirds of the 7-year-olds and nearly all of the 12-year-olds changed their drawings to accommodate the foreshortening (see figure 5.15). As Willats (1995) has argued, the older children were more effective than the younger ones in finding solutions to this unusual drawing problem. What they were doing was discovering increasingly complex 'drawing rules' in order to produce pictures that work better as representations.

Summary

The term *intellectual realism* is often used to describe the drawings made by young children. These pictures may depict a canonical view of an object rather than the view the child actually sees; they may also preserve the invariant features and structure of the scene rather than depict a particular view of it. In contrast, the term *visual realism* is used for those pictures that are drawn from a specific viewpoint, and these tend to be produced by older children and adults. Young children supposedly rely on an internal model of the object even when asked to draw a real one. This internal model tends to be generic in the sense that it represents a stereo-typical object of its class; it focusses on the defining features and structure of the object and those that are important to the child. The child is not forced to reproduce this model; she may be aware of what she can see but be dissatisfied with a visually realistic depiction of it and choose instead an intellectually realistic depiction. Thus, the younger child is not trying to draw a particular view of the object but rather a recognisable representation of it. There are problems with this notion of an internal model. In parti-cular, it is unclear how the child 'translates' it into a drawing and, although Willats has suggested a way that children might choose appropriate marks and shapes (picture primitives) to represent particular elements in the scene (scene primitives), this may not be universally applicable.

Young children often repeat a well-practised schema each time they draw, say, a human figure or a house. This conservatism suggests that internal models are relatively stable and a number of studies have demon-strated how difficult it can be to persuade children to change. However, a suggestion that they are 'locked into' a rigid procedure of movements has come under considerable criticism. Several studies have shown that young children do not reproduce a rigid sequence of movements each time they draw a particular object, but will vary the order from one occasion to another. Further studies have demonstrated that even very young children are capable of adapting their drawings. Thus, children are not as inflexible as some of the literature has led us to believe.

Although younger children tend to opt for intellectual realism, it should not necessarily be considered a childish mode of representation. It is clear that many non-trained adults use it and, despite the general trend towards visual realism, many artists have also exploited it. Neither can we assume that young children are incapable of visual realism. There are many examples of their awareness of how a scene appears from a particular point of view and their attempts to portray that view. It may be that in many research studies the tasks have biased the children towards producing an intellectually realistic picture, by, for example, asking them to inspect and name the object prior to drawing it or giving them insufficiently specific instructions. It seems, then, that although young children tend towards intellectual realism and older ones towards visual realism, these two modes of representation can coexist; they are not mutually exclusive. It does not follow, however, that young children are as expert at producing pictures in either mode as older children.

From about the age of 7 or 8 onwards children begin to favour visual over intellectual realism. It is unclear what influences this shift, although it is likely that there are many causes. It is not simply the development of an understanding of viewpoint, since children who can describe what can be seen from a particular viewpoint still have difficulty in representing the scene pictorially. Nonetheless, children who draw in a visually realistic way have a different strategy of looking compared to those who opt for intellectual realism: not only do they look longer at the model, they look at it more often – during the task as well as at the beginning of it. It is possible to encourage younger children to look more at the model by, for example, using more explicit instructions or involving them in a discussion of which parts of the scene are visible and which parts are not; further studies have manipulated the tasks in other ways, such as presenting the scene as a hiding game or presenting objects in contrasting orientations. It may be that an increase in the children's memory capacity is also important in enabling them to plan and produce more complex pictures. There is certainly a positive correlation between such an increase and the pictorial complexity that children produce. Although an increase in memory capacity might be necessary, it is unlikely to be sufficient to promote change. If we focus on the drawing activity itself it is likely that, when children are confronted with new problems, they actively seek out solutions and in doing so are able to alter and extend their repertoire. In addition, children may become increasingly more susceptible to the influence of other people's styles of drawing and to the kinds of representations in the mass media.

It appears that in producing a picture children are trying to be realistic – to present a 'good' representation of the scene. Realism does not have to be visual (photographic) realism, however. Intellectual realism is arguably just as valid, although, like visual realism, it also has its advantages and disadvantages. Although intellectual realism tends to be the more dominant mode of representation among younger children, by the age of about 7 or 8 years children show more interest in and admiration of visually realistic pictures, especially those drawn 'in perspective'. In the next chapter I shall discuss the way that children organise their figures on the page and how they learn to draw in perspective.

6 The spatial organisation of the picture

Whether a piece of paper or canvas is placed flat on a table or vertically on an easel or wall we tend to 'read it' in the same way: the top–bottom axis of the picture corresponds with the vertical dimension of our spatial world and the left–right axis to the horizontal dimension. At what age do children adopt this convention? As the surface of a picture has only two dimensions, we encounter a problem when we want to indicate the third dimension – that of depth. For this purpose many different pictorial devices have been developed, including partial occlusion of the farther object by a nearer one, diminution of the size of objects in the distance, slanting or converging lines of perspective, shading or 'modelling' of objects and tonal and textural gradation. Although these various devices come together in the system of linear convergence perspective, they can also be used separately; for example, partial occlusion but not convergence perspective was used in prehistoric cave painting and in Egyptian art (see chapter 8). Given the constraints of the dimensions of the page, how do children organise their drawings with regard to the spatial dimensions of the objects and scenes they want to depict? In particular, how do they solve the problem of depth? Furthermore, are children sensitive to the aesthetic composition of pictures as well as to their representation of space?

The orientation of figures on the page

When young children begin to draw recognisable objects they do not necessarily position them on the page in a conventional manner. For example, my daughter at age 2 years 10 months drew her first spontaneous 'tadpole' figure upright on the page. The next day, however, she drew 'a lady' across the page, even though there was no indication that the figure was meant to be lying down. A figure drawn on the third day was drawn upright. Nearly two months later her first two conventional figures (which included a separate torso with the arms attached to it) were drawn horizontally; subsequent human figures were drawn upright on the page. Sometimes children place their figures in different orientations on the same piece of paper (see figure 6.1). Rouma (1913), who also found

Figure 6.1 *Claire, aged 4 years 2 months, has drawn the members of her family in different orientations on the page.*

that several 3- to 5-year-olds drew their figures in a variety of different orientations, pointed out that for the very young child a sheet of paper lying on a table has neither a top nor a bottom and therefore there is no particular constraint on the way a figure should be orientated.

Goodnow and Friedman (1972) proposed that the direction of the figure is determined by the orientation of its facial features; children follow the vertical axis suggested by them. If the features have been drawn out of alignment with the axes of the page,[1] then the figure may appear to be leaning or even upside-down. Goodnow and Friedman presented children between 3 years 2 months and 6 years 7 months with two 'eyes' placed low down in a circle and another circle with the eyes placed sideways; the children were asked to complete the figures. The younger ones tended to draw their figures perpendicular to the axis of the eyes, resulting, respectively, in an upside-down figure or a horizontal figure. The older children, in contrast, altered the figures in various ways to make them vertical on the page. Similarly, both Freeman (1980) and Cox (1992), who placed the eyes on a diagonal slant, found that younger children tend to orientate towards the axis of the eyes whereas

---

[1] This, in turn, may have occurred because the child himself was not orientated perpendicularly to the edge of the paper (Golomb 1992).

Figure 6.2 *Some children have drawn their figures perpendicular to the axis of the mouth (a) or eyes (b); others have orientated their figures to the vertical axis of the page (c, d).*

older ones orientate towards the vertical axis of the page. Some children who started their completion in response to the orientation of the eyes then twisted the torso and legs so that the lower part of the figure was aligned with the vertical and, indeed, gave the impression of a vertical figure. The same effects were found when children were shown a circle with a curved mouth placed diagonally within it and were asked to complete the figure (see figure 6.2).

Early figures are often 'anchored' to the edge of the page and children may even rotate the paper, drawing figures on each side (see figure 6.3). Thus, the edge of the paper acts as the *ground line* for the figures. Children sometimes draw their own ground line (see figure 6.4), although this

Figure 6.3 *Denise, aged 3 years 6 months, has anchored each figure to the sides of the page.*

Figure 6.4 *Amy, aged 5 years 8 months, drew a ground line for her figure.*

occurs somewhat later: whereas only 1 per cent of 3-year-olds draw one, by the age of 8 years 96 per cent have done so (Wall 1959). Multiple ground lines are sometimes used when, for instance, two or more scenes are included on the same page. Ground lines are not necessarily horizontal. For example, Alice, aged 4 years 4 months, drew a circle for *Ring-a-ring-a-roses* and arranged her figures around it, although they themselves are indicated only by circles (see figure 6.5). Nine-year-old Deborah (see figure 6.6) also drew a circular ground line to guide the arrangement of her figures in *The farmer's in his den*, although these figures are much more detailed than Alice's. Other ground lines can be sloping, such as the sides of a hill or a pitched roof line (see figure 6.7). In these cases, children tend to draw their figures perpendicularly on the line, creating rather bizarre effects, such as people leaning precariously away from the hillside and chimneys in danger of toppling off roofs.

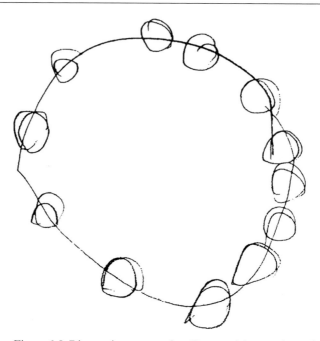

Figure 6.5 Ring-a-ring-a-roses *by Alice, aged 4 years 4 months.*

One of my students (Gillings 2003) investigated the influence of the ground line *and* the orientation of the eyes of the figure on 5-year-olds' and 8-year-olds' human figure drawing. All the children completed two figures: one with its eyes in conventional position and the other with its eyes drawn sideways. Half the children had a ground line already drawn just above the lower edge of the paper, the other half had no ground line. As expected, when the eyes were conventionally placed nearly all the children drew their figures vertically, whether they had a ground line or not. The sideways eyes produced some interesting results: when no ground line was present most of the children (78 per cent) drew their figure horizontally and did not appear to treat the lower edge of the page as a ground line; in the ground line condition, half drew their figure horizontally and half drew it towards the vertical, indicating that the predrawn ground line was effective, to some extent, in bringing the children's attention to the convention of drawing a figure upright on the page. This pattern of response was not significantly different in the two age groups.

It seems, then, that researchers have identified at least two sources of influence on the orientation of children's figures on the page. One is the way that the facial features were placed at the beginning of the drawing, and the other is the ground line. The positioning of the facial features has a particularly powerful effect, especially for very young children. However, by the age of about 5 or 6 years children are beginning to orientate

Figure 6.6 The farmer's in his den *by Deborah, aged 9 years.*

Figure 6.7 *Amy, aged 5 years, has drawn her chimneys perpendicular to the slope of the roofs.*

towards a ground line, whether it is the edge of the page or a line they have drawn themselves.

The perpendicular bias

The way that children attach a figure to a ground line – even when that line is sloping – or extend the body from misaligned facial features suggests a bias towards the perpendicular. In fact, children seem to be biased towards the perpendicular even in an abstract task. Ibbotson and Bryant (1976) asked 5- to 6-year-old children to copy a series of angles – a shorter line drawn onto a longer baseline at either 45 or 90 degrees (see figure 6.8). In each case the child had to copy the shorter line onto a predrawn baseline. Right angles were copied more accurately than the 45-degree angles and their copies of 45-degree angles tended towards the perpendicular (the average line was drawn at about 58 degrees). The bias towards the perpendicular occurred more when the baseline was horizontal or oblique than when it was vertical. It was not affected, however, by the mode of response: the results were similar when the children were asked to place a straight piece of wire onto a baseline instead of drawing it. One of my students (Keane 2003) has also compared different methods of response – asking children to draw the target line, to place a thin wooden rod or to move a rod onto the baseline on a pivot to produce the required angle – and has found no significant differences among them.

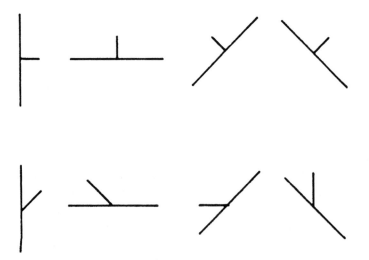

Figure 6.8 *Children can copy the figures on the top line correctly because they contain right angles. Younger children have difficulty in copying the figures on the lower line; they make the angle more perpendicular than it ought to be.*

The perpendicular bias is a very robust phenomenon: for example, it persists even when the experimenter has drawn a red line parallel to the target line that the child is then asked to produce (Bayraktar 1985). The bias does begin to fade, however, at about the age of 7 years, but, according to Bayraktar, is still evident among adults. Based on my own data, I would agree that it begins to fade at about the age of 7, but I have found no evidence for the bias among adults; indeed, it seems to have faded altogether at about age 10. Keane (2003), too, has found no significant bias among adults.

Although there is ample evidence from experimental studies for a perpendicular bias among young children, the bias does not seem sufficient on its own to explain the very definite right angles children often make in some of their spontaneous drawings. It is possible that in more meaningful contexts, such as figures placed on a hillside or a chimney drawn on a pitched roof, children over-generalise their knowledge that vertical objects normally intersect the baseline at right angles. In fact, this effect occurs not only in spontaneous pictures drawn from imagination but also in experimental studies where a two-dimensional model is available. For example, a number of studies (e.g., Phillips, Hobbs & Pratt 1978; Cox 1989; Lee 1989) have found that children copy nonsense or unnamed shapes more accurately than they copy recognisable or named models (such as cubes or tables). So, even when a model is available, the perpendicular bias will be activated if the model depicts a recognisable object known to contain right angles. (For further discussions of the perpendicular bias, see Bayraktar 1985, Bremner 1985 and Cox 1991, 1992.)

'To each its own space'

Borrowing from the ideas of Gestalt psychology (see appendix), Piaget and Inhelder (1971) argued that young children perceive objects as 'meaningful wholes' or '*Gestalten*'. It is as if the objects have boundaries around them that should not be violated. Because of this, young children are unwilling to draw the boundary of one object (or part of an object) across another. For example, human figures are usually drawn facing the viewer with all their body parts clearly displayed (see figure 5.9). In my data (Cox, 1993), 86 per cent of 5- to 6-year-olds, 83 per cent of 7- to 8-year-olds, 79 per cent of 9- to 10-year-olds and 87 per cent of adults drew a frontal figure when asked to 'draw a person'. Goodnow (1977) noted that young children seem to apply the 'to each its own space' rule (pp. 49–56), arranging the parts of a figure so that they do not cross one another. In my data, there were also low frequencies of overlap: 9 per cent at age 5 to 6 years, 3 per cent at age 7 to 8 and

3 per cent at age 9 to 10. If we accept that young children prefer to depict objects in such a way that they are recognisable (see chapter 5), then it is not surprising that they will be reluctant to compromise the clarity of their drawings.

Although children tend to draw frontal figures in the standard draw-a-person task (usually requested by an adult), they will often draw more 'experimental' figures for themselves (Goodnow, Wilkins & Dawes 1986, study 3), and researchers have investigated their ability to adapt their figures by altering the instructions. When asked to 'draw a person running' or 'walking very fast' (Goodnow 1978; Fujimoto 1979; Cox 1993; Smith 1993) children will modify their figures by, for example, drawing the legs wider apart and also drawing more profiles; even so, they do not necessarily overlap[2] or occlude[3] body parts – I found no cases among 5- to 6-year-olds, only 27 per cent among 7- to 8-year-olds and 58 per cent among 9- to 10-year-olds.

In these studies the children were asked to draw from *imagination*. If presented with a *model* in which, for example, one arm crosses the torso we might expect that more children would try to deal with this problem of representation, even though we know that young children do not always pay detailed attention to the model.[4] In fact, when Cox and Moore (1994) presented children with a model they found no occlusion or overlapping of body parts among 3- to 5-year-olds; however, among 6-year-olds 13 per cent drew occlusions and 47 per cent enclosed the arm within the torso contour, and among 8-year-olds 7 per cent drew occlusions and 93 per cent drew enclosures (see figure 5.11). In this study a standing model was presented, but in a study by Cox and Lambon Ralph (1996) the children saw both a standing model and a running figure viewed in profile. Here there was occlusion by the limbs in the running model which elicited more overlaps or occlusions in the drawings: 18 per cent among 5-year-olds, 58 per cent among 7-year-olds and 81 per cent among 9-year-olds. So, by age 7, and to a greater extent at age 9, children can modify their schemas[5] to reflect what they see, and in doing so are no longer constrained by the 'to each its own space' rule (see figure 6.9).

---

[2] The term *overlap* is used when, for example, the contours of an arm cross the contour of the torso, giving the impression that the arm is transparent.

[3] The term *occlusion* or *partial occlusion* refers to the masking of one body part by another, for example, when the contour of the torso is interrupted by an arm crossing 'in front of' it.

[4] Partridge (1902) found that young children drew frontal views of a lady even though the model in front of them sat in profile. However, Cox and Moore (1994) found that even some 4-year-olds were able to indicate the different views of a rotated figure by, for example, omitting facial features for the back view.

[5] See chapter 5 for a discussion of children's ability to alter their schemas.

Figure standing in profile   Running figure

Drawn by a boy aged 5 years 6 months

Drawn by a boy aged 7 years 4 months

Drawn by a girl aged 10 years 3 months

Figure 6.9 *Children's drawings of a model man standing in profile or running (Cox & Lambon Ralph 1996).*

Transparency drawings

Transparencies in children's drawings occur when contours are shown that should in fact be invisible. Examples are scenes in which one object is shown inside another, as if in cross-section – for example, a fœtus inside its mother or food inside someone's stomach (see figure 5.2). In cases such as these, the children seem to have had a deliberate intention to show what would normally be hidden. There are other cases, however, in which the transparency has resulted from a lack of planning. If young children draw their normal schema for a person (which is usually unclothed[6]) and

[6] Cox (1997).

Figure 6.10 *'Transparency' drawings (from Mann & Lehman 1976): a man wearing a coat (left), drawn by a boy aged 9 years; a lady in a long skirt (right), drawn by a boy aged 5 years.*

then add the clothes to it, a transparency is almost inevitable. Even older children may fail to consider what changes will have to be made to accommodate extra items of clothing. When Mann and Lehman (1976) asked children aged 4 to 9 years to draw a woman wearing a long skirt and a man wearing a coat, a third of the drawings were transparencies (see figure 6.10). Another typical example of a transparency is a person sitting on a chair. In order to avoid a transparency we have to implement the drawing rule 'draw what is nearer the viewer first and then draw the parts of the scene which are farther away' (Cox 1992). Thus, in this example the person should be drawn first and then the visible parts of the chair should be fitted around these contours. If this is carried out successfully then the contours of the person will occlude the hidden parts of the chair (see figure 6.11).

It has been suggested that transparencies also occur because young children cannot halt their schema of, for example, a hatpin piercing through an apple (a model originally used by Clark 1896–7) (see figure 6.12). When Crook (1985) asked children to draw a stick through a ball, 63 per cent of 5-year-olds produced a transparency. It was suggested that the children's knowledge of the structure of the scene (i.e., a single stick piercing right through the ball) elicited the drawing of a continuous line through the contour of the ball. However, the number of transparencies was greatly reduced (to 20 per cent) when the model consisted of two separate sticks that met in the middle of the ball, and was reduced to zero when there was a single stick with each half coloured differently. Thus, the way that the children draw the model may be related to their knowledge of its structure. It is unclear whether children themselves are concerned about their transparency drawings (although there are some anecdotal references to their acknowledgement of a problem[7]) or whether they

---

[7] For example, one of Mann and Lehman's (1976) children commented 'She bought a size too large!' (p. 46).

Figure 6.11 Someone sitting in a chair *by Amy, aged 9 years. The back of the chair has been successfully occluded but not the front edge.*

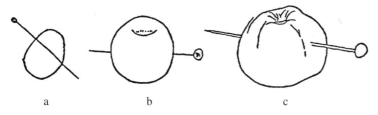

a   b   c

Figure 6.12 *When asked to draw a hatpin through an apple young children tend to draw the whole pin (a); older ones omit the middle section of the pin (b); eventually, children attempt to draw the model as they see it (c). (From Clark 1896–7.)*

simply accept the transparency as representing the structure of the scene rather than an actual view of it. It is clear, however, that a transparency is not always inevitable and the results of this and other studies discussed in chapter 5 have demonstrated that young children at or even below the age of 5 years are able to interrupt and alter their schemas. By the age of 8 to 9 years we see far fewer transparencies in children's drawings.

One object behind another

Transparency drawings seem to occur more often when two objects are 'structurally integrated' (Cox 1992), that is, when one object is *inside* another, *through* another or *on* another. In a sense, the objects in these scenes share the same space. In contrast there are relatively few transparencies when children draw one object *behind* another. In this case the objects occupy independent spaces and are only linked by our point of view, for example, 'the ball is behind the cup from where I am sitting' or 'the teddy bear is partly hidden by the ball from my angle of view'. If we changed our viewpoint then the spatial relationship between the objects would also change.

The reason why there may be fewer transparencies when one object is behind another may be that such a drawing could be misinterpreted, that is, one object might be seen to be inside another rather than behind it. Children are sensitive to these different spatial relationships. When Light and MacIntosh (1980) asked 6-year-olds to draw a tiny house inside a glass beaker, all the children drew the house within the contour of the glass. When asked to draw the house behind the glass, there was less agreement about the way it should be drawn, even though the two scenes looked very similar: 53 per cent drew the house within the contour of the glass, but 47 per cent drew the house and the glass separately. Of these 'separate' drawings, 64 per cent were in a vertical arrangement, with the house above the glass, and 36 per cent were in a horizontal arrangement, with the house to the left or right of the glass (see figure 6.13). Cox and Martin (1988) found similar results when 5-, 7- and 9-year-olds were asked to draw a cube inside or behind an opaque beaker. Although most of the children omitted the cube altogether, which would be in accord with what

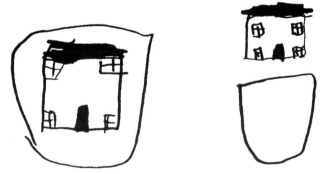

Figure 6.13 *When asked to draw a small house inside a glass most 6-year-olds draw the house inside the contour of the glass; when asked to draw a house behind the glass most children draw the objects separately, with the house either above or beside the glass (Light & MacIntosh 1980).*

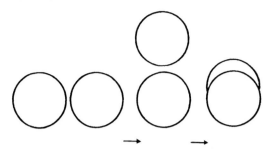

Figure 6.14 *When asked to draw one ball behind another young children draw them side by side; older ones draw them one above the other; from the age of 8 or 9 years children draw the farther ball partially occluded by the nearer one.*

they could actually see, 93 per cent of those who included it for the 'inside' relationship drew it within the outline of the beaker, but those who included it for the 'behind' relationship were divided in their response (40 per cent inside the outline, 55 per cent beside it and 5 per cent above it). It seems, then, that even 5-year-olds are aware that the spatial relationships they are representing are different and they may seek to mark that difference in the way they arrange the objects on the page.

When young children draw a scene in which one object only partially occludes the one behind it they also tend to separate the objects and place them either beside one another or above one another on the page. In fact, there seems to be an age-related shift (see figure 6.14), with the younger children drawing the objects side by side and the older ones drawing them vertically, and then around the age of about 8 or 9 years children draw a partial occlusion (Freeman, Eiser & Sayers 1977; Cox 1978, 1981).

There are many anecdotal accounts in the literature of children trying to indicate that part of the scene is 'behind' or 'at the back'. For example, if they are shown a head-on drawing of an animal and asked to add a tail, some children have tried to punch a hole through the paper; others have turned the page over and drawn the tail on the other side. My daughter, aged 4 years 3 months, drew a side view of a van with two windows; then she turned the paper over and drew two squares for the windows on the other side of the van. Since pictures do not possess a depth dimension, children have to invent or learn other, pictorial, ways of indicating it. Of course, if part of a scene is totally occluded from view then it should be omitted altogether from the picture. If it is partially occluded then only the visible part should be drawn and its part-contour should be attached to the contour of the occluding object. Children do not normally produce partial occlusions, however, until about the age of 8 or 9 years. It is not a lack of motor skill that prevents them from doing so, as most children can copy a predrawn partial occlusion by the age of 5 (Cox 1985); rather, it seems to be an unwillingness to draw only part of an object and to unify it with another which they know to be quite separate, although, as I discussed in chapter 5, there are some circumstances, such as the 'cops and robbers' task (Cox 1981), when younger children – even as young as 4 years – will attempt to use the partial occlusion device when drawing one object partly hidden behind another one along their line of sight.

Projection systems and depth cues

A number of different projection systems have been used at different times and in various cultures around the world (see chapters 8 and 10). They each have particular ways of dealing with the third, depth, dimension. In *orthographic* or *orthogonal* projection the vertical axis of the scene is represented by the top–bottom axis of the paper and the side-to-side relationships between objects are represented across the left–right axis of the page. The front–back dimension of the scene is not represented at all. So, for example, a tabletop will be shown as a single straight line, as if we are seeing its edge at eye-level. In this system, then, the depth of the tabletop is ignored. Examples of this kind of projection can be seen in classical Greek vase painting (see figure 8.11).

In *vertical oblique* projection the region of a tabletop will be shown but it is drawn as a rectangle with its sides joining the front edge at right angles; thus, the side edges coincide with the top–bottom axis of the page. In this system the shape of the table remains invariant. Examples can be found in mediaeval manuscripts (see figure 8.13). In *oblique projection* the side edges of the table are drawn parallel to each other but at an oblique angle to the front edge; the result is that the tabletop is shown as a parallelogram. Examples of this kind of projection can be seen in Japanese prints from the seventeenth to nineteenth centuries and also in European mediaeval painting (see figure 8.14). In both these oblique projections the parts of the scene that are farther away from the viewer are drawn higher up the page. In *linear convergence perspective* the sides of the table are drawn so that they tend to converge towards a vanishing point; the shape of the tabletop is trapezoidal (see figure 6.15, example 6). A number of depth cues are combined in this system, for example, size diminution, height on the page, convergence of depth lines and distortion of shape, resulting in its distinctive coherence (see figure 8.15).

A further style of drawing is classed as *divergent* by Hagen (1985). However, she argues that although diverging depth lines can be seen in mediaeval and Moghul paintings, they appear only very infrequently and cannot really count as a projection system. Indeed, she calls it a 'project system *manqué*' (p. 70). Nonetheless, Court (1992) reports *inverted perspective*, as she calls it, to be common in some present-day rural societies in Kenya (see figure 10.21).

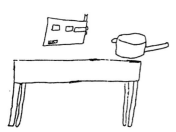

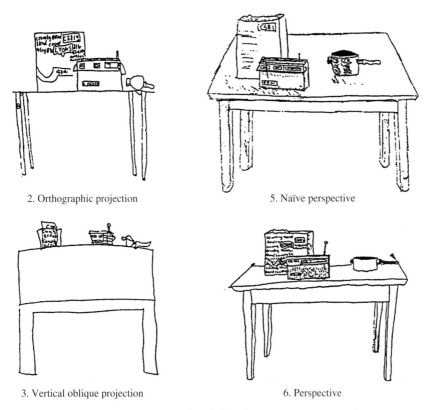

Figure 6.15 *Willats (1977) found that the projection systems above were related to children's increasing chronological age.*

Apart from divergent perspective, all these systems of projection occur in children's drawings too. In fact, Willats (1977) found that the systems are related to children's increasing chronological age (see figure 6.15). Of all these systems, that of linear convergence perspective preserves more of the phenomena of our 'visual geometry' (Bruce & Green 1990; Hagen 1985) and, because of this, may seem to be a more natural way of representing the three-dimensional world on a two-dimensional surface.

Yet, although artists before the Italian Renaissance used this system to some extent, it was not until the fifteenth century that the mathematical principles of perspective were formalised (Edgerton 1975). In Willats' (1977) study, although many of his older children drew a table in 'naïve' perspective rather few achieved the accuracy of true perspective. In fact, many adults as well as children are unable to draw correctly 'in perspective' (Hagen 1985; Luquet 1927/2001), and there is also evidence that both adults and children prefer representations that are not drawn in strict linear perspective (Hagen & Elliott 1976; Hagen & Jones 1978; Saenger 1981). Nonetheless, most children attempt to deal with the problem of depth in their pictures and by the age of 12 years will have some understanding of what it means to draw in perspective. However, they will not necessarily have developed expertise with all the depth cues at the same rate. I will not attempt to discuss all possible cues, as some, such as tonal and textural gradation, are very rare in children's drawings. I have already discussed the way children deal with the problem of drawing one object behind another, which implies depth in the scene. I will now discuss other depth cues that have also been studied extensively.

Size and height as cues to depth

Although the projective size of an object diminishes as it recedes into the distance we are often not aware of the extent of this effect, since our visual system tends to compensate by perceiving the real size of the object regardless of its distance from us, a phenomenon known as *size constancy*.[8] Nonetheless, children as young as 3 or 4 understand, for example, that a cyclist moving away from them appears to get smaller (Pillow & Flavell 1986). At age 5 years they also use the size of objects in predrawn pictures to judge which object is nearer the viewer and which is farther away (Nieland & Cox, cited in Cox 1992; Perara & Cox 2000).

In the system of linear convergence perspective artists use the size cue to indicate distance from the viewer although it is often difficult, even for them, to overcome the effects of size constancy without recourse to various mechanical aids (Willats 1997). If this is difficult for trained artists, it would not be surprising if young children found it difficult too, and, indeed, size as a cue to depth is normally absent from their drawings. A rare case is mentioned by Matthews (1999): his son, Ben, aged 4 years 3 months, drew a series of graded front views of a steam engine to show it coming towards us (see figure 6.16). Another child – 7-year-old Richard – tested by Littleton (1991, experiment 1), was asked to draw one ball behind another. He announced that he would draw the second ball smaller

[8] See also chapter 2.

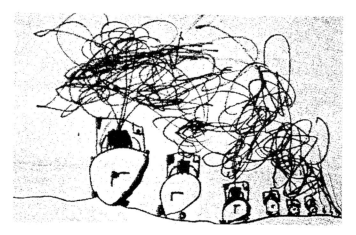

Figure 6.16 *Ben, aged 4 years 3 months, drew a graded series of views of a steam train to show how it appears larger as it gets nearer to the viewer (Matthews 1999).*

because it was farther away; he did draw it smaller even though he placed it by the side of the 'nearer' ball. Very few of Lewis's (1990) 7- to 10-year-olds used diminishing size as a depth cue in their drawings of a scene from imagination. Similarly, Cox, Perara and Xu (1999) found that very few children aged below 10 years used this cue, although it did increase at age 13 (see also chapter 12).

As well as appearing smaller, objects in the distance also appear higher in our visual field (at least, this is true for objects located below the horizon; objects above the horizon are lower in our visual field as they move into the distance). Height on the page as a cue to depth is used in a number of projection systems, although it is combined with the size cue only in linear convergence perspective. When the height cue is separated, experimentally, from the size cue it tends to be the size cue that children, from the age of 4 years onwards, use when interpreting distance in a predrawn picture (Cox & Nieland, cited in Cox 1992; Plant 1995). Hagen (1976) also found that 3- and 5-year-olds did not show sensitivity to the height cue and this led her to conclude that 'height in the picture plane functions informatively for young children [only] in conjunction with other depth cues' (p. 1013).

Usually, it is not until the age of 5 years that children begin to place a more distant object higher up the page (Freeman, Eiser & Sayers 1977) and, even then, they only do so when provided with a model and when they are given instructions that emphasise the depth relationship between the objects (Cox 1978, 1981). There is a problem with this interpretation of the height on the page cue, however. It is possible that children draw the nearer object closer to themselves (towards the bottom of the page) and the farther object away from themselves (towards the top of the page) but

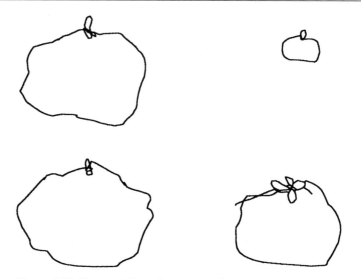

Figure 6.17 *Young children draw two apples, one near and one far away, the same size (left); from age 9 children begin to draw the farther apple smaller than the nearer one (right).*

without any notion that they are drawing a pictorial depth relationship. When Klaue (1992) compared children's drawings produced on a horizontal surface with those on a vertical surface she found that there was a clear influence of orientation: she concluded that drawings produced on a horizontal surface by children below the age of 8 years were more like *plans* of the scene, whereas those drawn on a vertical surface were more like the projected image of the scene. This finding supports the notion that height on the page is not necessarily a *pictorial* depth cue as far as children are concerned.

When Cox and Perara (2001, study 1) asked children to draw two apples, one near and one far away, most of their 4-, 5- and 7-year-olds drew two circles of the same size with one placed above the other. The same pattern emerged whether the children were drawing on a blank sheet or on a predrawn outline of a table. The co-ordination of the size and height cues began to occur at age 9, when 53 per cent of the children drew the more distant apple higher up the page and also smaller than the nearer one; 81 per cent of adults drew the apples in this way (see figure 6.17). There was no difference in response in a second study in which drawings from imagination were compared with drawings from a model. However, a construction task rather than a drawing task elicited more pictures in which the height and size cues were co-ordinated.

In summary, young children, at age 3 or 4 years, understand that objects appear to get smaller as they recede into the distance. They use this cue to judge distance in predrawn pictures, but they rarely use it in their own drawings. Three- to 5-year-olds do not use height to judge depth in predrawn pictures, but by age 4 or 5, in their own work, they place more distant objects higher up the page. By age 9 years they begin to combine these two depth cues in their own drawings.

Depth lines

Around the age of 7 years or so we begin to see children's spontaneous attempts to draw objects in depth – an example is a house where the side as well as the front elevation is shown; at first, the side is often on the same ground line as if it has been folded out (see figure 6.18). Later, the side is placed at an oblique angle to indicate that there is a change of plane (see figure 6.19). Although Hagen (1985) studied children's ability to draw an object in depth by asking them to draw a house, other researchers have asked them to draw a table (Willats 1977; Freeman 1980) or a cube (Derȩgowski 1977; Mitchelmore 1978; Chen & Cook 1984; Caron-Pargue 1985; Chen 1985; Cox 1986; Moore 1986; Nicholls & Kennedy 1992). In fact, the cube has been one of the most popular objects perhaps because it has square faces, which children are capable of drawing by age 5, if not earlier, and these faces lie in all three spatial dimensions, each bounded by a distinct edge. When asked to draw a cube many young children draw only a single square (Piaget & Inhelder 1956; Moore 1986; Cox 1986), which, according to Piaget and Inhelder and also Moore, may represent the whole object rather than only a single face of it. In Mitchelmore's (1978) study 7- to 15-year-olds were asked to draw a cube

Figure 6.18 *The two sides of Amy's house share the same horizontal ground line.*

Table 2 *The responses of children and adults asked to draw a cube (Cox 1986).*

	a	b	c	d	e	f
Condition 1						
7 years	18	20	8	9	8	
12 years		12		22	30	4
Adults		18		3	11	19
Condition 2						
7 years	11	33	4	10	6	3
12 years	2	18		8	24	9
Adults		22		1	5	22

Figure 6.19 *Amy has drawn the side of her house at an oblique angle to the front.*

that was placed in front of them in an oblique orientation. Most of the youngest children drew only a single square, and this response was not uncommon among 9- and 11-year-olds. Older ones drew several squares, often producing folding out drawings (Nicholls & Kennedy 1992 – see examples in *c* in table 2). From age 9 years onwards children tended to draw only the visible faces of the cube and also attempted to capture its oblique orientation. Interestingly, they seemed to use an oblique line simply to link up the squares in a multisquare configuration rather than to depict depth; the base of the cube was usually flat (see examples in *d* in table 2).

Most children are taught how to draw a cube by the time they are 11 or 12 years old (Cox 1986), and the way they normally do this is to draw a parallel oblique form. There are normally three faces: the front face is a square and the lines representing the receding edges of the other two sides are obliques but they are parallel to each other and do not converge towards a vanishing point (see example in *e* in table 2). Although this is not a view that is projected on to the eye, it is a convention widely used for many purposes, including illustrations in school textbooks. Some children and adults, especially those who have had special training in how to draw, have learnt how to draw the receding edges of the cube in linear convergence perspective. Even so, there are often rather low incidences of accurate perspective drawings reported (e.g., Kerschensteiner 1905; Munro, Lark-Horowitz & Barnhart 1942; Nicholls & Kennedy 1992; Milbrath 1998). The pattern of development in drawing a cube is so regular that a number of authors have used it to devise scales for scoring the drawings (e.g., Cox & Perara 1998).

A problem when asking children or adults to draw an object from observation, such as the cube presented in oblique orientation, is that they may not look at the model very closely and may 'automatically' draw a well-practised schema. In order to obviate this tendency I positioned the cube so that only the front and top faces were visible and the three-sided oblique parallel depiction would no longer be appropriate (Cox 1986). In condition 1 participants were simply asked to draw the cube. The same kind of pattern emerged as in other studies (see table 2). At age 7, 29 per cent of the drawings were single squares; a further 44 per cent consisted of two or more squares (see *b* and *c* in table 2); 27 per cent of the drawings included at least one oblique line (nearly half of these drawings were parallel obliques); there were no converging depth lines. At age 12 there were no single square drawings; 18 per cent drew two squares; 82 per cent drew some form of oblique solution (54 per cent of these included parallel oblique edges and 7 per cent drew converging depth lines – see *f* in table 2). Among the adults, 35 per cent drew two squares and 65 per cent drew some form of oblique solution (33 per cent of these were parallel obliques and 58 per cent were converging obliques).

In condition 2, before they started to draw, the participants were asked to point to the faces of the cube that they could see. This instruction tended to restrict them to drawing two faces. An interesting form drawn mainly by the 12-year-olds was a two-section figure in which the top face was a parallel oblique sloping to the side (see example in *e* in table 2).

Taken together, the results of these studies reveal a developmental trend in the way that children indicate the depth of three-dimensional objects. The youngest children draw depth lines that are perpendicular to the baseline. The next step is to draw depth lines which are still parallel to each other but oblique to the baseline. A few older children and some adults converge the depth lines.

Do young children avoid using obliques because they cannot draw them? The answer is 'no'. Seven-year-olds can correctly copy a line drawing of converging obliques (Cox & Littleton 1995, study 3) and can also use converging obliques to depict the top face of a wedge-shaped object whose sides really do converge (Cox 1989). It may be that some of the objects used by researchers are too complex, in the sense that children are concentrating on where to place the legs on a table, how to attach the roof on the house, how many faces they have to draw on the cube, and so on. In other words, the children may be more concerned with these 'peripheral' features than with the depth lines themselves. In order to focus their attention on the depth lines, Cox and Littleton (1995, study 1) asked 7-year-olds, 12-year-olds and adults to draw a simple black model road, 10 cm wide and 30 cm long and edged with grey. They were also asked to draw a doll's table and a cube. In fact, the road model did not have the predicted effect: the youngest participants continued to draw parallel depth lines just as they did in their drawings of the table and the cube.

Another reason why participants do not converge the depth lines may be that the objects presented to them are too near for any apparent convergence of depth lines to be obvious. Perhaps a stimulus with greater depth would be more effective. Littleton (1991; Cox & Littleton 1995, study 2) took children aged 7 and 12 years, as well as some adults, on to a footbridge so that they could look along the length of the road beneath (figure 6.20 shows the view with the sides of the road appearing to converge in the distance). They were asked to look at the road and then to draw a picture of it; they were also asked to choose a predrawn picture to represent it. Whereas the adolescents and the adults drew and selected a perspective solution, in which converging oblique lines represented the way in which the edges of the road appeared to converge, the younger children, in contrast, opted for a parallel solution (see figure 6.21).

It seems, then, that even when confronted with the apparent convergence of the edges in a real stimulus, children will, nonetheless, avoid using converging obliques to represent them. They either still do not notice the apparent convergence or they choose not to depict it. Either way, they appear to be focussing on the real structure of the object and not on how it happens to look from a particular angle of view, an explanation also supported by Luquet (1913, 1927; also see chapter 5).

Interestingly, when children were asked to copy the same scene from a photograph (Cox & Littleton 1995, study 3) 70 per cent of them converged the edges of the road, and when they were shown an even more dramatically converging road (see figure 6.22) all of them drew converging edges (study 4). One reason that they might use obliques when copying from a

Figure 6.20 *Children and adults were asked to draw this road (Cox & Littleton 1995).*

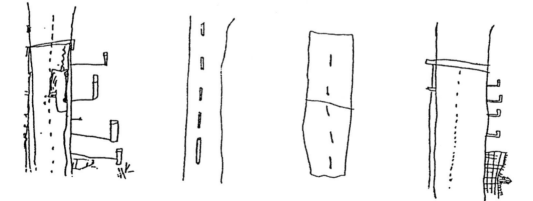

Figure 6.21 *The sides of the road were drawn parallel by the younger children (from Cox & Littleton 1995).*

Figure 6.22 *All 6- to 7-year-olds could draw a converging road when asked to copy this example (Cox & Littleton 1995).*

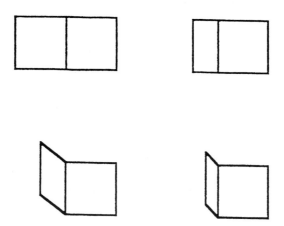

Figure 6.23 *Children were asked to draw equal-width (top left) and half-width (top right) models with both sides presented in the frontal plane, and the same models with one side receding at a 45-degree angle (lower row) (from Nicholls 1995).*

photograph or line drawing rather than from the real road is that the oblique edges of the road may be more obvious in contrast with the rectangular frame of the picture. This possibility could be tested by, for example, asking children to view the real scene through a rectangular view-finder and also to copy a photograph without a rectangular surround.

Whereas most studies have concentrated on the number of faces or the kind of projection that children draw, Nicholls (1995) has investigated children's use of *foreshortening* to represent the face of an object that lies in the depth plane. She showed children two models, each consisting of two hinged sections of card (see figure 6.23). The equal-width model consisted of two equal-sized squares; in the half-width model, one section was a square and the other was a rectangle, half the width of the square. When these models are placed so that one square faces the viewer but the second section is turned away, the depth edges appear shorter, making the whole area of this section appear smaller; the shape of the section is no longer rectangular, the top and bottom edges tend towards convergence and the farther vertical edge appears shorter than the nearer vertical edge.[9] Nicholls investigated whether children are sensitive to these aspects of the projection or whether they will try to preserve the rectangular structure of the object in their drawing.

In experiment 1, 5- to 6-year-olds and 7- to 8-year-olds were asked to draw each model when it was facing the viewer (i.e., in the frontal plane) and also when one section was turned back at an angle of 45 degrees (i.e., receding). When the sections were in the frontal plane both age groups used lines of more or less equal length to represent the width of the equal-width model and a shorter line to represent the width of the narrower section of the half-width model. With the equal-width model, more than half of the older children used oblique lines to show the receding section; in contrast, very few of the 5- to 6-year-olds did so. It seems, however, that these younger children were not insensitive to the appearance of this receding surface. Both they and the older children tended to shorten the lines that were meant to represent the receding edges (compared with their length in the frontal plane), thereby producing a narrower section with a smaller area. Thus, these children used foreshortening even though they did not use oblique lines. Whereas the older children shortened the receding lines of both the equal-width model and the half-width model, the younger children only did so for the equal-width model; for the half-width model the younger children used similar proportions for both the frontal and the receding conditions. One reason for this may be that the 45-degree angle was too small for the younger children to notice the difference between the half-width model's appearance in the frontal and the receding planes.

In her second experiment, Nicholls contrasted a 45-degree angle and a 75-degree angle from the frontal plane to find out whether this larger angle of recession would encourage the children to draw a correspondingly narrower section. Equal-width and half-width models were used as in experiment 1 (see figure 6.24). Both age groups used shorter lines to depict the receding section of both the equal-width model and the half-width 75-degree model compared with the 45-degree models, supporting the suggestion that perhaps the angle of recession in the first experiment was not large enough to make the projected size of the half-width model obvious. Not surprisingly, the younger children reduced the size of the receding section less than the older children did, indicating that they were not as sensitive to alterations in proportion. Nicholls concluded that

---

[9] Note that the illustrations in figure 6.23 are schematic and do not show the apparent convergence of the receding edges.

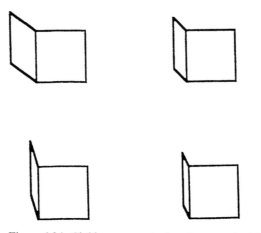

Figure 6.24 *Children were asked to draw equal-width and half-width models receding at a 45-degree angle (top row) and at a 75-degree angle (lower row) (from Nicholls 1995).*

children younger than 8 years of age can use foreshortening, even though they do not use converging lines, and claimed that, in reducing the proportions of the receding section of the model, they are attempting to show something of the projected appearance of the model from their point of view. This finding that children are able to indicate the change of the appearance of an object tilted away from the viewer supports that of Willats (1992b), who found that about two-thirds of 7-year-olds and nearly all 12-year-olds used foreshortening to show the apparent changes of shape of a figure holding a plate.[10]

It seems that the use of oblique lines – particularly converging obliques – is resisted by young children when drawing an object in depth. It is not because they cannot draw converging obliques nor because they are totally insensitive to the changes in projection of an object seen 'in depth'. Rather, they seem to be intent on preserving some of the invariant structure of the object and it is not until about the age of 9 years that they begin to be able to represent objects according to their correct perspective projection.

Drawing it all together

All the different aspects we see in linear convergence perspective – occlusion, size diminution, converging lines, foreshortening and so on – come together in a coherent system that gives a convincing representation of the way a scene looks from a particular vantage point. We should not

[10] See chapter 5 for a fuller account of this study.

assume, however, that the child's acquisition of all these devices is uniform. Willats (1985) did not find a consistent relationship between children's use of overlap or occlusion and any particular projection system, that is, a child attempting linear perspective might also draw overlapping outlines and, conversely, a child drawing objects in vertical oblique projection might also use partial occlusion to indicate one object behind another. This finding indicates that projection systems and occlusion may be different representational issues for the child. And Matthews (1999) has also pointed out that the developmental trajectories for various kinds of pictorial device may be different, albeit interrelated, and whether devices are employed or not may vary according to a number of different variables – the kind of object to be drawn, the structure of the scene and so on. Even when researchers show that, with certain experimental manipulations, very young children can be made more aware of the way a scene looks and will attempt to use at least some of the drawing devices, we should not lose sight of the fact that their expertise is not as developed nor as easily harnessed as that of older children. In other words, it is important not to conclude that just because we can demonstrate that young children can employ certain pictorial devices in certain circumstances that therefore there is no development taking place.

According to Piaget and Inhelder (1956) the general shift towards drawing more realistic pictures that occurs in mid- to late childhood coincides with children's ability to adopt a particular point of view as well as an understanding of the Euclidean spatial concepts of, for example, angles and proportion. However, this explanation for change is not supported by the evidence, since children who are aware of what can be seen from a particular point of view are not necessarily able to represent that view pictorially (e.g., Ives 1980, 1983[11]). And, as Golomb (1992) has pointed out, 'we should not expect progress in projective geometry and in perspective-taking tasks to automatically translate into perspective drawings' (p. 126). The difficulties that children have are more directly related to the special domain of pictorial representation. According to Willats (1997), the problem is 'primarily a drawing problem, rather than a problem in seeing or becoming consciously aware of one's own viewpoint' (p. 306) and the solution occurs, again according to Willats, with children's acquisition of a wider repertoire of drawing devices, either through their own observation and experimentation or by direct tuition. Nonetheless, this acquisition is also related to developments in aspects of general cognition such as an increase in working memory capacity and planning ability (see, e.g., Cocking & Copple 1987; Morra 1995).

---

[11] See chapter 5 for more details of this study.

Composing the scene

The pictures produced by very young children are often made up of unrelated items with no particular organisation to the scene as a whole. Older children, however, will organise the items into a *composition*.[12] One of the early noticeable arrangements is the lining up of figures along the horizontal axis of the page. The bottom edge of the paper or a specially drawn ground line may serve as the anchor for a line of figures, or the ground line may simply be imaginary.

Another particularly early characteristic of the way a picture is organised is what Golomb (1992) has called *figural centering*. As the term suggests, one figure is placed in the centre of the page, giving it both prominence and stability. Along with this placement of individual items there are also attempts at symmetry where groups of figures or other objects are balanced around a central point or axis. We might see this symmetry not only in terms of groups of items but also in their size, shape, colour and so on. Although these various aspects may be seen in 5-year-olds' drawings, the expertise and complexity of this symmetrical organisation becomes more developed in much older children, especially if they also include the depth cues of overlap or occlusion. In fact, in older and more talented children[13] we see pictures that are not equally balanced. For example, a large object on one side of a mid-point might be balanced by two smaller objects on the other side. Asymmetric arrangements can have the effect of making the composition appear more dynamic. Also, the shape of groups within the composition can suggest movement (e.g., a triangular arrangement of items might suggest an upward movement) and the use of perspective depth lines can direct the viewer's attention 'into' the picture.

There are some potentially confounding variables that may affect the compositional strategies children use. One of these is the topic of the drawing. When Golomb (1992) analysed the drawings of children aged 3 to 13 on six different topics she found that whereas a topic such as 'the family' elicited a 'lined-up' arrangement reminiscent of a family photograph, the theme of 'three children playing' or 'a birthday party' led to more centric and symmetrical pictures, particularly by the older children. The same pattern of development in composition had been found by Barnhart (1942) in the drawings of children enrolled in the Cleveland Museum Art School. Other variables that might affect the way children

---

[12] The principles of balance and other aspects of our aesthetic response to the organisation of a picture were first investigated by Gestalt psychologists (e.g., see appendix) and, later, Arnheim (1974) built on these ideas in his analysis of the relationship between visual perception and art.

[13] See chapter 9.

a

b

c

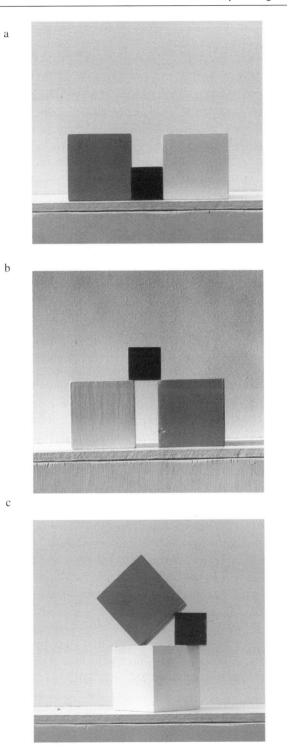

Figure 6.25 *Composition by second and third grade pupils (a), a fifth grade pupil (b), and a sixth grade pupil (c) (Milbrath 1998).*

compose their pictures are their level of representational skill and the order in which they draw the items on the page. Barnhart found that both of these were related to children's level of compositional form.

Milbrath (1998) devised a method of studying composition in children's pictures without these confounding factors. Given that children can appreciate the aesthetic elements of pictures before they can produce them themselves, Milbrath predicted that without these production constraints children might be able to demonstrate a greater compositional competence. She asked children aged 6 to 17 years to make an arrangement from a number of precut two-dimensional shapes or three-dimensional wooden blocks, from which they could draw a still-life picture that would be pleasing to them. As predicted, children were able to demonstrate a higher level of composition than they could achieve in their own drawings. The younger children showed symmetry in their arrangements and the older ones were more experimental, composing asymmetrical and dynamic arrangements even though the visual balance of the composition was often jeopardised (see figure 6.25). It seems, then, that the problems children encounter in their own representational drawing may overshadow any attempts they might make to form a pleasing composition. Nonetheless, since Milbrath's findings also indicate that children are more attuned to aspects of composition than had been previously demonstrated, this is a dimension of picture production that we might be able to encourage through discussion or carefully designed tasks.

Summary

Very young children do not organise their pictures in a coherent fashion. Indeed, they do not even orientate their figures in a conventional way on the page. Gradually, though, they learn the pictorial conventions, and increasingly acquire a number of pictorial devices. At first, these may be applied only to isolated figures in the picture rather than to the picture as a whole, and children may be biased towards local cues such as the accidental orientation of slanting eyes or the perpendicular bias when drawing figures on to a sloping baseline. Other tendencies, such as the 'to each its own space' rule, serve to separate figures and parts of figures, often giving the picture a 'wooden' appearance.

Young children are sensitive to different kinds of spatial relationship between objects (e.g., in, on, through and behind), but the way they 'translate' these relationships on to the page is often puzzling to adults. In their 'transparency' drawings items are shown which would not be visible in reality. In fact, these drawings may occur because of a lack of planning or because the child has followed the structure of the scene rather than its visual appearance. When drawing one object hidden behind another children often separate the two on the page. Again, they may be attempting to show the structure of the scene (i.e., the fact that the two objects occupy separate spaces) rather than its appearance from a particular viewpoint.

One of the more difficult problems about pictures is how to represent the depth dimension. In this chapter I have discussed some of the research which has investigated children's ability to use a number of pictorial devices for this purpose, including occlusion, size and height cues, and depth lines. Although there are age-related increases in the ability to use each of these devices, they do not necessarily develop uniformly in the same child, but may have different trajectories depending on the kinds of objects the child wants to draw, the structure of a scene, and also the child's own individual interests. Although linear convergence perspective is a most effective system for showing how a scene looks from a particular viewpoint (*visual realism* in Luquet's terms), we should remember that it is only one way of representing the world. It is not necessarily the best way, nor the system of projection that children or adults automatically choose or try to emulate (see chapter 8). Nonetheless, to acquire the skilful use of all the drawing devices in this system is a considerable achievement and not one that comes easily to most people. It usually requires expert tuition (see chapter 12). Alongside their developing ability to represent the spatial world in their pictures, children have also been shown to be sensitive to aesthetic composition. We know, however, that this aesthetic dimension may be overshadowed by their difficulties in solving the representational problems and may not normally be evident in any sophisticated form in their own pictures.

7   Children's ability to depict expressions of emotion

Central to discussions on the nature of art has been the notion of expression of emotion (e.g., Collingwood 1938; Goodman 1976). Indeed, 'the expression of emotion has long been considered the *raison d'être* of visual art' (Callaghan 1995, p. 3). One way of tackling this issue in relation to children's pictures is to consider children's understanding of emotional expression in ready-made pictures, as I did in chapter 3. The conclusion I drew was that children as young as 2 years of age can recognise some depicted facial expressions of emotion and that, at about the age of 5, they are just beginning to understand non-literal or metaphorical ways of suggesting emotion. In this chapter I shall consider children's ability to convey emotion in their own pictures. Does this development also proceed from the literal to non-literal? Does it occur at a later age than children's understanding, that is, does production lag behind comprehension?

The literal depiction of emotions in facial expressions

Drawings of facial expressions are considered to be *literal* representations of emotion (Goodman 1976), and in one of the first detailed discussions of portrait painting de Piles (1708) advised painters to attend to facial expression. Even if the face is not painted accurately from an anatomical point of view, it is still considered as the 'seat of emotional expression' (Spiegel & Machotka 1974, p. 168). According to Gombrich (1960), we readily interpret almost any lines inside an oval contour as a facial expression and we easily recognise the cartoonist's use of simplified and stereotyped expressions even though they are not objectively realistic (Gombrich 1972). Participants in research studies who have been asked to draw a whole figure which is, for example, happy, sad or angry have focussed on the facial features rather than on other bodily gestures (Golomb 1992; Morra, Caloni & d'Amico 1994). In fact, in Golomb's study nearly 25 per cent of her 6-year-olds drew only the head for each of their figures and omitted the rest of the body altogether.

The face, then, seems to have a special status in the expression of emotion, although, as Brunswik (1956) and Robertson (1962) have warned, it has many variables and a certain expression is not necessarily related to only one particular feature. We might expect, though, that young children, compared with older ones and adults, will not be able to alter many aspects of a face in their drawings. Indeed, it is well known that individual children often use the same graphic schema for their human figures and, therefore, all their figures may look very similar over a series of drawings. Nonetheless, although we see this conservatism in their pictures it does not follow that children are completely inflexible and, in fact, there is a considerable amount of evidence that they can adapt their schemas in various ways (see chapter 5). We would expect to see the same findings in their depiction of facial expressions of emotion, that is, we would expect to see that, if given appropriate tasks and instructions, even young children might be able to alter the faces of their figures in a fairly simple way but that this ability will develop with increasing age. Since some emotions are understood earlier than others (see chapter 3), we would expect that this pattern would also be mirrored in children's own drawings. In particular, 'happy' is the emotion that seems to be most easily recognised, followed by sad and angry; the less well understood emotions are disgust, fear and surprise.[1]

Even though children can recognise at least some facial expressions of emotion both in real faces and also in pictures by age 2 years, they might not be able to depict those expressions themselves. In fact, at age 2 years only 15 per cent of children can draw a recognisable face on a ready-drawn circle, whereas 80 per cent can do so at age 3 and 95 per cent at age 4 (Schulenburg 1999). If most 2-year-olds cannot draw a recognisable face then it follows that they will also be unable to draw different facial expressions of emotion. So, we would expect to find that children's ability to draw these expressions will develop later than their ability to comprehend them in ready-made pictures. In other words, production will lag behind understanding, a pattern found in many studies of drawing (Golomb 1992; Fayol, Barrouillet & Chevrot 1995; Jolley, Knox & Foster 2000)[2] as well as in other domains (e.g., Dale 1976).

When Golomb (1992) asked 6- to 12-year-olds to draw a happy, a sad and an angry child the participants concentrated on the face and it was the mouth, in particular, that they altered. Morra and colleagues (1994) tested children of a similar age range (6 to 11 years), asking them to draw a happy, a sad and a scared person. Again, the children concentrated on the face and altered the orientation of the mouth. In order to focus on the face itself Missaghi-Lakshman and Whissell (1991) gave 7- to 12-year-olds outlines of faces and asked them to draw the six basic expressions.

---

[1]   Darwin (1872) claimed that there are six basic facial expressions of emotion: happiness, sadness, fear, anger, surprise and disgust.

[2]   There are some studies, however, in which comprehension and production have been found to occur at the same time, for example Taylor and Bacharach (1981), Moore (1986) and Brooks, Glenn and Crozier (1988).

A number of subsequent studies (e.g., Sayil 1996, 1997a, 1997b; Zagòrska 1996; Larkin 2001; Skipper 2001) have also adopted this method, although not all have included all six basic emotions. There are similar findings, however, regarding the ways in which children adapt the faces in order to convey different emotional expressions. Depictions of a *happy* face generally include an upwardly curving mouth. Golomb (1992) found that the youngest children tended to draw a single curved line while the older children made it into a two-dimensional 'heart' shape. Older children often draw curved eyebrows and include eyelashes on their happy faces. *Sadness* is generally indicated by a downwardly curving mouth. Again, Golomb found that her youngest children drew a single line while the older ones drew a two-dimensional shape. Tears are often included in a sad face: in Golomb's study tears were added by 10 per cent of the 6-year-olds, 90 per cent of the 8-year-olds and 50 per cent of the 11-year-olds. Older children sometimes draw inwardly pointing eyebrows (/\). For *anger* Golomb's younger children tended to draw a straight line or included teeth or a heavy dot above the lips; the older children drew a zigzag or wavy mouth and included teeth. Older children also draw outwardly pointing slashes for the eyebrows (\/) and a wrinkled brow. When depicting *fear* children sometimes drew vertical lines for the hair and wide eyes. A *surprised* face often has an open mouth and sometimes wide eyes. A protruding tongue is often added to a *disgusted* expression (see figure 7.1.)

Missaghi-Lakshman and Whissell (1991) asked twenty-nine adults to guess the emotion intended for each face drawn by their children, aged 7, 9 and 12 years. The happy and sad faces were best identified, followed by angry and surprised, and then disgusted and afraid. Sayil (1996) also found that her 6-year-olds drew happy and sad expressions more successfully than they drew surprised and angry ones. Younger children were included in a study by Zagòrska (1996). She asked 4- and 5-year-olds to draw joy, sadness, fear and anger. The expression of joy was the easiest to draw and the expression of anger the most difficult.

Two of my students (Larkin 2001; Skipper 2001) also tested children aged 4 to 5 years as well as an older group aged 6 to 7 years. In addition, Skipper also included a group of adults.[3] Three adult judges independently decided which emotion each picture was intended to depict. If two or more of the adults judged a picture to convey a certain emotion then the picture was deemed to have been a successful depiction of that emotion.

Not surprisingly, the younger children were less successful at conveying emotion than the older children: the younger ones were successful with an average of only 2.08 (Larkin) or 1.75 (Skipper) expressions (out of a total of 6), whereas the older ones were successful with an average of

---

[3] Many studies have not included an adult group, as it has often been assumed that they will be able to depict all facial expressions successfully.

4–5 years   6–7 years   Adults

Happy

Sad

Angry

Surprised

Disgusted

Frightened

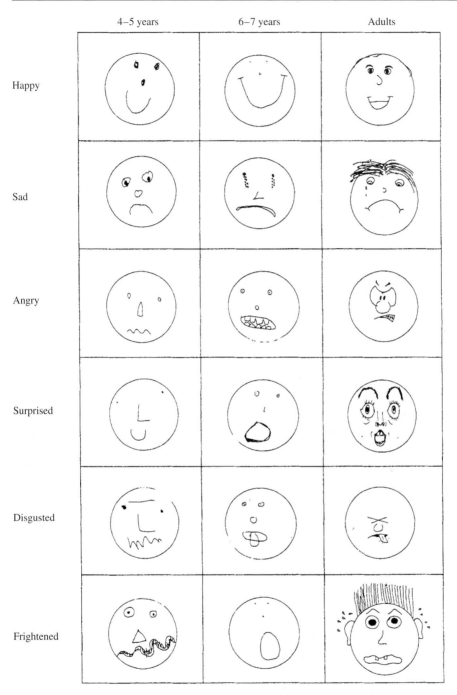

Figure 7.1 *Children's drawings of the six basic facial expressions of emotion (from Skipper 2001).*

Table 3 *Successful depictions of the six basic facial expressions of emotion by three age groups in studies by Larkin (2001) and Skipper (2001).*
(As percentages)

| | 4–5 years | | 6–7 years | | Adults |
	Larkin	Skipper	Larkin	Skipper	Skipper
Happy	85	80	100	85	95
Sad	62	60	85	90	90
Angry	31	15	35	35	60
Surprised	15	10	8	20	60
Disgusted	8	5	38	30	55
Frightened	4	5	15	10	45

2.81 (Larkin) or 2.70 (Skipper); interestingly, the adults conveyed emotion successfully in an average of only 4.05 pictures, not all six of them. As can be seen from table 3, happy was the emotion most easily conveyed, closely followed by sad. On the whole, only a minority of the younger children were successful with angry, surprised, disgusted and frightened. Even though this increased for the older children, less than half of them were successful and, in fact, even many adults failed to convince the judges of the emotion they were trying to depict.

There is general agreement that happy is the emotion most successfully depicted, followed by sad. The four other emotions are much less well depicted, and there is no clear order of difficulty. Why are there these differences? One reason may be that we are more familiar with expressions of happiness and sadness and that this makes it easier for us to depict these two emotions (Bridges 1932). Although there is some similarity in the pattern of responses in depiction and recognition tasks, both adults and children have more difficulty in depicting the emotions than in recognising them.[4] This difficulty may result either from their lack of understanding of exactly which facial features are involved in particular expressions or because they have not learned the conventional pictorial schemas for them. Interestingly, Skipper (2001) found no significant correlation between children's recognition of the expressions of emotion and their ability to draw them, a result also reported by Sayil (1996). In other words, some children may be good at recognition but poor at drawing, and vice versa.

As Missaghi-Lakshman and Whissell (1991) have pointed out, children need to learn a number of conventionally accepted symbols in order to

---

[4] See chapter 3 for a discussion of the findings relating to recognition of facial expressions of emotion.

depict different facial expressions. Very young children are unlikely to have learned all of them and therefore they will be unable to depict all the emotions and unable to depict them as effectively as older children will. One of the earliest accepted symbols is the up-curved mouth used to denote a happy face. In fact, most young children (66 per cent of 2- to 4-year-olds in Schulenburg's 1999 study) draw an up-curved mouth even when they are simply asked to draw a face, that is, not necessarily a happy face; a minority draw a (roughly) straight line or an enclosed shape. This suggests that the 'happy' face, as denoted by an up-curved mouth, is the preferred face that children draw from an extremely young age. So, of all the facial expressions, they will have had the most practice at drawing this one. We might suppose that the down-curved mouth for a sad face is then relatively easy to learn, as it is simply the same symbol but turned upside-down; further alterations to the mouth such as drawing a wavy or jagged mouth for angry or an open mouth for frightened or surprised might take longer to perfect. It is also likely that children draw happy and sad expressions more often than they draw angry, disgusted, frightened and surprised expressions.

Some facial expressions, such as frightened and angry, are only successful (or, at least, more successful) if they involve alteration of the eyebrows. This region of the face may be an area that children pay less attention to, and Sayil (1997b), among others, found that few of her 6- and 8-year-olds drew appropriate eyebrows for each emotion. She noticed that although they had difficulty in drawing oblique lines,[5] they also seemed not to pay attention to these details. Sayil concluded that they prefer to depict emotion with the shape of the mouth, a finding consistent with that of other researchers. When Cunningham and Odom (1986) asked 5- and 11-year-olds to complete a series of tasks matching and recalling photographs of different facial expressions, they found that the children were more likely to remember and evaluate information from the mouth region first, the eye region second and the nose last. Thus, the mouth seems to be the most salient feature.

The research on children's ability to draw facial expressions of emotion mirrors, to some extent, their comprehension of these expressions in ready-made pictures. In particular, happy is the emotional expression most successfully drawn, followed by sad. The other four basic emotions – angry, frightened, disgusted and surprised – are less well depicted and their order is less clear. The earliest feature to be altered is the mouth; alterations to the eyebrows and additions such as tears (for sad) and a protruding tongue (for disgusted) appear later. As expected, there is a time lag between children's understanding of emotional expressions in pictures

---

[5] However, Cox (1989) and Cox and Littleton (1995) found that 7-year-olds have no difficulty with drawing obliques.

and their ability to produce them themselves. Whereas 4-year-olds – and even 2-year-olds – show some discrimination among the different depicted expressions, they are not very successful at drawing these differences themselves; the evidence from current studies shows that children are beginning to depict the differences at age 4 to 5 years, but that further development takes place well into middle childhood and perhaps beyond. Interestingly, children's developing ability to draw facial expressions of emotion is not related to their memory capacity, at least not between the ages of 6 and 11 years (Morra, Caloni & d'Amico 1994). This suggests to Morra and colleagues that drawing a person's emotions is not really a problem-solving activity that demands attentional capacity, rather it may simply involve recalling the features of a person experiencing particular emotions, which even quite young children should be able to do. I would suggest, though, that it also involves learning the symbols conventionally used to denote different facial expressions of emotion.

Conveying mood in pictures by non-literal means

Whereas facial expressions convey mood in a literal way, there are also *non-literal* or metaphorical ways in which this can be achieved. One is through the *abstract* or formal properties of a picture: for example, upward and curved strokes as well as bright colours are thought to convey a positive mood whereas downward and angular strokes and dark colours convey a negative one. Another way of conveying mood metaphorically is through the picture's *content*: for example, a blooming tree can suggest happiness whereas a leafless tree can suggest sadness. Adults generally agree on the meaning of both of these strategies – abstract and content expression – for expressing emotion, and are also consistent in their use of them (Werner & Kaplan 1963).

Although abstract and content expression are often combined in the same picture, it is possible to analyse them separately. Ives (1984) found that content expression did not occur to any great extent in his study until the age of 16 years. It is suggested that this late onset is because the drawer must conceive of a metaphor (e.g., a leafless tree for sadness) and then, usually, adapt the abstract properties (using downwardly curving lines) in order to bring about the mood required (see figure 7.2). In contrast, both Jolley, Cox and Barlow (2003) and Jolley, Fenn and Jones (2004) found evidence to suggest that content expression occurs earlier than abstract expression.

Since far more studies have investigated children's use of abstract rather than content expression in their pictures, I will concentrate on abstract expression. According to Winston and colleagues (1995), the most likely abstract properties to be shown in children's drawings are line, colour and

Figure 7.2 *In abstract expression (left), the curved lines indicate happiness and the drooping lines, sadness; in content expression (right), a fruitful tree indicates happiness and a withered tree, sadness (from Ives 1984).*

size, and these have been the most prominently researched in the literature. However, young children are mainly concerned with subject matter, and Parsons (1987) claimed that they do not consider the abstract properties of pictures until at least the age of 9 years. Indeed, some earlier studies have provided evidence in support of this assertion (see chapter 3). Even so, a few studies have provided evidence to the contrary: for example, O'Hare and Cook (1983) found that 8-year-olds can recognise the differences in the use of colour among a set of pictures and that 6-year-olds can discriminate pictures according to an artist's use of line (O'Hare & Westwood 1984). Some later studies (e.g., Steinberg & DeLoache 1986; Callaghan & MacFarlane 1998) have controlled for subject matter and have demonstrated that, indeed, children as young as 6 years are sensitive to the differences between pictures in terms of their abstract, stylistic features.

Even though children are sensitive to these abstract properties in ready-made pictures (see chapter 3), they may have difficulty in reproducing them themselves. Carothers and Gardner (1979) found that although their 10-year-olds were sensitive to the line quality and the mood of a picture and were able to choose a ready-drawn completion for an unfinished picture, they could not draw it; by the age of 12 years, however, children could both choose and draw the completion themselves. Similarly, O'Hare and Cook (1983) found that 8-year-olds could detect differences in colour style between pictures but were unable to reproduce these differences until the age of 11 years. In contrast, Wilson (1992) found that when children were asked to draw what happened after the incident depicted in Munch's *The Scream* (see figure 3.1), even 5-year-olds used undulating lines in imitation of those used by Munch. However, children's ability to detect and imitate certain aspects of the style of other artists does not necessarily indicate that they can use abstract properties in a deliberate way in their own spontaneous artwork.

The expressive use of line

Ives (1984) examined children's ability to produce expressive drawings by asking 4- to 16-year-olds, as well as adults, to draw various kinds of tree: happy, sad, angry, quiet, loud and hard. Four adults were asked to judge the pictures. The results revealed that the preschool children typically responded in a literal way by drawing a face on the tree to make it, for example, happy or sad (see figure 7.3). The use of abstract expression in terms of whether the lines were curved or angular, thick or thin, or upward or downward increased with age: whereas 4-year-olds tended to use only one kind of abstract expression, older children increasingly used a combination of these means of conveying different moods. Winston and colleagues (1995) also asked their children, aged 6, 9 and 12 years, to draw a happy and a sad tree. Like Ives, they found that the younger children tended to use literal representations and that the use of abstract means of conveying the emotions increased with age – older children were more likely to use line direction and also colour.

In order to compare children's ability to depict emotions in a literal or a non-literal way, Morra and colleagues (1994) asked children aged 6 to 11 to draw a person, a tree or a ship. Each child drew only one topic but drew it three times, as happy, sad and scared. The ability to modify the shape and lines of the drawings increased with age, especially from age 7. The person was the most easily modified, followed by the tree and then the

Figure 7.3 *A 4-year-old's use of literal expression: a happy tree (left) and a sad tree (right) (from Ives 1984).*

ship, indicating that children's ability to convey emotion in a literal sense (i.e., by facial expression) precedes their ability to convey it through non-literal or metaphorical ways. Just as Ives had found, so also in this study, facial features were added to the tree and ship drawings. Later modifications included alterations in the shape or direction of the limbs, branches and sails and alterations to the quality of the line (e.g., 'trembling' lines to indicate fear). Morra and colleagues found no significant correlation between children's ability to draw facial expressions of emotion and memory capacity, but they did find a significant relationship when non-human topics were involved (tree, $r = .63$; ship, $r = .50$). They suggested that as memory capacity increases children are increasingly able to co-ordinate the information involved in the process of metaphorical thinking.

The expressive use of colour

As these studies indicate, children at about 6 to 7 years of age are beginning to be able to adapt the *lines* in their drawings to convey different moods. It may be, however, that another abstract property, namely *colour*, can be used at an earlier age. Young children seem to be particularly sensitive to colour, and in chapter 3 I suggested that colour may be the most salient abstract property of a picture for them. They will cite colour as a reason for liking or disliking a picture, and will use it rather than shape or composition for classifying pictures; they also use bold colours in their own work (Harrison 1990; Machotka 1966; Rump & Southgate 1967). Colour may be highly salient, but can children use colour to express emotion?

Golomb (1992) reported that very young children use colours idiosyncratically but then, at about age 4, begin to restrict them in realistic ways (e.g., blue for the sky, green for the grass), although she also reported a great deal of playfulness in the choice of colour for different objects. By the age of 6 to 8 years, however, the realistic use of colour is elevated almost to a rule. Children from the age of about 7 years are in a 'schematic stage',[6] according to Löwenfeld and Brittain (1970), and are concerned primarily with colouring objects realistically; only at the age of about 14 years do they develop emotional reactions to colour. In our everyday speech we make links between colour and emotion, for example, 'red with anger', 'feeling blue', 'green with envy' and so on, and both Odbert, Karwoski and Eckerson (1942) and Wexner (1954) found considerable

---

[6] Löwenfeld proposed three distinct stages in younger children's drawing development: scribbling (aged 2–4 years), preschematic (aged 4–7 years) and schematic (7–9 years). From age 9 children become more interested in realism and the representation of three-dimensional space; later they become concerned with emotions and aesthetics.

agreement among college students in their choice of colours associated with a set of adjectives describing various moods. These stages correspond loosely to Parsons' (1987) developmental account (see chapter 3) in that there is a shift from a concern with realism to a consideration of the expressive possibilities of colour.

Guilford (1940) claimed that our emotional response to colour (bright colours for positive emotions and dark colours for negative ones) is biological. An alternative explanation is that it is the result of learned associations. Lawler and Lawler (1965) argued that a good test of these claims would be to ascertain the strength of association in young children, who would have had less time to learn the mood–colour associations. Although these researchers provided only two colours and asked their 3- to 4-year-olds to colour in only one picture (a happy or a sad girl), there was a clear association between happy and yellow and sad and brown, an association also found by one of my students (O'Neill 1997) in 4- to 5-year-olds, 7- to 8-year-olds and adults who were asked to give a verbal response to each colour named by the experimenter. Lawler and Lawler argued that their results provided support for Guilford's biological claim. It should be pointed out, however, that by the age of 3 or 4 children have had plenty of time to learn these colour–mood associations from a variety of sources, including, for example, pictures in storybooks.

Whether or not colour associations are innate or learned, children at quite an early age can use colour in their pictures as an expression of emotion in a non-literal way. One reason they may be able to demonstrate this so early is that they do not have to acquire a skill in using colour; they merely have to choose appropriate colours from those available. In contrast, some degree of skill is required to vary the line quality of a picture in a non-literal way and also even to vary the shape of a mouth or eyebrows in a literal facial expression of emotion.

Many of the studies on the use of colour have been criticised on the grounds that researchers have provided the children with only a limited number of colours (Corcoran 1954; Golomb 1992). Indeed, Kellogg (1969) dismissed the study of children's use of colour on the grounds that their choices are simply limited by adults. Mindful of this problem, Golomb (1992) provided eight coloured crayons (black, blue, brown, green, red, orange, purple and yellow) in her investigation of children's use of colour. She asked 6- to 12-year-olds to draw a happy, a sad and an angry child. As I have already indicated earlier in this chapter, the children altered the facial features, in particular the shape of the mouth. They did not alter the posture of the figure or the quality of the line, and, interestingly, there was no clear relationship between the depicted emotion and colour.

In case this task might have seemed too bland for her children, Golomb gave them a second task in which she asked them to draw some emotionally felt experiences – a happy and also a frightening dream. Not surprisingly, these themes produced very different pictures, for example, birthday parties and children winning prizes for the happy dreams versus ghosts and Halloween scenes for the frightening ones. The colours also differed, at least for the younger children, with bright and more numerous colours being used for the happy dreams and darker colours used for the frightening dreams.

In Callaghan's (1994) study, the children were younger – aged 4 to 9 years – and were given a free choice of subject matter: they were simply asked to draw one happy, one sad, one excited and one calm picture. An adult artist then classified the four pictures drawn by each child. There was a high degree of consistency (.72 overall) between these classifications and the intentions of the children. Callaghan reported that children of all ages used colour, with bold primary colours being used more often for the happy and excited pictures, pastel shades for the calm ones, but a range of colours for the sad pictures (see plates 1, 2 and 3 for examples of children's depictions of different emotional states).

Callaghan and MacGregor (1997) pursued this idea of asking children to draw a felt emotion. At home, 5- to 9-year-olds were invited to draw happy, sad, excited, calm and angry pictures when their parents judged that their children were actually feeling these emotions; the children were also asked to draw these pictures out of context when they were in a research lab. Like Golomb, Callaghan and MacGregor found that certain themes were linked with certain emotional states, especially when the drawings were produced at home, but they also reported the use of colour to differentiate the drawings.

Although both Golomb and Callaghan and MacGregor have reported colour differences in children's pictures of differently emotionally charged topics, the colours may have been chosen not with the emotion in mind but simply because they were appropriate for the topic. A drawing of a dead cat on a road (i.e., a sad drawing) may be a dark picture because the road is a dark colour. A picture of dolphins in the sea is likely to be blue (a calm picture) because of the nature of the topic. A picture of a party (a happy or excited picture) is likely to be bright because the party clothes, presents and decorations at children's parties are usually bright and varied. In other words, topic and colour are often confounded. Therefore, we do not know whether children are aware of conveying emotion via colour in their pictures or whether they are simply colouring the objects realistically.

Some studies have controlled for the subject matter of the picture by, for example, asking children to colour in a set of faces. Although faces convey emotion in a literal sense, other aspects of them, such as their colour, can convey it in a non-literal or metaphorical way. Zentner (2001) asked 3- to 4-year-olds to choose a colour to go with a happy, a sad or an angry facial expression. Bright colours (particularly yellow) tended to be chosen for happy, and dark colours (particularly blue) for sad, although there was no association between angry and any particular colour. One of my students (Platten 2003, study 1) asked 6- to 7-year-olds, 10- to 11-year-olds and some adults to choose a colour (from a set of eight) for three facial expressions (happy, sad and angry). As in Zentner's study, her participants tended to choose yellow for the happy face (50 per cent of the younger children, 65 per cent of the older ones and 95 per cent of the adults) and also dark colours (black, brown or blue) for the sad face, although this latter tendency was not very strong and did not differ among the age groups. Unlike Zentner's study, there was an association between red and angry, although this was not significantly different at different ages.

Like Morra and colleagues (1994), Platten also compared children's responses to different facial expressions and to trees labelled with different emotions. With increasing age, yellow was chosen for the happy face; yellow was also chosen for the happy tree by 50 per cent of the participants, although there was no relationship with age. Dark colours tended to be chosen for both the sad face and the sad tree, although an increasing tendency with age was not significant. Whereas the angry face elicited red, the angry tree tended to elicit both red and black, and again there was no significant increase in this tendency with age.

Although we see some regularity with which certain colours are linked to specific emotions, there may also be some differences in colour preferences according to age. Alschuler and Hattwick (1947) found that very young children have a general preference for 'warm' colours whereas older children prefer 'colder' colours such as blue and green. There may also be variation in colour preferences among individual children. Boyatzis and Varghese (1993) reported considerable variation in the emotions that colours evoke. Reactions seemed to be both gender-related and also dependent on personal experience. For example, one girl said that pink made her happy because she had a pink dress; several boys said that black made them feel excited because they wore black in karate lessons; and one girl said that red made her sad because she thought of Jesus on the cross with blood all over the place. It would seem important to take these findings into account when investigating children's choice of colour to depict different emotions.

And this is exactly what Burkitt, Barrett and Davis (2003a) have done. Their children were first asked to order ten colours in order of preference. Next, they were asked to colour in some outline drawings of a nice, nasty and neutral man, dog or tree. The drawings were then analysed in terms of children's own individual colour preferences as well as the actual colours used. At all ages, from 4 to 11 years, children tended to use their more preferred colours for the nice figures and their least preferred colours for the nasty figures; they used intermediately rated colours for their neutral figures. These findings were repeated in a further study (Burkitt, Barrett & Davis 2004). In both studies black tended to be chosen for the nasty figures. Whereas a wide range of colours was used for colouring in the nice figures in one study (2003a), the primary colours were mostly used for the nice figures in the other (2004). Primary colours were used for the neutral figures in the earlier study and secondary colours for the neutral figures in the later one.

Whereas children do not begin to use line as an abstract form of expressing emotional mood in their pictures until about the age of 6 to 7 years, their use of colour for this purpose seems to occur somewhat younger – beginning at about 4 to 5 years and possibly even at age 3. It is unclear whether this indicates that colour–emotion associations are innate, as even at a young age children will have had the opportunity to learn them. Although a number of studies have reported that children use bright colours for positive emotions and dark ones for negative emotions, we should also bear in mind that there may be individual differences in their colour choices.

The expressive use of size

As well as varying line and colour in order to suggest a particular emotion, we can also vary the *size* of the objects in the picture. Varying the size of figures to denote their importance and status is a well-known feature of, among others, Egyptian art. Löwenfeld and Brittain (1970) claimed that in children's artwork too size is a reflection of the emotional importance of what is being depicted. So, for example, certain parts of the human figure or particular members of a family group may vary disproportionately in size, reflecting their emotional importance to the child. A number of studies have supported this claim (e.g., Craddick 1963; Sechrest & Wallace 1964; Fox & Thomas 1990).

Among the methodological problems with some of the early studies is the lack of control of factors affecting the planning of the drawing (see Freeman 1976; Cox 1992). For example, children might draw a larger figure because they intend to draw a lot of detail within its contours or they might draw one figure smaller than another because there is insufficient space left on the page (Freeman 1980; Thomas & Tsalimi 1988; Henderson & Thomas 1990). In order to reduce the need for children to plan for any detail they might want to include in their figures Thomas, Chaigne and Fox (1989) asked children aged 4 to 7 years to copy the shaded outline of a figure (see figure 7.4) and then to copy it again, imagining it either as a nice person or as a nasty person; the drawings were completed on separate sheets of paper. The nice person was drawn larger and the nasty person smaller than the neutral figure; a further group of

Figure 7.4 *Children were asked to copy the shaded outline of a figure.*

children who drew the neutral figure twice did not alter the size of their two figures. This effect of size occurred also when the children were asked to draw a nice and a nasty magic apple, demonstrating that it is not confined only to depictions of people. These results were supported by Burkitt, Barrett and Davis (2003b), who asked children aged 4 to 11 years to copy a shape of a man, a dog and a tree. The figures were given either positive (nice, kind, pleasant and friendly), negative (nasty, horrible, mean and unfriendly) or neutral characterisations. The children's feelings towards the figures were assessed independently and were found to be in the intended direction. The positively described topics were drawn larger than the neutral ones and the negative ones were reduced in size relative to the neutral ones (although this reduction effect was less consistent than the size increase of the positive figures).

These particular studies of size and emotion have used rather unusual models – outline figures – which most children would not usually draw. In order to investigate whether the size effect occurs in a more natural drawing task Burkitt, Barrett and Davis (2004) asked children aged 4 to 11 years to draw the topics in the absence of a model. They drew a neutral figure (a man, a dog or a tree) and then a nice and a nasty figure (in counterbalanced order), all on separate pieces of paper. Children increased the size of their nice figures compared with the neutral ones. However, the reduction in size for the nasty figures was less reliable; in fact, the reduction only occurred for the trees and not for their drawings of the man or the dog. Whereas children across the 4-to-11 age range increased the height and width of their 'nice' drawings, there was an age difference when the area of the drawings was measured: the younger children (4–8 years) increased the area but the older children (aged 8–11) did not. As regards the nasty figures, whereas the younger children drew them smaller than the neutral ones, the older children tended to draw them larger than their neutral ones. A content analysis was carried out to check that the nice figures had not been enlarged in order to include more details in them and this was confirmed not to be the case.

Despite some discrepancies in these results it might seem that children draw according to the convention that larger figures represent those with a positive emotional charge and smaller ones, those with a negative charge. However, not all studies have supported this conclusion. Cotterill and Thomas (1990), for example, found that when children were asked to draw both their figures on the same sheet of paper rather than on separate sheets the size effect was reversed: the nasty figure was the larger one and the nice figure, the smaller. Jolley (1995) also found this reverse effect when children were asked to judge whether ready-drawn large and small figures were nice or nasty; this was the case for figures of a man, a dog and an apple. In a further set of studies in which children were asked to draw the figures themselves, Jolley manipulated a number of variables: the stimulus (shaded outline, non-shaded outline and no stimulus), the instructions (the man was simply characterised as nice or nasty, or the children were asked to pretend that they had to meet him), whether the drawings were made on the same sheet of paper or on separate sheets, and whether the nice man was contrasted with the nasty man or whether each man was contrasted with a neutral figure. In these tasks there was no evidence that children significantly varied the size of the nice and nasty characters. Furthermore, Jolley found that individual children were inconsistent in their responses. In particular, the size differences between drawings of a nice and a nasty man correlated at only .41 between two drawing sessions.[7]

If children were responding to the convention that positive figures are drawn larger and negative ones smaller then we would not expect to see this variation in findings, and, in particular, we would not expect to find the reverse size effect in some studies. A different explanation put forward by Thomas and colleagues (1989) is that children are responding to the task with an 'appetitive-defensive mechanism', which encourages them to increase the size of nice topics in order to identify more strongly with them and to decrease the size of nasty topics in order to reduce their perceived threat. This explanation is not convincing also, in the light of the inconsistency of response (particularly of children's drawings of negative topics) and, again, the reverse size effect found in some studies. More worrying still are the lack of significant effects and lack of consistency in individual children's responses in Jolley's (1995) study. The current position regarding the research findings on size of figures in children's drawings is that it is by no means clear that children consistently use size to differentiate emotionally charged figures, and that the two main explanations are not at all convincing. It should be pointed out, however, that most studies have concentrated on 'nice' and 'nasty' figures. Other kinds

---

[7] Swensen (1968) reported that the reliability of size across the same person's drawings of the human figure was only 51 per cent.

of contrasts may produce different results. Ives (1984), for example, found that some 4-year-olds used size to show the difference between a quiet (small) and a loud (large) tree. He argued that young children appear to be able to convey expressivity in an abstract way if there is a cross-modal similarity between two dimensions (in this case, size and sound).

When we consider the three kinds of abstract expression in children's drawings that have received the most attention from researchers, we find that the findings are more straightforward for line and colour whereas those relating to the size effect are the least reliable and convincing. It appears that at about the age of 6 to 7 years children can vary the quality of the line in their drawings to reflect different sorts of emotional moods. Their ability to use colour for this same purpose occurs earlier – beginning at the age of 4 or 5 years or even at age 3 according to one study (Zentner 2001).

Is there a linear increase with age in children's ability to draw expressive pictures?

Most of the studies mentioned so far in this chapter that have included a developmental perspective have shown that there is an increase with age in children's ability to express emotion in their pictures. This pattern of development receives further support from Jolley, Cox and Barlow (2003), who asked children aged 4 to 14 and adults to draw happy, sad and angry pictures. These pictures were then assessed by artists for abstract expression (including separate assessments for colour, line and composition), content expression (the number of different subject matter themes through which the mood of the picture was expressed) and the overall quality of expression (i.e., how well the intended mood was conveyed). There was a slow but steady improvement in the emotional expressivity ratings of the pictures across the age range; in fact, there was a significant shift from ages 4 to 5, a plateau from 5 to 9, another shift from ages 9 to 11, and then another plateau from 11 to 14, and then some evidence of another shift from age 14 to adulthood. A similar study by Jolley, Fenn and Jones (2004) has also shown a slow improvement in the expressive drawings of children aged between 4 and 9 years.

In contrast, there is another view that the pattern of development is somewhat different. Gardner and Winner (1982) and Strauss (1982) suggested that young children's drawings are very expressive but that there is then a decline in emotional expressivity after the age of about 7 years, with a subsequent rise in adolescence; thus, development supposedly follows a U-shaped pattern. In order to test this prediction Davis (1997) tested children aged 5, 8 and 11; she also added two groups of 14-year-olds (some self-declared artists and some non-artists) and two groups of adults (a group of professional adult artists and some non-artists). Each participant drew three pictures: happy, sad and angry. Judges scored each picture in terms of its expression (the extent to which it embodied emotion through its aesthetic properties), aesthetic balance and appropriate use of line and composition (in relation to the emotion supposedly expressed in the picture). When these scores were combined the 5-year-olds scored 7.9 out of a possible 12 whereas the 8- and 11-year-olds scored much lower (6.2); the 14-year-old and adult non-artists also scored low. The 14-year-old artists scored more or less the same as the 5-year-olds and the adult artists scored higher still (9.5). Thus, Davis' data seem to show an L-shaped development when the older children and adults were non-artists but a U-shaped one when they were artists. In either case, there appears to be a dip in performance around the age of 8 years, when children seem to produce pictures that are less expressive than those they produced at a younger age. The reason for this, according to Davis and others, is that children at this age are striving for visual realism and, in their attempts to do this, become more fussy and less bold in their execution of their artwork.

The different developmental patterns found in these different studies may be due to a variation in the beliefs of the judges regarding children's expressivity – particularly the expressivity shown in young children's drawings. Some judges may be more traditional in their assessment of pictures, in the sense that they see young children's drawings as less skilful both in terms of representation and emotional expressivity compared with the drawings of older children. Some judges, on the other hand, may be biased towards seeing young children's drawings as expressive even if they are not technically skilful. Davis (1997) has raised this issue and points out that 'the celebration of the artistry of young children derives from and is unique to a modernist perspective' (p. 152). Indeed, the notion that young children's art is somehow more innocent, uninhibited and 'pure' has been reinforced by, for example, Kandinsky's claim that children look at the world with unspoiled eyes (Miesel 1970) and Picasso's assertion, 'Previously, I used to draw like Raphael but it's taken my whole lifetime to learn to draw like children do' (De Meredieu 1974, p. 13). It is not surprising, also, that if modern artists have consciously tried to paint like young children,[8] then we will see similarities in their styles (Pariser 1995; Fineberg 1997).

That adults' judgements may be biased one way or the other has been demonstrated by Pariser (1995), who has tried to replicate Davis' study with drawings collected from the Chinese community in Montreal which were then evaluated by both North American and Montreal Chinese judges. The North American judges identified a U-shaped development whereas the Chinese judges did not. Pariser explains these findings in

---

[8] Artists such as Kandinsky, Klee, Miró and Picasso were interested in and influenced by children's art.

terms of a western reverence for expressiveness versus a Chinese appreciation of technical control in drawing (see chapter 12). Kindler (2000) also
found no evidence of a U-shaped curve of development when she asked
eight judges (including children as well as adults) in Taiwan to rate a set of
children's drawings (a person, a classmate and a cartoon) on a three-point
scale. There was, however, an increase in perceived artistry with age, with
no decline in late childhood or adolescence. Kindler and her colleagues
(Kindler et al. 2001; Kindler et al. 2002) have discovered that a U-shaped
curve of development tends to occur when the judges are 'modernists'
whereas a more linear relationship occurs when they are 'traditionalists',
and this difference occurs regardless of country. Thus, when assessing the
overall shape of development with regard to children's ability to express
emotion in their pictures, we should bear in mind who is doing the judging
and the fact that judges with different beliefs about young children's
drawings may make very different assessments.

Summary

In chapter 3 I concluded that children at quite a young age – at
4 years and perhaps even at age 2 – show some ability to discriminate
between pictures of different facial expressions of emotion. In contrast to
their understanding of this literal means of conveying emotion, their understanding of non-literal or metaphorical means comes later – beginning at
about the age of 5 years. If we accept these findings then we might expect
that children's ability to convey emotions in their own pictures would
follow the same pattern, that is, the depiction of emotional expression by
literal means occurring at an earlier age than that by non-literal means.
We might also expect that there will be a developmental lag between
children's ability to understand emotional expression in the drawings of
others and their ability to produce such drawings themselves.

As regards the literal expression of emotion, children are beginning to
be able to draw different facial expressions at the age of 4 to 5 years. Of the
six basic emotions, happy is the one most successfully drawn, followed by
sad; there is no clear order of difficulty for angry, afraid, surprised and
disgusted. The earliest feature to be adapted is the mouth, whereas alterations to the eyebrows and additions such as tears (for a sad face) appear
later. With regard to the non-literal or metaphorical means of conveying
emotion in pictures, I have reviewed the evidence from studies that have
investigated the abstract properties of a picture (line, colour and size) and
also its content. Since there is conflicting evidence between the few studies
that have concentrated on content expression, it is difficult to draw any
conclusion on this issue at the present time. I have therefore focussed more
on abstract expression. With regard to the use of line, we can conclude

that at about 6 to 7 years of age children are beginning to vary its quality in their drawings of different emotions. For example, they use upwardly-curving lines for positive emotions and downwardly-curving ones for negative emotions. With regard to their use of colour in non-literal ways, this seems to occur at an earlier age, at about 4 to 5 years or even younger. Bright colours, particularly yellow, are used for positive emotions and dark colours for negative ones. It is difficult to come to a conclusion about the use of size to differentiate emotions in children's drawings due to the lack of consistency of the findings.

Is it the case that the pattern of literal followed by non-literal development found in children's understanding of the pictorial expression of emotions is also found in their ability to convey emotional expression in their own pictures? The answer to this is not straightforward. The answer is 'yes' if we consider the findings regarding their use of line: whereas literal means of conveying emotion appear at about the age of 4 to 5 years, their use of line in a non-literal way occurs later, at ages 6 and 7. However, if we consider their use of colour then this occurs at a younger age, 4 to 5 years. It is unclear whether the reason for this early use of colour in non-literal ways is a biological reponse or a learned response. Either way, children do not have to acquire a graphic skill to use colour (they merely have to choose one), whereas some skill is needed to vary, say, the line when drawing an angry mouth or the branches of a 'trembling' tree.

When we consider the developmental lag between comprehension and production, this pattern seems to hold true for the literal expression of emotion: at age 2 years children recognise at least some facial expressions of emotion in both real faces and in pictures, but their ability to vary different facial expressions in their own drawings occurs much later – beginning around 4 to 5 years. The age at which children understand non-literal means of conveying emotion in pictures varies according to different studies, and, as I have already pointed out, according to different means of expression (e.g., line, colour). Understanding the use of line occurs around 5 years of age, and its use in children's own pictures at about age 6 to 7. Understanding colour occurs at around 4 years of age and its use, around 4 to 5 years. It seems, then, that there is a developmental lag between understanding and production.

Does the ability to convey emotion in pictures continue to increase as children get older? Most studies have concluded that it does, although development may be slow. In contrast, it has also been claimed that this ability is high among very young children, declines in middle childhood when children are preoccupied with visual realism and then rises again in adolescence, particularly for more artistically talented pupils. It seems that the kind of developmental pattern we see may depend on who the judges are. 'Modernists' who believe that very young children's art is intrinsically expressive tend to give high ratings to these children's pictures; traditionalists, on the other hand, tend to be more concerned with the representational features of the pictures and rate them less favourably compared with those of older children.

In this chapter I have tackled the issue of emotion in children's pictures by examining studies that have asked ordinary children to depict particular emotional states. Another approach is to study the drawings of children with emotional problems – those who may, for example, be traumatised by illness, war or sexual abuse. According to many clinicians and therapists the pictures of these children may reveal their feelings even when the children have not intended them to do so. In chapter 11 I shall consider the evidence for this claim that children's emotional state can be revealed through their artwork.

8 The development of children's pictures and the history of art

We can see some general trends in children's artistic development. They include an early exploration of the kinds of marks or forms that can be made in any particular medium, an increasing interest in creating representational pictures, a development from simple to more complex figures, and a tendency towards intellectual realism in the early years giving way to an interest in and, for some, a mastery of visual realism in later childhood and adolescence (see chapters 4, 5 and 6). Whereas their earlier concerns are directed more at the representational aspects of a picture, older children become interested in the emotions that pictures can express and also in the formal or abstract properties of a picture, such as its line and colour (see chapters 3 and 7). Some writers (e.g., Luquet 1923; Eng 1954; Gablik 1976; Gowans 1979; Damerow 1998) have claimed that there are similarities between these changes in children's artwork and the changes in art over prehistorical and historical time. The claim, or at least the implication, is that the artistic productions of societies are a reflection of the cognitive level of their members, in the same way that children's work supposedly reflects their changing and increasing cognitive abilities. This is a version of the 'ontogeny recapitulates phylogeny' argument (Haeckel 1906), that the development of the individual re-enacts the development of the species. In this chapter I shall investigate the evidence for this claim. First of all I shall discuss the emergence of artistic activity among early humans and compare it with young children's first attempts at drawing. I shall go on to trace some developments in art over historical time and compare them with artistic developments within the child. I shall argue that although there have been innovations in technique and style at various times and in different cultures, this development is neither inevitable nor universally the same. Similarly, although we also see developments in children's art, the pattern is not predetermined but, rather, is influenced by the artistic styles children experience in the culture they happen to live in and also by their particular purposes and intentions when producing a picture, as well as their own increasing motor and cognitive skills.

The beginnings of art

Fragments of pigment as well as paint-grinding equipment dating from between 350,000 and 400,000 years ago have been found in a cave at the hilltop site of Twin Rivers in central Zambia (Barham 2002). The mineral-based pigments include yellow, light and dark red, brown, pink, purple and blue-black. All of the minerals used to produce these pigments would have been found within 2–5 km of the site, and it is thought that the collection, transportation and processing went on over the course of 100,000 or more years of intermittent occupation.

It has been argued that iron minerals have chemical properties that would have made them useful ingredients in medicines (Velo 1984) or as preservatives of animal hides (Keeley 1980; Audouin & Plisson 1982), but their main use historically has been as pigments (Knight, Power & Watts 1995). The variety of different minerals transported to the Twin Rivers site indicates a use other than the merely functional. It suggests that people were interested in the different *colours* that could be produced. It is not known how these pigments were used, but a likely explanation is that prehistoric people mixed them with animal fat and used them for painting their bodies. If this was so, then it indicates that they may have been participating in ritualistic behaviour such as initiation ceremonies, hunting rituals or other social events. So far, these finds are the earliest indication of some kind of aesthetic or artistic behaviour among prehistoric humans, and they date from a time before the shift from archaic *Homo sapiens* to anatomically modern humans, *Homo sapiens sapiens*, about 100,000 years ago. Even if pigments were used in some kind of ritual there is a great deal more we do not know – for example, whether they were painted on surfaces other than the human body, whether they coated a surface or were painted as marks or designs, whether these were 'abstract' or figural, and whether they were intended simply to be decorative or were symbolic or representational.

Perhaps the oldest evidence for graphic decoration or symbolism has been found at Blombos cave in South Africa (Henshilwood et al. 2001). As well as a range of stone and bone tools, such as an awl, there are also a number of pointed ochre 'crayons' thought to have been used to apply areas of colour or design on to an abrasive surface. Even more significant, though, are pieces of deliberately engraved ochre dated at approximately 70,000 years ago and made by anatomically modern humans. The ochre surface was not accidentally scored with a knife as a by-product of some other activity; on the contrary, it was deliberately rubbed down and then a criss-cross pattern was engraved on it with a pointed implement. It is not known whether these marks were simply decorative or whether they had some other meaning. Of course, early humans could have been making marks, designs or even images at an earlier date if they made them on their bodies, on animal skins or bark, or in the mud or sand as other more recent hunter-gatherer societies do (e.g., the Warlpiri in Australia); temporary marks and images or those made on perishable surfaces would not have survived the ravages of time.[1]

The origins of image making

Gombrich (1960) speculated that early humans noticed that natural cracks or marks in nature (on a rock surface, for example) sometimes resemble the shape of real animals or humans,[2] and that this fortuitous discovery led to the deliberate production of such outlines. Davis (1986), however, has argued strongly against this claim, mainly on the grounds that there is no empirical evidence except for the occasional incorporation of a natural feature of the rock surface into Palaeolithic[3] pictures, and this may simply have been the artists' ingenuity in incorporating natural features into their already thought-out designs. In contrast to Gombrich's position, Davis claims that 'Objects are not seen as marks; rather, marks are seen as objects' (p. 199). In fact, it may have been the use of marks that paved the way for later image-making.

Early humans had been scratching marks on bones and stones for hundreds of millennia (Bahn 1997), although we can only speculate whether some of these had any symbolic or notational significance. Prolific mark-making increases the probability that, sooner or later, a mark will be seen as a thing. It is then only one step further to seeing the contour 'as the object' (i.e., standing for or depicting the object), rather than thinking that it is the real object itself. A closed contour, in particular, can often be seen as a natural object against a background (Arnheim 1974; Golomb 1992). Once one mark or shape had been interpreted as a representation then, potentially, other marks could be interpreted in this way too.[4] A certain way of depicting an object can then become a convention, recognised and understood by all members of a community. Thus, rather than assuming that modern humans suddenly, around 40,000 years ago, became gifted with a new artistic capacity, Davis (1986) explains the emergence of representation as arising out of the prior elaboration of mark-making. And this

[1] Bahn (1995) has argued that prehistoric cave art may be unrepresentative and uncharacteristic of the period and that it is very likely that most rock art was produced on exposed, open-air surfaces.

[2] Bahn (1997) reported the finding in the South African cave of Makapansgat of a water-worn cobble of ironstone resembling a human face, which may have been transported from twenty miles away by Australopithecines about 3,000,000 years ago.

[3] The Upper Palaeolithic period (or Upper Old Stone Age) dates from approximately 35,000–7,000 BCE.

[4] Note that this idea is similar to Luquet's (1927/2001) claim that young children move from scribbling to representational drawing by a process of fortuitous realism, that is, noticing a resemblance between their meaningless scribbles and real objects (see chapter 4).

could have occurred at several different places and at different times. He assumes that a number of sign systems would have been in operation at the same time – visually recognisable images, marks and patterns, as well as language – to convey meaning. These various symbol systems, Davis argues, paved the way for culture to develop. Interestingly, image-making is not just culture-bound (see chapter 10) but can also be culture-creating.

Davis' explanation of the origins of image-making has not gone uncriticised, as he himself recognises. There are, perhaps, not as many early marks as we would expect if, as Davis claims, they formed the basis for later image-making. In fact, it is not clear that simple marks were the earliest graphic form. It is possible that other types of marks – possibly ones with symbolic meaning – were made on materials that have since perished or were only intended to be temporary, painted on human bodies or drawn in the sand or mud. Even if we cannot understand the meaning of early marks and designs they may, nonetheless, have had a meaning and may even have had some visual similarity to whatever they were meant to denote. A further complication is that the three-dimensional figurines found across Europe seem to be older than most of the two-dimensional imagery (Hahn 1972), and it is unclear how the idea for these would have arisen from the making of non-figural marks and signs. Thus, difficulties in interpreting the meaning of marks and also the chronology of their production hinders our speculations as to how representational art originated.

Prehistoric figural art

The rock paintings of the Kondoa and Singida districts in Tanzania contain some of the oldest figural art. They may have been produced around 40,000 years ago[5] and, if so, then they predate the figural art produced in Europe. Around 35,000 years ago anatomically modern people moved into Europe. They made necklaces from bone ivory, shells and teeth and also engraved images of animals or parts of animals, as well as the human form, especially the female, on blocks of rock (Davis 1986). Modern humans also produced female figurines carved in ivory, bone or stone, and animals such as horses, mammoths and cave lions, dating from about 32,000 years ago. These three-dimensional images, which also carry marks, probably predate the engravings and paintings – in Europe, at least.

There is evidence that Neanderthals (*Homo sapiens neandertalensis*), who were descended from a line of archaic *Homo sapiens* but who were dying out by about 35,000 years ago, also produced jewelry by piercing animal teeth for

[5] Pettitt and Bahn (2003) warn of the difficulties in dating prehistoric art. Some radiocarbon dates conflict with the dates suggested by the style of the images, suggesting that the samples may have been contaminated in various ways or that the images were produced using much older materials.

necklaces. However, it appears that they did not begin to produce these until modern humans had arrived, and we assume that they copied the technique from their anatomically modern neighbours. There is some evidence that Neanderthals made deliberate scratch marks on bone (Marshack 1976), but it is not clear whether these were symbolic in some way. There is, however, no evidence of their ever having produced figural art, and this lack indicates to Stringer and Gamble (1993) that Neanderthals did not use art in the same kinds of negotiations and ceremonies that *Homo sapiens sapiens* was involved in. Perhaps this lack of image-making (or other representational systems) among Neanderthal groups served as a major drawback in their ability to create a more complex and enduring culture.

The 'golden age' of Palaeolithic artwork was between 20,000 and 10,000 years ago, when there was a proliferation of engravings (petroglyphs), sculptures and paintings on rock faces and in caves mainly in France, Spain and Portugal. Using flint tools, engravers and sculptors produced remarkable friezes in half-relief as well as three-dimensional figures. 'Art galleries' of paintings were developed, sometimes in obscure caves where scaffolding must have been erected in order to reach some of the higher surfaces (Leroi-Gourhan & Allain 1979); indeed, sockets for scaffolding survive at Lascaux. The vast majority of the images are of animals (see figure 8.1), although there are a few humans[6] or human-like figures (such as the head of a bison set upon the legs of a human), as well as some geometric patterns, 'showers' of dots and unidentified configurations.

Further south, in Spain and into North Africa, rock paintings have been found not only in caves but also on rocks and cliffs out in the open. As in the north, much of the art concerns animals,[7] but these are often accompanied by humans, in particular by hunters. Although they are often grouped into a scene, the figures themselves are more sketchy and less realistic than those further north. Indeed, these more southerly rock-shelter images are from a later date – 7,000–4,000 years ago – and are referred to as Mesolithic (Middle Stone Age).

A variety of painting techniques has been identified. For example, as well as applying paint with the hands or fingers, the mineral-based pigments were also applied with brushes or pads made from moss or animal hair. Artists sometimes applied the paint as a wash and may have sprayed paint on to the rock surface by blowing it through a hollow bone; they may also have used blocks of ochre as 'crayons'. Several examples of 'negative' hand prints standing out against a coloured background show that they knew the technique of stencilling; there are also a few examples of 'positive' imprints, where the artist dipped a hand in paint and then pressed it onto a wall.

---

[6] According to Bahn (1997), 75 per cent of Palaeolithic human depictions are actually portable, that is, scratched on stones or bones.

[7] Bahn (1997) has documented regional differences in the kinds of animals depicted.

Figure 8.1 *Palaeolithic cave art, Lascaux, France.*

According to Halverson (1992) there are no representations of vegetation[8] and no landscapes in Palaeolithic art. There appear to be few, if any, scenes in which the artist has deliberately arranged two or more animals into a composition. One possible example, however, is in the Chauvet cave (in the Ardèche region of France), discovered in the 1990s, where two bison are shown facing one another, perhaps fighting (Chauvet, Deschamps & Hillaire 1995). Occasionally the artists incorporated natural features of the rock surface into their depictions. In one example the painted contour of a bison's back follows the line of a crack. Presumably, this was a deliberate use of the rock feature by the artist. Another example is of a series of stags' heads painted just above a naturally dark area of rock, which gives the overall impression of deer swimming in a river. We cannot know for sure whether this interpretation is correct; indeed, it is unlikely, given the dearth of scenic depictions elsewhere in Palaeolithic art (Halverson 1992) and also the fact that it is quite common that only parts of animals are drawn (Lorblanchet 1977): for example, the head and the back or the underside of the body and part of the legs.

In general, the engraved and painted animals are depicted in profile. Often they are in complete profile but sometimes they are in 'twisted

[8] However, Tyldesley and Bahn (1983) reported a very few cases.

perspective', with, for example, the horns shown from the front on an otherwise profiled figure. Bahn (1997) has noted that frontal views of ibex and a horse are a later development – around 10,000 years ago. In the Chauvet cave there are some examples of three-quarter and full-face animals – an owl is shown full-face. Although there is some occlusion within a single animal, such as the nearer legs and body masking parts of the legs on its 'other' side, there are few cases of partial occlusion of one animal by another. In the Chauvet cave, however, there is a set of multiple outlines, as if the artist was trying to suggest a herd of rhinoceros. There is also an animal with many legs, which might possibly have been an attempt to indicate movement. Whereas there are few if any unambiguous cases of one animal partially occluding another, there are many cases of overlap where complete outlines of animals are superimposed on others. There are no clear cases of the use of diminishing size to indicate that an animal is farther away in the distance. In fact, there is no evidence of what we call 'linear convergence perspective' in Palaeolithic art (Halverson 1992).

We are perhaps most familiar with reproductions of the spectacular multicoloured cave paintings, but these actually constitute the lesser part of Palaeolithic art, most of which is, in fact, engraving. Most of the engravings and indeed the paintings are outline figures, and Halverson (1992) has pointed out that, above all, Palaeolithic art is an art of outline.

The purposes of Palaeolithic art

Although we can easily recognise most of the figures in rock art, including many animals which are now extinct (such as the mammoth and the woolly rhino), we do not know why these images were produced or how they were used. As there are so many depictions of animals, we may speculate that they were related in some way to hunting – perhaps in initiation ceremonies for young hunters or religious rites involving animal spirits. Clearly, there is more to art than simply recognising the depicted objects. In order to appreciate it fully we must also know something about the context in which it was produced, the use to which it was put and the knowledge, beliefs and interpretations that contemporaries brought with them when engaging with these images. And this is the case not only for art of the Palaeolithic period but for art at any time (Baxandall 1972; see also chapter 3).

In the first half of the twentieth century the interpretation of Palaeolithic art was largely based on comparisons with the traditional practices of present-day societies. For example, Reinach (1903) claimed that Palaeolithic art, like the art of Australian Aborigines, was produced in order to gain some control over hunted animals as well as to ensure their fertility, and Breuil (1952) argued that the artists hoped to acquire for themselves the strength and ferocity of some of the more dangerous animals they depicted. However, this kind of simple ethnographic analogy has fallen out of favour, mainly on the grounds that we should not compare the complex societies of Palaeolithic times, stretching over many thousands of years, with a single modern society now living in marginal circumstances and which has had a long history of contact with other cultures. In fact, there is probably no society today that is equivalent to the societies of Palaeolithic times (Lewis-Williams 2002).

The idea that at least some Palaeolithic art was linked with shamanism has been around for some time (e.g., Lommel 1967). More recently, Lewis-Williams (2002) has provided evidence for this view derived from a combination of his study of the rock art of South Africa, a knowledge of Bushman practices and an understanding of neuropsychological research into altered states of consciousness. Essentially, the idea is that the shaman goes into a trance-like state by dancing or, perhaps, with the use of hallucinogenic substances, and in this altered state predicts the future, cures the sick, controls animals and so on (Bourguignon 1989; Dobkin de Rios & Winkelman 1989). Shamanism appears to be a feature of all hunter-gatherer societies (Vitebsky 1995). However this altered state of consciousness is achieved, the participant experiences certain forms of mental images or 'entoptic' phenomena, such as dots, zigzags, wavy lines, grids and U-shapes in the early or 'lighter' stages (Tyler 1978). Examples of these images are also found in South African rock art and in European Palaeolithic art (see figure 8.2). As participants go deeper into altered consciousness they try to make sense of these images by seeing them as objects or important experiences (Horowitz 1964, 1975). Recognisable but sometimes distorted images of both humans and animals can be found in rock art and may have been representations of the kinds of images experienced by someone in an hallucinated state.

Neurological research has demonstrated the experience of certain basic mental images among participants who were given hallucinogenic drugs in controlled laboratory conditions (e.g., Siegel & Jarvik 1975; Siegel 1977; Asaad & Shapiro 1986) (see figure 8.3). As the images in the early stages of a drug-induced state are derived from excitation of the nervous system, it is assumed that all people, regardless of cultural background, are capable of seeing them (Hedges 1983; Whitley 1988). Huichol Indians in Mexico have reported almost identical imagery while under the influence of peyote, an hallucinogenic drug, as do participants in the laboratory; this imagery is also evident in Huichol weaving and art (Siegel 1977). Some of the patterns – particularly the zigzags – are also commonly reported by people who suffer from migraine headaches. Unfortunately, as Lewis-Williams (2002) points out, the universality of entoptic images themselves does not help us with their meanings in Palaeolithic art, nor with the ways in which they were used; both the meanings and their uses are 'always culturally controlled and historically situated' (p. 159).

Even though we do not know precisely in what ways they were used, pictures were a very early form of representation, predating writing by

Figure 8.2 *Marks on a cave wall, Montespan, France (from Capitan 1923).*

Figure 8.3 *Visual hallucinations seen by adults undergoing controlled intoxication with cocaine (from Siegel 1977).*

many thousands of years. In fact, the earliest writing systems were based on pictures and were probably developed in the fourth millennium BCE (see Robinson 1995 for an overview of the history of writing). Hundreds of small clay tablets inscribed with pictographic signs have been found near Uruk, Iraq, dating from approximately 3,300 BCE. These early writing systems used simplified pictures representing objects that had associated meanings. We still use this idea today on, for example, the washing instruction labels in our clothes and the male and female symbols that denote men's or women's public lavatories. It is likely that, in a similar way, the images produced by Palaeolithic people also carried associated meanings that are not explicit or obvious (to us) in the images themselves.

'Primitive art' and the art of young children

A number of authors (e.g., Luquet 1923; Eng 1954; Kellogg & O'Dell 1967) have attempted to make links between the art of primitive people and pictures of modern-day children. By 'primitive people', Eng (1954) meant those of Palaeolithic times who, she believed, were at a very primitive stage of mental development. She also regarded the artwork of some 'primitive races' of recent times, such as Bushmen, Eskimos and a few Indian tribes, as similar to Palaeolithic art, and many 'present-day savages' were deemed to be at a lower level of artistic representation. Clearly, the terminology reflects the attitudes of her time.[9]

Eng claimed that the development of the species is reproduced in the child. Therefore, we should see the same stages of development in the art of these early artists as we do in that of young children. She believed that both ancient art and child art begins with scribbling, and gave examples of 'scribbled' animals in early Palaeolithic art (Capitan & Peyrony 1921) that echoed the scribbled human figures drawn by her niece at age 2 years and 7 months (see figures 8.4 and 8.5). In both cases the heads are more detailed and recognisable whereas the bodies are incomplete. In both, the figures are superimposed on each other in a tangle of lines and without definite orientation. Further examples of wavy lines (Cartailhac & Breuil 1910), zigzags and so on (Capitan 1923) have also been classified as Palaeolithic scribbles (see figures 8.6 and 8.2) and compared with similar marks and patterns made by young children. In more recent times, Blatt (1994) and Damerow (1998) have also noted the apparent similarities between Palaeolithic art and young children's drawings.

One problem with these claims is that the authors are trying to impose their own interpretation on to the finished products without knowledge of

---

[9] Sully (1895) also compared the aesthetic senses of 'savages' and children, and considered children to be superior.

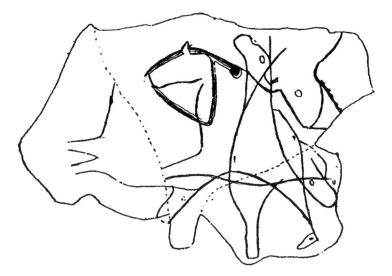

Figure 8.4 *Palaeolithic engraving (from Capitan & Peyrony 1921).*

Figure 8.5 *Scribble with indications of heads and body lines, by Margaret,
aged 2 years 7 months (Eng 1954).*

the context in which they were made or used. It may be that the
Palaeolithic lines and scribbles had some kind of meaning that is simply
not obvious to us. As discussed above, they may have been incorporated
into shamanistic practices. They may have been tallies, recording the

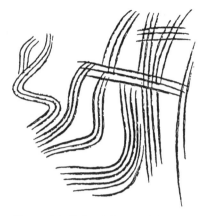

Figure 8.6 *Palaeolithic 'scribble' (from Cartailhac & Breuil 1910).*

making, storing or exchange of food or goods, or recording events or periods of time such as the phases of the moon. Another possibility is that they could be representations of tactics in a hunt or a diagram of, for example, a bear-trap, or a kind of map of a journey.[10] It is important to remember that lines and shapes might refer not to the visual appearance of objects but to an action or event, akin to young children's gestural or action representations (see chapter 4). Thus, although there are marks from Palaeolithic times that resemble young children's scribbles we do not know whether or not these marks had any symbolic meaning nor whether they were used in the same way. Moreover, as pointed out earlier in this chapter, we cannot be sure that these so-called scribbles predate representational forms, as other imagery painted temporarily on bodies or on other perishable surfaces will not have survived.

Most Palaeolithic pictures are of animals, with a few not-so-well executed human figures; in contrast, young children's pictures tend to be more concerned with the human figure.[11] In each case the artists are supposedly depicting the subject matter that is of most importance to them. There is, however, some doubt about the chronology; if the many Palaeolithic figurines found across Europe predate the engraved and painted animals then the early dominance of human figures would be similar in both ancient societies and modern child art. Even so, the Palaeolithic figures were mainly carved three-dimensional forms rather than two-dimensional images. Deręgowski (1998) has suggested that humans do not have such typical contours as most quadrupeds, whose bodies have a pronounced ridge, and that this makes the human form more difficult to draw. This could be the reason for

---

[10] Many modern-day paintings by Australian Aborigines refer to journeys, often in connection with hunting or locating plants and other sources of food (see chapter 10).
[11] Although the human figure is a popular topic in western children's drawings, children in rural areas of Africa are more likely to draw animals (Court 1992; see also chapter 10.)

the rarity and relatively late appearance of human figures in rock art. On the other hand, it may be that the human figure is not very prevalent in rock art because rock art focussed on animals; possibly, art associated with the human figure was mainly reserved for body painting or portable objects, such as figurines. In other words, different media may have been used for different purposes and different subject matters. When two-dimensional representations of human figures do appear – in the Ndedema rock shelters, for example – nearly all are depicted in a lateral view; this contrasts with the frontal views drawn by most children (Pager 1972).

Incomplete depictions of animals were discussed by Luquet (1923), who claimed that Palaeolithic artists, as well as modern-day children, missed out items of lesser interest, for example, eyes, ears and sometimes the arms of the human figure. However, we do not know why these items were omitted or why many of the animals are incomplete. It may have been, as Luquet believed, that artists only depicted their primary, defining features. On the other hand, they may have been practising an outline contour of a particular part of the animal, or perhaps they were teaching younger hunters about specific body parts. In other words, they may have had a particular reason for depicting incomplete figures and may not have intended to draw whole images. It is inappropriate, then, to claim a similarity between Palaeolithic art and children's art when we cannot know our ancestors' motives for these particular depictions.

When we examine drawings of complete animals we see in Palaeolithic art, as in child art, examples of mixed perspective and transparencies (e.g., the internal organs and skeleton of an animal may be shown and an arrow head may be visible even though it is supposed to be embedded in the animal's side).[12] Most of the animals depicted by Palaeolithic artists and also by African Bushmen are shown in profile or at least in lateral view; this is also the case in children's art. Although in neither Palaeolithic art nor in child art do we see the use of linear convergence perspective, nonetheless the animals produced by many of the Palaeolithic artists have more vitality and are also more naturalistic (Eng 1954); in contrast, children's images often seem stiff and less naturalistic. Indeed, as Rouma (1913) pointed out, the average child or even the average modern adult cannot draw as well as Palaeolithic artists, who were probably the more artistically gifted members of their communities and were also, no doubt, well practised at their art. Not all 'primitive' people were equally skilled at art: the best art has probably been produced by hunter-gatherers while some of the settled and more advanced people (so-called) have been less skilful. Rouma concluded that as the art of primitive people is so dependent on their environment, their occupations, their ideas and so on, then a comparison with children's pictures is not really useful.

[12] See chapter 5.

Figure 8.7 *A man (left) and his dog (right), by a boy aged 3 years 9 months.*

Although there are some similarities between Palaeolithic art and the art of young children, it would be unwise to stretch the parallels too far, as, for example, Luquet (1910) did by claiming that the Palaeolithic images of 'masked dancers' are actually the artists' inability to relinquish their animal schemas when drawing the human form, in a similar way that young children sometimes use a well-practised human form as the basis of their drawings of animals (see Eng 1954; see figure 8.7). It is surely unlikely that an accomplished artist, albeit from Palaeolithic times, could not draw a recognisable human and had to resort instead to drawing the head of a bison on the legs of a man. A simpler interpretation is that such a figure is meant to be a human wearing a mask or headdress as part of a dance or rite, or is camouflaged as he takes part in a hunt, or that the figure is a shaman who, in a ritualised trance-like state, experiences himself as an animal (Lewis-Williams 1981). Thus, we should not jump to the conclusion that art from an earlier time resulted from a more primitive mind (Clottes 1996). On the contrary, as Gombrich (1960) argued, historically earlier art forms were the result of the demands of the culture at their time and the motivations and intentions of the artists.

Historical developments in artistic styles and techniques

In order to decide whether or not the development of children's art parallels that of the history of adult art we need to consider, first of all, whether in fact there is a pattern of development in art over time. Although

Figure 8.8 *Wall painting from the tomb of Nebamun: hunting in the marshes (Thebes, Egypt, c. 1400 BCE).*

we might be tempted to think of the history of art as an orderly sequence of achievements which began in prehistoric times and which has culminated in 'better' forms of picture-making in more recent times, Hagen (1985) has challenged this notion of a 'grand evolutionary march' (p. 59). She surveyed artistic styles in a number of broad geographical regions (Europe, Africa, the Middle East, the Far East and the Americas) and claimed that there has been no universal sequence of development. For example, mixed-perspective pictures occur as an earlier art form in some cultures but not in others. It is certainly true that mixed perspective can be seen in Palaeolithic art, when an animal is drawn in profile but the horns are 'twisted' and viewed from the front (see figure 8.1). It can also be seen in the paintings of ancient Egypt: a 'full-face' eye is painted on a profile face, the shoulders are shown from the front whereas the arms and legs are painted from the side, and both feet are shown from the inner side so that a figure will appear to have, for example, two right feet (see figure 8.8). As well as these early examples there are further examples of mixed-perspective drawings during more recent eras, such as the mediaeval period in Europe. In the fourteenth-century Luttrell Psalter we see both ends of the courtly carriage,

Figure 8.9 *A 'folding out' picture of a courtly carriage – Luttrell Psalter, fourteenth century.*

Figure 8.10 A Young Boy with a Crayfish *by Pablo Picasso.*

which, in reality, would not be possible from a single vantage point (see figure 8.9). But even in more recent times the Cubists of the twentieth century showed many facets of the same object in a single picture (see figure 8.10). Thus, these mixed-perspective pictures, which may be

Figure 8.11 *Achilles and Ajax playing a game – Greek vase, signed by Exekias, sixth century BCE.*

regarded as examples of intellectual realism[13] (rather than visual realism), have occurred at different times throughout history – and in prehistory.

Similarly, many different projection systems have been used at different times and in different cultures. For example, in Greek art we see tabletops depicted as a straight line (see figure 8.11), as if we are looking at them at eye-level (orthographic or orthogonal projection). In Egyptian art there is a bird's-eye view of a rectangular pool (vertical oblique projection), with the trees on each side 'folded out' (see figure 8.12). In European mediaeval paintings we see tabletops also depicted as rectangles, even though they would not project this shape to the eye if we were looking at a real scene (see figure 8.13). We also see examples of oblique perspective in which the side edges of the tabletop are depicted as slanting parallel lines and the front and back edges are the same length (see figure 8.14). Since its formalisation during the Italian Renaissance, linear convergence perspective, or a variant of it, has often been considered to be the apogee of artistic development (see figure 8.15). In Europe it became the yardstick, indeed almost a straitjacket, for the way a picture should be organised, and various later movements, such as Cubism (Rosenblum 1960), had a hard time convincing people that there might be other legitimate ways of depicting the world. While linear convergence perspective was the norm of western painting, however, oblique perspective was the preferred

[13] See chapter 5.

Figure 8.12 *Wall painting from the tomb of Nebamun: garden with a pond (Thebes, Egypt,* c. *1400 BCE).*

system of sixteenth- to eighteenth-century Indian Moghul painting and seventeenth- to nineteenth-century Japanese prints. Linear convergence perspective was not developed by all cultures independently and was not adopted by all cultures even when they encountered it. Since there appears to be so much variation in styles of depiction, Hagen (1985) concluded that there is no development in art. (See chapter 6 for examples in children's pictures, and chapter 10 for examples of these different features and projection systems in other cultures.)

Hagen's assertion may be going too far, however. Although different kinds of depiction have been used at different times and in different cultures this does not disprove the idea of development in art, since development does not necessarily have to follow a strict sequential order, nor does it have to be universal (see also chapters 7 and 10). We can still accept the notion of development in the history of art if we look at

Figure 8.13 *The table in this mediaeval painting is in vertical oblique projection – Sir Geoffrey Luttrell dining with his family, Luttrell Psalter, fourteenth century.*

Figure 8.14 A perfumer's shop *from John Lydgate's* Pilgrimage of the Life of Man *(1426). Note the oblique projection of the table.*

the broad changes within one culture, although even then the progression might not be very orderly.

According to many art historians the history of western art was, for a long time, a journey towards a more convincing way of representing the visible world (Vasari 1885–7; Gombrich 2002). Although not completely

Figure 8.15 *Linear convergence perspective in Renaissance art* – Annunciation *by Carlo Crivelli, c. 1495.*

unknown to earlier artists, linear convergence perspective was developed in the fifteenth century as a formal and mathematical system – the earliest account by Brunelleschi appearing in about 1425 (Edgerton 1975; see also Spencer 1966 and Grayson 1972 for translations of Alberti's *De Pictura* of 1435). What artists were trying to do was to depict the detail and layout of a scene as if viewed through a window (see figure 8.16). This picture-as-window idea produced a more credible sensation of looking into a real scene and was being developed around the same time as other investigations of the natural world by, for example, Galileo, Leonardo da

Figure 8.16 *An artist drawing a scene through a gridded window (from Hieronymous Rodler and Johann II of Bavaria*, Ein schön nützlich Büchlein und Unterweisung der Kunst des Messens, *1531)*.

Vinci and Harvey.[14] The pictorial cues to depth, such as foreshortening, partial occlusion, size diminution and shadow projection, are not mere artistic conventions, however; our perception of the three-dimensional environment depends on these kinds of information, which are contained in the structure of ambient light (Hagen 1980). As well as an interest in the way that the structural features of a scene are projected on to the eye, artists had long been interested in the depiction of light, particularly since the introduction of oil paints, which enabled them to create more luminous effects. The Impressionists of the nineteenth century pursued this interest further, downplaying the need to paint an accurate picture of the physical structure of a scene and focussing instead on one's momentary experience of it in terms of light and colour. Although Gombrich (1960) did not believe in a predetermined development in the history of art, in his last book (2002; also see review by Hall 2002) he concluded that primitive art really is primitive and, although earlier artists mastered certain technical skills, later techniques such as linear convergence perspective can be considered superior – that is, if the artist's intention is to produce as visually realistic a picture as possible.

---

[14] *On the Movement of the Heart and Blood in Animals*, 1628/1962.

As well as developments in visual realism we can also trace changes over time in the emotional expression in pictures. When we see artworks from an earlier age – for example, from Palaeolithic times – we rarely feel that they convey any sense of emotional expression. If emotion was involved in the way that these images were used then it is likely that it was conveyed in complementary ways – through gesture, storytelling or dance, for example. Similarly, when mediaeval artists painted narrative scenes involving traumatic events the facial expressions are often rather bland and we must 'read in' the emotions ourselves, as viewers, from our own knowledge of the stories. In fact, with a few exceptions, emotional expression did not seem to be a major concern in western art until the beginning of the Italian Renaissance. Gradually, though, the emotional dimension became more important, and by the beginning of the twentieth century the Expressionist movement focussed mainly on emotional expression rather than on, and often at the expense of, a visual likeness to the object or scene. The Surrealists, influenced by the psychoanalytic movement, also wanted to get beyond reality and concentrated on our deeper and perhaps more disturbing mental states.

In contrast to Hagen's claim that there has been no development in art, we can see that there have been some broad developments over time – both in the introduction of graphic devices and projection systems as well as in the emotional mood of a picture – although not in all cultures. Although some 'modernist' artists in the twentieth century began to shun the notion of representation altogether, concentrating instead on the formal or abstract qualities of pictures, such as line, shape and colour, other artists never abandoned representational art or its emotional dimension. Indeed, these concerns are much in evidence in the work of contemporary artists, although here they may not necessarily be as an end in themselves. The styles and techniques that have been developed at different times and in different cultures do not necessarily replace each other in a sequential way, rather, they are retained in the artistic repertoire in order to be used according to the artist's purposes.

Parallels between the development of art history and children's art

I have argued, contrary to Hagen's claim, that we can see some developments in the history of art. Can we see parallels between these historical developments and the development of artistic ability within the child? I will take the development of projection systems and the development towards emotional expression as examples.

In the case of visual realism in western art, linear convergence perspective was a late development. If we look at children's use of projection systems (see chapter 6), we also find that linear convergence perspective makes a late appearance and that systems used before the historical formalisation of perspective are used by younger children. It is only at about the age of 14 years that children converge the side edges of their drawings of a tabletop, and even at this age they do not shorten the lines sufficiently or make the angle acute enough, so that their version of perspective is said to be 'naïve'. A more accurate attempt at linear convergence is rarely seen among adolescents and even among adults. There is some evidence, then, for a parallel development between the historical development of projection systems and that in children's art.

A concern with the depiction of emotion also appears to be a later development from an historical point of view, and this is also the case in children's art (see chapter 7). Whereas their earliest pictures show little emotional expression,[15] by age 4 to 5 years children can successfully draw a happy face and are quite good at drawing a sad face; the ability to depict other facial expressions comes later. By age 4 to 5 children can also use colour to suggest different emotions – bright colours for positive emotions and dark ones for negative emotions – and at about the age of 6 to 7 years they can use line for the same purpose – upwardly curving lines for positive emotions and downwardly curving lines for negative ones. However, their ability to convey emotion in their pictures seems to develop slowly through the primary school years, although it increases significantly as they move into adolescence.

By considering these two examples – the use of projection systems and the depiction of emotion – we can see that there is some similarity in the pattern of development between art history and children's art. It should be made clear, however, that these examples have been taken from developments in western art and the developmental pattern of western children. We cannot assume that either of these patterns is universal (see chapter 10). Similarly, in the same way that styles and techniques developed at a later time in history do not necessarily replace earlier ones, so in children's art also, earlier styles may be retained and incorporated into a larger repertoire as the child develops.

Causes of artistic change

Since the history of art in different cultures does not necessarily follow the same pattern, it follows that there is no inevitability about artistic developments in any one culture. Things could have turned out differently. At some points in history and in some cultures certain artistic styles have lasted for a long time. These periods of conservatism in art may be

---

[15] We should, however, bear in mind that 'modernists' tend to judge young children's pictures as expressive whereas traditionalists do not (see chapter 7).

related to the purpose of art during that particular period. If there is a concern with the faithful reproduction of traditional forms of depiction, then there is little impetus for change. In ancient Egyptian art, for example, the conventions of depiction were virtually unchanged for 3,000 years. Although to our eyes the figures may look flat and contorted, the artists were 'merely following a rule which allowed them to include everything in the human form that they considered important' (Gombrich 1954, p. 36). Similarly, important men were depicted as much larger than their wives, children and servants (see figure 8.8). Artists were not depicting what they could actually see from a particular viewpoint. However, by employing this size convention they were able to convey to the viewer the importance and status of certain people in that society. These conventions or rules were not applied haphazardly, but very carefully and consistently. In fact, Egyptian artists had to undergo a very strict apprenticeship in learning the conventions of depiction. Even when artists do try to be innovative there may be forces militating against them. For example, if they try to paint what they see they may still be influenced by existing ways of depiction. According to Gombrich (1960), it is extremely difficult to be innovative and to shake off traditional styles, as they seem to exercise a conservative hold over the artist and, indeed, the viewer. Gombrich discussed the case of Constable, who while trying to draw exactly what he saw, nonetheless could detect the influence of Gainsborough in his own painting of nature.

Presumably, the principles of linear convergence perspective could have been worked out at an earlier time and in other cultures, since people would have had the cognitive ability to do so and some artists already used it, albeit in an intuitive way. The reason why it was formalised in fifteenth-century Italy was that artists were responding to a new scientific way of thinking about the world. As Bremner (1996) has emphasised, 'a society possessing a particular level of knowledge will explore problems thrown up by that level of knowledge, which will in turn determine the form that the next level of knowledge takes' (p. 518). This notion can be traced to Vygotsky's (1962) cultural-historical approach to the development of societies and their individual members (see chapter 12). Along with developing more technologically sophisticated tools to cope with the physical environment, societies also develop ways of co-operating and communicating, for example, through speech, writing, number systems and picture-making. Whereas societies can and do evolve new ways of thinking about the world, these changes are not in any sense predetermined or inevitable. And this also applies to the historical changes we see in styles and techniques in art.

Although we see some historical development in the techniques and styles that artists have used, we should not assume that change is always linked to new technical achievements. Sometimes artists 'rediscover' techniques and styles from earlier times or from other cultures and incorporate them into their own work. For example, van Gogh was influenced by Japanese prints imported into Europe during the nineteenth century and Picasso and others were influenced by the art of so-called 'primitive' cultures as well as children's art. Furthermore, the role of the artist in modern western societies, at least, is to find new ways of seeing and thinking about the world; we expect artists to be innovative and to challenge our conventional ways of seeing and thinking. Thus, developments in art are not only directly tied to the development of new materials and techniques but also to the ideas and intentions of the artists, their contact with other artistic traditions and society's expectations of them. Although there have been developments in the history of art, we should see them not as a predetermined and orderly sequence occurring in all societies but rather as an accumulated repertoire of techniques, ideas and concerns which is then available as a resource for artists at any time and in any place.

Just as the historical development of art is not predetermined, systematic or universal, similarly the development in the individual child does not have to be strictly sequentially ordered. There is evidence for unevenness – for example, there may be periods of scribble even after recognisable figures have been produced, tadpole figures might reappear after conventional figures have already been drawn and so on (see chapters 4 and 5). Nonetheless, there do seem to be broad shifts in children's abilities and concerns, as I have outlined above and in other chapters. Although these are to some extent related to increases in motor skills, memory capacity and so on, they do not exactly mirror a developmental change in a child's cognitive ability. Authors such as Gablik (1976), Gowans (1979) and Damerow (1998), who claim such a close link, have relied too heavily on an acceptance of Piaget's (1952) theory of cognitive development, which itself has been the target of criticism in the last thirty years or so (Flavell 1971; Brown & Desforges 1977; Brainerd 1978; Halford 1989). In the same way that changes in art history are related to cultural demands and artists' intentions (Gombrich 1960), so the changes in children's art are also related to the kinds of artworks children see around them and their own changing intentions – although, in the case of children, these influences also interact with developments in their mental capacities and skills (see also chapters 10 and 12).

We can see some broad patterns in children's artistic development and to some extent these parallel some of the developments in the history of art. Artistic development over historical time appears to be a response to the changing requirements of societies and the intentions of individual artists. In the case of children, development is an interaction between their own cognitive development, their intentions and the influence and help of those around them.

Summary

Coloured pigments may have been used as long ago as 350,000 to 400,000 years, although we cannot be sure that they were used for aesthetic or artistic purposes. The earliest deliberately marked artefacts are dated at about 70,000 years ago and the earliest recognisable pictorial representations around 40,000 years ago. The making and use of graphic marks and pictures has been an activity of modern humans; as far as we know, no other species or even archaic humans have developed a system of pictorial representation. Palaeolithic art mainly consists of engravings and some paintings, animal subject matter and outline drawings, with figures mainly in profile or mixed- or semi-profile. The purposes of this artwork can only be guessed at.

There are some similarities between the art of prehistoric times and that of young children in western cultures: for example, in both there are incomplete figures, transparencies and mixed perspectives; in both there is no systematic use of perspective or diminution of size of an image to indicate its distance from the viewer. However, there are many differences. For example, although most children scribble before they draw recognisable figures, we cannot be sure that Palaeolithic artists produced non-representational marks before representational forms; one of the main problems is that we can only guess at the meaning of the marks made by Palaeolithic people, why they were made and how they were used. Despite the charm of young children's drawings, many Palaeolithic artists drew in a more skilful and animated way than most children and, indeed, most modern adults, and, based on what survives, their subject matter was mainly animals rather than people.

The idea of an orderly historical development in artistic style is hard to maintain, as the pattern is in fact not very orderly, nor is it universal. Art in different societies and at different times serves different functions: in ancient Egypt, for example, it was important for artists to continue with strict conventions of picture-making, whereas in the European Renaissance artists were amongst the vanguard of thinkers and innovators tackling the problem of visual reality. A concern with emotional expression has also been relatively recent. So, although innovations seem to come about in relation to certain prominent problems and concerns and are then added to the repertoire of techniques at an artist's disposal, there is no predetermined or inevitable progression in the history of art.

As with art history, it is also difficult to argue for an orderly set of stages in the developing child's artwork. Although we might expect that developmental changes in motor control and cognitive development will affect children's picture-making, we also need to take into account the *intentions* of the child. Furthermore, it is important to recognise that children are not producing pictures in a vacuum, but are creating them within a social and cultural context. The relationship between cognitive development and the development of art is likely, therefore, to be *indirect*, and, as Lindström (2000) has pointed out, artistic development is now 'described as the growth of a gradually more differentiated repertoire, with different options co-existing and being available for different purposes rather than replacing each other in a hierarchical order. In this perspective, there is not one but multiple end-points of development' (p. 11).

9 Artistic development in special populations

So far in this book I have discussed the artistic development of children with average cognitive abilities but have said little about those who fall outside this average range, who may be below or, indeed, above average. These children constitute 'special populations' and may include those who have an intellectual disability for which there is no obvious reason, as well as those whose abilities are associated with particular conditions such as Down's syndrome. Does their development follow the same or a different pattern? Talented[1] child artists might also be considered a special population. Although most of these children tend to be above average in mental ability, some of them have an intellectual disability – some well-known savants with autism are a case in point. Whatever the child's level of ability, we generally think of pictorial art as a visual medium. Is it possible, then, for children with a visual impairment to understand and even produce pictures? I shall examine the abilities of blind children in order to assess what effect a visual impairment has in the artistic domain and to what extent this medium really is reliant on visual ability.

Children with a non-specific intellectual disability

An issue going back to the early twentieth century is whether the development of children with an intellectual disability is basically the same as it is for those in the average range, or whether their development has a different pattern. The debate tends to be polarised between the idea of a developmental *delay* (Zigler 1969) versus the idea that there may be an actual *difference* in the development of these children (Morss 1985; Wishart 1993).

In 1913 Rouma included a group of 'feeble-minded' as well as typically developing children in his study of children's drawing ability. He considered that the intellectually disabled children produced drawings that were reminiscent of those of younger children. In other words, they were performing in accordance with their mental age rather their chronological

---

[1] I shall follow Milbrath (1998) in using this term rather than 'gifted', since the latter tends to be associated with a very high IQ, which is not necessarily related to artistic talent.

age. This suggests that intellectually disabled children are proceeding at a slower rate than their typically developing peers. In contrast, a number of other researchers (Schuyten 1904; Kerschensteiner 1905; Lobsien 1905; Burt 1933; Goodenough 1926) claimed that there are differences between the drawings of these two groups of children. Particularly noticeable were the unusual proportions of the human figures drawn by the intellectually disabled children compared with children of the same mental age, and the lack of coherence among the parts of their drawings as well as the extra details they included (Earl 1933; McElwee 1934; Israelite 1936; Spoerl 1940).

Unfortunately, these early studies suffered from a number of methodological shortcomings, which, according to Golomb and Barr-Grossman (1977), makes it impossible for us to decide between the 'delay' hypothesis and the 'difference' hypothesis; particularly problematic was the failure to include a control group with the same mental age as the intellectually disabled children. These authors carried out their own study, comparing the human figure drawings of children with a non-specific 'familial'[2] intellectual disability (with chronological ages between 4 years 4 months and 13 years 1 month and mental ages between 3 years 7 months and 5 years 6 months) and typically developing children (with chronological ages between 3 years and 5 years 10 months and mental ages between 3 years 7 months and 5 years 5 months). Thus, the intellectually disabled children were matched for ability with a typically developing but much younger group. The drawings of the two groups were very similar, with no noticeable differences between them in terms of the structure of the figures, their proportions or the addition of bizarre details. The only difference was that those intellectually disabled children with a mental age of 4 and 5 years drew more details than did the typically developing 4- to 5-year-olds. In general, then, this study supports the delay hypothesis although, to some extent, it does support those earlier studies which also noted that intellectually disabled children drew extra details.

Whereas Golomb and Barr-Grossman included intellectually disabled children from both the severe (i.e., below IQ 50) and the mild (IQ 50–70) range, a number of studies have concentrated on one or the other. Cox and Braga (1985) included children from a school for pupils with mild mental impairments – their average chronological age was 12 years 7 months but their average mental age was 7 years 11 months. They were matched with two groups of typically developing children: one was a chronological age match and the other was a mental age match. All the children were asked to draw two cubes in different spatial arrangements: one beside the other, one on top of the other, and one behind the other.

---

[2] 'Familial' refers to the fact that there appeared to be no specific pathological disorder in these children and their disability was therefore assumed to be associated with normal genetic variation in ability and/or a less stimulating environment.

Figure 9.1 *Human figure drawings by a 10-year-old (left), a 6-year-old (centre), and a child aged 10 but with a mental age of 6 (right) (Cox & Cotgreave 1996).*

The cubes were drawn from observation. The responses of the intellectually disabled children were similar to those of the typically developing children with the same mental age; both groups produced less 'mature' drawings than the typically developing 12-year-olds.

Cox and Cotgreave (1996) also included children in the mildly disabled range – their average chronological age was 9 years 11 months and their IQs ranged from 50 to 70. Each child was asked to draw a person and this was scored according to Koppitz's (1968) thirty developmental items (see chapter 11). Their drawings were compared with those of a group matched for chronological age (an average of 10 years 4 months) and another for mental age (an average of 6 years). The intellectually disabled children scored more like the 6-year-olds than the 10-year-olds – so, more like their mental age than their chronological age (see figure 9.1). When asked to identify which group had drawn each picture, twelve teachers[3] could easily identify the typically developing 10-year-olds' drawings, but they

---

[3] Four teachers were teachers of children with a mild intellectual disability and eight taught typically developing 5- to 6-year-olds. None was a teacher of the children who took part in this study.

frequently confused the drawings of the intellectually disabled children and the typically developing 6-year-olds. These results suggest a developmental delay in the drawings of intellectually disabled children.

Children with a severe intellectual disability were included in a study by Cox and Howarth (1989). Their average chronological age was 9 years 2 months but their average mental age was 3 years 9 months. Most of the group of fifteen had a non-specific intellectual disability, but three had Down's syndrome. Among the tasks they were asked to perform was a human figure drawing. Again, there were two comparison groups, one matched on chronological age and the other matched on mental age. The drawings were classified into five categories:[4] scribbles, shapes, tadpole figures, transitional figures and conventional figures (Cox & Parkin 1986). The intellectually disabled children's figures were more similar to those in the group matched on mental age than to those of their same-aged peers, although they actually lagged behind those in the mental age group. The reason for this lag may have been because the intellectually disabled children's average mental age was, in fact, eleven months behind that of the group matched on mental age. In other words, the matching of these groups was not as close as one would have liked. Bearing this in mind, the results still suggest a developmental delay.

In general, then, these studies show that children with a non-specific intellectual disability perform less well than their same-aged peers and more like younger children who have a similar mental age. This finding supports the developmental delay hypothesis, although there is a hint that these intellectually disabled children might also add more details to their drawings, which, arguably, could be evidence for a difference between them and typically developing children.

The drawing ability of children with Down's syndrome

One of the difficulties of studies involving children with a non-specific intellectual disability is that because the cause of their condition is not known (or at least not known to the researcher) groups of such children may have a range of different kinds of problems, which may or may not have a direct bearing on the way they draw and which may affect the tasks in different ways. Interpretation is more straightforward if studies include groups of children with the same kind of impairment, as their drawing ability might then be assumed to be affected in the same kind of way.

---

[4] It would have been difficult to use established scoring systems, as some of the children did not draw recognisable figures at all.

Down's syndrome is probably the most common condition associated with intellectual disability, accounting for approximately seventeen in every 10,000 births in the UK, and there are a number of studies that have investigated the drawing abilities of these children. Clements and Barrett (1994) found that children (aged 5 to 17 years) with Down's syndrome performed consistently lower than typically developing children matched for mental age on a set of drawing and picture selection tasks. Similarly, Eames and Cox (1994) found that their 16-year-old Down's syndrome children scored lower than younger children with a similar mental age on a series of drawing tasks. The Down's syndrome children tested by Cox and Maynard (1998) all had a severe intellectual disability. Their average age was 9 years 3 months and their mental age, 4 years 3 months. They were compared with typically developing children matched for chronological age (their average age was 9 years 3 months and their average mental age was 9 years) and others matched for mental age (their average age was 4 years 6 months and their average mental age was 4 years 3 months).[5] All the children were, first of all, asked to draw a man from imagination and then a man from a model. The drawings were scored according to Koppitz's thirty developmental items. If we consider the drawings from imagination then the average score of the Down's children was the same as that of the group matched on mental age (7.77 points), whereas the group matched on chronological age scored much higher (20.25). On the model task the Down's children achieved a lower score than the group matched on mental age (7.29 and 9.12, respectively), but, even so, were closer to this group than to the group matched on chronological age (22.88 points) (see figure 9.2).

The results of these studies suggest that drawing development in Down's children is delayed rather than different, although the delay may be greater than might be expected from the children's mental age. There were, however, some aspects of the children's behaviour in the Cox and Maynard study which might lead us to conclude that the difference hypothesis should not be abandoned. In particular, unlike the groups matched on chronological and also on mental age, the Down's children did not improve their score in the model task compared with the drawing from imagination. A possible explanation for this result may be the Down's children's supposed problems with attention. Stratford (1985) has argued that these children have a tendency to switch their attention from one dimension of a task to another and then to become confused. In the Cox and Maynard study (1998) the switch would be from drawing from imagination and then to drawing from a model. In fact, the Down's

---

[5] Importantly, in this study each Down's syndrome child was matched individually with a child of the same chronological age and one with the same mental age. The matching was therefore more rigorous than in many studies in which the groups are matched only on their average scores.

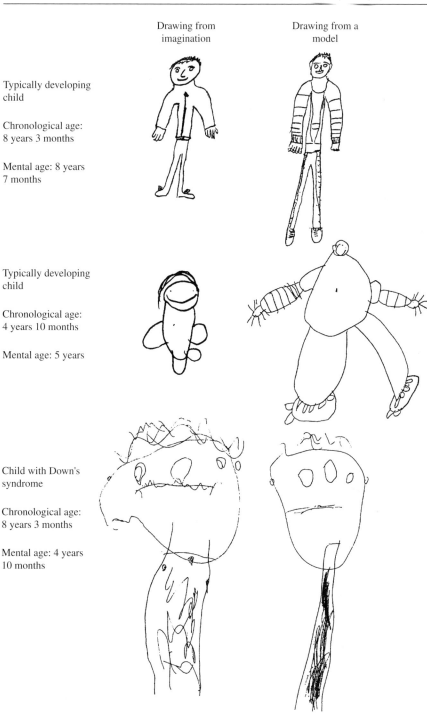

Figure 9.2 *Drawings from imagination and from a model by typically developing children and a child with Down's syndrome.*

children did not appear to be confused at all. They looked at the model when the experimenter pointed to it but then completely ignored it while they drew their usual schema for a man. Their drawings in the model task were very similar to their first drawings and some were actually less detailed. In contrast, the children in the groups matched on chronological and mental age added more body parts and more items of clothing when drawing from the model.

There are a number of developmental deficits linked to Down's syndrome: for example, there may be problems of motor control (Henderson, Morris & Frith 1981; Anwar & Hermelin 1982; Connolly et al. 1993; Jobling & Gunn 1995; Jobling 1998), vision (Woodhouse 1998) and planning (Clements & Barrett 1994). It is not clear, however, whether these particular problems are responsible for the lower level of drawing ability observed in most Down's syndrome children. What does seem to be clear, though, is that unlike that of typically developing children, Down's children's drawing ability is not significantly related to their mental age. In the Cox and Maynard study (1998) the correlations between task scores and mental age were .15 (drawing from imagination) and .06 (drawing from a model) in the Down's syndrome group, but .77 (imagination task) and .74 (model task) among the typically developing children. This pattern of results has also been reported by Clements and Barrett (1994) and Laws and Lawrence (2001). Although, on the whole, Down's syndrome children draw in a similar way to much younger children there is wide variation, which is independent of mental age. Laws and Lawrence illustrate this point with the examples of a well-executed drawing by one of the most delayed children in their group and a very immature drawing produced by a more able child (see figure 9.3).

One of the problems that may cast doubt on the research findings, not only for studies of Down's syndrome children but also for others with intellectually disabled children, is the measure used to match the groups for mental age. Ideally, one might suppose that a full IQ assessment should be made, based on both verbal and non-verbal tasks. This is rarely undertaken, however, because of the length of time it takes to administer such a test and the burden it imposes on children who may have a very limited attention span. In any case, as drawing is largely a non-verbal task it might be more appropriate to match the groups on non-verbal rather than verbal test scores.[6] Although some researchers (Eames & Cox 1994; Cox & Cotgreave 1996) have opted for non-verbal matching, many (Cox & Howarth 1989; Clements & Barrett 1994; Cox & Maynard 1998; Laws & Lawrence 2001) have opted to match on verbal test scores. Bearing this issue in mind we might reasonably conclude that the drawing ability of

---

[6] Scores on drawing tasks are more closely related to non-verbal (or performance) scores than to verbal scores (Abell, von Briesen & Watz 1996; Abell, Wood & Liebman 2001).

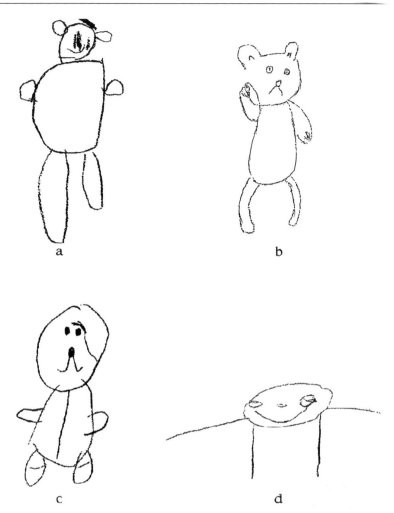

Figure 9.3 *Bears drawn by (a) a typically developing boy aged 5 years
4 months (MA 4 years 10 months), (b) a typically developing girl aged 8 years
6 months (MA 8 years 3 months), (c) a girl with Down's syndrome aged
9 years 3 months (MA 3 years 2 months) and (d) another girl with Down's
syndrome aged 11 years 6 months (MA 5 years 4 months) (Laws &
Lawrence 2001).*

children with Down's syndrome lags behind that of their same-aged peers.
Their performance is similar to that of younger children with the same
mental age and may even be more delayed than this. However, within a
Down's syndrome group, unlike a group of typically developing children,
drawing ability is not correlated with mental age. There is also some
evidence that children with Down's syndrome attend to a model even
less than typically developing young children do, but it is unclear whether

problems of motor control, vision and planning are accountable, even in part, for their poorer drawings.

Talented child artists

There have been few cases of exceptional artistic talent among very young children (Lark-Horovitz, Lewis & Luca 1973; Feldman & Goldsmith 1986). In fact, in a study of children taking art classes at the Cleveland Museum, Lark-Horovitz and colleagues reported no cases below the age of 11 years. Nonetheless, as we can see from the childhood drawings of famous artists such as Klee, Picasso and Toulouse-Lautrec (Pariser 1987, 1997), a talent for drawing may manifest itself at quite an early age. Of course, even though some children display a technical talent early in life this does not necessarily mean that they will go on to be gifted adult artists (Langer 1953).

According to Winner's (1996) review, talented teenage artists tend to be above average in intelligence but do not do particularly well at school and are not especially interested in academic subjects. They are, on average, at about the sixtieth percentile in terms of position in class. Interestingly, quite a high proportion of them are left-handed or, at least, non-right-handed.[7] A disproportionate number of males are non-right-handed. In terms of cognitive tasks, talented artists tend to do better on non-verbal (or performance) tasks than on verbal tasks. In particular, they excel at a number of different visual abilities, which include visual-spatial skills (e.g., recognition of shapes hidden in complex designs), visual imagination (the ability to recognise incomplete pictures) and visual memory (both short-term and long-term) for colour, composition, form, line quality and content (Milbrath 1998). As well as performing less well on verbal tasks, these talented artists also have a higher incidence of reading problems, such as dyslexia, compared with other children. Indeed, their enhanced visual abilities are not highly correlated with their verbal IQ scores.

Despite the different profile of abilities[8] between talented and non-talented artists a number of researchers, such as Golomb (1992) and Pariser (1995), consider that the drawing development of artistically talented children follows a normal path but is greatly accelerated. Golomb (1995) has described the development of an artistically talented

---

[7] Mebert and Michel (1980) reported that 21 per cent of art students were found to be left-handed compared with 7 per cent of other students at the same institution; 48 per cent were non-right-handed in contrast to 22 per cent of other students. 'Non-right-handedness' includes people who are strong left-handers, weak left-handers, not strongly right-handed or who are ambidextrous.

[8] Uneven profiles of abilities are important evidence in favour of Gardner's (1993) theory of 'multiple intelligences' as opposed to the unified notion of intelligence advocated by Piaget (1970) and the neo-Piagetians (e.g., Case 1992).

boy, called Eitan, who was drawing recognisable figures at age 2 and by the age of 4 was beginning to experiment with indicating volume and drawing the different facets of an object. He went on to master various spatial projection systems, such as oblique projection and then linear convergence perspective. This order of development appears similar to that in the normal population.

In contrast to this view that differences between talented and less talented child artists are simply a matter of developmental rate, Milbrath (1995, 1998) has argued that the results of her study of talented and less talented child artists, aged 4 to 14 years, indicate that the developmental path of artistically talented children is different from that of the less talented. For example, talented children begin to draw three-quarter views of figures by ages 5 and 6 whereas less talented children rarely do this, preferring frontal or, at a later age, profile views. Similarly, many talented children are beginning to use foreshortening at the age of 7 or 8 years whereas few less talented children do this even at age 13 or 14. By age 13 to 14 many talented children are using shading and shadow to indicate a light source; in contrast, this is very rare among less talented children of the same age. Milbrath points out that the level of detail and skill of the talented children in her study was never matched by those of the less talented, and the less talented children never caught up to the level of the talented. In fact, the older the children became, the more divergent their artwork seemed to become. These findings suggest that talented artists may be using different mental processes.

Milbrath believes that most children learn to see the world in terms of categories and concepts and that their perception tends to be dominated by these 'object-centred' descriptions. When they draw they rarely do so from a model, but rely on generic internal models, which tend to result in stereotypical and canonical figures (see chapter 5). Unless they receive specific teaching, most children do not successfully overcome the tendency towards producing object-centred representations, and when they recognise that these drawings do not look sufficiently realistic they may become disillusioned with drawing altogether. In contrast, those children who develop an artistic talent have a heightened visual sensitivity that enables them to see the world in terms of visual surfaces and apparent shapes (Lark-Horovitz, Lewis & Luca 1973; O'Connor & Hermelin 1983; Hermelin & O'Connor 1986; Rosenblatt & Winner 1988). Whereas most people 'see' a brick, for example, as a solid object with rectangular sides, the artistically talented may see it in terms of, say, three visible surfaces, none of which has a rectangular shape from their particular viewpoint. When they draw from a model these talented individuals are likely to look more closely at it than are less talented children, but even when not drawing from a model their superior visual memory skills allow them to call up *particular* visual memories, which they can then use as models instead of relying on generic internal models. There is, then, an emphasis on *figurative* processes among the talented child artists, in contrast to a reliance on *conceptual* processes in the less talented.

As well as having enhanced visual abilities, talented child artists are also more focussed on the actual process of drawing and become aware of the discrepancies between their own efforts and what they really see. They are interested in solving graphic problems and develop varied and flexible drawing schemas from an early age. Since they are interested in and, indeed, fascinated by the pictorial domain they are usually prodigious drawers and are interested in the challenges of representation, often tackling complicated spatial compositions and perspective when other children shy away from them. Although most talented artists are skilful at drawing or painting a range of topics, some tend to specialise. For example, a talented girl discussed by Lark-Horovitz, Lewis and Luca (1973) was keen on drawing horses (see figure 9.4), a boy studied by Wilson and Wilson (1977) excelled at drawing the human figure in the style of the Marvel comics (see figure 9.5) and a girl studied by Tan (1993; Ho 1989) specialised in painting monkeys and other animals (see figure 9.6).

Savants with autism[9]

A discussion of artistically talented children would not be complete without mention of those who are generally lower than average in terms of mental functioning but who happen to be exceptionally good artists. Nearly all of these 'savants' are also autistic to some degree, and most are male. Autism can be diagnosed on the basis of three particular behaviours: severe social impairment, severe communication difficulties, and the absence of imaginative pursuits such as pretend play (Frith 1994; Happé 1995). Individuals with autism often, but not always, have low mental functioning, and their verbal IQ scores tend to be lower than their performance (non-verbal) scores. Autism is rare,[10] savants with autism are very rare,[11] and savants with autism *and* an artistic talent are very rare indeed.[12] Because of one or two high-profile cases, such as Nadia Chomyn (Selfe 1977, 1995) and Stephen Wiltshire (1987, 1991), who have shown

[9] Individuals with a general intellectual disability but with one exceptional ability used to be termed *idiot savants*. More recently, Howe (1989) has referred to them as *retarded savants*. Since most are individuals with autism, I shall refer to them as *savants with autism*.

[10] Surveys in Europe, Japan and North America report an incidence of between 4 and 10 cases in 10,000 births (Sigman & Capps 1997).

[11] Rimland (1978) reported that only 10 per cent of individuals with autism have exceptional talents.

[12] Saloviita, Ruusila and Ruusila (2000) found only 16 per cent of artistically talented individuals among their sample of savants.

Figure 9.4 *Drawings of horses produced by a talented girl between the ages of 5 and 11 years (Lark-Horovitz, Lewis & Luca 1973).*

outstanding drawing ability (particularly with regard to visual realism), it is often assumed that many other children with autism may have this talent to some degree. After all, people with autism tend to have uneven cognitive ability profiles, with higher performance on non-verbal tasks compared with verbal tasks. In this respect their profiles are similar to those of talented artists. In fact, superior drawing ability is not common among

Figure 9.5 *Cartoon figures drawn in the style of the Marvel comics by a teenager called Anthony. Reprinted with the permission of Brent Wilson.*

children with autism (Fein, Lucci & Waterhouse 1990; Lewis & Boucher 1991; Charman & Baron-Cohen 1993; Eames & Cox 1994). Eames and Cox matched their groups of autistic children, Down's syndrome children and two groups of typically developing children (one matched with the chronological ages of the autistic children and one with their mental ages) more closely than had been achieved in previous studies. Even so, the children with autism did not display any special drawing ability. They performed well below their chronological age, and even lower than a group matched for mental age (although higher than the children with Down's syndrome). Although we assume that some abilities or characteristics of autism contribute to the talent of autistic savants (since most savants are also autistic), they are either not present or not sufficient to promote talented artistic performance in the majority of individuals with autism.

As Winner (1996) points out, savants with autism are similar to other talented child artists in a number of ways; for example, they usually have higher scores on non-verbal tasks than on verbal ones, they have very

Figure 9.6 Performing acrobatics *by Wang Yani, aged 4 years (Ho 1989)*.

good visual memory skills, they excel at visual realism and they are prodigious and keen drawers. As well as these similarities there are also some noticeable differences. Savants with autism tend not to draw people (although 'CZ', studied by Cox and Eames 1999, is an exception – see figure 9.7) and tend not to draw expressionist pictures or pictures to do with emotional states. Even when Stephen Wiltshire went to art school and expanded his repertoire to include portrait and figure paintings his preferred topic was still the urban landscape devoid of people (Pring &

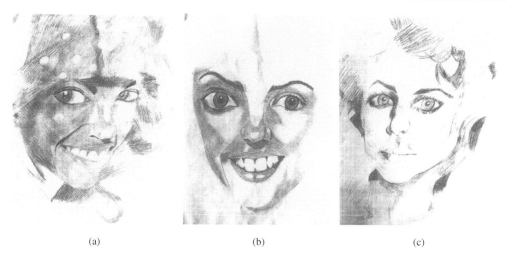

(a)   (b)   (c)

Figure 9.7 *Drawings by a teenage girl ('CZ') with autism, studied by Cox and Eames (1999).*

Hermelin 1997). As well as a preference for non-human topics in their pictures, savants with autism tend not to show their pictures to other people or to talk about them (although Stephen Wiltshire seemed to take pleasure in communicating in this way). These tendencies reflect the social and communication problems that most autistic people have.

Whereas most children, including talented artists, tend to sketch the general structure of a picture before they fill in the details, savants with autism tend to focus on the details, perfecting them as they go along. Watching an autistic savant drawing resembles peeling away an opaque covering to see the finished drawing gradually emerge underneath. Frith (1989) has argued that this focus on detail is due to a weak central coherence in the cognitive processing of individuals with autism. *Central coherence* is a term used to describe our tendency to process information as a coherent whole, that is, the general gist takes precedence over the details. This process may be disturbed in individuals with autism. Pring, Hermelin and Heavey (1995) tested part–whole processing in children with autism as well as in typically developing children and concluded that there is 'a facility in autism for seeing wholes in terms of their parts, rather than as unified gestalts' (p. 1073). Despite this preoccupation with detail, savants with autism still manage to end up with an integrated drawing. Whereas some talented artists have a preference for certain topics, savants with autism tend to be obsessed with particular kinds of subject matter: Nadia Chomyn was very keen on horses (although not exclusively so), Stephen Wiltshire specialised in buildings, 'BX' was obsessed with the Forth bridges (see figure 9.8) and 'CZ' with faces, particularly the pop singer Kylie Minogue's face (see figure 9.7).

(a)

(b)

(c)

Figure 9.8 *Drawings of the Forth road and rail bridges by a teenage boy ('BX') with autism, studied by Cox and Eames (1999).*

It is tempting to characterise all savants with autism in a similar way, perhaps with a view to finding the key to their talent. But these children are individuals and they display individual differences. To start with, they choose different subject matter for their drawings. CZ (Cox & Eames 1999) goes against the trend of choosing non-human topics by drawing faces. Whereas most savants prefer a linear style, CZ again goes against this trend by building up her pictures with shading. In fact, CZ's cognitive profile is also rather different in that she has poor visual memory compared with that of most artistic savants and talented artists. Whereas most savants draw from memory, CZ copies from photographs. Such a task does not require a particularly good visual memory. It may be that she chose a copying task because she lacks a good visual memory; on the other hand, it may be that her obsession with a copying task has contributed to the stagnation of her visual memory skills. Although most savants with autism are not really aware that others are interested in their work, Stephen Wiltshire seemed to take pleasure in their interest. As Selfe (1995) has pointed out, 'autistic individuals do not form a homogeneous group' (p. 226), and in fact they 'differ substantially from one another' (p. 227).

There are, then, a number of ways in which talented child artists are similar, whether or not they have autism. In particular, their performance on non-verbal tasks is usually better than on verbal tasks and their visual memory skills are enhanced. Their pictures often show striking visual realism. However, there are also notable differences between talented artists and savants with autism – in particular, autistic savants' choice of non-human rather than human topics and their drawing style, which focusses on detail rather than on overall structure. Despite these similarities and some differences between talented artists and savants with autism, savants with autism are all individuals with individual predispositions and cognitive abilities.

Biological differences in the brain

The superior visual abilities of artistically talented children have been attributed to differences in the way the brain is organised (Winner 1996). In most people the left hemisphere of the brain (associated with language) is dominant. In the artistically talented (and some other talented individuals such as musicians, for example) brain organisation is more bilateral, so that the right hemisphere, associated with visual-spatial skills, becomes more involved in left-hemisphere tasks (Winner & Martino 1993).[13] The suggestion, then, is that the brains of artistically

[13] It is important to stress that there is no strict dichotomy of left and right processing as the two hemispheres are connected, allowing the right hemisphere to be involved in language functions (Gazzaniga 1988) and the left in some spatial processing (Mehta & Newcombe 1991).

talented people, compared with those of less talented individuals, may be predisposed to excel at 'right-hemisphere' tasks such as drawing.

This bias towards right-hemisphere tasks and deficits in relation to left-hemisphere (verbal) tasks, as well as other characteristics such as non-right-handedness, reading problems such as dyslexia and being male, has prompted speculation about a biological cause for these phenomena. Geschwind and Galaburda (1987) suggest that an elevated level of testosterone at the foetal stage of development may be responsible. Since males are exposed to more testosterone than females – their own and their mother's – they may be particularly prone.[14] Geschwind and Galaburda claim that if this exposure occurs after about the twentieth week of gestation then certain areas of the left hemisphere of the brain (relevant to language) may fail to develop. Areas of the right hemisphere (and possibly adjacent areas of the left) will develop in order to compensate. The authors claim that this will result in a cluster of abilities and disabilities: the children will be good at right-hemisphere activities such as spatial and artistic tasks and also possibly the calculator ability (in the left hemisphere), but may have some verbal deficits (such as dyslexia, delayed speech and stuttering). Some children may display a more extreme form of this profile, which manifests itself in autism.[15] There will be a tendency towards non-right-handedness. Elevated testosterone levels can also affect the development of the thymus gland, which is important in the development of the immune system. Thus, these children may be prone to allergies and auto-immune diseases.

If, as this theory claims, a higher level of testosterone after the twentieth week of gestation retards the growth of certain areas of the left hemisphere of the brain, leading to a compensatory growth in adjacent areas as well as in the right hemisphere, then we might expect to see these corresponding areas of retardation and growth in the brain itself. In fact, autopsies on the brains of four autistic savants (see Treffert 1989) have not yielded conclusive results, as only one of them showed left-hemisphere damage. However, as Winner (1996) has pointed out, this is only a very small number of cases and, anyway, the technique used may be too crude. Indeed, X-rays of the brains of a number of autistic individuals, including a few autistic savants, have revealed that fifteen out of seventeen showed left-sided abnormalities (Hauser, Delong & Rosman 1975). MRI scans have shown that some people with autism have larger or heavier brains, with an increased cell density in some areas (Piven et al. 1991). This suggests an increase in neurons, perhaps due to a failure of 'pruning'[16] in brain development

[14] Children who had higher levels of foetal testosterone have been found to exhibit more male-like abilities and behaviours (e.g., less eye contact, a smaller vocabulary and lower social skills) when they were tested at ages 1, 2 and 4 years (see Baron-Cohen 2003).

[15] Asperger (1944) suggested that autism is an extreme variant of male intelligence.

[16] 'Pruning' refers to the cull of brain cells that occurs in the foetus towards the end of gestation (Hamburger & Oppenheim 1982; Huttenlocher 1994).

(Happé 1999), and may provide some support for the notion of central coherence, which is supposedly weak in many individuals with autism and which may contribute to the particularly detailed drawing style adopted by many artistic savants. A number of studies have suggested a biological basis for the impairment in social and emotional behaviour that is also associated with autism – impairment in the cerebellar, mesolimbic and temporal lobe cortical regions of the brain (Critchley et al. 2000); other studies have suggested amygdala dysfunction (Baron-Cohen et al. 2000). It is unlikely, however, according to Happé (1999), that autism will prove to be the result of damage to only one particular brain area.

There is, then, some support for Geschwind and Galaburda's theory. However, most brain development evidence relates only to individuals with autism who are mostly without a particular talent. As Winner (1996) has pointed out, we need studies that reveal differences between those who do not have a particular talent and the savants with autism who obviously do. It is clear, however, that many savants with autism do not display the full cluster of abilities and disabilities that the theory predicts. Selfe (1995) points out that although some are left-handed others are right-handed, some have poorly developed language skills whereas others have well-developed language skills, and some have contradictory brain dysfunction (e.g., Nadia Chomyn displayed abnormal electrical discharges on the right side of the brain, not the left). As well as needing more detailed studies of individuals with autism who do and who do not have a special talent for art, we also need studies of talented individuals who do not have autism at all. It may be that there will be no detectable damage or enhanced growth in the brains of artistically talented people, even though processing may occur in different areas compared with that in non-talented individuals. In order to identify the locations of processing in artistically talented and non-talented people, with or without autism, we would need data from functional MRI and MEG scans.

Practice makes perfect?

By the age of about 11 years most typically developing children have difficulties with representational drawing which, in many cases, discourages them from drawing altogether. Talented children, in contrast, seem to have solved many of the problems and relish the challenges that face them. It is a myth, however, to suppose that their success is effortless. As Howe (1989, 1990) has pointed out, this is far from the case. Talented children, in whatever domain, invariably put in a great deal of effort and practice, which is usually self-motivated and often encouraged by their parents and teachers. In fact, one of the causes put forward to explain their exceptional talent, whether it be in the visual arts or in other domains, such as music or maths, is the amount of effort and practice that the individual invests. Thus, although a child may have an aptitude for a certain activity, this aptitude will usually be supported by his or her own motivation, commitment, curiosity and propensity for hard work and experiment, as well as by other people's help and encouragement.

Talented artists, with or without autism, are keen drawers. Rimland (1978) and O'Connor and Hermelin (1988) point out that the autistic tendency to be obsessive may result in certain individuals with autism practising a task so much that they excel in it. Practice undoubtedly helps, and, as I have already pointed out, talented non-autistic artists also practise their skills a great deal. Ericsson, Krampe and Tesch-Romer (1993) found that levels of achievement in music, chess, bridge and athletics correlate highly with the amount of practice individuals engaged in. It is difficult to identify practice alone as the cause, however, since these individuals are likely to have an interest and perhaps an aptitude for their chosen task and they will be highly motivated to pursue it. One would want to assess the effects of practice among non-talented individuals, although practice without interest or motivation might be difficult to sustain.

If visual–spatial information is largely (but not solely) processed in the right hemisphere of the brain, then we might reasonably suppose that there is a bias towards right-hemisphere processing in artistically talented individuals. We cannot be certain, however, that such a bias is innate or inherited. It is possible that talent could be nurtured through persistent practice, and the frequent exercising of their skills in artistically talented children could have brought about alterations in their brain structure. After all, we know that animals raised in stimulating environments have larger cortical areas of the brain and better neural connections than those raised in impoverished environments. A similar effect might occur in humans too (although it is unlikely in the case of savants with autism, such as Nadia Chomyn, whose talent often appears apparently without prior practice). In other words, even if artistic talent is found to be associated with neurological changes in the right hemisphere of the brain, unless this can be assessed very early in life, we do not know whether it is the cause or the effect of talented performance. Of course, the choice of explanation may not have to be so stark: it is possible, indeed likely, that talent will be shown to be the result of neurological differences in the brain *as well as* in the way and extent to which a particular skill has been practised and nurtured.

The pictorial abilities of blind children

When we look at a picture we do so with our eyes. We see its lines, shapes, colour and texture. But of course we do more than this. We identify objects in the picture (if it is representational), we appreciate its composition and we interpret its meaning. Nevertheless, we still think of art appreciation as primarily a visual enterprise. Similarly, we tend to think of the production of pictures largely as a visual process, even though we know that other factors are involved, such as motor control of the hands and fingers as well as the cognitive skills associated with translating our ideas into pictorial form.

How important is vision for artistic understanding and production? Is it possible for people who are blind to appreciate pictures and, indeed, to produce them? Although blind people cannot detect the features of a picture by visual means, they can, of course, use touch. Many artists, such as van Gogh, have applied paint thickly so that it creates a tangible texture. But this does not necessarily enable a blind person to recognise the objects represented in the picture. However, by using a raised-line technique[17] it is possible for blind people to feel the contours of depicted objects with their fingers. Even so, one might imagine that since most objects do not have raised contours around them, and since blind people will not have had the experience of seeing the outer contours of objects against their background, then they might have difficulty in recognising objects represented by a raised outline. On the other hand, neither do sighted people generally see objects 'frozen' in a fixed position against a background. But according to Gibson's theory of visual perception (Gibson 1979; also see appendix), people 'pick up' typical invariant shapes of objects from the continually changing visual array. It is possible that blind people do something similar, based on their experience of exploring objects by touch. If so, then blind people should be able to recognise a depicted object by its 'typical' raised contour, and the same outlines that sighted people use to identify depicted objects could also be used by blind people, if they can access them by touch.

Both blind children and sighted children (who have been blindfolded) generally identify raised-line pictures after a longer exploration time than would be needed in a visual inspection, and achieve a lower accuracy than can be achieved by sighted participants (Kennedy 1974; Millar 1994). Nonetheless, blind children can identify raised-line pictures. A study by D'Angiulli, Kennedy and Heller (1998) included children aged 8 to 13 years. After a practice phase the children were asked to identify a set of eight raised-line drawings: a face, a bottle, a cup, a person, a telephone, an umbrella, scissors and a key. A group of blind children explored the drawings, as did a group of sighted children who were blindfolded (the 'active sighted' group). In a 'passive sighted' group, who were also blindfolded, the experimenter guided the child's finger twice around the figure.

---

[17] A simple kit includes a rubber-coated board on which is placed a plastic sheet. Raised lines are produced when a ball-point pen is used to draw on the sheet.

On the first test, the blind children recognised more pictures than did the passive sighted children and far more than the active sighted. Although performance improved for all three groups on a second test, there was still no significant difference between the performance of the blind group and the passive sighted group; both were better than the active sighted group. This result is not surprising, as blind children would be better at exploring by touch (even though they had not used raised-line pictures before) and the passive sighted group were given guidance in this form of exploration. What is perhaps more interesting is the fact that the pictures recognised by the blind children were also the ones frequently recognised by the sighted children. The authors claim that this is key evidence that both blind and sighted children are interpreting pictures in the same way.[18] What is important is their knowledge of the shape of common objects. That blind children are able to identify objects from their outlines indicates that object recognition does not rely on vision alone.

It is worth pointing out that the objects depicted in the raised-line drawings were familiar ones to all the children. They were also shown in their typical orientation. Furthermore, some of the objects, such as the face, the scissors and the key, are basically 'flat' objects whose depicted shapes could perhaps be more easily identified. We do not know whether blind children would perform so well if the objects were unfamiliar, if they were depicted in a less typical orientation, or if they were bulky three-dimensional objects that extended more equally in all three spatial dimensions. What is clear is that a raised outline, like a visual outline, can be used to indicate an occluding edge (where one surface overlaps another) or where two surfaces meet at a corner. It is not essential to use vision to perceive these facts; both can be discerned by touch. So, recognition of objects from their outline by the blind and the sighted is probably based on processes that have much in common, a claim made by both Millar (1994) and Kennedy (2000).

What of blind children's ability to produce drawings themselves? Millar (1975) compared the drawing ability of blind children aged 6, 8 and 10 years with that of sighted but blindfolded children. All the children were asked to draw a human figure using the raised-line technique. Although most of the blind children had used a raised-line kit before in some experiments on spatial ability, they had not previously been asked to draw a representational figure. The 6- and 8-year-old blind children were not very successful and often did not produce a recognisable figure at all. Although they had no difficulty in recognising real body parts, they had not learned and did not invent ways of representing these forms on a

---

[18] In a later study, D'Angiulli and Kennedy (2000) demonstrated that sighted children who were blindfolded but given guided exploration correctly identified almost as many pictures as sighted adults who were also blindfolded.

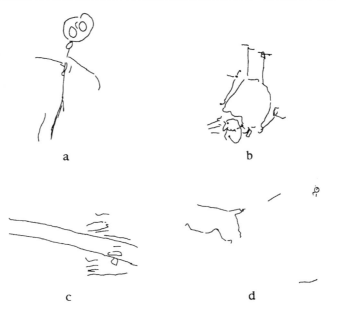

a

b

c

d

Figure 9.9 *Human figure drawings by (a) a blind girl aged 11 years 4 months, (b) a blind boy aged 9 years 3 months, (c) a blind boy aged 8 years 6 months and (d) a blind girl aged 6 years (from Millar 1975).*

two-dimensional surface. There was, then, a distinct developmental lag between the blind children's and the sighted children's performance on this task. The 10-year-old blind children had considerable success. However, whereas nearly all the sighted children drew their figures upright, many of the blind children initially drew their figures upside-down, horizontal or in near horizontal orientations. When told about the rule, however, they quickly drew their figures aligned with the 'floor' at the bottom of the page. The sighted children produced more accomplished drawings. Nonetheless, the blind 10-year-old children were able to produce recognisable figures, including the main body parts and placing them in the correct relationship to each other. Furthermore, they used the same kinds of shapes as did sighted children – a circle for the head, a circle or a vertical line for the body and so on. In fact, their performance was not significantly worse than that of the sighted children (see figure 9.9).

The fact that the blind 10-year-olds used the same kinds of shapes for their figures as did the sighted children shows that the blind children did not have a problem in using flat shapes to stand for three-dimensional forms. Their choice of shape also indicates that the shapes used in pictures are not arbitrary – a circle is an acceptable representation of a head because it preserves something of the shape of a real three-dimensional head. This information can be felt as well as seen and is therefore available to the blind as well as the sighted. According to Millar, the younger blind children had not yet thought of the possibility of using two-dimensional shapes to stand for three-dimensional objects. The fact that they had not made this discovery at an age when sighted children have suggests that vision provides important information, giving sighted children an advantage. Nonetheless, despite this developmental lag, it shows that this discovery can be made through touch and that vision, although extremely useful, is not actually essential.

The raised-line figures that Millar's children were asked to draw and the depicted objects used by D'Angiulli and colleagues (1998) did not include the occlusion of one part by another or linear convergence perspective. In other words, there was no depth information in these pictures. Now, depth in a picture is generally related to a particular vantage point or point of view. We may see an object partially obscured by a nearer one and, as we look into the distance, a farther object is higher up our visual field and also appears smaller than a similar object nearer to us. Furthermore, parallel lines seem to become more convergent with distance, and lines and surfaces are foreshortened. Without the ability to see, can blind people understand these phenomena and will they indicate them in their drawings?

Kennedy and Campbell (1982) familiarised blind children aged 5 to 15 with the extent of a wall in a small room; the children were taken from one end of the wall to the other. Then they had to stand facing the wall and were asked to point to its corners (the right arm to one corner and the left arm to the other). When they were far from the wall (4 metres away) the angle made by their arms was narrower than when they were nearer to it (one step away); the distance between their hands was also smaller when they were farther away than when they were close to the wall. This understanding of the changes in distance and angle in relation to the changing position of the viewer seems to be inherent in our spatial experience and is not dependent solely on vision. Similarly, an understanding of the apparent change of shape in relation to a viewer's position is not dependent on the ability to see. Kennedy (1980) reported asking three blind children (aged 6, 8 and 10) to point to the perimeter of a plate. When pointing from above the plate their fingers described a circle whereas when pointing from the side they described an ellipse. Since blind people as well as sighted have this understanding, then it would not be surprising if they also understand the principles of perspective in a picture. As Kennedy (1983) has pointed out, perspective is not merely an artificial convention; it has some intuitive basis in our experience and understanding of the world (see also Hagen 1980).

Kennedy (2003) has reported the drawing ability of a girl called Gaia, who has been blind since birth. Since her preschool years she experienced raised-line drawings drawn for her by her mother and she also drew in this way herself. Gaia was given a series of drawing tasks in two separate sessions (three months apart) when she was aged 12 and 13. In contrast to some other studies in which blind children have had no previous experience with raised-line drawings, Kennedy's study provides us with data from a blind child who has experienced and produced raised-line drawings from a very early age. It is useful to be able to compare her drawings with the ordinary pencil drawings of sighted children who have also been drawing for this length of time. What we find is that Gaia's drawings are remarkably similar in many ways. They were well executed, with clear and controlled lines. Her human figure drawings were similar to those made by sighted children aged between 10 and 12 years (see figure 9.10), and she used some of the depth cues commonly used by sighted children at this age – for example, she used partial occlusion to show one object behind another (see figures 9.11 and 9.14), height on the page to show one object farther away (see figure 9.12) and foreshortening to show the elliptical shape of the rim of a glass when it is tilted (see figure 9.13).

Two depth cues that Gaia did not use were diminishing size with distance and converging perspective lines. Sighted children usually combine diminishing size and height on the page by about the age of 9 years, and some children are starting to experiment with linear convergence perspective at about the age of 13 or 14 years (Dubery & Willats 1972). Interestingly, Gaia used divergent perspective for several objects, such as a tabletop (see figure 9.14) and a slanting roof. Although only a minority of sighted children have been reported to use divergent perspective in, for example, a cube drawing (Cox 1986; Nicholls & Kennedy 1992), Kennedy (2003) suggests that it might actually be more prevalent than has previously been reported and, for some children, may be only a small

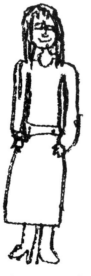

Figure 9.10 *A human figure drawing by Gaia, a blind girl aged 13 years (Kennedy 2003).*

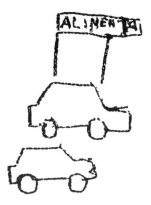

Figure 9.11 *Crossed pencils drawn by Gaia (Kennedy 2003).*

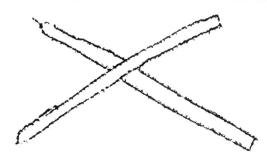

Figure 9.12 *Gaia's drawing of two cars on a street, one farther than the other, and a store (Kennedy 2003).*

Figure 9.13 *Gaia's drawings of a glass from above and from the side (left), upright, tilted and lying down on the table (right) (Kennedy 2003).*

developmental step away from using convergence perspective.[19] After all, the notion of using obliques has already been grasped and all that is needed is that their direction be reversed. Thus, Gaia's use of divergent perspective should not necessarily be seen as an anomaly or a typical feature of blind children's drawing development. Studies (e.g., Heller & Kennedy 1990; Heller, Kennedy & Joyner 1995) of blind adults' use of

[19] Divergent perspective is common in both children's and adults' drawings in rural Kenya (Court 1992) and was also used by some artists in Moghul India (see chapters 6 and 10).

Figure 9.14 *Table and chairs drawn by Gaia (Kennedy 2003)*.

raised-line drawings indicate that those who have been blind from early in life tend to produce 'folding out' drawings of a model house, whereas those who became blind later in life tend to produce side-view depictions; in contrast, at least some sighted but blindfolded people attempt perspective views. However, Kennedy (1997) has also found that some blind adults use partial occlusion, foreshortened shapes, diminishing size and converging lines to indicate depth.

The research evidence shows that the blind can recognise raised-line drawings and can produce them themselves. They can use lines to represent objects (such as the body parts of a stick figure), as outlines of solid objects or as interior detail. The important relationships include boundaries, corners and edges – all features of a surface layout that can be shown by lines. Lines activate this faculty whether by vision or by touch, and the blind have the same kind of perceptual faculty as the sighted for apprehending these features. Furthermore, they do not need extensive prior instruction or knowledge of pictures. Drawing development in the blind proceeds in much the same way as that in sighted children. Kennedy (1980) believes that the principles that underlie pictorial representation belong to a perceptual system that is greater than vision alone, and the body of research to date suggests that the artistic domain, particularly with regard to the use of line, is not solely a visual medium, even for sighted people, but rather engages us at a broader perceptual and cognitive level.

Summary

In this chapter I have discussed the artistic development of certain special populations. I have included children with a non-specific intellectual disability as well as those with the well-known condition of Down's syndrome. These children generally function below average in terms of mental ability. Their drawing ability also tends to be below that expected for their chronological age and is more in keeping with their mental age. Among Down's syndrome children, in particular, the lag is more pronounced, as a number of studies have found that these children perform even lower than younger children matched on mental age. Although the findings still support the notion of a delay in the development of children with an intellectual disability, several studies have also identified ways in which these children may differ from typically developing children, such as their inclusion of more details in their pictures and the lack of correlation between their drawing ability and mental age within their group.

Although many talented child artists are above average in mental ability, they are not necessarily academic high-fliers. They have superior visual skills, are highly motivated to engage with the challenges of pictorial representation and are usually prodigious drawers. A number of talented artists, such as savants with autism who have an intellectual disability, share a number of characteristics with talented artists who are not autistic; however, there are also some differences, which are mainly in the topics they choose to draw and in a drawing process that focusses on detail rather than on the overall structure of a picture. The causes of artistic talent, whether associated with autism or not, are unclear, although one speculative but controversial theory postulates changes in structure in the foetal brain as a result of exposure to excessive testosterone. The evidence, however, is not conclusive and, in addition, does not rule out the role of non-biological factors, such as the individual child's motivation and practice as well as the support and encouragement provided by parents and teachers. Indeed, both biological and environmental influences may be important. The likelihood of environmental influences seems less in cases of savants with autism, however, as their talent seems to appear without prior practice. It may be that these cases lie at the extreme end of the autistic spectrum and represent particularly pathological and anomalous development (Selfe 1983, 1995).

Although we think of art as being primarily a visual medium, and most talented artists have superior visual abilities, evidence from blind children indicates that visual experience is not actually necessary for understanding and producing outline pictures. Surprisingly, perhaps, we do not have to see in order to recognise pictures or to be able to draw. Studies of blind children show that a lack of vision is not an impediment to producing pictures and that blind children can draw as long as they can feel the lines. Their development proceeds more slowly but in much the same way as that of sighted children, indicating that representational drawing is not solely visual but also taps into a more basic perceptual and cognitive level.

10 Cultural influences on children's artwork

It is widely accepted that making pictures is a cultural phenomenon rather than something we are innately programmed to do. If this is so then we might expect to see differences in the art produced by different cultures and, indeed, we know that societies in different parts of the world and at different times in history have chosen different topics and different ways of depicting them (see chapter 8), and that some societies have produced no representational art at all. However, the spread of the mass media in modern times has resulted in certain pictorial forms being more common than others. In particular, styles of the so-called developed countries are more prevalent than those of more traditional, rural communities. Since most research has also been conducted on children in western countries it is not surprising that their pattern of understanding and production of pictures is better known and has often been regarded as being both universal[1] (Kellogg 1969; Kellogg & O'Dell 1967) and reflecting a cognitive development that for Piaget (1970), at least, is broadly similar for everyone. But does children's understanding and production of pictures *really* develop in the same way universally? If we agree that art is primarily a cultural activity then it would be surprising if children's appreciation of art as well as their own artistic efforts were *not* affected by the culture they are exposed to. In this chapter I shall consider the differences and similarities between different cultures, both in children's understanding of pictures and in their styles of picture-making. I shall also discuss the different ways that cultural influences may be transferred to and absorbed by children.

Cross-cultural studies of object recognition in pictures

First of all, it would be useful to establish whether people in all cultures are capable of understanding representational pictures, that is, whether they are able to recognise *what* is being depicted, an issue already discussed in chapter 2. One theory of picture perception (the ecological theory of Gibson 1979) maintains that all people naturally have the ability

---

[1] This notion also underpinned the development of the Draw-a-Man or Draw-a-Person tests to assess children's intellectual level (see chapter 11).

to recognise depicted objects; another theory (the constructivist approach of Gregory 1972, 1974) maintains that pictorial conventions have to be learned.[2] So, how do people in non-pictorial cultures respond to pictures when they first see them? Although human beings have been drawing or painting representational pictures for thousands of years (see chapter 8), there are some cultures that, at least until very recent years, have had no established tradition of representational art. If naïve viewers in these cultures recognise the objects in pictures then we can at least conclude that object recognition in pictures is universal.

One problem is, of course, to decide which kinds of pictures we should choose as our 'test' items. From a series of studies by Deręgowski and his colleagues (Deręgowski, Ellis & Shepherd 1973; Shepherd, Deręgowski & Ellis 1974; Ellis, Deręgowski & Shepherd 1975) we can conclude that colour photographs of objects presented no problem for participants in Scotland and Rhodesia. Even though the two groups were rather poorly matched for age and education, they were, nonetheless, similar in their ability to recognise photographs of faces and cups. Some studies (Deręgowski 1971; Deręgowski & Serpell 1971) have used black and white photographs, which, one might argue, are less realistic than coloured images. In some cases recognition of objects was slow, especially for unfamiliar objects and by older Zambian participants, but on the whole these photographs caused no major problems for either Zambian or Scottish people. Anecdotal reports by travellers in Africa in the nineteenth and early twentieth centuries reveal that indigenous peoples not only recognised the images in photographs projected on to a screen, but were often frightened by them (see chapter 2).

Line drawings might seem to be even farther removed from reality than photographs. On the other hand, they might be easier, in the sense that much of the redundant information is pared away and one is left with more crucial information for recognition of the object (Kennedy 1974). And that crucial information may be the outline that denotes the contour of an object against its background. Although there is normally no such outline around real objects, nonetheless our visual system has been particularly adapted to detect edges or contours created by abrupt changes of colour, texture or light (Attneave 1954). Thus, outlines in a drawing or painting exploit one of the fundamental properties of our normal visual processes[3] (see Latto 1995). Halverson (1992) has argued, along Gibsonian lines, that we use the same basic processes to recognise an object in a picture as we do to recognise the real object. It should not be surprising, then, if outline pictures, either line drawings or silhouettes, are

---

[2] See appendix for more details of these theories.
[3] Interestingly, the earliest known pictures, from Palaeolithic times, exploit this aspect of perception by concentrating on the *outlines* of animals seen in profile (see chapter 8).

also easy to recognise. Indeed, outline drawings should maximise the likelihood of recognition. Biederman and Ju (1988) have demonstrated that outline drawings are in most cases just as effective as colour photographs for the recognition of depicted objects; the extra information in the photographs appears to be redundant for this purpose. It is not necessary for a picture to indicate depth in order for us to recognise the depicted object. We can recognise both line drawings and silhouettes even when, particularly with a silhouette of a face in profile, there are no cues to the third dimension. A number of studies have found no difficulties with line drawings of familiar objects among children or adults in various different cultures (Brimble 1962; Jahoda et al. 1976).

I will discuss one such study in more detail. When Kennedy and Ross (1975) tested the Songe tribe in a small village in Papua New Guinea they were principally concerned with the recognition of objects in outline drawings. At the time of the study the Songe painted and carved abstract patterns but produced no figural art. A few villagers, mainly men, had had some contact with western influences when they travelled outside the village, but the older people had had no formal education and very little outside contact. Although the children and teenagers in the village were being educated at a school, this was about six miles' walk away and schoolbooks were not brought home.

The researchers compiled a set of line drawings that included a palm tree, a Songe-style house, a canoe, human figures, hands, birds, common and uncommon animals, a fire, a river, a car and an aeroplane. When presented with each picture, each participant was asked to say what it was. There were prompts if he or she did not recognise the object at all, and follow-up questions if no further information was spontaneously volunteered.

In general, with a few exceptions, most pictures were correctly identified by most of the villagers. Participants across all ages were 90 per cent correct with pictures of familiar objects. For the unfamiliar objects the youngest participants (aged 10 to 19 years) were 97 per cent correct, those aged 20 to 39 were 91 per cent correct and those over 40 were 68 per cent correct. Strictly speaking, this study is not cross-cultural, as only the Songe people were tested and no other comparison group was included. We do not know how westerners, for example, would have responded to the tasks, although, of course, we assume that they would have performed very well. Nonetheless, Kennedy and Ross's results indicate that line drawings of objects are easy to recognise even with no, or very little, prior exposure to pictures. However, perhaps not all aspects of line drawings are equally easy to understand. For example, the Songe villagers had some difficulty with the depiction of the movement of flames and water or a change in colour or texture on a bird's plumage (see figure 10.1). These kinds of depiction are conventional in the sense that, although there is

Figure 10.1 *The Songe of Papua New Guinea could easily identify familiar objects in line drawings. However, some pictures were more difficult, including a fire (left), a river (centre) and a bird's plumage (right) (Kennedy & Ross 1975).*

little obvious correspondence between the lines in the picture and the aspects of the real scene that they are supposed to denote, we understand their meaning through repeated exposure. It would be difficult to grasp their meaning straightaway, with no prior familiarity or explanation. In a review of the early literature, Coppen (1970) concluded that simplicity in drawings enhances their comprehension; however, Winter (1963), in her recommendations for the design of safety posters in the workplace, also warned against the use of conventional symbols (e.g., 'pain stars') that might not be understood by people in all cultures.

The evidence indicates that pictorially naïve viewers are able to recognise depicted objects either immediately or after a short explanation (Deręgowski, Muldrow & Muldrow 1972; Kennedy & Ross 1975). Outline drawings of familiar objects do not present a major problem. The evidence, then, supports Gibson's (1979) ecological theory.

Cross-cultural studies of the perception of depth in pictures

Whereas some cross-cultural studies have concentrated on people's recognition of objects in pictures (what Deręgowski, 2000, has called *epitomic* pictorial perception), others have focussed on the way that depth is interpreted (*eidolic* perception). As the picture plane itself has no depth dimension, the artist has to employ particular pictorial devices to indicate the three-dimensionality of an object or the depth of a scene. Even so, it is still possible that observers might misinterpret them or fail to perceive the depth altogether. Some of the most well-known studies were conducted by Hudson (1960, 1962), who devised a pictorial depth perception test consisting of a number of line drawings of a hunting scene (see figure 10.2) and a flying bird scene, and also a photograph of a model of the hunting scene. In each picture the depth cues of size of object,

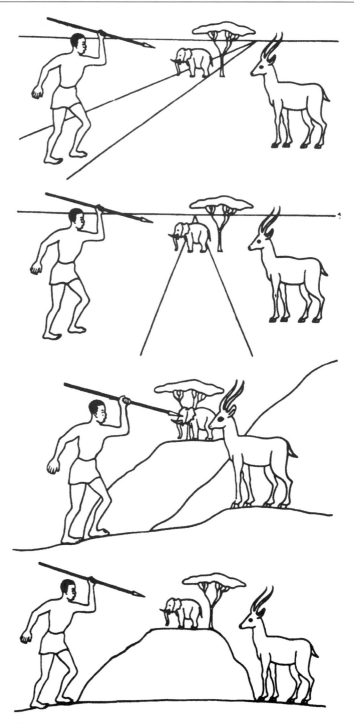

Figure 10.2 *Scenes used in Hudson's (1960, 1962) pictorial depth perception test.*

partial occlusion, linear convergence perspective and height on the page were varied (see also chapter 6). Hudson administered the test in South Africa to a number of different black and white groups – children and adults – asking them questions about the distance of objects from one another in each picture. He concluded that the white participants tended to be three-dimensional picture perceivers whereas the non-whites tended to be two-dimensional picture perceivers, and he explained that this difference was the result of different amounts of experience with pictures. Such a conclusion is in line with the constructivist account of picture perception, that is, our perception of pictures depends on our familiarity with the pictorial devices used in them.

Criticisms regarding the methodology of Hudson's work led many researchers to claim that it is not possible to draw any conclusion from his results, nor to accept his test as valid (Miller 1973; Jahoda & McGurk 1974; Haber 1980; Jones & Hagen 1980). Indeed, later revisions of the test, using more appropriate cultural content and correct principles of perspective, revealed all the non-white groups as well as the white groups to be three-dimensional picture perceivers (Page 1970; Omari & MacGintie 1974; Leach 1975; Opolot 1976; Hagen & Johnson 1977).

It appears, then, that people in societies with no, or very limited, pictorial experience are, nonetheless, able to perceive depth in pictures. A note of caution is sounded by Deręgowski (1980), who argues that it is not surprising that people from different cultures will all respond similarly to the revised, more visually realistic pictures. This does not invalidate Hudson's work, the aim of which was to find out if people from different cultures differ in their interpretation of pictures. For this purpose, it was valid to use pictures that were not necessarily visually realistic and were composed of localised pictorial conventions. The differences in interpretation of depth in the pictures could have been due to cultural differences in the perception of these pictorial conventions.

Bearing this argument in mind, it seems that pictorially naïve people and people in different cultural groups will perceive depth in a picture if it has been constructed according to accurate perspective principles. And this is in accord with Gibson's (1979) theory. Where a picture diverges from this system there is more variation in the way it is interpreted by people in different cultural groups, and this evidence is in accord with Gregory's (1972, 1974) constructivist approach to visual perception.

Similarities and cultural differences in our understanding and appreciation of art

It is one thing to be able to recognise depicted objects and understand the spatial layout of a picture, but quite another to understand and appreciate the aesthetic qualities of pictures. Much of the research on appreciation of art has been conducted with participants within the western aesthetic tradition (see chapter 3); it may be that people in other cultures with different artistic traditions do not necessarily discuss pictures in the same way (Winner & Gardner 1988). Whereas the modernist movement in twentieth-century western art may have been reluctant to consider cultural differences, postmodernist thinking has viewed art and aesthetic responses as forms of *cultural* expression that may differ from one culture to another. Whereas the Gestaltists[4] argued for universal principles or laws of aesthetics, McFee (1978) has questioned whether aesthetics can be universal, and Feldman (1987) has argued that our understanding of the arts is *not* based on universal principles, values or concerns but on culturally specific ones, a view endorsed by Hart (1993).

Ford, Prothro and Child (1966) compiled sets of realistic and abstract paintings, each set containing three pictures that had been rank-ordered according to preference by American artists or art teachers. In Fiji six local people who were skilled in carving or basket-making were asked to state their preferences among these pictures. The correlation of .56 between their choices and those of the Americans was significant but modest. In Greece the correlation between the judgements of four local craftsmen and the Americans was much lower (.28); however, when the judgements were made by two artists the correlation was high (.86). The authors interpreted these results as supporting the idea of cross-cultural agreement in the judgement of art. However, it seems to me that this conclusion is unwarranted, given the variation in the correlations and the very low number of participants.

Winner and Gardner (1988) gave an anecdotal report of the *differences* between cultures – namely, western and Chinese attitudes.[5] Whereas westerners believe that art should 'open the viewers' eyes and show them something in a new way' (p. 256), even if this means depicting an ugly subject, the Chinese believe that art should be about beautiful subjects, beautifully crafted.[6] In Parsons' (1987) stages of thinking about art the Chinese view would have to be placed no higher than stage 2 (see chapter 3). Winner and Gardner speculate, however, that Parsons would not necessarily relegate the Chinese to this lower stage, but might simply exclude them from the analysis altogether on the grounds that stages 3 to 5 are largely dependent on the western aesthetic tradition and that other cultures (and he specifically mentions the Chinese) may think about art in completely *different* ways.

---

[4] See appendix.
[5] Also see Lowry and Wolf (1988), Winner (1989), Cox, Perara and Xu (1998) and Cox, Perara and Xu (1999).
[6] Also see Kindler and Darras (1998), Kindler, Pariser, van den Berg and Liu (2001) and Kindler, Pariser, van den Berg, Liu and Dias (2002).

When Kindler, Darras and Kuo (2000) asked children whether an ugly thing can be art they found some cultural differences: whereas Canadian children (of European ancestry) agreed that an ugly thing can be art, French and Asian children tended to deny that it can. However, many studies have found similarities among cultures when children were asked about their preferences for specific pictures. For example, Chan, Eysenck and Götz (1980) found similarities in aesthetic reactions among children in Japan, Hong Kong and England, and Machotka (1966) found similarities between French and American children aged 6 to 18 years in both their preferences and reasons for choosing certain pictures. Kuo (1993) found that Taiwanese and American children aged 7 to 15 were broadly similar in knowledge of and judgement about art, but that the American children scored higher on art appreciation. Whereas these studies were truly cross-cultural, others which have been carried out in different single cultures can also help inform our view of what is universal or culture-specific. A pattern that seems to emerge is a preference among younger children for realism and colour, with complexity emerging later (Machotka 1966 – France; Rump & Southgate 1967 – UK; Goude 1972 – Sweden; Bell & Bell 1979 – Australia; Kindler 1993 – Canada).

The evidence, then, regarding adults' and children's understanding and appreciation of art shows some cultural differences and some similarities. Cultures may have different general ideas about art (e.g., whether ugly subject matter can be art), but when children are asked for their preferences among specific pictures they are broadly similar.

Children's drawings in different cultures

When studying children's artwork in different cultures we might consider whether the same topics are important universally. For example, in developed countries the human figure appears very early in young children's drawings and remains popular and important. Because of the presumption that the human figure is of universal importance, Di Leo (1970) claimed that 'The Goodenough Draw-a-Man Test is probably as close as we have come to the ideal of a culture-free test of intelligence' (p. 224).[7] Yet, we know that the depiction of the human figure was not very common in Palaeolithic art (see chapter 8) – at least, not in the cave art in France, where the depiction of animals is much more prevalent – nor in children's drawings in some other cultures in more recent times. In a study conducted on the island of Alor, in the former East Indies, Du Bois (1944) found that human figures appeared in only 7 per cent of boys'

---

[7] Goodenough's (1926) Draw-a-Man Test was originally standardised on a sample of children in the USA (see chapter 11).

drawings and 1 per cent of girls' drawings. The boys were much more likely to include plants, animals and buildings and the girls, plants, tools and buildings. In her studies of children in Kenya, Court (1989) found that when rural Kikuyu children were given a free choice of subject matter, houses were drawn much more frequently than people. Similarly, only about a quarter of a group of twenty-one Luo 11- to 18-year-olds and twenty-four Samburu 10- to 18-year-olds drew people. Furthermore, when human figures were included they were rather small and without detail and were accompanied by other, more significant imagery, such as boats (among the Luo) and animals (among the Samburu). The low incidence of the human figure in these cultural groups contrasts with the much higher incidence (76 per cent) among a group of twenty-five Kamba 10- to 15-year-olds, who although they more often drew human figures also drew them very simply, without detail or expression, and placed them in social and active contexts.

Aronsson and Andersson (1996) demonstrated that children in different cultures present the human figure in different ways. These researchers asked children in Sweden and in Tanzania (one group in a traditional school and another in a refugee settlement) to draw a picture of themselves (and their classmates, if they chose) and their teacher working in the classroom. The African children drew themselves much smaller in relation to the teacher and with fewer details than did the Swedish children; they also placed the teacher more centrally on the page and set her apart from the pupils (e.g., behind a desk) (see figures 10.3 and 10.4). These tendencies were even stronger in the drawings made by children in the traditional school compared with those in the refugee camp. The authors claim that these representational differences in 'social space' reflect differences in pedagogic practices and child-rearing ideologies, which are reckoned to be more *sociocentric* in the African groups (particularly in the traditional group) but more *child-centred* in Sweden.

Since the depiction of the human figure is not equally popular in all cultures, children in some cultures are likely to be less practised at drawing it. When they do draw it they may situate it in a social context rather than drawing it for its own sake, and this may result in a less detailed representation. A less practised and detailed figure may receive a lower score on the Draw-a-Man Test (Goodenough 1926). Indeed, when children's Draw-a-Man figures from other countries have been compared with those in the USA the scores have been different, even when children have attended western-style schools (Anastasi & Foley 1936; Harris 1963). Dennis (1957) found that children in Egypt and the Lebanon aged 5 to 10 generally scored lower and declined in the level of their scores after age 5. Sundberg and Ballinger (1968) also found that the scores of Nepalese children declined from age 7 onwards. Interestingly, however, the difference is not always in favour of white American children;

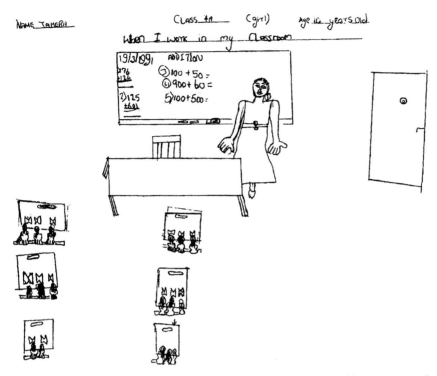

Figure 10.3 When I work in my classroom *by a 10-year-old Tanzanian girl (Aronsson & Andersson 1996).*

Figure 10.4 *A pupil–teacher drawing by a 10-year-old Swedish girl (Aronsson & Andersson 1996).*

Havighurst, Gunther and Pratt (1946) found that native American children, aged 6 to 11 years, obtained higher scores than their white peers.[8]

Because of cultural differences in the importance of a particular topic (or of drawing in general), as well as differences in amount of practice, it is not particularly interesting to investigate whether one culture's depictions are better or worse than another's. A more interesting question focusses on the *ways* that depictions differ from culture to culture. When making these comparisons it is useful to concentrate the investigation on the same topic, and even though it may not be popular to the same extent in all cultures, I shall choose the human figure as the main example in this present discussion. In western countries we are familiar with a particular pattern of development of the human figure (see figure 10.5). After a period of scribbling, children usually draw tadpole figures, which basically consist of a head and two legs, although other details such as facial features, arms, feet and hair may also be included. Some children go on to draw a 'transitional' figure in which the arms are placed on the legs rather than on the head and a torso may be located between the legs. However, many children omit this form and move directly to drawing a conventional figure in which the torso has a separate contour below the head and both the legs and the arms are attached to it. With increasing chronological and mental age children add more details to their figures and the proportions become more realistic. Single lines for the limbs are replaced with double lines. Instead of adding each detail as a separate item and with a separate contour, parts of the figure may be drawn with a continuous contour. Front-facing figures give way to experimentation with profile figures and figures engaged in action. There is more indication of depth when, for example, one body part overlaps or partially occludes another. An extra impression of depth is added when some teenagers use shading to enhance the three-dimensionality of their figures.

Despite this familiar pattern there is considerable variation in the way that children and, indeed, adults in different cultures draw the human figure. Paget (1932) published a study based on over 60,000 drawings of non-western children collected from all over the world. Many of the examples in studies such as this have come from children who have lived in largely non-pictorial cultures and who have not drawn before. Instead of drawing a circle containing facial features children in a number of African cultures have been observed to draw a 'pin-head' with no facial features at all (Paget 1932; Fortes 1940, 1981; Reuning & Wortley 1973). In western children's drawings we are used to seeing the facial features placed within an outline of the head and, similarly, features of the torso

---

[8] Whatever the direction of the difference, it is inappropriate to use the Draw-a-Man Test to assess intellectual maturity in other cultures if test norms have not been established for those particular cultural groups.

Figure 10.5 *Typical western pattern of development in children's drawings of the human figure.*

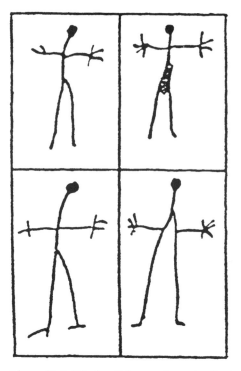

Figure 10.6 *'Pin-head' figures drawn by Bemba children (Rhodesia) (from Paget 1932).*

placed within or attached to a contour representing the torso region. In contrast, there have been examples in both Africa and India of a different way of depicting the body parts. In some cases, although the facial features are included, there is no contour for the head; in other cases, the head contour does not enclose the facial features but is separate from them (Paget 1932). There are also examples of the whole figure drawn in a chain-like way (Paget 1932; Werner 1948; Hudson, cited by Deręgowski, 1962): starting from the head, each item is added like links in a chain or items on a list; each one may be drawn directly below and touching the one above or, in some examples, may be connected by a line running vertically through the figure (see figures 10.6, 10.7 and 10.8).

We see some differences in the way that figures are drawn even in cultures that have a well-established tradition of pictorial representation. Features that are particularly distinctive are the different styles of hair and dress and, to some extent, different physical features.[9] Pfeffer (1984), for

---

[9] Paget (1932) suggested that some of the shapes used to depict, for example, the nose actually reflect the physical differences between different racial groups. Half his sample of Burmese children emphasised the nostrils, reflecting the prominence of the 'wings' of the nostrils, whereas Indian and Arab children chose a more slender shape, in keeping with their own nose shape.

Figure 10.7 *Omission of a facial boundary. From left to right, figures drawn by a 7-year-old Iranian girl, a 9-year-old Kenyan girl, a 10-year-old Lunda boy (Rhodesia), and a 9-year-old Bakongo girl (Portuguese Congo) (from Paget 1932).*

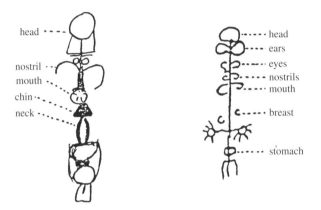

Figure 10.8 *'Chain' figures drawn by a 6-year-old girl from the Belgian Congo (left) and a 6-year-old boy from India (right) (from Paget 1932).*

example, found that 40 per cent of a sample of 8-year-old Yoruba children in Nigeria drew their figures with African hairstyles, 25 per cent of them drew them in traditional dress, and 50 per cent drew African facial features (see figure 10.9). These percentages do not seem particularly high and may reflect the fact that the children in this study were not specifically asked to draw a cultural or racial figure. When Dennis (1966) asked black and Indian children to draw a negro figure they were easily able to depict negroid features and dress. Similarly, when Frisch and Handler (1967) asked black children to draw a negro person 80 per cent of them drew negroid features.

It is perhaps not surprising that features such as dress and hairstyle as well as some facial features differ in the drawings made by children in different cultural or racial groups. After all, the children are drawing features that are distinctive of real people. There are, however, differences in the way that figures are depicted which do not seem to reflect an actual difference in the way different cultural or racial groups appear. Rather, the

Figure 10.9 *Human figure drawings by a 9-year-old boy (left) and a 10-year-old girl (right) from Nigeria.*

different forms seem to occur simply because of a different choice of graphic convention. One example is the way that the torso is drawn.[10] Typically, in the drawings of young western children the torso is circular or oval in shape; later, it is adapted to reflect the shape of the clothes – for example, a dress or blouse and skirt for a female and a shirt or jacket and trousers for a male. Stick figures are actually rather rare in western children's drawings and when they do occur it is often (but not always) because adults have taught their children to draw in this way (Kellogg & O'Dell 1967).

A real torso does not have a regular geometrical shape. Although it is generally longer than it is wide and may appear angular, particularly at the shoulders, it also has rounded contours and is usually narrower at the waist. We could reasonably choose to depict it in a number of different ways, including some or all of these features. It is interesting, then, that some cultural groups favour particular shapes more than others. In contrast to the shapes preferred by western children many, in countries in Africa and the Middle East, draw a rectangular torso (see figure 10.9). This is so common that Wilson and Wilson (1984) call it the 'Islamic' torso. In Paget's (1932) data there were several examples of bi-triangular

---

[10] Cultural variations in the way that other parts of the human figure are drawn are outlined in, for example, Paget (1932); see also Cox (1993).

Figure 10.10 *Bi-triangular figures drawn by 7-year-old and 10-year-old Bergdama boys in South West Africa (now Namibia) (from Paget 1932).*

Figure 10.11 *Bi-triangular figures drawn by a 14-year-old Zimbabwean girl (Andersson 2003).*

torsos among the drawings of children in South West Africa (now Namibia) (see figure 10.10). When Andersson (2003) visited this region over sixty years later, during 1995–7, he collected a few drawings, in both Namibia and in the neighbouring part of Zimbabwe, in which children had drawn this same kind of torso (see figure 10.11).

We see an even more dramatically different choice in the way the body can be drawn in the art of some Australian Aboriginal groups. For example, the U-shape used by the Warlpiri in central Australia to represent a whole person appears strange to western eyes (Munn 1973; Wales 1990; Cox & Hill 1996; Cox 1998) (see figure 10.12). One reason why graphic symbols[11] such as this need to be simple is because of the way they are used in traditional storytelling. Typically, it has been women who tell stories and illustrate them as they go along by drawing

[11] Munn (1973) claimed that there are sixteen or more of these traditional symbols in the Warlpiri culture.

Figure 10.12 *Artists working on their paintings at the Centre for Aboriginal Artists, Alice Springs, Australia.*

in the sand.[12] They use simple forms that can be drawn quickly, erased and replaced with others as the plot unfolds.[13] However, this in itself does not

[12] Australian Aboriginal cultural and religious life centres on the *dreaming* or *dreamtime* (Sutton 1991), a period beyond living memory when the ancestors and supernatural beings created and shaped the world and laid down the laws of social and religious behaviour. These events provide the great themes of Aboriginal art practised not only by recognised artists but also by ordinary adult members of the community.

[13] One presumes that the visual symbols are not meant to 'stand alone', but are always interpreted in the context of verbal storytelling or ceremonial ritual.

Figure 10.13 *Two-eyed profile figures once common in European and North American children's drawings. Reprinted with the permission of Brent Wilson.*

explain why a U-shape, rather than any other, is used to represent a person. At first glance it may appear to be completely arbitrary, with no visual likeness to a real person, but it may in fact have been derived from an aerial view of a person seated on the ground.

As well as different kinds of depiction in different cultures, we can also see differences within a culture over a period of time. When Rouma (1913) listed a set of stages for the development of the human figure in children's drawings he included a transitional stage between an earlier full-face figure and a later profile figure. One of the main characteristics of this transitional stage is that there are two eyes set in a profile outline of the head (Wilson & Wilson 1982) (see figure 10.13). According to Wilson (1985), this form was very common in western Europe and North America

Figure 10.14 *Overlapping trouser legs drawn by Spanish-speaking Californian children in the early 1920s. Reprinted with the permission of Brent Wilson.*

during the late nineteenth and early twentieth centuries, but all but disappeared after this time. A much more local style was a figure with overlapping trouser-legs drawn by Spanish-speaking Californian children between 1917 and 1923 (see figure 10.14). Back-mounted arms were another feature of this local style (see figure 10.15). Interestingly, this style had also been noted in Italy by Ricci (1887) about forty years previously, and it is possible that it could have 'travelled' to the USA with Italian immigrant children in the 1920s. Among my large collection of children's human figure drawings collected mainly in the UK in the late twentieth century there are no examples of two-eyed profiles, overlapping trouser-legs or back-mounted arms. One assumes that these were 'fashions' in children's drawings, some more localised than others, which died out and were superseded by other, preferred styles. Wilson (1992) suggests that they may have died out because of the introduction of inexpensive comics, which provided children with a range of possibilities for ways of drawing the human figure.

Although in all societies with a pictorial tradition there is at least some visual or spatial similarity between a real human figure and the way it is depicted, there is also a good deal of evidence that children (and indeed

Figure 10.15 *Back-mounted arms drawn by Italian children in the 1880s (above) and by Californian children in the 1920s (below).*

adults) in different societies depict the human figure in different ways. Some of these differences reflect actual physical features between people or differences in their dress and hairstyle; others seem to be the result of a choice among possible ways in which a human being could be represented in a picture and may be the dominant or even the sole form of representation in any particular cultural group. Particularly marked differences are seen in very different cultures, for example, in developed countries versus traditional, rural and often preliterate societies. As well as differences between cultures we also see differences within a culture, but at different points in time. Both the style prevalent in a particular culture or at a particular time are likely to be passed on through cultural means and later in this chapter I shall discuss the various means that might be responsible.

Is there a universal pattern of development in children's pictorial representation?

It has been claimed that although we see cultural differences in the pictures of older children and adults, the early graphic efforts of young

...า are universal. For example, Kellogg and O'Dell (1967) claimed ...Children of the world, wherever they live, make all their early ...ngs in the same way' (p. 77), and 'The art of young children every-...e is identical' (p. 105). Indeed, in most cultures with a pictorial ...ition nearly all young children scribble and make simple shapes, ...atever the style of figure they develop later on (see chapter 4). ...ribbling may be an important activity for young children in order to ...ractise manipulating the pencil and experimenting with the kinds of lines and shapes that can be produced with it. Based on his research with his own three children, Matthews (1983, 1984) has claimed that the series of mark-making movements that young children produce forms the basis for their later drawing activity. Furthermore, based on his study of forty children in a London nursery and forty in a nursery and kindergarten in Singapore, Matthews (1994) has claimed that this process may be universal. We should be cautious about this claim, however, as scribbling has not been investigated in a large number of different cultures. Some older children, who have not had the opportunity to draw before, also experiment with lines and shapes before they draw a recognisable figure, although this experimentation may be very brief. Scribbling may be less necessary for older children since they already possess more developed motor and cognitive skills, which may enable them to succeed quickly in a representational drawing task (Martlew & Connolly 1996).

When children begin to produce recognisable figures these are not necessarily the same in all cultures. This is not surprising since, according to Vygotsky (1978), a child's development takes place *within* a cultural context; cultural influences are integral to that development and are observable from a very young age. In his socio-cultural approach to development, Vygotsky argued that development involves the mastering of *cultural tools* that mediate higher mental functioning. These tools include technological devices such as calendars, clocks, books and calculators, and concepts or symbol systems such as language, writing, mathematics and pictures. With regard to pictorial representation, Vygotsky's theory would predict that different cultures may use different graphic symbols to represent the same object. The mastery of cultural tools, such as representational pictures, takes place largely through social interactions with parents and others and, in this way, children benefit from the accumulated knowledge of previous generations (see chapter 12).

One of the first recognisable attempts by western children to draw a human figure is the tadpole form. This is the case in a number of cultures and may even be seen among rural adults drawing for the first time (Cox & Bayraktar 1989). However, some children in other cultures have been observed to draw the facial features but without a surrounding head

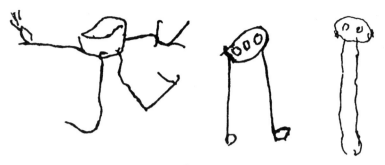

a

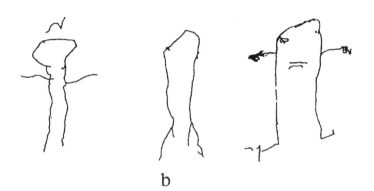

b

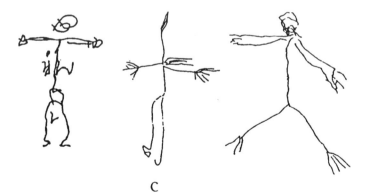

c

Figure 10.16 *Different forms of the human figure drawn by children in the Jimi Valley, Papua New Guinea: (a) tadpole forms, (b) contour figures, (c) stick figures (Martlew & Connolly 1996).*

contour (Paget 1932) and in their study of children in the Jimi valley of Papua New Guinea Martlew and Connolly (1996) found that, although some children drew tadpole figures, others produced other kinds, notably a contour figure and, to a much lesser extent, a stick figure (see figure 10.16).

Thus, these authors claim that there may be different routes into the representation of the human figure.

Although representational art was traditionally unknown in the Jimi culture, one assumes that western-style pictures have become available, perhaps on school materials and on imported commercial goods. It is unlikely, then, that even the unschooled children were complete novices at recognising pictures, and their idea of how a human figure should be depicted might well have been derived from western-style models. So, why is it that some of them drew contour and stick figures rather than tadpole forms? In fact, these styles are not unknown among western children's figure drawings. For example, both the contour type and the stick type occur in the longitudinal data collected by Fysh[14] (see Cox 1997). There are also examples of facial features drawn with no surrounding contour.

All these ways of drawing a human being are reasonable solutions to the problem and are not merely arbitrary or random attempts (Golomb 1992). Interestingly, Fysh's preschool children in the UK did not use the above styles consistently over time. Children who at first omitted a head contour very soon included one, and those whose figures started off very stick-like did not necessarily continue to develop them into a more advanced stick figure. In fact, most children who drew alternative forms switched to tadpole figures quite early. So, although different forms may represent their object equally well, some 'experimental' styles may be replaced by other, more prevalent forms in the child's culture. Since Martlew and Connolly's (1996) study was not longitudinal we do not know whether individual children would have continued to develop exclusively along contour, stick or western lines. It may be that the alternative forms they produced for the researchers were short-lived, just as those observed in the UK seemed to be.

One presumes that the particular style of figure that a child produces is the result of her attempt to reconstruct the figures that are generally available in pictures she sees around her. In the Warlpiri culture of central Australia the traditional way of drawing a human figure is very different, and when young Warlpiri children draw in this style they do not draw tadpole figures but, rather, simplified versions[15] of the U-shape used by adults (figures 10.17, 10.18). However, when they draw at school, where they are also exposed to western-style pictures, they may draw in a western style.[16] Thus, what the young child draws depends on the target image she is

---

[14] The human figure drawings collected by Amelia Fysh are held at the National Arts Education Archive, Bretton Hall, University of Leeds, UK.

[15] A single curve is used by younger children whereas older children tend to use an outlined U-shape more like the adult form (see figures 10.17 and 10.18).

[16] In fact, there are examples of both western and Warlpiri styles within the same picture (see figures 10.17 and 10.18).

Figure 10.17 *Detail from a drawing by a 6-year-old Warlpiri girl. Both tadpole figures and the Warlpiri U-shaped form have been used. This detail is from an original drawing collected by Rosemary Hill.*

Figure 10.18 *Detail from* Groups of people chatting around camp fires, *drawn by an 8-year-old Warlpiri girl. The Warlpiri symbol has been used for most of the figures, but the baby is a conventional western form. This detail is from an original drawing collected by Rosemary Hill.*

aiming for, and what she produces will bear some resemblance to that image even though it is likely to be a simplified version. The sparse data available[17] on the style of Warlpiri children's drawing suggest that whether they draw in the traditional or the western style, their figures become more complex as the children grow older. However, these data are not longitudinal, so we do not have an account of how an individual child's mastery of both the Warlpiri style and the western style develops over time. Nonetheless, it is reasonable to conclude that the development of depiction, in terms of the actual images produced, is not universal because the intended pictorial image is not universally the same. It sometimes only seems that way because a certain kind of image has become so widespread and therefore children in most cultures have a similar goal in mind when they learn how to draw a person. Nonetheless, it appears that there may be a universal progression in the sense that children generally shift from simple to more complex graphic forms, which is in line with Arnheim's (1974) and Golomb's (2002) claims.

As far as we know, children in all pictorial cultures scribble and experiment with the lines and shapes that they can make with a pencil. This may be a universal phenomenon, although older children in non-pictorial cultures who have been asked to draw for the first time may take only a very short time for this experimentation. When we look at children's early attempts at drawing the human figure we find that they often experiment with different forms before settling to a more conventional form for their particular society. The cultural variation in the images that children produce does not disprove the notion of universality, however, as according to Matthews (1999) 'universality does not mean homogeneity' (p. 156). Since children's own creativity in finding graphic equivalents for the figures they want to draw interacts with the pictures they see around them, variation is bound to occur.

Sources of the cultural diversity of graphic representation

How do children acquire the particular styles of depiction prevalent in their own culture? If a certain way of drawing already exists then it is likely that each generation of children is ushered into this style through formal or informal tuition by others and/or by their own attempts to copy what they see in the art around them. Wilson (1985) maintains that children learn to draw by studying the graphic models available in their culture, and Goodnow, Wilkins and Dawes (1986) also claim that children's drawings are shaped by the pictures available in their

[17] The children's drawings were collected by Rosemary Hill when she visited Yuendumu to produce a television programme on children's drawings for the BBC/Open University.

culture. Even when, as in the West, artists try to be innovative and find new ways of expression, they often find that they are influenced, unwittingly, by existing artistic styles (Gombrich 1960). It is difficult not to be influenced by them, even when we try to draw 'from life'.

Graphic models are available in books, magazines and advertisements and on many items of merchandise. Models of more localised graphic conventions appear on the work produced by local artists and craftsmen. For example, the pin-head figures (see figure 10.6) reported by Paget (1932), Fortes (1940, 1981) and Reuning and Wortley (1973) have been seen more recently on pots and other products made by adults in southern Sudan (Elatta 1992). Bi-triangular designs, similar to the figures drawn by some schoolchildren in Namibia and the neighbouring part of Zimbabwe (see figure 10.11), have also been seen as decorative features on woven baskets and on the carved sides of drums, as well as on other artefacts (Andersson 2003). Similarly, Court (1992) noticed that the cross-hatching technique (see figure 10.21) used by Kamba children in Kenya was also used by the adults when decorating calabashes (gourds). Australian Aboriginal storytellers, as well as drawing figures in the sand, also produce their more formal artwork in a very public way, so that children are able to witness the process as well as see the final figures that emerge (see figure 10.12). Kindler (1994b) has described how her 5-year-old son, Jan, started to draw in the Haida style of the north-west coast of Canada after he became interested in the prints and carvings of a local artist and saw this traditional style of art in the Museum of Anthropology and a gallery of Indian crafts (see figure 10.19). Jan incorporated this style into his pictures of hockey players and even invented a new video-game character using his version of the Haida style (see figure 10.20). With regard to the way objects are portrayed in depth, Court (1994) has pointed out that the divergent perspective common in Kenyan children's drawings of tables is widespread in that culture (see figure 10.21); it has a long-standing tradition in east Africa, from Ethiopian manuscripts to contemporary sign painting and on word charts in schools.

When Wilson and Wilson (1977) interviewed 147 American teenagers about the source of the graphic images in their pictures they found that nearly all of them could be traced to the popular media. Some children are particularly influenced by the cartoon-style of comics and films. Manga comics (see figure 10.22) are read by children and adults alike in Japan and account for nearly 40 per cent of all books and magazines sold there (Schodt 1983). Manga styles are not only enjoyed in a passive way, however, as some Japanese children join manga clubs and make their own comics. Wilson (1997b, 2000) found that the manga style was evident in two-thirds of the graphic narratives produced on request by 6-, 8-, 10- and 12-year-old children.

Figure 10.19 *Haida representation of a beaver.*

Children may be shown how to draw by adults and also by other children. This tuition may be informal, when a young child asks its parent to draw something, or formal, when it occurs in a classroom. The effect of schooling has often been to expose children to western imagery through books and other educational materials, and may have been responsible for the decline in the use of local styles. When Fortes (1940) collected

Figure 10.20 *Jan, aged 5, invented a video game character based on the Haida style (Kindler 1994b).*

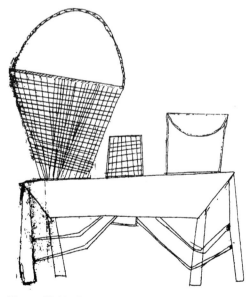

Figure 10.21 *Divergent perspective is common in Kenyan children's drawings (Court 1994).*

Figure 10.22 *Illustration from a Japanese manga comic.*

drawings from both unschooled Tallensi children and those in a boarding school in what was then the Gold Coast of west Africa, he noticed that the figures drawn by the children at the school were much more western in style. Thirty-five years later (Fortes 1981) the drawings collected from local schoolchildren, who were the descendants of those in his original sample, were also in a western style but were more skilfully produced than those drawn by the earlier generation. Martlew and Connolly (1996) also found that, in the Jimi Valley, the more schooling children had the more detailed and visually realistic their drawings became and also the more western in style.

A western style of drawing could also be inadvertently passed on to children who have not drawn before and who live in a culture without pictorial art. If a child (or an adult) has never seen a representational picture and has no idea what it means to draw, then researchers may give at least some minimal demonstration of how the task could be done. Most studies have not reported what this picture was like, but even one example could be sufficient to influence what the children themselves draw. Thus, their figures may not be the naïve drawer's own ideas but their attempt to reproduce an example presented to them by researchers. The main cultural influence could be the researcher's own western style of drawing!

Where a strong style of drawing already exists, however, this may be upheld and even formally taught in school. In Japan, for example, where the teaching of art is very structured, we see a typically Japanese style among children's figure drawings. When Cox and colleagues (2001) compared the human figure drawings of children in Japan and in the UK they found that although the Japanese figures were not constructed differently, they were more skilfully drawn and were more highly rated than those in the UK (see figure 12.4 and also chapter 12). As well as being influenced by a more structured art curriculum, these drawings may also have been influenced by the children's exposure to and practice at drawing manga figures. In some areas of China where, up until the 1990s at least, art teaching has been very formal (Winner 1989; Cox, Perara & Xu 1998, 1999) we again see typically Chinese styles of drawing (see plates 4–6). Efforts are also being made in the Australian Warlpiri culture to maintain their traditional style of depiction in the schools.[18] In Yuendumu, for example, the teachers print their own books and materials using both Warlpiri and western images. The two styles are not necessarily kept separate, however, as some adult artists and children will use western and Warlpiri imagery in the same picture.

As well as being responsive to what is formally taught, children also respond to teachers' expectations or to what they think teachers' expectations are. Goodnow, Wilkins and Dawes (1986) found that 6- and 7-year olds' drawings of a man produced on request were more detailed and in proportion than their own spontaneous drawings, but were also presented in a static and full-face orientation; in contrast, some of the 7-year-olds experimented with various action postures in their spontaneous figures,

---

[18] This contrasts with Kaneda's (1994) report that the traditional craftwork of Nepalese adults and children has been abandoned since the influx of foreign goods to local markets.

even though these might be only sketchily drawn. So, the artistic conventions of adults is a very potent source of influence on children's artwork. Whether the influence is formal or informal, a certain style is being presented as an example which children may then be instructed or choose to follow.

As well as tuition from adults, such as teachers or parents, children may also be influenced by and, indeed, taught to draw by their peers. In fact, Paget (1932) argued that, although children may invent their own graphic symbols, they also copy the drawing styles of other children, which are passed on from generation to generation in a similar way to that of children's playground games (Opie & Opie 1969). Paget (1932) regarded the bi-triangular figures in South-West Africa as a local convention only among the children. They did not reflect the adult convention for human figures in that region,[19] although, as Paget noted, they could have been influenced by the triangular abstract designs in adult craftwork of that area. Wilson (1985) has also drawn our attention to certain local or regional styles that seem peculiar to children, such as overlapping trouser-legs and back-mounted arms (see figures 10.14 and 10.15).

There are, then, several potential sources of cultural influence on children's drawings, and these are not necessarily mutually exclusive. They include the availability of images that children can copy, as well as tuition from adults and children in formal and informal settings. Since it might be difficult if not impossible to carry out studies rigorous enough to test these various possibilities, we shall probably be unable to come to a firm conclusion about this issue and, therefore, these ideas about potential influences on children's drawings may have to remain speculative. It is important to remember, however, that just because there are cultural influences on children's art, this does not mean that there is no development, since children still have to grapple with how they can produce the particular form they are aiming for and *that* may depend on developmental factors as well as on individual skill and motivation. Thus, it is reasonable to assume that there is an interaction between children's intrapersonal development and the influences of the culture in which they are brought up.

Summary

Research evidence shows that people in different cultures have no difficulty in recognising familiar objects in pictures. Even pictorially naïve

---

[19] Interestingly, this bi-triangular form has been observed more recently on local craft objects made by adults in the Sudan (Elatta 1992) and in Namibia and Zimbabwe (Andersson 2003).

adults and children are successful with no or little instruction. They also need no or only minimal explanation regarding spatial depth relationships in a picture. With regard to the understanding and aesthetic appreciation of art in different cultures, there is some evidence that both adults and children have different general ideas of what constitutes art (e.g., whether ugly subject matter can be art). However, when children are asked about their preferences for particular pictures there appears to be more similarity among cultures with young children preferring realism and colour and older ones preferring complexity.

Children's very early experimentation with mark-making may be universal, although we need more evidence in support of this claim. What is less contentious is that their early attempts to draw the human figure tend to be simple schemas and these are elaborated and become more complex as children grow older. The actual styles of drawing, however, vary from culture to culture, and it is clear that the western style of depiction is not inevitable. Although there may be some limit to the number of possible ways objects can be drawn, the variation is quite wide and different cultures have adopted many reasonable and 'legitimate' styles of depiction. Indeed, a number of styles can and do emerge, even in western children's drawings. However, children quickly conform to the style that is more prevalent or valued in their own culture. In some cases, such as the Warlpiri in central Australia, children seem equally happy with western and traditional styles, as both of these have a valued place in their society. Within any particular culture the sources of the images are varied and include the popular media, school materials and both adults' and other children's pictures. Children may learn to draw through formal or informal tuition and also through their own interest in copying the pictorial images they have available to them.

The importance of considering drawings in different cultures is that it helps us to identify what is universal and what is not. Given the variation in styles of drawing it is clear that if there is anything universal about children's development of picture-making it is likely to be at a rather general level such as a shift from simple to complex figures.

11 Professionals' use of children's drawings

Drawings are used in a variety of ways by a number of different professional groups, such as educational psychologists, clinical psychologists, child psychiatrists, paediatricians, counsellors, investigators in criminal cases (e.g., police or social workers) and therapists of various kinds. Unlike many psychological tests, drawings do not need extensive training on the part of administrators or special practice on the part of the children. Most require only paper and pencil and are quick to administer. An attraction is that drawing is an enjoyable activity for most children and therefore, compared with other forms of testing, is much less likely to cause resistance or anxiety. Another advantage is that drawings are not overly dependent on language and therefore should not penalise children whose language skills are less well developed. Various surveys have found that tests based on human figure drawings are popular and widely used by psychologists, especially in the USA (Sundberg 1961; Prout 1983; Lubin, Larsen, Matarazzo & Seever 1985; Archer et al. 1991; Watkins et al. 1995; Thomas & Jolley 1998) and also in Hong Kong (Tsoi & Sundberg 1989). Drawings are not always used as part of a formal test, however. In fact, responses to my enquiries in the UK indicate that clinicians and therapists tend to use drawings in an informal way, as a means of engaging children in talking about their families and what is bothering them. In this chapter I shall investigate the way that drawings are used by various professional groups[1] and assess the claims that are made about them.

The use of drawing tests to assess children's intelligence

For at least a hundred years psychologists have known that certain aspects of children's drawings correlate with an increase in age, and Schuyten (1904) was among the first to try to establish norms based on these changes. Claparède (1907) suggested that drawings might be used as an indication of intellectual ability, and Ivanoff (1909) scored drawings

---

[1] I have not included teachers here as the use of drawings in education is covered in chapter 12.

on a six-point scale and then compared these scores with teachers' ratings of children's general abilities. Rouma (1913) found that aspects of children's human figure drawings, such as the number of body parts, and their relative proportions were more strongly related to mental age than to chronological age. He described a set of developmental stages specifically relating to human figure drawings.

The first formal test of intelligence, based on the human figure drawings of nearly 4,000 children, was Goodenough's (1926) Draw-a-Man Test. In order to make fair comparisons among children it is important that the topic should be the same for all of them. The human figure is a good choice since it is very commonly drawn by children in most cultures. The test is based on drawings of a man because, it was argued at the time, men's clothing is less varied than that of women and children. Goodenough's test was revised by Harris (1963), becoming known as the Goodenough–Harris Test. It requires the child to draw a man, a woman and oneself. Points are awarded for the number of body parts, their relative proportions, the way they fit together, the control of the line, and so on. There is a total of seventy-three points for a male figure and seventy-one for a female figure. Harris preferred to regard the test as a test of 'intellectual maturity' rather than intelligence. Like Goodenough, he also acknowledged that girls tend to score higher than boys on both figures and this is taken into account when converting the raw scores into IQ scores.

Koppitz (1968) wanted to simplify the scoring system and produced her own Draw-a-Person Test, partly based on the Goodenough–Harris Test but also on her sample of nearly 2,000 children's drawings. There are thirty *developmental items*, which can be applied to a male or a female figure (see table 4). Naglieri (1988) has also devised a test based on over 2,000 human figure drawings. In his Draw-a-Person Test the child draws three figures: a man, a woman and oneself. There are sixty-four scoring items for each figure. This system is supposed to take into account dress and fashion of the figures and does not penalise children with fine motor control problems. In all these tests the raw score can be converted into an IQ score, although in the Koppitz system it converts to a broad band of IQ scores rather than to an exact score.

The reliability of these tests based on inter-rater reliability is quite high – over .90 for all three drawing tests. The test–retest reliability varies depending on the time interval between the two tests: whereas Goodenough reported a correlation of .94 between the Draw-a-Man scores of figures drawn on successive days, McCarthy (1944) reported a correlation of .68 when the drawings were made one week apart. Far more important, though, is the validity of the tests, and this can be assessed by correlating the drawing test scores with scores on well-known intelligence scales such as the Stanford-Binet Intelligence Scale (Terman & Merrill 1960) and the revised Wechsler Intelligence Scale for Children (WISC-R) (Wechsler 1974).

Table 4 *The thirty developmental items in Koppitz's (1968) Draw-a-Person Test.*

1. Head	16. Arms correctly attached to shoulders
2. Eyes	17. Elbows
3. Pupils	18. Hands
4. Eyebrows or eyelashes	19. Fingers
5. Nose	20. Correct number of fingers
6. Nostrils	21. Legs
7. Mouth	22. Legs in two dimensions
8. Two lips	23. Knees
9. Ears	24. Feet
10. Hair	25. Feet in two dimensions
11. Neck	26. Profile
12. Body	27. Clothing: one item
13. Arms	28. Clothing: two or three items
14. Arms in two dimensions	29. Clothing: four or more items
15. Arms pointing downwards	30. Good proportion

Kamphaus and Pleiss (1991) listed a number of these correlational studies along with their correlation coefficients, which are positive but not always as high as one would wish. For example, correlations for the Goodenough or Goodenough–Harris scores range from .38 to .74, for the Koppitz scores .45 to .80, and for the Naglieri scores .51. However, from their review of the literature, Motta, Little and Tobin (1993) note that correlations are generally only in the .40s and .50s.

Often the correlations have been calculated using the drawing test scores and the IQ scores derived from the whole battery of an IQ test. Since drawing is mainly a non-verbal activity, it might be more appropriate to correlate the drawing scores with the IQ scores based only on the 'performance' (i.e., non-verbal) subtests. Where this has been done, the correlations between drawing and performance IQ are higher than between drawing and verbal IQ. For example, Abell, von Briesen and Watz (1996) found that the correlation between the Goodenough–Harris scores and the WISC-R verbal scores was .28, but between the Goodenough–Harris and WISC-R performance scores it was .51; Abell, Wood and Liebman (2001) found these correlations to be .46 and .57, respectively. The correlation between the Koppitz scores and the WISC-R verbal scores was .23, but between the Koppitz and the WISC-R performance scores it was .32 (Abell, von Briesen & Watz 1996). The correlation between the Naglieri scores and the WISC-R verbal scores was .35, but between the Naglieri scores and the WISC-R performance scores it was .48 (Abell, Wood & Liebman 2001). Even though the correlation between the drawing test and children's performance IQ is consistently higher, none of these correlations is very impressive. Interestingly, they tend to underestimate a child's IQ. For example, Abell and colleagues found that the average score for 100 6- to 15-year-olds was 91.71 on the Goodenough–Harris Test, 91.95 on the Naglieri test but 100.02 on the WISC-R (99.65 on the verbal scores and 100.55 on the performance scores). There are sound reasons, then, to be cautious about the use of these drawing tests.

Even Goodenough and Harris (1950) believed that when the Draw-a-Man Test is administered to children of a similar cultural background, it can be valuable only 'as a crude measure of "general intelligence"' and 'cannot serve as a satisfactory substitute for individual tests of the Binet type' (p. 399). It would not be appropriate, then, to use such a test on its own to make any serious judgement about a child's ability or his future. However, if a child cannot or will not tolerate a long battery of tests, then a drawing test might be an attractive option. Nonetheless, the validity of such tests is not very high, leading some authors to a much stronger conclusion: 'human figure drawings should not be substituted for other well-established intelligence and achievement tests. The data fail to support the use of human figure drawings even as an additional measure' (Aikman, Belter & Finch 1992, p. 119); 'human figure drawings are seriously flawed as a screening test for intellectual performance and are not useful as a predictor of academic achievement' (Motta, Little & Tobin 1993, p. 167); and 'must be used with the greatest of caution, if at all' (Abell, Wood & Liebman 2001, p. 213).

The use of drawing tests for clinical assessment

Clinical psychologists, working in hospitals or health centres or in private practice, use a variety of tests to help them make a psychological assessment of their clients. Two recent studies have surveyed the use of these tests (including drawings) in clinical practice. One was carried out by Watkins, Campbell, Nieberding and Hallmark (1995) in the USA and the other by Bekhit, Thomas, Lalonde and Jolley (2002) in the UK.

The results showed that clinicians in both countries spend a considerable amount of time in 'face-to-face' interviews with their clients. However, compared with their North American colleagues British clinicians spend less time on formal testing and, in particular, were far less enthusiastic about projective assessment procedures.[2] Whereas 96 per cent of the American clinicians favoured the use of a projective assessment[3] based on a free drawing, only 3.8 per cent of the British sample did so. In fact, the

[2] A projective procedure refers to a task or activity into which the client is assumed to project her feelings or emotional state.
[3] Archer, Maruish, Imhof and Piotrowski (1991) also reported the popularity of projective testing in the USA.

majority of the British clinicians claimed that they never used projective techniques, and those who did so spent only about 1 per cent of the assessment time on them. The British study also investigated the use of the more formal[4] drawing tests, such as the Draw-a-Person Test (Machover 1949), the House-Tree-Person Test (Buck 1948) and the Kinetic Family Drawing (Burns & Kaufman 1970), and found that they were recommended by very few clinicians. In contrast, the Machover test, the House-Tree-Person Test and the Kinetic Family Drawing have been found to be in the top ten tests used by both clinicians and school psychologists in the USA (Prout 1983; Lubin et al. 1985). Clearly, there is a huge difference between clinicians' practices in these two countries and, in particular, the extent to which drawings are used.

One of the most well-known projective tests is Machover's (1949) Draw-a-Person Test, in which the child is asked to 'draw a person' or 'draw somebody'. This figure is presumed to represent the child herself – it is 'intimately tied to the self in all of its ramifications' (pp. 348–9) – and distortions of the figure are considered indicative of the problems the child has with her own self-image. Then the child is asked to draw another person (of the opposite sex to the first one) on a separate sheet of paper. This second figure is supposed to represent an important person in the child's life.

In fact, this test is not really a test at all in the conventional sense, but a vehicle for the clinician to interpret the figures, taking into account the body parts that have been included or omitted, their size, shape and position on the page, the quality of the line, the amount of erasure, and so on. The interpretation is psycho-dynamically orientated,[5] imbuing each aspect of the drawing with symbolic meaning. As an example of her technique, Machover (1951) shows a picture drawn by 8-year-old Peter (see figure 11.1) who had been referred to a clinician for behavioural problems – in particular, he was aggressive, restless and attention-seeking. The picture is interpreted as depicting Peter and his mother,[6] despite the fact that Peter said it was a boy and his sister. The boy's central location on the page is said to be Peter's attempt to force himself into the centre of attention. If this were true then it would be true for nearly everyone since, given this drawing task, the vast majority of children and adults draw their figures in the centre of the page. Although the stance of this figure is said to be 'wide and assertive' (p. 364), both the figures are drawn in a frontal and canonical way, quite typical of an 8-year-old child's drawing (see

[4] By *formal* I mean that the topic of the picture is specified by the clinician.
[5] This Freudian view assumes that despite their overt subject matter the drawings also have some 'deeper' symbolic meaning.
[6] Peter attempted to draw the second figure on the reverse side of the paper but then drew it on the same side as the first. Machover comments that Peter must always be close to his mother physically and cannot tolerate even graphic separation.

Figure 11.1 *Picture drawn by 8-year-old Peter, who was referred to a clinician because of behavioural problems (from Machover 1951).*

chapter 5).[7] Machover sees a lot of sexual significance in the drawing: for example, she claims that the belt cutting off the lower part of the boy's body suggests sexual anxiety. The problem is that trousers with a belt are bound to divide the figure. The female figure also has a belt (or a waist-band), but is not interpreted as being sexually anxious. Peter says the nicest part of his drawing of the boy is his tie, which Machover says represents 'phallic strength' (p. 363).

One problem with this kind of projective assessment is its lack of reliability. In fact, Anastasi (1976) reported that different clinicians did not agree on the way that certain features of the drawings should be interpreted. Another problem, and arguably the more important, is

[7] Machover's approach was devised mainly for use with adolescents and adults; no allowance for normal development seems to have been made when interpreting children's drawings.

whether this approach is valid. At issue is the assumption that the depicted figures reflect psychological characteristics and problems of the drawer. We should not accept this assumption without independent confirmation that this is the case (Golomb 1992). One way we could assess it would be to compare different clinical groups to see if their drawings differ; for example, one could compare the drawings of a group high in aggression with those of a group low in aggression or a group low in self-esteem versus a normally adjusted group. Over the years there have been a number of reviews of such studies (e.g., Swensen 1957, 1968; Roback 1968; Klopfer & Taulbee 1976; Kahill 1984; Motta et al. 1993), but these have found little support for the projective approach. With regard to Machover's various claims, there is contradictory evidence or insufficient evidence and, in addition, some issues are simply not testable. At best, her technique might be useful as a 'rough and ready' means of detecting adjustment problems at a gross level (Cox 1993), but this might tell clinicians no more than what they would already know by simply observing the child's behaviour or by referring to behavioural reports. A number of researchers (e.g., Klopfer & Taulbee 1976; Kahill 1984; Thomas & Jolley 1998) have concluded that in the clinical context drawings are best reserved as a focus for discussion about a child's problems rather than for a diagnostic purpose.

Other tests also based on the psycho-dynamic approach are the House-Tree-Person Test and the Kinetic Family Drawing Test. In the House-Tree-Person Test (Buck 1948) children are asked to make separate drawings of a house, a tree and a person. The house is considered to be a projection of the child's feelings relating to his or her own home and those living there. The tree is supposed to be representative of the child's psychological development and his feelings about his wider environment. The drawing of a person is said to reflect the child's feelings about his own body and his self-concept. The drawings are evaluated on the presence or absence of certain features, details, proportions, perspective and colour. In the Kinetic Family Drawing Test (Burns & Kaufman 1970) children are asked to draw a picture of everyone in their family, including themselves, engaged in some kind of activity. The distance between the figures and their interactions are believed to reflect the child's self-concept and the dynamics of the family relationships. The clinician looks for mood, proximity, isolation, size, interactions and so on. The problem is that some of the supposed effects are not reliable. In chapter 7 I reviewed some of the findings relating to the size of figures as a reflection of children's positive or negative feelings towards different people and concluded that this effect cannot be accepted as reliable. The current position is similar regarding proximity. Although Gray and Thomas (unpublished paper) found that their 5- to 8-year-olds drew a friend closer to an image of themselves than they drew a 'foe', this effect only occurred when the drawings were on separate sheets of paper; the effect was not reliable when children were asked to draw the friend and foe on either side of a self-image, all drawn on the same sheet. Similarly, Thomas and Gray (1992) found that children draw themselves closer to images of their friends than to classmates that they dislike, but this effect was only found when children drew the figures in a left-to-right sequence across the page. A further problem is that Acosta (1990) failed to find a relationship between the closeness between figures in children's drawings and the actual closeness between family members. Using the Kinetic Family Drawing Test, Joiner, Schmidt and Barnett (1996) examined the size, detail and line heaviness in the drawings of psychiatric inpatients aged between 6 and 16 years. They found that none of these three indicators significantly related to various standard measures of depression and anxiety.

A rather different problem with this test is that the administrator is instructed to leave the room while the child completes the drawing and therefore, as Golomb (1992) has pointed out, will have no knowledge of the planning problems the child may have had; so, for example, some figures may have been drawn smaller and more cramped, not because of any emotional problems the child has with those people, but perhaps because they were drawn later and there was less space left for them on the page. In the same way that we can criticise the Machover test, so with these other tests we can criticise the assumptions on which they are based, the subjectivity of the interpretation, and their reliability and validity.

Another kind of human figure drawing test is the Draw-a-Person Test devised by Koppitz (1968). As well as scoring the figures for thirty developmental items they can also be scored for thirty *emotional indicators* (see table 5). The attraction for many psychologists is that the test yields a score and, because of this, may seem to be more objective and systematic than the approach based on a clinician's psycho-dynamic (and, critics would say, subjective) interpretation. Unlike Machover, Koppitz made some attempt to take into account the normal development of children's drawings; in fact, the test was specifically designed for children from age 5 years. An emotional indicator was only scored if it was unusual in the human figure drawings of normal children at that particular age. Koppitz also attempted to test the validity of her claim that emotionally disturbed children would have more emotional indicators in their figure drawings than would normal children. She compared the human figure drawings of 76 normal and 76 emotionally disturbed children between the ages of 5 and 12 years and found that there were indeed more emotional indicators in the disturbed group's drawings than in those of a well-adjusted group. In fact, 76 per cent of the normal children had no emotional indicators at all; a further 18 per cent had only one indicator and 5 per cent had two. In contrast, 75 per cent of the emotionally disturbed children had two or

Table 5 *Emotional indicators in children's drawings.*

Emotional indicators	Koppitz (1968) – minimum age for scoring		Catte & Cox (1999) – minimum age for scoring	
	Boys	Girls	Boys	Girls
1. Poor integration of parts	7	6	6	5
2. Shading of face	5	5	No longer valid	No longer valid
3. Shading of body/limbs	8	7	No longer valid	No longer valid
4. Shading of hands/neck	7	7	5	5
5. Gross asymmetry of limbs	5	5	5	5
6. Slanting figure	5	5	5	5
7. Tiny figure	5	5	7	8
8. Big figure	8	8	No longer valid	No longer valid
9. Transparency	5	5	5	5
10. Tiny head	5	5	5	5
11. Crossed eyes	5	5	5	5
12. Teeth	5	5	No longer valid	No longer valid
13. Short arms	5	5	No longer valid	No longer valid
14. Long arms	5	5	5	5
15. Arms clinging to body	5	5	5	5
16. Big hands	5	5	5	5
17. Hands cut off	5	5	6	7
18. Legs pressed together	5	5	No longer valid	No longer valid
19. Genitals	5	5	5	5

20. Monster/grotesque figure	5	5	5
21. Three or more figures spontaneously drawn	5	5	5
22. Clouds	5	5	5
23. No eyes	5	5	5
24. No nose	6	8	6
25. No mouth	5	5	5
26. No body	5	5	5
27. No arms	6	6	5
28. No legs	5	5	5
29. No feet	9	7	7
30. No neck	10	9	11
		No longer valid	

more indicators and only 9 per cent had no indicators. Further comparisons were made between children rated as aggressive and those rated as shy, and between neurotic children with a history of stealing and those with a history of psychosomatic complaints such as stomach upsets and headaches. A difference in the number of emotional indicators was found in both these comparisons. It appears, then, that Koppitz's test has some external validity in discriminating between the drawings of normal children and those who are emotionally disturbed.[8]

In an attempt to replicate Koppitz's study Catte and Cox (1999) compared 44 emotionally disturbed boys[9] aged from 7 to 11 years 8 months with 44 normal boys of the same chronological age (CA group) and a further 44 normal boys with the same mental age as the clinical group (MA group[10]). Individual children were matched across these three groups not only on chronological or mental age but also on social background. Thus, the groups were considered to be more tightly matched than those in Koppitz's study. We found that significantly more (59 per cent) of the emotionally disturbed boys scored two or more indicators compared with the boys in the other two groups (27 per cent of the CA group and 41 per cent of the MA group); in fact, these two control groups did not differ significantly from each other. So, both this and Koppitz's study found that the majority of the emotionally disturbed children scored two or more indicators whereas a minority of the normal children did so.

Since Koppitz's study was carried out in the 1960s in the USA we wondered if some of the indicators might no longer be valid for today's children in the UK, or if they might be valid but at a different age or for one sex rather than the other. So in a second study we compiled new norms based on the human figure drawings produced by 1,598 children (boys and girls) aged 5 to 11 years. We found that some items were no longer valid because they violated Koppitz's criteria for inclusion as emotional indicators – that they must occur rarely (less than 15 per cent) in normal children's drawings or that their frequency should not increase as children get older. We compiled a revised list of indicators – a total of twenty-three for boys and twenty-five for girls (see table 5). When the original drawings in our study were rescored we found that a minority of boys in all three groups had two or more indicators (32 per cent of the clinical group, 5 per cent of the CA group and 9 per cent of the MA group). Even so, the clinical group still scored significantly higher than the other two groups.

---

[8] Koppitz warned clinicians against making judgements about individual indicators in a drawing and recommended that only the total number of indicators should be considered. The reason is that problems and anxieties may be expressed in different ways by different children and in different ways by the same child tested on different occasions.

[9] Boys only were included in this study because they represented the vast majority of children classified as emotionally disturbed. They were all full-time pupils at special schools for children with emotional/behavioural difficulties.

[10] Koppitz did not include a group such as this.

A potential problem with the study was that the children's drawing skill had not been taken into account and some children's poor drawing skill might have accounted for the greater number of emotional indicators in their figures. In a further study (Cox & Catte 2000) the drawings of the emotionally disturbed boys were scored according to the Goodenough–Harris scale (Harris 1963), in which scores are awarded for the number of items included in a drawing, the proportions of the figure, the skill with which parts have been joined together and the quality of the line. It was felt that since the scores are based directly on the children's drawings then this might be an appropriate way of matching contrasting groups of participants in order to compare their emotional indicator scores. The comparison group consisted of 44 well-adjusted boys aged 6 to 11 years. Each emotionally disturbed child was matched with a normal child with a similar chronological age and a similar Goodenough–Harris score.

Since there is some overlap between items on the Goodenough–Harris scale and Koppitz's emotional indicators, there was a danger that a drawing could be penalised twice. In order to eliminate this possibility the confounding items were removed from the list of revised indicators, leaving a total of thirteen.[11] The majority of children in both groups scored either none or only one indicator; 16 per cent of the emotionally disturbed boys scored two indicators and only 5 per cent of the normal boys did so. There was no significant difference between the two groups. We concluded that the higher scores awarded to the disturbed boys in the previous study were mainly due to their lack of drawing skill.

Even though the drawings of these two groups of boys could not be distinguished by the application of Koppitz's emotional indicators, it remained a possibility that they might be distinguishable by some other means. The chosen method was the 'intuitive method of identification' (Dieffenbach 1977), in which judges are asked to inspect the pictures and identify which ones were drawn by the clinical group and which by the comparison group. Interestingly, out of twenty judges,[12] only one was able to differentiate successfully above chance level (correctly identifying 68 per cent of the drawings). It seems that when groups of disturbed and well-adjusted children have been carefully matched on a number of relevant variables then their drawings cannot reliably be distinguished.

The results to date on the use of human figure drawings for clinical assessment do not look promising, and Motta and colleagues (1993), among others, have argued that human figure drawings should not be used for this purpose. Even if this method were valid we might wonder

---

[11] These are items 1, 4, 5, 6, 7, 9, 11, 15, 16, 19, 20, 21 and 22 in Koppitz's original list.

[12] The judges in the Cox and Catte (2000) study were not experts, as previous research had shown that experts (including art therapists) are no better than non-experts (Hiler & Nesvig 1965; Stricker 1967; Ulman & Levy 1973; Arkell 1976; Motta et al. 1993; Catte 1998).

why clinicians would bother to make this assessment when behavioural observation or reports would do the job just as well. Despite the many criticisms of the use of drawings in clinical assessment, the activity of drawing may still be a useful one. For example, it can be used as a non-threatening means of establishing rapport with a child when a stark face-to-face interview might be too confrontational. The drawing itself can provide a focus for discussion and this might be particularly useful for children who are reluctant to speak about their experiences and feelings or who might have difficulties in expressing themselves.

The use of drawings in therapy

Therapists are likely to be dealing with children who are experiencing emotional problems and who may well have been severely traumatised by war or conflict or by physical, sexual or psychological abuse. Quite often therapists use drawing or painting as part of the therapeutic procedure. Art is generally a non-threatening and pleasurable activity and is particularly useful if children cannot express their concerns in words; indeed, it may be a means of revealing information that they are fearful of expressing overtly (Burgess & Hartman 1993). By making their experiences visible in their pictures, and thereby putting some distance between these events and themselves, their trauma may be reduced (Burgess, McCausland & Wolbert 1981). After reviewing and criticising a number of drawing tests, Malchiodi (1998) pointed out that most therapists do not use drawings for assessment purposes but to help children solve problems, express their feelings and to work through situations, memories or emotions that may be troubling them.[13] In fact, the fundamental tenets of art therapy involve communication, control and resolution of emotional conflicts through art-making (American Art Therapy Association 1996).

Many therapists ask children to make a free drawing and/or a drawing of themselves and their family. Although some use the drawings only as a springboard for discussion others will go further, interpreting them in a psycho-dynamic way combined with assumptions from 'folk psychology' rather than from any proven effects based on systematic research. There is a common assumption that a picture is a 'window on the mind' – that, even though a child may not be able to talk about his feelings or what has happened to him, nevertheless this information will be there in a drawing if we know how to 'read' it. As one therapist commented, 'Like dreams they [children's drawings] are an expression of their unconscious mind, something which is not normally accessible' (Wilson 1993, p. 37). It is as

---

[13] The drawings are usually used in conjunction with other techniques and information, such as observations, psychological assessments and self-reports.

if pictures are tapping into our underlying feelings, and that the child cannot help but reveal herself in a drawing. If this assumption were true then drawings would be very helpful to therapists in their efforts to monitor the emotional state of mind of a child.

There are problems with this view. One is the assumption that the child's picture is a direct reflection of what is in his mind. We know that children – and especially young children – do not or cannot draw everything that they know or see (see chapters 4 and 5). If this is the case regarding their physical environment, then it may also be the case regarding their feelings and emotional state. Another problem is that clinicians and therapists may be unfamiliar with the normal development of children's drawings and may misinterpret what they see as an unusual feature or way of drawing but which may be typical for a child of a certain age. Without an understanding of the difficulties and cognitive constraints on picture production, they may not realise that the way something has been drawn may simply be the result of planning problems and lack of space on the paper rather than of any underlying emotional problem. A further issue is that children sometimes copy images from other people (other children, their parents, cartoon figures in comics, etc.). If images have been copied then it would not be clear whose feelings or emotional state the picture reflects. Indeed, the cultural influence on the way children draw is an important consideration (e.g., Wilson 1985; see also chapter 10). It is important, therefore, that therapists become familiar with the literature on children's normal drawing development.

Two examples of children's pictures given to a child psychotherapist and art therapist for comment are shown in figures 11.2 and 11.3; these were published in a magazine for parents (Wilson 1993). The therapist's comments suggest that she did not know who the depicted figures were meant to be but had simply made assumptions about them (Ian has drawn his parents and Michael has drawn his father and himself – and the dog). She emphasises the size differences between the figures and assumes that these differences reflect the children's feelings about the characters and also themselves (based on Löwenfeld and Brittain's 1970 view that the size of figures or particular body parts indicates their emotional importance).

In fact, one figure may be smaller than another because in reality there *is* actually a size difference – between, for example, a small boy and his father. Although the size difference in the picture may be disproportionate, this may be because children at this age are not very good at size-scaling – at getting the relative sizes in proportion (Selfe 1983). The difference in size may also have come about because of lack of planning. If the larger figure was drawn first and has taken up most of the space, then there is less space left for the next figure (Selfe 1983; Thomas & Tsalimi 1988; Henderson & Thomas 1990). At the outset the child may not have intended to draw a second figure and, therefore, may not even have

Figure 11.2 *Commenting on 3-year-old Ian's drawing a therapist said, 'This is a typical drawing for his age consisting of two figures with just a head and a body of sorts. If he's drawn his parents, it could be he feels one parent is much stronger than the other.'*

thought about reserving a place for it. A further problem for the interpretation of the size of the figures is that even when children are asked to draw nice and nasty figures they do not use size consistently to differentiate them (see chapter 7).

Although the therapist in this case did not mention the colour of the drawings,[14] clinicians and therapists often assert that children's choice of colour may be associated with their underlying emotional status. In chapter 7 I reviewed some of the literature which shows that there is a general tendency even among quite young children to link brighter

[14] The original drawings were in colour.

Figure 11.3 *A therapist commented on 5-year-old Michael's drawing, 'The whole drawing smacks of insecurity and if it's a figure of his family with his father in the centre, it looks as though he's represented himself as exceedingly small. This could denote a feeling of helplessness.'*

colours with positive emotions and darker colours with negative ones. Even so, there is also a great deal of individual variation reflecting children's personal experiences. For example, contrary to common assumptions Boyatzis and Varghese (1993) reported that many of their children associated red with excitement and happiness and not with anger or sadness and that black evoked positive emotions in many children. There are dangers, then, in making assumptions about a particular child's use of colour as this may not coincide at all with the therapist's assumptions about the meaning of those colours.

It is often assumed that the drawings of traumatised children will also reflect something of their experiences or feelings. Magwaza and colleagues (1993) asked children in South African townships to draw an event they had experienced in their lives. These children came from areas with on-going civil conflict and violence. Eighty-four per cent of the children drew action figures associated with or engaged in violence and 22 per cent of these drawings depicted the consequences of violence, such as burning houses, corpses and ambulances. In contrast, Wilson (1995) found that refugee children displaced by the fighting in Bosnia either refused to draw soldiers or drew them much smaller than did children in a matched control group of non-refugees. They were happy to draw other topics, such as idealised pictures of their old homes or how they would like to live. In some cases, then, children will depict their bad experiences but in others they will not and seem to want to avoid them or escape from them altogether.

As well as the content of the drawings, researchers have also investigated other aspects. Jolley and Vulic-Prtoric (2001) found no reliable effect of size and proximity when they tested Croatian children aged 7 to 10 years whose fathers had been soldiers in the 1991–5 war. For half the children their fathers had survived, but for the other half they had been killed. The children were first asked to make a portrait of themselves by filling in the details of an outline figure. Next, they were asked to draw a neutral man and then another man, or a Croatian soldier, or an enemy soldier. There was no significant difference between the two trauma groups with regard to the size of the figures or their proximity. It is possible that there was no difference because the children were tested eighteen months after hostilities had ceased. On the other hand, it may be that there simply are no reliable effects of size (see chapter 7) or proximity (see earlier in this chapter).

Another study that failed to find substantial differences is Forrest and Thomas' (1991) study of bereaved children. The drawings of those who had lost a parent or a sibling in the last four years were compared with drawings produced by a control group. The children were asked to draw a person, themselves, their family and a topic of their choice. There were no differences between the two groups when the person and the self drawings were scored according to Koppitz's emotional indicators. There was no difference in the height of the figures drawn by the two groups, or in the size of the free-choice drawings. And, based on the topic of the free-choice drawings, seven judges could not tell any better than chance which were drawn by the bereaved children and which were not. The only significant finding was that all of the bereaved children included themselves in the family drawing whereas only half of the non-bereaved children did so (having just drawn a picture of themselves immediately beforehand). One reason why there may have been almost no significant differences between the drawings of the bereaved children and those of the control children is that the particular measures chosen for investigation by the researchers simply did not discriminate between the two groups. Another reason is that although the bereaved children may have been upset by the death of a family member they may, nonetheless, have made a very good adjustment to this loss and therefore did not draw in a markedly different way from the control children. It remains a possibility, of course, that drawing itself is an activity that fails to show any differences.

According to Jolley (personal communication, 2003), the evidence for children's consistent use of size towards positive or negative topics is most likely to come from case studies in which children are known, for example, to fear a particular illness or a specific person. Golomb (1992) described the human figure drawings of a girl called Ayana during the course of her abdominal illness. Her figures had been normal for a 6-year-old prior to the illness. At the beginning of the illness her figures had large abdomens but when the illness became more advanced Ayana began to draw figures with no torso at all. The suggestion is that the enlarged abdomens of the earlier figures reflected the importance of the abdomen at that time; the later omission of this body part was supposedly a way of minimising or avoiding the seriousness of the problem. Although this interpretation seems plausible, it is only one case study and perhaps a selective one at that. Nonetheless, an issue pointed out by Golomb is that drawing is a personally meaningful process for the child, who expresses some of her thoughts and feelings in her choice of theme, the manner in which she draws her figures, uses colour and structures the composition. We should not necessarily expect to see similarities among the drawings of these children. Although we should take into account the social and cultural context in which a drawing is made, the child's developmental level, her motivation for drawing, her practice with the medium and graphic talent, we should also take seriously the child's own thoughts about her drawing or painting, as she is a privileged informer.

Another particularly distressing trauma is sexual abuse, and when genitalia appear in children's drawings adults may be alarmed and take it as a sign that sexual abuse has actually occurred. Since genitalia appear very infrequently in normal children's drawings[15] (Ames & Ilg 1963; Koppitz 1968; Rosen & Boe 1968; Di Leo 1970 & 1973; Briggs & Lehmann 1989; Cox 1997), Di Leo (1970) assumed that there must be some special reason if a child has included them. One reason could be that abuse has occurred, but other reasons might include a child's concern about bed-wetting or a preoccupation with an impending operation such as circumcision. Even when we know that children have been sexually abused, very few of them depict genitalia in their drawings. Hibbard, Roghmann and Hoekelman (1987) found that only 10 per cent (5 out of 52 cases) of those alleged to have been abused included genitalia, and this was not significantly different from the 2 per cent (1 out of 52) of a comparison group who included them. Interestingly, five of the six children who included genitalia did so on a completion drawing;[16] only one child did so on a free drawing. We cannot say that the inclusion of genitalia in a drawing indicates sexual abuse; on the other hand, their absence does not

---

[15] When genitalia do occur they tend to be in very young children's drawings, that is, those aged below 5 years (Ames & Ilg 1963; Furman 1991).

[16] An outline contour of a human figure was provided for the children to complete.

necessarily mean that a child has not been abused. Various studies of child abuse have severe limitations (see review by Trowbridge 1995). Many have small samples, the drawings have not been collected under controlled conditions and subjective or unsystematic methods of analysis have been employed (e.g., Burgess, McCausland & Wolbert 1981; Goodwin 1982; Kelley 1984; Wohl & Kaufman 1985; Yates, Bentler & Crago 1985). Many studies have not employed a control group, and those that have done so have often not used a suitably matched group; unless groups are similar, except for the sexual abuse, differences cannot reasonably be attributed to sexual abuse itself (Kinard 1994). Frequently, reliability is either not assessed at all or, where this has been done, proves to be low – as low as 42 per cent in a study by Cohen and Phelps (1985). And, of course, there is the problem of projective interpretation, whose limitations I have already pointed out in this chapter.

A major problem with the interpretation of the drawings, then, is that in many cases no differences are found between the drawings of traumatised children and those of control groups, or that the effects are not consistent when, for example, some children choose to draw the objects of their fears whereas others prefer to avoid them. Whether or not there are observable differences between the drawings of distressed and non-distressed children, art therapy may still be a useful way of helping children on the road back to normality. Unfortunately, despite the claims for its efficacy, there are rather few studies that have tested it. Kelley (1984), for example, claimed that although the drawings of children at the start of therapy were frequently of a lower developmental level than expected, they were more age-appropriate at the later stages of therapy. A problem with this claim is that it is not clear how long the children were in therapy and so the changes could have been due to normal drawing development. Males (1990) assessed the effects of art therapy on intellectually disabled males and females, comparing their drawings with those of a control group who had no therapy. Since the drawings of both groups improved over time, it cannot be concluded that the therapy had produced the change. Dalley (1980, 1984) has admitted that research into art therapy, particularly in the UK, has been rather sporadic and unsystematic, but has suggested that a practicable way of obtaining information would be to ask the patient. Although case studies are used as evidence for the efficacy of a treatment, it ought to be possible to devise a more rigorous evaluation.

Using drawings to facilitate children's memory for events

When children are victims or witnesses of a crime they may be interviewed by police officers, social workers or counsellors and may even be required to give evidence in a court of law. Nonetheless, historically, there has been a bias against using the testimony of young children on the grounds that they suffer from illogical thinking and do not sufficiently understand the moral implications of their testimony (Ross, Miller & Moran 1987; Qin et al. 1997). Furthermore, it was argued, they may not be able to recall events accurately or may even make up information. Research studies have shown that children may encode different details of an event compared with adults (King & Yuille 1987) and may have a different perspective on the same event (Leichtman, Ceci & Morse 1997). Children may provide answers that they think will please the interviewer (Ceci & Bruck 1993) or may answer questions that they do not fully understand (Saywitz 2002). Children are also seen as more suggestible than adults (Ceci & Bruck 1993) and their memories more distorted or damaged by suggestive interviews (Qin et al. 1997). They are often regarded as being less credible than adults (Ross et al. 1990), and less weight is assigned to their testimony. Other potential problems are that children may be afraid or embarrassed to verbalise what they have experienced (Saywitz et al. 1991).

Despite all these potential difficulties research studies have demonstrated that children's memory for events increases linearly with age (Goodman & Reed 1986; Baker-Ward et al. 1993; Bates, Ricciardelli & Clarke 1999) and their verbal accounts become more coherent and complex (Fivush, Haden & Adam 1995). It seems, then, that children do possess the competence to be reliable witnesses, and that age is no longer grounds for refusing testimony. However, if children are simply asked to recall as much as they can they may not be very forthcoming. In contrast, they respond better to direct questioning. The problem with this technique, though, is that it results in more errors and could also be seen as 'leading' the witness. It would be useful, then, if we could find other ways to facilitate children's memory for events and their ability to provide relevant information. The use of their drawings is a possibility.

In Butler, Gross and Hayne's (1995) study children visited a fire station and afterwards were asked to recall as much as they could about the visit. Those children who were asked to draw as well as tell their experiences recalled more than those who were simply asked to tell, although this was the case for 5- to 6-year-olds but not for 3- to 4-year-olds. A number of subsequent studies have also found that drawing helped children's recall (Brennan & Fisher 1998; Gross & Hayne 1998; Wesson & Salmon 2001; Jolley, Apperley & Bokhari 2002; Salmon, Roncolato & Gleitzman 2003),[17] including Rowlands' 2003 study, which used a more ecologically valid event, namely a (video-recorded) theft. Drawing and telling not only

---

[17] However, Salmon and Pipe (2000) and Davison and Thomas (2001) found no evidence that drawing aided recall.

increases the amount of recall but it also does not increase the number of errors that children make compared with children who are asked to give a verbal report only. Furthermore, drawing continues to aid recall even when there is a long time gap between the child witnessing an event and then reporting on it (Gross & Hayne 1999). Rowlands found that drawing as well as telling enhanced recall for children as young as 3 and up to age 8 years; in fact, the amount that children recalled when they were able to draw and tell was often comparable to or even greater than the recall of children one or two years older who were asked to give only a verbal report of what they had experienced. Some studies (Brennan & Fisher 1998; Edwards & Forman 1989) have reported improvements up to the age of 10 years, but although drawing has been used in clinical work with teenagers up to age 16 (Pynoos & Eth 1986), further research is needed in order to assess whether drawing actually enhances recall for both teenagers and adults.

An important finding in Rowlands' (2003) research is that drawing aids recall under 'free recall' questioning, whereas it does not appear to do so under direct questioning. This is particularly useful as free recall questioning is less adult-directed and therefore less open to the criticism that children have been given leading questions. It is important to note, though, that younger children (aged 3 years 6 months to 5 years) are only deemed to recall significantly more if the drawings as well as the interview transcripts are available to the adult judges and are included in the scoring process; the older children (aged 6 years 6 months to 8 years) recall more even when their drawings are not part of the scoring process. The point is that the drawings themselves may contain additional information that the children do not verbalise. For example, although a child may say that a particular person in the video had been carrying a bag she may colour the bag red in her drawing; thus, information about the colour of the bag is revealed only in the drawing.

Rowlands also found that children who were asked to draw and tell about their experiences spent longer in the interview than children who were asked to tell only, and the interview duration became longer as age increased. In contrast, children who were asked only for a verbal report spent similar amounts of time in the interview regardless of age. At all ages, the longer the children spent in the free recall phase of the interview, the more correct information they recalled. The representational quality of their drawings was also judged to be better as age increased.

Why does drawing have a facilitative effect on recall? It appears that it encourages children to spend longer in the interview and to produce more detailed pictures, potentially providing more information about the event they have witnessed. The drawing itself may act as a retrieval cue: having drawn one part of an event, this in turn may trigger memories for other aspects (Butler, Gross & Hayne 1995; Gross & Hayne 1998, 1999; Wesson &

Salmon 2001). These cues remain physically present in the picture, enabling children to refer back to it in order to remind themselves of what occurred. Thus, the drawing can be used to cue recall, providing a 'scaffold' (Greenhoot et al. 1999) and reducing the demands of the free recall task, which is reckoned to require high levels of cognitive processing (Gee, Gregory & Pipe 1999).

It seems, then, that drawing is an activity that might be useful not only as a focus for discussion about a child's problems in a clinical or therapeutic setting, but also as an aid to a child's recall of events. Although I have discussed the findings in relation to children's eye-witness testimony, there are also obvious applications in other domains, for example as an aid to understanding and learning in an educational context.

Summary

Various kinds of professional groups ask children to produce drawings which are then used in a number of ways, including the assessment of intelligence and clinical or emotional status. Although the reliability of the scoring of the drawings has generally been found to be high, their validity has not. In fact, the evidence suggests that drawings should not be used instead of the more well-established tests of intelligence and achievement, nor should they be used in addition to them. Similarly, in clinical practice the research evidence does not support the use of drawings as part of the assessment of children's emotional problems. In fact, it is difficult to establish general rules for differentiating between the drawings of normal children and those of children with emotional problems.

Despite this rather negative conclusion there may still be a use for drawings in these contexts. Since drawing is a pleasurable activity for most children, it can be used as a means of establishing rapport in a clinical setting. The drawing itself can also be used as a focus for discussion with a clinician or therapist. Whether or not the activity of drawing helps in the child's improvement or recovery in a therapeutic context is not proven. There are many assumptions about the meaning of children's drawings (and, indeed, adults' as well), but very little evidence. Many of the claims have not been adequately tested, and those that have, have often been found to be unreliable.

Therapists need to understand what is normal in the development of children's drawings, and should take this into account when making an assessment based on a drawing and also judging a child's improvement. It may be that improvement in the drawings over time is simply the normal development of the ability to draw. It is also important to consider that distressed or traumatised children may be functioning at a developmental level lower than their chronological age would suggest. Therefore although their drawings might seem unusual when judged against those of normal children of the same age, they may in fact be normal for a slightly younger child. So, they may be delayed but not aberrant.

A more recent and promising use of children's drawing is as a facilitator for their memory for past events. A number of studies have demonstrated that asking children to draw as well as to give a verbal report produces better recall. This effect seems to hold for children of all ages. There are a number of practical uses for this procedure. For example, children who have been the victim of or a witness to a crime can be helped to give a fuller account if they are asked to draw as well as tell about their experiences. Eliciting greater recall would also be useful in counselling and therapeutic interviews as well as in part of the educational process.

12   Children's art and education

In our education system particular emphasis is placed on literacy and numeracy, and, in the primary school, reading, writing and arithmetic are still the 'core' subjects. If pupils have difficulty with them then this may be a cause for anxiety, and remedial help may be offered. But education is broader than this. Eisner (1989) argued that 'Education is an enterprise whose general aim is to expand the forms of literacy that individuals can employ' (p. 24) and these forms include words, numbers, sounds *and* visual images. Certain meanings are more appropriately expressed in one form than another; each was invented to do something that the others cannot do. Some people – adults and children – may be more responsive than others to particular forms of communication (Moore & Bedient 1986; Riding & Douglas 1993; see also Gardner's, 1993, theory of multiple intelligences). In order to be fully educated, however, all of us need to be able to 'read' and use all these forms and, Eisner (1989) argued, the school curriculum should aim to develop all of them.

Many people, including some art educators, take the view that art should not be formally taught, since this will stifle children's natural creativity and encourage them to produce stereotyped and 'wooden' images. The teacher should do no more than set up a stimulating environment in which the child's artistic creativity can unfold. Others, in contrast, take issue with the notion of a naturally developing child immune from the influences of the culture in which he or she is raised and argue that children are, in any case, influenced by the graphic images they see around them, even if these are not formally taught. They argue that the development of children's artistic ability, like that of most other abilities, is at least in part a *social* as opposed to a lone process. In this chapter I shall outline this debate further and consider the ways in which art is taught in different countries and in schools with different educational philosophies. I shall also consider art as a study skill, particularly in relation to observational drawing. Finally, I shall discuss the teaching of art appreciation in the school curriculum.

Freedom of expression in art

In the late nineteenth century and the first half of the twentieth century art educators and authors such as Cizek (see Viola 1936),

Löwenfeld (1939) and Read (1956) were instrumental in leading a revolt against an earlier, overformal approach to art education in schools. Whereas previously children were required to copy examples from textbooks (see Cox 1992; Korzenik 1995) or from models set up by the teacher, they were now encouraged to work spontaneously and freely. This shift towards freedom of expression was justified on the grounds that it allowed the child's natural talent and imagination to develop,[1] and Kellogg and O'Dell (1967) argued that children should be left untutored and unhindered by adult forms of representation.

One problem with this non-directive approach, however, was that the role of the teacher was reduced to one of 'dispenser of art materials and fountain of emotional support for the child' (Eisner 1976, p. 7). And, according to some, the romantic notion that children will produce original and creative works of art if left alone 'may have kept many children from receiving the kind of art education that might have helped them to develop as artists' (Wilson 1992, p. 23). Hiller (1993) went as far as to say, 'our progressive legacy based upon natural untutored development has resulted in artistic deprivation for generations of students' (p. 35).

Eisner (1972) criticised the non-directive approach on the grounds that it was 'based on the assumption that the child develops best from the inside out[2] rather than from the outside in' (p. 51) and 'seemed to pay scant attention to the fact that a child or adult could be positively as well as negatively influenced by social and cultural factors' (p. 19). Others (e.g., Wilson 1985) also opposed to the rather idealistic view of children's artistic ability developing in a natural and unspoiled way have argued that children pick up ways of drawing from many different sources and that their graphic images are not necessarily the result solely of their own originality and creativity. In fact, according to Wilson and Wilson (1984), in societies where graphic images are very limited children's own repertoires also tend to be limited, which in turn allows them only a restricted means of expressing themselves. Although we would not wish to impose ready-made graphic schemas on children in an authoritarian way, adult intervention might help them resolve some of the problems they encounter when trying to express themselves as well as help them expand their skill, thereby opening up even greater opportunities for expressing their ideas in pictorial form. Anyway, as Kindler (1995) has pointed out, children 'do not grow up in a visual and aesthetic void' (p. 12) but, from the beginning, are exposed to visual images, many of them produced by adults. Furthermore, children's experiences with art occur in a *social* context, as I shall discuss later in this chapter. So, the influence

---

[1] This idea can be traced back to Rousseau (1762/1964) in the eighteenth century.
[2] That is, an innate unfolding of ability as the child grows older.

of adults and adult-produced images is inevitable. What matters, according to Kindler, is not the presence but the quality of this influence.

Influences on children's art

Although there is plenty of evidence that children invent graphic schemas for themselves (when, for example, they use a tadpole form to stand for the human figure) and adapt them to fit their own pictorial requirements (see chapters 4 and 5), there are various sources of influence on the ways that children draw (see chapter 10). For example, children copy from or are taught by other children. Paget (1932) argued that this is one of the main influences on children's drawing and the styles are passed down in the same way that children learn games from other children, without the intervention of adults (Opie & Opie 1969). When Kindler (1994a) observed children aged 3 to 5 years in the classroom she found that the art-making activities of many of them took place in a social context with other children, providing the children with opportunities to observe and talk about their pictures.[3] And when Geiger (1977) included some older children in an 8-year-olds' art group she found that the younger children's drawings took on some of the characteristics of those of the older ones.

It is also clear that in many if not most cultures children are influenced by the graphic images produced by adults – in formal art or craftwork, in the mass media or in pictures drawn for children either spontaneously or on request. For example, Wilson (1992) reported a study in which 5- to 10-year-olds were shown a copy of Munch's *The Scream* (see figure 3.1) and were then asked to draw what happened next. Although no reference was made to the style of the painting, even the 5-year-olds tried to imitate the undulating lines that Munch used. Australian Aboriginal children also see adults using traditional graphic symbols in their paintings, in body painting for ceremonies, in educational materials at school and as illustrations in the sand to accompany their storytelling (Cox & Hill 1996; Cox 1998). The children are not necessarily taught this style of drawing in a formal way, but simply observe what they see and then attempt to produce it in their own artwork. These children also see western styles of depiction, especially when they start school. So, they are exposed to both styles of depiction and will use both of them in their own pictures, sometimes separately but sometimes combining them in the same picture (see figures 10.17 and 10.18).

---

[3] See also Cocking and Copple (1987), Thompson (1999) and Boyatzis and Albertini (2000).

The important influence of images in the mass media was identified by Wilson and Wilson (1977) when they interviewed 147 American teenagers about the source of the graphic images in their pictures; most of the images could be traced to the popular media or 'how to draw' books. Similarly, in Japan many children are influenced by the style of manga comics and films. Indeed, Wilson (1997b, 2000) found that this style was evident in two-thirds of the graphic narratives produced on request by 6-, 8-, 10- and 12-year-old Japanese children. Many art educators and authors, including Arnheim (1978), have decried the influence of popular culture on children's art, believing it to stifle their natural creativity. Others, however, have pointed out that children can learn graphic principles such as foreshortening from these images, and apply them flexibly and in inventive ways in their own work (Wilson & Wilson 1987).

It is clear, then, that children are not isolated from the graphic images available in their environment but readily assimilate them. Their own artistic development does not proceed in a vacuum but is open to 'outside' influences, which include the images produced by other children and by adults.

The support of adults

There is some evidence that a completely non-interventionist approach may result in very young children being uninterested in art. For example, Kindler (1995) observed that although art materials were plentiful in one particular daycare centre for children below the age of 3 years, the children rarely experimented with them unless a teacher was present and became involved in what the children were doing. This was in stark contrast to the children's more spontaneous involvement in the housekeeping corner and the car-racing area. This observation led Kindler to speculate that the mere availability of materials is not sufficient to stimulate young children's art-making and that adult input may be essential.

Many art educators, however, are uneasy with the idea of adults intervening further than merely providing the appropriate materials and giving general encouragement. As they see it, adult input might result in children copying adult drawings, which in turn will lead to the production of their own stereotyped images. Löwenfeld and Brittain (1970), for example, exhorted parents and teachers not to allow their children to copy anything. Although I would not wish to advocate a diet of copying, copying does not necessarily lead to stereotyped images, as Pariser (1979) found when he made a freehand and enlarged copy of Dürer's *Rhinoceros* and asked children (aged 8 to 9 years) to use it as an aid when illustrating Kipling's story, 'How the Rhinoceros got his Skin'. There was great diversity in the children's pictures, with some concentrating on the m features of the animal (e.g., its bulk, the horns, the texture of the sk and others experimenting with the graphic devices in the picture, such cross-hatching and stippling. Pariser did not explicitly ask the childr to copy the rhinoceros and neither did they, rather, they used t picture as a stimulus or starting point for expressing their own idea. As Matthews (1999) points out, 'Children simply do not copy what is already there, but bring something new to these exemplars' (p. 157). Copying involves children in a detailed examination of the structure of a drawing. It does not necessarily result in an imposed adult image, but can enable children to discover new ways of drawing that they can then use and develop for their own purposes. Until quite recently it has been common for artists, as part of their training, to copy the work of established artists, but this has not prevented them from finding and pursuing their own style, although this can sometimes be a difficult process (Gombrich 1960).

Luquet (1927/2001) believed that adult intervention is perhaps unnecessary up until about the age of 11, when children become concerned with visual realism and are keen to learn about it. When they seek help themselves they will be keener to implement it than if it is imposed on them. It seems to be the case that without tuition most children and, indeed, most adults do not develop their representational skills in art much beyond that acquired in late childhood. Kindler (1992), though, has evidence that dissatisfaction with their own pictorial productions is common among children as young as 6 or 7 years. At whatever age children express dissatisfaction, it seems to me that adult intervention is appropriate, especially if children explicitly seek it.

Learning within a social context is the central assumption of Vygotsky's (1962, 1978) approach to children's development. Although development depends on the child's current competence, this competence also interacts with the support provided by others. Vygotsky notes that the child is accelerated in his achievements if helped by adults or older children, compared with his achievement if left to struggle with problem-solving on his own, a difference Vygotsky described as the *zone of proximal development*. The effective teacher will guide the child by asking questions, making suggestions and generally leading the child towards solving a particular problem but without giving him the solution in an authoritarian kind of way; usually the instruction will be phased so that, at the beginning, the teacher will have high involvement but this will be reduced as the child 'takes off' on his own.

Many studies have provided evidence in support of Vygotsky's approach, which is sometimes referred to as 'scaffolding' (Bruner 1964; Wood, Bruner & Ross 1976). For example, Wood and Middleton (1975) showed how 4-year-olds could, at first, construct a set of wooden blocks only with help from an adult (usually their mothers) but that gradually this help was diminished as their performance improved. A study by Freund (1990) showed that children as young as 3 years improved in their ability to classify objects when they worked inter-actively with their mothers compared with children who worked alone (even though they received feedback on their performance). Thus, tuition can be said to take place, but it is not in the form of overt and didactic instruction. Indeed, Rogoff (1990, 1998; also Rogoff et al. 1993) argued that cognitive growth is shaped as much if not more by informal adult–child transactions – which she calls 'guided participation' – as by formal teaching or educational experiences. It should be stressed, how-ever, that it is not simply a matter of the adult's facilitating the abilities in the child that would have developed anyway; rather, the child's abilities would not have developed *without* this interaction (Lock et al.1989).

In the domain of drawing, Yamagata (1997) has noted how, in a shared drawing task, mothers will talk not only about the topic of the drawing but also about the method of drawing and the relationship between the drawing and the object it represents (see also Boyatzis 2000; Braswell 2001). Pemberton and Nelson (1987) found that their preschool children benefited from mutual drawing sessions with an adult, where the adult gradually introduced more complex figures as she and the child drew together on the same page. The children's own drawings improved compared with those they had completed in a pretest and compared with those of another group who simply had the encour-agement of the adult while they were drawing by themselves. The authors suggested that the children in this first group benefited from seeing more complex images than they themselves could draw, but also that it was the interactive experience of the process that was mainly responsible for the improvement in their representational skills. Matthews (1999) has also emphasised the way in which his own children's drawings were frequently assisted by discussions with their parents about pictures and about how they 'work'. He believes that adult–child interaction is crucial for development and that children's art does not develop very far without interpersonal support.

So, how exactly can or should adults – especially teachers – engage with children in their art-making? Although many art educators are comfortable with the idea of encouraging children and discussing their ideas and intentions, they may still worry about their interference in a process which they may believe should be spontaneous. As Freeman (1990) has noted, 'It seems to be the case that the closer one gets to the chalk face – the children producing marks on the page – the more resistance one finds among many educators to a joint enterprise approach' (p. 54).

Approaches to art education at different times and in different places

In the UK, as in many other countries, there have been changes in the school art curriculum over time. In the late nineteenth and early twentieth centuries lessons were very formal, with a lot of emphasis on technique and a considerable amount of copying. Later, particularly from the 1950s onwards, a laissez-faire approach took over. Wilson and Ligtvoet (1992) compared children's drawings in the 1930s and in the 1980s and found that the earlier drawings were more detailed and were drawn with more care, perhaps reflecting the expectations of teachers at that time (see figures 12.1 and 12.2).

More recently, since the early 1990s, art (actually, art and design) has become obligatory and more structured, and has been designated a 'foundation subject' in the English National Curriculum (DFE 1995; DFE&E 1999a & 1999b), with its own formalised programme outlining the aims and expectations for teaching art to children from 5 to 14 years in state schools.[4] Some art educators, such as Herne (1996), have complained that there is a bias towards figural rather than non-figural art, and that observational drawing is particularly prominent. Nonetheless, many primary school teachers have welcomed the programme on the grounds that it gives serious consideration to art and design in the curriculum (Clement 1994). Some, however, who are not art specialists, have found the requirements of the programme too vague and have expressed uncertainty about their ability to teach it. Indeed, Clement found that over 61 per cent of headteachers felt that their staff would need further support and 55 per cent of the teachers themselves said they would need extra guidance. When Sweden underwent a similar change in its art curriculum most teachers, particularly at the primary level, did not change their practices but continued to treat art as an opportunity for pupils to relax and use their imagination rather than as a challenging activity; many felt that their training in art education was inadequate (Lindström 1997).

As well as changes in approaches to art teaching over time we also see variation in the school curricula for art in different countries and, often, between regions within a country. Some countries have a 'hands-off' approach; others provide general guidelines and suggestions; yet others have a very detailed and prescriptive curriculum. China is an example of a formal and prescriptive approach, although this varies somewhat among different regions (Lowry & Wolf 1988; Winner 1989; Cox 1992). In Nanjing up until at least the 1990s teachers would demonstrate how to

---

[4] Interestingly, the art curriculum for primary schools was soon slimmed down in order to give more time to raise standards of literacy and numeracy (Prentice 1999).

Figure 12.1 *Dutch children's drawings of two girls picking apples, 1937 (Wilson & Ligtvoet 1972).*

draw particular objects. For example, in the panda lesson (see figure 12.3) the teacher would give step-by-step instructions on the blackboard. The children were then asked to draw their own pandas using the dotted examples in their art book as a guide. After that, they might be allowed to draw their own 'free' versions. In this way the children were given detailed instructions on how to draw a schema for each object. We see in Chinese children's drawings a certain stylised way of drawing

Figure 12.2 *Dutch children's drawings of two girls picking apples, 1986 (Wilson & Ligtvoet 1972).*

that appears to reflect the kinds of schema they have been taught (see plates 4 to 6).

   Not all Chinese schools employ such a rigid way of teaching, although their art lessons are usually more structured than those in European and North American schools. In Beijing in 1995 I observed a number of art

Figure 12.3 The panda lesson, *from a Chinese primary school textbook.*

lessons given by an art specialist in a state primary school. Each lesson had a clear aim, such as the depiction of movement or the blending or contrast of colours. In one lesson with 7-year-olds the teacher began by writing the name of the topic (e.g., swimming) on the blackboard and then talked about and demonstrated arm and leg movements associated with different kinds of swimming strokes. She chose a few children to draw figures on the blackboard, while the rest of the class started to make their own drawings on paper using felt-pens. The teacher moved around the class making comments and giving encouragement to individuals. Then she interrupted the class's activities in order to discuss and make critical points about the drawings on the blackboard. Towards the end of the lesson she showed the children some pictures on the same topic drawn by another class (see plate 4). Over the course of a school term the children might complete ten pictures, each of which would be awarded a grade and then the child would be given an average grade in art for that term.

The Chinese approach emphasises technical proficiency even for quite young children.[5] And this is for a very sound reason. Teachers believe that without technical proficiency children cannot be creative – they cannot give pictorial form to their ideas. The notion, often expressed in the West,

---

[5] Jolley (personal communication, 2004) has reported that the recently (2002) revised art curriculum in Kunming now includes more expressive and creative drawing for 3- to 6-year-olds, although there is still considerable emphasis on copying what the teacher draws.

that children should be left to their own devices without interference from adults was greeted with amazement and derision. Copying and reproducing traditional images is seen as a legitimate activity in order to learn particular techniques.[6] However, it became clear during my school visits that Chinese children do not solely depend on copying adults' two-dimensional figures. They also draw three-dimensional objects from observation as well as pictures completely from their imagination.

In the same way as not all Chinese art education is as rigid as some people believe, so in the West lessons are not necessarily as free as we might expect. Although most primary school teachers in the UK are not art specialists, many give advice about technique even though this tends to be transmitted to individual children in an informal way rather than to the class as a whole. Children in British classrooms also observe and draw three-dimensional objects, and sometimes may be encouraged to look carefully and copy from pictures in books. So, the teaching approach in the UK cannot be described as completely laissez-faire.

It is difficult to assess whether these different emphases in art education have differential effects on children's artwork. We can certainly see differences in the *styles* of drawing between different countries. For example, when Cox, Perara and Xu (1999) asked five judges to guess which of a randomly shuffled pile of pictures of a scene had been drawn by British children (aged 6 to 13 years) and which by Chinese children they found this a relatively easy task; just over 92 per cent of the pictures were correctly allocated. The scene had been drawn from imagination but included the following items: the sun shining in the sky, birds flying, and a house on a hill with a garden that has trees and flowers growing in it. Another set of judges was asked to specify the differences in the styles of the pictures produced by children aged 7, 10 and 13 years. They said that the British children tended to focus on the house whereas the Chinese children drew a wider landscape, often with many hills. The Chinese pictures also tended to be more detailed and colourful, and had a greater sense of depth (see plates 5 and 6).

Although there might be noticeable differences in style between the drawings produced in two different cultures, can one set of drawings be judged to be better than another? When Cox, Perara and Xu (1998, 1999) compared the pictures drawn by children (aged 6 to 13 years) in state schools in the UK and in China they found no systematic differences between the children's pictures of the scene drawings described above. There were also no significant differences in the drawings of a person or of a horse drawn from imagination and also from models. The pictures were rated by two British art advisers and a Chinese researcher familiar with

---

[6] Pariser (1991, 1997) points out that, for the Chinese, the question of originality is much less important than the lifelike quality or *ch'i* of the image.

children's drawings. Each picture was rated on a five-point scale where 1 = very poor, and 5 = excellent. There was good inter-rater reliability among the scores awarded by these raters. No specific criteria were given to the judges since, as in previous research (Cox, Eames & Cooke 1994; Cox, Cooke & Griffin 1995), judges rated pictures similarly even when a general instruction was given. When asked to write down the criteria they thought they were using the judges mentioned similar things – a sense of vitality of the object in question, the shape of its different parts and their interrelationships, the amount of detail, proportions, composition, representation of occlusion, three-dimensionality, and maturity, confidence and originality of the drawing.

Also included in this study was a group of children (also aged 6 to 13 years) attending, for half a day, a private weekend art school in Beijing; they went to normal state primary schools during the week. For their drawings from imagination as well as from observation these children gained higher scores – usually significantly higher – than did the children in state schools in both the UK and China (see plates 5 and 6). This pattern was maintained across the age range. A set of five judges compared the pictures of the scene drawn by the state school children and the weekend art school children. They noticed that the scenes drawn by the art school children were more life-like, more realistically coloured, were better composed and better proportioned; they also contained more depth cues. Our subsequent analyses of depth cues showed that the most frequently used were the partial occlusion of one object by another and, to a lesser extent, attempts to show the side as well as the front of the house. The art school children used these depth cues more and at a younger age than the children in state schools (both in China and the UK). Interestingly, relatively few children, particularly below the age of 10 years, indicated depth by diminishing the size of objects in the picture (see also chapter 6).

The weekend art school children receive more tuition than children who do not attend, and this tuition includes a greater range of techniques and styles. The classes are taught by art specialists and are just as formal as in state schools. Of course, it is not possible to say that the children's high artistic ability is the result of this extra tuition, as these children are likely to be more highly motivated and may already possess greater aptitude for art than those who do not attend.

Whereas we found no significant differences between the drawings of children in state schools in the UK or China, a cross-cultural study comparing the figure drawings of 7- and 11-year-old children in the UK and in Japan did reveal differences (Cox et al. 2001).[7] The raters were both British and Japanese. On two of the tasks (a man standing still and facing

---

[7] See also Toku (2002), who compared the drawing skills of children in Japan and those in the USA.

the viewer, and a man running to the right) the Japanese children's drawings were rated more highly than those produced by the British children for both age groups. On the third task (a man running towards the viewer), the drawings of the Japanese children received higher ratings than those of the British children, although this difference was not significant except for girls at age 7. Although the drawings by the Japanese children generally received higher ratings, they were not different from the British children's drawings in terms of the way different body parts were drawn, for example, whether the arms and legs were drawn symmetrically or asymmetrically, or whether the limbs were foreshortened. So, the Japanese children did not construct their figures in a different way but, nevertheless, they drew them more skilfully (see figure 12.4).

It is, of course, difficult to identify what might be the cause of the difference in ratings. It is unlikely to be a formal way of teaching,[8] since no significant differences were found in the study comparing children's pictures in the UK and in China, although the lessons in Beijing turned out to be not as prescriptive as we had been led to believe. One influence that might be important in Japan is the prevalence of manga comics throughout Japanese society. Children of all ages – and adults – not only read these comics but many also use the manga images as models for their own drawings (Wilson 1997b, 2000). However, we can only speculate about the reasons for the difference in the ratings of the drawings between the two countries, as it is very difficult if not impossible to control all possible variables when conducting a cross-cultural study. For example, although we assume that differences in art ability (or the abilities that underpin them) among different cultures are not innate, we cannot rule this out.

A comparison can be made, however, between different approaches to art teaching within one country. For example, Cox and Rowlands (2000) compared the drawing ability of children in Steiner, Montessori and traditional schools in the UK. Care was taken to ensure that each school was a good exemplar of its avowed educational approach. The focus in the Steiner philosophy is on 'artistic imagination', with an emphasis on expression and fantasy (Steiner 1965; Edmunds 1975; Ginsburg 1982; Wilkinson 1993; Meighand 1995). Montessori (1912, 1918, 1965) education focusses more on reality, and encourages copying and observational drawing and discourages fantasy.[9] The approach of traditional schools lies somewhere in between. Children (aged 6 to 7 years) in these different

[8] Although art lessons in Japan are not as formal as some of those observed in China, children in Japan are issued, each year, with a new art textbook in which they can see examples of children's work and also those of famous artists. Pupils are not necessarily expected to copy these images, but they are available as models for their own work.

[9] However, today's Montessori schools allow for increased provision of art in the curriculum compared with the original approach (e.g., Merz 1996; Schneider 1996).

	UK		Japan	
	7-year-olds	11-year-olds	7-year-olds	11-year-olds
Task 1. Man standing and facing the viewer	Mean score: 2.5	Mean score: 4.75	Mean score: 3.25	Mean score: 4.75
Task 2. Man running towards the right	Mean score: 3	Mean score: 4.25	Mean score: 3.25	Mean score: 5
Task 3. Man running towards the viewer	Mean score: 2.5	Mean score: 3.5	Mean score: 3	Mean score: 5

Figure 12.4 *Typical examples of 7- and 11-year-olds' human figure drawings by British and Japanese children. The drawings were rated on a 1–5 scale (Cox, Koyasu, Hiranuma & Perara 2001).*

schools were asked to complete three drawings: a free drawing from imagination, a scene from imagination (using the same instructions as described above for the British–Chinese study) and an observational drawing (a model man in a running pose).

When the drawings were rated independently by two raters, the Steiner children's free and scene drawings received the highest ratings (see plates 7 and 8). There was no significant difference between the ratings of the Montessori and traditional children in the free drawing but, in the scene drawing, the traditional children scored higher than the Montessori children. The raters noted that the Steiner children's drawings tended to fill the whole page and did not leave an air gap.[10] Steiner drawings were more detailed and colourful, with more use of shading. As expected, the Steiner children included more fantasy items in their free drawings.

Given the emphasis on observational drawing in Montessori schools, we expected that these children would achieve higher scores on the observational drawing task. But, in fact, the Steiner children received the highest scores and those for the other two schools were not significantly different. The raters noted that the Steiner figures were more in proportion and that there was a tendency for Steiner children to use shading (often building up an image with shading rather than with outlines) and to use line as a contour rather than to construct the figure in segments. This result is surprising since the Steiner children had had no practice in observational drawing. However, they seemed to spend more time looking at the model, ensuring that their pictures were as accurate as possible; the Montessori children and the traditional children appeared not to concentrate on the model and often drew stereotyped schemas. It is possible that the Steiner children's normal attention to detail in illustrating and decorating their schoolwork generalised to this new task. Also, it may be that they were interested in the observational task because it was new to them and, consequently, attended more carefully to the instructions.

The emphasis on art in Steiner schools and the greater amount of artistic training among Steiner teachers may have accounted for the Steiner children's superior drawing ability. However, since Steiner teachers claim not to give direct tuition in drawing it could be that the main influence is their positive attitude towards art, regarding it not just as a 'filler activity' (Hargreaves & Galton 1992) but as integral to most aspects of the curriculum, and their expectation that the children's artwork will be of a high standard. We should be cautious, however, in jumping to the conclusion that the children's artistic ability is the direct result of the Steiner approach to art education. Although this may be the case, it is also likely that Steiner schools attract more artistically minded parents who nourish artistic creativity in their own children. Since the children in schools advocating different educational approaches have not been randomly assigned to them but have been self-selected, we cannot know whether the educational approach itself is having a causal effect.

We can see differences in style between children's pictures completed at different historical times, in different countries and in schools with

---

[10] The air-gap refers to the space between the sky and the ground, often left blank in young children's drawings (Hargreaves, Jones & Martin 1981; Lewis 1990; Cox & Chapman 1995).

different educational approaches. In some cases the pictures produced in one culture or approach have been judged superior to those in another. The reasons for these differences are not clear. It is difficult to conclude that they are the result of the different art education approaches themselves since, inevitably, the studies cannot control for all relevant influences. Indeed, they are unlikely to be the result of a more formal approach since Chinese children in state schools, where art education is very formal, are not judged to be better artists than state school children in the UK. Moreover, children at Steiner schools in the UK, where art education is very informal, are judged to be better artists than their peers in state or Montessori schools. It is my guess that the most positive factors influencing children's artwork are in fact a very encouraging and creative attitude towards art on the part of teachers and parents as well as the children themselves. This would explain the excellent art work produced by many Chinese children at weekend art schools, Japanese children brought up in the pervading culture of manga comics, and British children in Steiner schools which encourage the artistic imagination.

Assessing the effectiveness of art teaching

There are many different approaches to art education and an enormous number of books to help teachers apply them (e.g., Smith 1983, 1998; Clement 1993; Gentle 1993; Matthews 2003). Many teachers may approve a particular approach on an intuitive and personal basis, that is, if the children's experiences and their artwork seem to confirm the teachers' expectations then they will be content to continue with their chosen approach. A way that we could be more certain that an approach has a *causal* effect on what children produce is by randomly allocating individual children or classes of children to different kinds of teaching programme. We would then know that any differences in the children's artwork would be due to the different programmes and could not be due to any inherent differences in a particular group relating to culture or parental influences.

This experimental method has been used to assess the effects of 'negotiated drawing', an approach to representational drawing devised by Cooke (1986), originally for teaching children aged 5 to 7 years. The children are engaged in conversation with the teacher about a particular topic, which might be a very realistic one, such as 'How to fry and egg', or a fantasy theme, such as 'The dancing skeleton' (Cooke, Griffin & Cox 1998). Other activities might also be included such as drama, storytelling and problem-solving. For example, the skeleton lesson was originally devised for a class of children who had been studying bones and had also been involved in some drama relating to a series of amusing books

Figure 12.5 The skeleton lesson, *using the negotiated drawing approach (Cox, Cooke & Griffin 1995)*.

about a family of skeletons. The lesson begins with children being introduced to a life-size inflatable skeleton. The teacher invites the children to help him draw the skeleton on the blackboard by giving verbal guidance. Through careful questioning on the teacher's part the children examine the shapes of the skeleton, their relationship to each other and their proportions. The teacher also makes deliberate errors in order to draw attention to ambiguities in the children's instructions or to relationships they have not yet noticed (see figure 12.5).

The skeleton is then placed within an imaginative 'frame'. In one case he is sad because he has forgotten how to dance, and the children are invited to teach him. When they are asked to draw a picture showing how they taught the skeleton to dance, the children can refer back to the real skeleton and are allowed to alter the position of its limbs to help them make their picture. The teacher's drawing, which was not necessarily completed, is erased from the blackboard so that the children cannot copy it. What this approach does *not* do is to impose a particular schema on the children or to prematurely teach conventions such as 'perspective'. Rather, the teacher focusses on the process of observing objects and the way that shapes can be 'extracted'[11] and used in children's own pictures. In essence, it is an approach designed to help teachers and children engage together with the *process of drawing* as an enjoyable but challenging activity.

In order to evaluate the effectiveness of this approach a set of ten lessons was given to classes of children aged 5 to 7 (Cox, Eames & Cooke 1994; Cox, Cooke & Griffin 1995). In one condition, Cooke, an artist and advisory art teacher, gave the lessons himself, using the negotiated drawing approach. In a second condition, the ten lessons were delivered by a

[11] However, Arnheim (1997) has emphasised that the child does not so much extract or select from the observed facts but, rather, *creates equivalents* of them.

'supply' teacher who, like Cooke, was also a visitor to the schools; she was a non-art specialist who had been trained to use the negotiated drawing approach. We wanted to see whether the negotiated drawing approach could be used effectively by a non-art specialist. In a third condition, Cooke gave the same ten lessons but used a 'normal' teaching approach, that is, using the same objects and scene-setting devices but omitting the attention to the drawing process itself. In a final condition, children were given a set of ten lessons by their class teachers along normal[12] lines. There were two classes of children in each of these four conditions.

At the beginning of the study the children were assessed for non-verbal reasoning (Raven, Court & Raven 1990) and drawing ability (a human figure drawing scored according to the Goodenough–Harris system and the Koppitz developmental items – see chapter 11). They were also asked to complete three drawings: an observational drawing of a telephone, a drawing entitled *Brushing your teeth* and another entitled *A strange zoo*. These drawings were rated on a five-point scale. There were no significant differences among the conditions on any of these measures.

Although children in three of the experimental conditions had lessons on the same ten topics, the children who were taught by their class teachers only had two lessons the same as the others – the magic bicycle and daffodils – and the other eight lessons were on topics of the class teacher's choice. Consequently, direct comparisons across all four conditions could only be made with these two topics; in addition, however, all children had completed drawings on the same three topics at the beginning and at the end of the study. The judges were three school art advisers. Using a five-point scale they independently rated each drawing. Agreement among them was very high: for example, 90 per cent of the telephone drawings received exactly the same rating from all three judges or the same rating from two judges with the third judge only one category rating apart.

In order to conclude that the negotiated drawing approach is effective higher scores should be awarded to the drawings produced in the lessons taught by Cooke and by the supply teacher, and lower scores to the pictures produced in lessons taught in a more traditional way. Although the differences between the conditions were not always significant they were generally in this predicted direction. This result not only applied to the magic bicycle (see figure 12.6) and daffodil (see figure 12.7) drawings but also generalised to the three drawings completed at the end of the study (the same tasks which were also given at the beginning of the study – an observational drawing of a telephone (see figure 12.8), a drawing entitled *Brushing your teeth* and another entitled *A strange zoo*).

[12] A common way that teachers teach art is to tell a story or incident, often related to a classroom project, or to use interesting or dramatic objects as stimuli. But the teacher rarely focusses on the observation of objects or on the drawing process itself.

Figure 12.6 The magic bicycle. *On a 1–5 scale the judges rated the upper drawing 1 and the lower drawing 5 (Cox, Cooke & Griffin 1995).*

The 'negotiated drawing' approach is consistent with the ideas of Vygotsky outlined earlier in this chapter. It is also consistent with some of Luquet's (1927/2001) ideas. For example, in discussing the ways that teaching could be effective in relation to drawing, Luquet argued that suggestions should not be made overtly but, rather, that adults should draw in front of the children, making deliberate mistakes, and should then talk about their reasons for correcting those mistakes. But any intervention should not destroy the child's spontaneous enjoyment of drawing. Of course, our study was only of modest proportions, comparing only one approach with normal art teaching. Critics may also argue that the

Figure 12.7 Daffodils. *On a 1–5 scale the judges rated the upper drawing 1 and the lower drawing 5 (Cox, Cooke & Griffin 1995).*

assessments focussed solely on the drawings themselves and ignored the children's experiences during the process. Despite these criticisms an experimental research method is able to provide objective evidence regarding the efficacy of different approaches to art teaching.

Observational drawing in the curriculum

In the mid-nineteenth century Ruskin (1857) espoused the value of drawing, believing that it teaches us how to notice things rather than

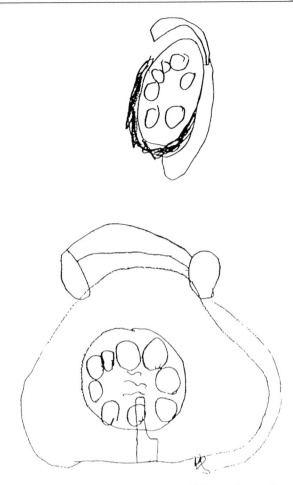

Figure 12.8 Telephone. *A 6-year-old boy's observational drawings before and after the programme of negotiated drawing lessons (Cox, Cooke & Griffin 1995).*

how merely to look, and that, in recreating the objects in pictorial form, it gives us a deeper (and conscious) understanding of their details and construction.[13] Luquet (1927/2001), like Ruskin, argued that one of the main roles of the drawing activity is that it helps develop a sense of observation. The observation of the objects involves the creation and refinement of children's internal models. In fact, Luquet claimed, drawing in an *intellectually realistic* way (see chapter 5) encourages a sense of

---

[13] The relationship between drawing something and knowing it remains an important idea (see Rosand 2002).

observation; since it involves drawing the invariant shape of objects it forces the child to look closely at things and to mentally 'dissect' them. Van Sommers (1995) also takes the view that 'Unless we draw from life regularly, we do not necessarily store information about objects in our memory in a way that is optimally useful for drawing' (pp. 46–7). He gives the example of a bicycle: even though we might know how to ride it, we might not have a detailed visual image of its constituent parts and how they are linked together. Indeed, van Sommers reports that objects such as bicycles are 'notoriously badly drawn' (p. 45), with intelligent adults depicting them with the chain directly joining the front and rear wheels. Some authors (e.g., Edgerton 1980) argue for the importance of drawing not only in helping us to understand things but also to help us think out problems, such as when Leonardo da Vinci, in his notebooks, seemed to be solving mechanical problems through drawing. As well as being an aid to observation, understanding and problem-solving, drawing may also help us to remember things and become better able to recall them (see chapter 11). There are many claims for the benefits of drawing, not least that it is 'the essential, core activity in art and design education, without which it is impossible to achieve meaningful work of quality' (Clement 1992, p. 121).

Since talented drawers have enhanced visual attentional abilities and visual memories (see chapter 9), perhaps these tendencies could be encouraged in less-talented drawers. Some art educators (e.g., Thistlewood 1992) have claimed that observational drawing is of prime value within an art and design curriculum and, indeed, it is given high priority in the English National Curriculum (DFE 1995; DFE&E 1999a & 1999b). Drawing from observation is important because it 'introduces children to a convention of representational image making which involves careful looking, critical thinking and decision making' (Cooke, Griffin & Cox 1998, p. 3). One of my students (Robinson 2002) compared the drawings of 11-year-olds who were given practice at observational drawing with those of another group who drew from imagination. At the beginning of the study both groups drew two pictures from imagination – a man and a bicycle – and there was no significant difference between the groups in the ratings of the drawings.[14] On each of the next three days the children in the 'observation' group drew from a model man and a real bicycle; the 'imagination' group drew these same topics from imagination. Finally, both groups drew the man and the bicycle from imagination.

---

[14] The judges (two undergraduate students, a secondary school art teacher and a primary school art specialist) used a five-point rating scale. They agreed exactly on 77 per cent of the drawings and were within one point of each other for the remaining 23 per cent.

Figure 12.9 *Drawing a bicycle from imagination. Left: a 10-year-old boy's pretest and post-test drawings both scored 3 (on a 1–5 scale); they did not improve after three sessions of drawing from imagination. Right: an 11-year-old girl's drawings improved from 3 to 4.5; she had had three sessions of drawing from observation. (From Robinson 2002.)*

The ratings for the observational drawings were higher than for the original imaginative drawings. The ratings for the observational drawings also increased over the three sessions, whereas those drawn from imagination did not. The observation group's final drawings, which were produced from imagination, received higher ratings than those of the imagination group. In fact, the drawings in the imagination group did not improve. So, not only did the drawings from observation improve with practice but the children also transferred this improvement when they were asked to draw again from imagination (see figure 12.9).

Although observation may help children to see more details in the objects and scenes themselves and, as Luquet (1927/2001) pointed out, although intellectual realism is a particularly good system for showing all these details, there is a problem when children want to draw in a visually realistic way. One of the main features of visual realism is that it takes a particular point of view *vis-à-vis* the scene and attempts to reproduce something that approximates the image projected on to the eye. Although linear convergence perspective is not the only system that children may want to learn, it produces very powerful visual and spatial effects in a picture. To be able to draw in this way is part, and arguably an important part, of an artist's repertoire of skills.

Many teachers believe that children will adopt visual realism if they simply look more carefully at the scene. Edwards (1986, 1992), however, realised that this is not enough. Despite her exhortations her students complained that even though they were looking carefully at an object they still could not draw it to their satisfaction. The reason is that, as Ruurs (1987) points out, seeing and drawing are not the same thing: 'An artist drawing after nature must reduce three dimensions to two: this involves a process that does not occur in the course of normal observation' (p. 6). Thus, children, and indeed adults, may need special help to achieve their goal.

Edwards (1986, 1992) describes a number of ways in which students can be encouraged to look at the model itself and not fall back on stereotyped images.[15] One such procedure is to focus intently on the model's edges and slowly to trace the contour on paper. Another is to concentrate on the spaces within and around a model (a chair, for example) rather than on the structure itself. Edwards claimed that, over a number of weeks, adult students who used these techniques improved their visually realistic drawings. Edwards also advocates the use of a perspective frame if students wish to draw exactly what they see from a fixed viewpoint. Perspective frames of various designs have been used by many renowned artists, such as Leonardo da Vinci, Dürer and van Gogh (see illustrations in Cox 1992). A *camera obscura* is thought to have been used by Vermeer in the seventeenth century; this device helps render the details of the subject matter more accurately. The *camera lucida* projects an image of the object on to the drawing paper by means of a four-sided prism and may have been used by Ingres in the early nineteenth century. Since the introduction of photography many artists also use photographs to help them in the process of picture-making. And, more recently, computer graphics programs have been used by a wide variety of people, such as architects, designers and artists. Children can also use them. For example, Olsen (1992) taught children aged 3 to 7 years to draw a scene of a house, garden and sky with a computer drawing program. Even 3-year-olds could manipulate and alter the icons (such as a rectangle) on the screen. This enables children to draw shapes more accurately than they could do by hand, and to make corrections with ease.[16]

Although some art educators, such as Kellogg and O'Dell (1967), object to drawing from observation on the grounds that it 'may stifle the pride, the pleasure, the confidence so necessary to the growth of a creative spirit' (p. 17), this view is not shared by all. And, indeed, Milbrath (1995) argues

[15] Edwards claimed that in order to draw successfully in a visually realistic way we need to tap into right-hemisphere skills (seeing an object as a configuration of lines and shapes on a flat surface) and bypass the tendency to name and categorise the object (a predominantly left-hemisphere activity), which tends to trigger stereotyped schemas (Bremner & Moore 1984; Cox 1989; Lee 1989). See also Springer and Deutsch (1989).

[16] Other researchers (e.g., English 1987; Matthews & Jessel 1993) have taught young children to use computer paintbox programs.

that 'drawing accurately what one sees represents technical mastery over line and form' and technical mastery is 'a skill most children who draw find motivating' (p. 103). The introduction of computer programs may also seem to many people a step in the wrong direction in that it might result in picture-making becoming too mechanistic. But it can also be seen simply as artists taking advantage of whatever technology is available to help them, just as they have always done. Commenting on the use of computers in art, the artist Richard Hamilton (interviewed by Buck 2003) has pointed out that they are a tool, just as oil paint or photography are tools, but that with a computer program it is easier to manipulate the images. Rather than leading people away from traditional methods of drawing, David Hockney (interviewed by Rothschild 2003) believes that computer graphics programs are highly motivating and may lead people back to conventional drawing.

Teaching art appreciation

Around fifty years ago Herbert Read (1956) proposed that the art curriculum should include appreciation of art as well as drawing and painting from observation and for self-expression. However, unless teachers, particularly in primary schools, happened to be interested in art this aspect of art education was rarely explored. Now, though, the National Curriculum in England (DFE&E 1999a & 1999b) includes the requirement that children should have knowledge and understanding of the work of famous artists, craftsmen and designers from different times and in different cultures. They should be able to see these works, preferably in the original but more likely as reproductions, and be able to examine the styles of different artists, their techniques and the way they have interpreted various kinds of subject matter. Even so, the teachers' choice of which adult artworks are shown to the children is dominated by the availability of materials in the school. Clement (1997) found that there is actually quite a narrow range of pictures available, mostly by nineteenth- and twentieth-century artists. The most frequently used for children of all ages are pictures by van Gogh, Picasso, Monet and Matisse.

Clement also found that from the teachers' point of view the main aim of introducing children to adult artists' work is to help them learn about different aspects of picture-making such as colour, pattern and texture, line, and so on, which they can then apply to their own art-making. In order to facilitate an understanding of artists' techniques children are often encouraged to reproduce a certain artist's style or to incorporate it in their own interpretations of the subject matter. So, for example, children might examine a reproduction of Picasso's *Guernica*, discussing with the teacher the circumstances which gave rise to the picture (the horrific bombing of civilians) and the emotions it conveys, as well as the techniques Picasso used. The children are then encouraged to use the techniques themselves, such as limiting the colour range to black and white and intermediate greys in order to explore the use of tone for dramatic effect (see McInally 2003).

Freeman and Parsons (2001) see the study and understanding of artworks and children's own art-making as an essential combination. Of great importance is that the teacher should talk about artworks – those of adults and of the children themselves – in order to get a sense of how children understand them and, equally, how they do not. Clement (1997), however, found that there is in fact minimal emphasis on talking about the meaning of a picture and how ideas in art develop and change, although these aspects are introduced as children get older and are more prevalent in the secondary school.

The task for art education is more difficult these days, with the shift from modernism to postmodernism (see chapter 3). The modernist concern was with the supposed fundamental truth or essence of a work of art, the notion that there is one 'correct' way to understand it. The postmodern, or contemporary, view is that there may be many meaningful ways. Critics do not necessarily agree about a picture, and people with an art or a non-art background may make different judgements; in addition, people in different cultures seem to have different criteria about works of art (Kindler & Darras 1998; Kindler, Darras & Kuo 2000; Kindler et al. 2001; Kindler et al. 2002). Art education is no longer concerned in a direct way with teaching or encouraging children to grasp an essential point or message intended by the artist; rather, as Parsons (1996) argues, the task is to investigate the ways in which students find meaning in artworks, how they relate artworks to various contexts and come to entertain multiple interpretations of them. This more relativistic approach does not mean, though, that one cannot make comparative judgements about pictures. As Gardner, Winner and Kircher (1975) pointed out, 'All works of art are not equally good, and one's experience is impoverished as long as this view is uncritically embraced' (p. 76).

Summary

Most young children are keen to draw. This usually takes place within a social context – often with an adult – and, indeed, children's artistic development seems to be best promoted in this kind of way. It is important to realise that this development is an interaction between what children generate themselves and the socio-cultural influences and support they receive, a view that is consistent with Vygotsky's theory of development. Although this support may be relatively informal in the early years, it seems that more formal guidance or tuition is appropriate in later childhood and beyond, if children are to develop their artistic abilities to any great extent. As well as being influenced by adults, children are also affected by the discussions they have with other children, by other children's graphic images and by the images available in the mass media. Thus, children's picture-making is not simply an automatic consequence of maturation but involves a learned set of abilities which, although related to children's developing motor and cognitive skills, is also influenced by the culture in which they live.

The art curriculum in schools has changed over time, and varies from country to country and in schools with different educational approaches. When we find differences in the style or quality of children's artwork it is difficult to conclude that it is the different approaches to art education that have caused them. There are other variables that cannot be controlled in comparative research studies and which may be responsible. And it may be that it is the presence of an encouraging and creative atmosphere that is more important than the actual teaching programmes themselves. We are more able to come to a conclusion about a particular teaching programme if we use the experimental research method, and there is some evidence that at least one approach – 'negotiated' drawing – is helpful in improving children's picture-making. Various authors and researchers have argued that drawing is the core activity in art education and that drawing from observation is particularly important in sharpening children's observational skills and their understanding of the objects and events they draw. There is some evidence that practice at observational drawing not only improves children's ability to draw in this way but also generalises this improvement to their drawings from imagination. However, in order to draw in a visually realistic way children – and adults – may need special tuition and the use of artistic aids, such as a perspective frame, to help them draw what they see.

As well as the production of pictures and other artworks, appreciation of the work of adult artists is now part of the formal art curriculum in the UK. However, the range of work that children see is very limited and examples are used mainly as a stimulus to the children's own art-making rather than as a means of promoting their understanding and appreciation of art. This situation may be exacerbated in the primary school, where most teachers are not art specialists and may have little knowledge of works of art. A reluctance to discuss artworks in a critical way may also be a function of the postmodern climate, in which teachers and others are uncertain about discussing the meaning of pictures and making comparative judgements about them.

Children produce pictures for a number of reasons – to explore and play with ideas, to communicate information, to express feelings and emotions, as well as for sheer pleasure. They need a rich and varied art curriculum so that they can acquire the pictorial skills to implement these aims, not least to their own satisfaction. However, even though there is a formal art curriculum in the UK there is still disagreement about what it should include. Many favoured approaches have not been tested in order to ascertain their effect on children's picture-making, and therefore their implementation is based largely on ideology and intuition rather than on any objective evidence. Many art educators will maintain that it is not possible to evaluate art in an objective way. But even those who are not averse to the idea may, nonetheless, disagree about what it is we should be evaluating. For example, some may be biased more towards technical accomplishment whereas others may tend towards expressive qualities in a picture. Yet others may argue that individual pictures should not be the focus of any evaluation, but that we should be looking at a child's development over a series of pictures, as he explores and develops a theme. And yet others may consider that the child's experience in the process of art-making is as important as what is actually produced.

Whatever changes there may be in the art curriculum in the future, it is important that it retreats neither to a completely 'hands-off' approach nor to teaching in a dry and mechanistic way. Despite the modern pressure for schools to meet targets some areas of the curriculum can be more relaxed and art should be one of these – remaining as a space within which children can feel less constrained and be free to experiment. At the same time, children need to be engaged in the process of understanding and making pictures and also need to receive help in order to achieve their goals. Art lessons are no longer seen solely as opportunities for free expression; neither are they viewed as a support for other subjects in the curriculum; furthermore, they are no longer treated as providing free time for teachers. They may include these benefits, but the modern art curriculum requires planning, engagement and instruction in order to give children a fully rounded education.

13 Picturing the future

As newborn babies we demonstrate some fairly sophisticated visual capabilities, and it seems, therefore, that we are predisposed to perceiving and processing information in a visual way, although there are undoubtedly individual differences in the extent to which this is the case. Human beings have capitalised on this visual predisposition by developing a pictorial symbolic system that can be used to represent and communicate desires, feelings and intentions. We think of art, then – in the sense of drawing and painting – as a visual medium. Young children are not born fully-fledged in this respect, but are artistic novices who, if they are to participate fully in their culture, must master this symbolic system. Indeed, whether or not individuals are especially 'tuned in' to the visual world, they must be competent in this visual form of literacy (Eisner 1989) or intelligence (Gardner 1993) in order to be considered fully educated members of our society. In the preceding chapters I have traced children's developing ability to understand and appreciate the pictures they see around them and their ability to produce their own pictures. In this final chapter I highlight various points already discussed in this book or which have arisen from these discussions; I also suggest issues relating to the pictorial world of the child that I believe would benefit from further research. I have not intended to produce a summary of the issues and conclusions of the whole book, since I have already given a summary at the end of each chapter. My selection here reflects my own personal choice and I recognise that other researchers may have chosen differently.

Not surprisingly, children's understanding of the world of pictures tends to precede the production of their own pictures. Young children appear to require no or only minimal tuition in order to recognise familiar objects in pictures. However, there is a great deal more to understanding a picture than its ability to represent aspects of the visual world; it also has the ability to refer to or evoke emotional mood through both literal and non-literal means, and, furthermore, it can be understood as an aesthetic object and as a cultural artefact situated in a particular society at a particular time. All this takes time to master and children continue to develop their understanding of pictures long after they have begun to produce them themselves. However, research evidence indicates that even quite young children in the primary school are sensitive to some of these aspects of art appreciation and have some potential for engaging in critical discussions about art. An obvious application of this knowledge is in art education, and indeed art appreciation is now included in the English National Curriculum. It seems to me that this is an area in which research studies could be useful in evaluating the effectiveness of various approaches to teaching art appreciation in schools.

Since children are novices when it comes to learning how to draw or paint, it is not surprising that their earlier efforts reflect their attempts to explore and control the medium. We call this the 'scribbling' period. It seems that nearly all typically developing children go through such a period, in which they are experimenting with the materials. Although researchers have not been able to support Kellogg's (1969) claim of an extensive repertoire of detailed and varied scribbles for all children, they have, nonetheless, shown that most children show some variation in the marks and shapes they make before they go on to use these forms in a representational way. For example, Matthews (1983, 1984) has described the downward stabbing movements, sideways sweeps, and forwards and backwards 'push-pull' movements observed in a number of children, which seem to arise from the different body movements and gestures that the child makes in the space around him. Whether these particular kinds of movements are universal, as Matthews claims, remains to be confirmed. Interestingly, older children and adults who have had no previous experience with picture-making also spend some time – however short – making apparently non-representational marks and shapes before they produce recognisable forms. That older children need less time in this respect is not surprising, as their more advanced motor control and cognitive capabilities should help them to grasp a new medium more quickly.

Whereas some researchers have denied that scribbles are representational, others have shown that there is sometimes some representational intent behind them. Matthews (1984) and Wolf and Perry (1988) give examples of the way in which children's scribbles may leave a visible trace of an 'action' or 'gestural' representation of a movement or an event. Not all researchers, however, would accept these scribbles as true representations. Golomb (1992), for example, insists that representations must bear some visual similarity to the objects they stand for in order that they can be correctly recognised independently of the child's gestures or verbalisations made at the time. Although I understand the point, it seems to me that this is rather a strict criterion and I would be reluctant to relegate action or gestural representations to some prerepresentational or non-representational category. In fact, I would suggest that we abandon the notion of distinct categories and, instead, explore the possibility that there might be transitional forms of representation leading eventually to unambiguous and undisputed representational forms.

When children begin to draw representational forms they are not attempting to make a copy of the real object but, rather, are engaging in a 'search for equivalents' (Arnheim 1974) – finding lines and shapes that will stand for the real object and bear some resemblance to it. The structure of an object itself may restrict the options and some solutions may be more convincing than others or more appropriate for the purposes for which they are required. Even so, different cultures vary in the particular forms of depiction they favour. Taking the human figure as an example, we could choose to represent it in many different ways: the head can be shown as a dot, a circular region or a region with a profiled contour; the torso can be drawn as a single vertical line, a broad, shaded vertical area or a contoured area of many different shapes. Not all parts of the figure need be drawn. Whereas most pictorial cultures have chosen to represent either a frontal or side view some, such as the Warlpiri, have chosen a U-shape, which perhaps reflects the outline shape of a seated figure seen from above. And it is not only in different cultures that there is variation in the way that certain topics, such as the human figure, are depicted. Individual children experiment with different forms of representation and may have their own preferences. We see variation among children in any one culture. For example, children in the Jimi Valley in Papua New Guinea (Martlew & Connolly 1996) have produced different forms of the human figure (e.g., tadpole, contour and stick figures). Also in the UK there is a similar variety among very young children (see Cox 1997 for an account of the longitudinal data collected by Fysh). All forms bear some visual resemblance to aspects of a real human figure but, in the UK data at least, most children who have experimented with less typical forms will abandon them and then conform to the more typical style. Thus, although the search for equivalents may be universal, the potential solutions to this problem are very varied. Choices are made by individual children and also by whole societies. It seems to me that it would be useful to think in terms of *universality* with regard to the *process* underlying children's search for suitable representational forms and *variation* in the *actual forms* that they produce through this process.

In discussing young children's early attempts to find visual equivalents of the objects they want to represent, Arnheim (1974) claimed that they start with simple lines and shapes and graduate to more complex forms, and this 'law' applies to the representation of single objects as well as to a whole composition. When drawing the human figure, for example, children in a number of different cultures draw 'tadpole' forms, which may be as minimal as a roughly drawn circle with two lines extending below it; in time, extra details will be added and the structure will be reorganised to include a torso. Complexity may refer not only to added details but also to the modification of the figure when, for example, the child experiments with figures in action or figures seen from an atypical point of view. When asked about their preferences for particular pictures, younger children in a number of different cultures prefer realism and colour whereas older ones prefer complexity. Arnheim's claim for a universal simple-to-complex development seems to be borne out by all the research studies so far and, in fact, it would be rather surprising if it were not. However, there is little in the way of longitudinal data, and in order to confirm the claim for universality we need to check whether depictions of figures in other cultures, albeit drawn in different ways, nonetheless follow the same simple-to-complex pattern.

The way that young children draw, not from the objects themselves but from an internal model of the object (Luquet 1927/2001), has attracted much attention and criticism. One difficulty that critics have identified is the supposed rigidity of the internal model, which, although it explains why young children tend to draw stereotyped, generic forms rather than the particular objects they can actually see, does not account so well for the variability in many children's drawings and the flexibility that can be demonstrated under experimental conditions. In fact, this criticism may have come about through a misunderstanding of Luquet's idea. For Luquet, the internal model is analogous to a photograph of the object the child wishes to draw. The important parts, as far as the child is concerned, will be more in focus than others. However, according to Costall's translation of Luquet's work, the more focussed and important parts of the internal model are not necessarily the same each time the child accesses it. If this is the case then Luquet's idea can explain the variability in children's drawing as well as their conservatism.

A limitation of Luquet's account, however, is that he did not explain *how* children select the marks and shapes for their figures. Willats (1981, 1985, 1987) has attempted to bridge this gap by suggesting how the child chooses appropriate lines and shapes depending on the bulk or extendedness of the object in question – the process of matching picture primitives to scene primitives. One problem with Willats' account is that it focusses on the child's quest to invent a solution without reference to how objects are typically represented in her culture. In western cultures, for example, most children draw a roughly circular shape to stand for a head. But this is also the typical way that adults represent a head. We do not know if the child is thinking about the shape of a real head or whether she is trying to reproduce the way she has seen other people draw. In Warlpiri culture young children draw a version of the U-shape that adults use to represent a person. Presumably, Warlpiri children are not concerned with how one might draw a head, a torso and so on, since these details are simply not shown in traditional Warlpiri depictions. These children are not drawing from life but from their knowledge of *pictures* of a human being in their culture. If this is the case in Warlpiri culture then it may also be true in others. Thus, children may not be drawing real people (or their internal representation of real people), but may be trying to copy or capture the human forms they have seen in pictures (when, for example, adults or other children have drawn for them). This notion that children's attempts at depiction are not (only) informed by their own mental analysis of real objects but by their desire to replicate what others are doing when they draw a picture owes a great deal to Vygotsky's (1962, 1978) ideas. In particular, children's development involves and is heavily dependent on the acquisition of the 'cultural tools' prevalent in their own society, and this process takes place in interaction with others rather than as an independent and isolated quest on the part of the child.

Given this process, we would expect to find diversity in the kinds of pictures produced in different societies. Nowadays, however, it is increasingly difficult to find a culture that has not come into contact with western styles of pictures. With increasingly global communication systems one wonders whether the cultural diversity of representational forms will shrink and whether the artistic traditions of minority and isolated groups will disappear altogether. If this happens it may appear to future researchers that the prevalent universal style is a natural and inevitable form of depiction whereas, in fact, it would have come about because of a certain culture's domination and control of the media. Universality, then, does not mean that culture is not important. Phenomena and behaviour that are universal may result largely or even completely through cultural means.

An assumption made by many authors regarding the nature of children's developing artistic ability is that development is stage-like. This notion has applied particularly to the tendency for younger children to construct their pictures according to intellectual realism and older ones to attempt visual realism (Luquet 1927/2001). In fact, this stage-like interpretation is based mainly on Piaget's (1970) general theory of cognitive development, in which children develop through an orderly sequence of stages towards a more logical way of thinking; at any one stage their thinking will be similar in all cognitive domains. However, Luquet's idea of 'stage' is much more flexible than this. He did not see intellectual and visual realism as discrete and sequentially ordered stages; although these systems of representation typically emerge in this order and younger children may favour one and older children the other, they both remain in a child's repertoire to be used when the need arises. Evidence in support of this position comes from the many research studies that have shown how younger children, in some circumstances, can and do opt for visual realism and how older ones (and adults) sometimes choose intellectual realism. It seems more useful, then, to think of children's artistic development as an increasing repertoire of representational systems, some of which may be more difficult to master and may therefore appear at a later stage of a child's development. There is, however, no predetermined goal or end point, no inevitable progression towards visual realism.

Change in children's artistic development comes about in many ways. Abilities that are involved in the artistic enterprise – motor control, attention, memory skills, planning and organisational skills and so on – are developing as the child gets older. We know, however, that there are other important influences on development. Some children seem to have a special aptitude for the pictorial world and are internally motivated towards exploring its possibilities and problems. Through their own efforts these children will master the medium, gain practice and set challenges for themselves, but often they will also have the support and encouragement of families and teachers. Indeed, an artistically orientated environment either at home or in school may stimulate even the less talented child's interest in art and encourage higher standards in children's own artwork. It would be useful to conduct more studies in order to identify the kinds of educational programmes that will best support children's work. Rigorous research evaluations might also help allay the disquiet among some art educators about the extent to which art is adequately taught and also provide evidence in support of art education in the light of current fears about its being reduced in order to give more time to the 'basics' of literacy and numeracy.

Since the 'cognitive revolution' of the 1960s (see Gardner 1985; Baars 1986) research on children's artistic development has tended to veer towards its more cognitive aspects and less towards its aesthetic side, although some researchers (Gardner 1980; Winner & Gardner 1981) never lost sight of this dimension. In more recent years, however, more researchers have become interested in children's understanding of the feelings and emotions that pictures can convey or evoke and also in children's ability to depict or convey emotional expression in their own pictures. Although the research evidence sometimes lacks consistency, it seems to indicate that children's efforts are directed more towards achieving a convincing visual representation than to the emotional or aesthetic aspects of their pictures. To some extent this order of priorities might be inevitable, although it might also result from the bias in parents' and teachers' own understanding and attitudes about art. More research into children's abilities regarding this emotional and aesthetic dimension of art, as well as their response to art appreciation programmes which encompass it, would be a welcome and fruitful enterprise.

There have been various approaches to the nature of intelligence, one of which argues that there are distinct kinds of intelligence. Gardner (1993), for example, originally proposed seven distinct kinds, which, he argued, are linked to different areas of the brain and may follow different developmental courses. Visual-spatial intelligence would, presumably, be the kind of intelligence that underpins the artistic domain. Some evidence does seem to point to a pattern of independent abilities. For example, injuries in particular parts of the brain often affect one kind of ability and leave others intact. Some individuals, such as savants with autism, are intellectually disabled but excel in one ability, and there are a few famous cases of autistic savants who have produced remarkable pictures. Even if the brain were not organised initially in a modular way, it could become so if talented individuals with a particular bias towards certain kinds of processing and activity, such as picture-making, were to practise and master this activity to a particularly enhanced degree (Karmiloff-Smith 1992).

I think it would be a mistake, though, to use this evidence to claim that art is a distinct domain with a special biological basis in the brain for all typically developing individuals. As evidence against this notion, critics point out that different kinds of ability are often not as independent from each other as Gardner has claimed: individuals who are above average on one ability are often above average on all of them; although talented child artists are not necessarily academic high-fliers they are, nonetheless, generally above average in their schoolwork. Thus, although we tend to talk about art as a distinct domain with clearly defined parameters, we should remember that it also relies on fundamental perceptual and cognitive processing, which is also important in other activities. Surprisingly, perhaps, art need not be solely a visual activity, since even blind people can understand and make pictures with raised-line kits. I would also point out that not all aspects of artistic ability are preserved in talented artists who also have autism. For example, although autistic savants focus on the visual appearance of a scene and may be able to represent it in a very realistic way, most of them are completely uninterested in the human and emotional dimension of art, often omitting people from their pictures altogether.

I am aware that in this book I have been rather critical of the use of children's drawings as a basis for testing their intelligence or emotional stability. The reason for this is that although existing tests have been found to have quite high reliability, their validity leaves a great deal to be desired. In fact, many researchers warn against their use altogether. Whereas few educational psychologists these days would use a drawing test as the basis for decisions relating to a child's educational needs, it seems that far more clinicians and therapists routinely use children's drawings, either formally or informally, to help diagnose their emotional problems and assess the progress of their treatment. Unfortunately, these professionals often interpret the drawings in an intuitive or psychodynamic way, and the research evidence provides little support for this approach. I believe that professionals must rethink their use of children's pictures. For example, I have suggested how drawings can be used as a focus for discussions with children in a therapeutic setting and have also outlined some interesting research that drawings may enhance children's memory for events they have experienced. Research studies could pursue these leads and also perhaps explore new ways that drawings could be used by professionals.

It is likely that children, as well as adults, have been producing pictures for hundreds or, indeed, thousands of years. Even without materials such as paper and pencil they could have made marks with their fingers in sand or mud. But, since very few children's pictures exist from before the 1800s, we presume that their artwork was not valued and neither parents nor teachers considered it interesting enough to keep. Since the nineteenth century, however, there has been a growing interest in children's pictures by researchers and professionals, as well as by parents. There are now many collections of children's pictures in formal research and educational archives and also as part of ordinary families' memorabilia; the number of books and journal articles is increasing. This great interest in children's artwork is set to continue.

Appendix
Theories of visual perception and the perception of pictures

There are a number of different theories about the way we perceive objects in our normal environment, including those we see in pictures. In this appendix I give a brief outline of those theories that have been mentioned in preceding chapters. For further criticisms and discussions of these theories, see Hagen (1980), Costall (1985), Bruce and Green (1990), Tarr and Bülthoff (1995) and Hodgson (2002).

Gestalt theory

For the founders of the Gestalt theory (Wertheimer 1923; Köhler 1925; Koffka 1935; see also Ellis 1969) the task of perception is to recognise objects in the environment according to the organisation of their constituent parts. However, we do not perceive separate elements. Perception is not a set of distinct sensations but depends on the relationships among the elements, which we then perceive as whole forms or *Gestalten*. Some basic shapes have an intrinsic aesthetic appeal and are regarded as 'good forms'. Thus, our perception of the whole object is more than the sum of its parts. This occurs because the brain imposes organisation on the visual information projected on to the retina.

Visual perception, then, cannot be understood simply by analysing the parts of an object or scene; rather, the process follows certain 'laws' that reflect the way the brain functions. There are a number of laws of organisation. For example, according to the adjacency or proximity principle, when two figures are seen in close proximity to each other they are more likely to be grouped together perceptually (see figure A1). We also tend to group together figures that are similar (the similarity principle; see figure A2) and we tend to 'complete' figures that have gaps in them (the law of closure; see figure A3). Since these laws of perception are supposedly innate they will be the same for all people everywhere regardless of the culture they have been raised in.

The constructivist approach

Gregory's (1972, 1974) constructivist approach to visual perception is a variant of the 'picture theory' of perception – the idea that our perception

Figure A1 *The law of proximity. We see three pairs of lines rather than six single lines.*

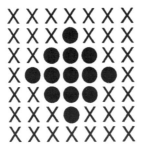

Figure A2 *The law of similarity. We perceive similar elements (dots) as belonging to the same form.*

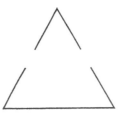

Figure A3 *The law of closure. We tend to perceive the incomplete figure as a complete triangle.*

of real objects is based on successive two-dimensional retinal snapshots. The problem is that these images are inherently ambiguous and open to a number of different interpretations. For example, Costall (1985) shows us a photograph of what may be a gravestone and its shadow on a nearby wall; equally, however, we could be looking at one or even two archways in the wall (see figure A4). Even though this photographic image is a true projection of a real scene, we are not certain how to interpret it. Gregory maintains that we put forward hypotheses, based on our past experiences, of what the image is most likely to be. Thus, we *construct* an interpretation of the visual input we receive. Perception is, therefore, an *indirect*, secondary and inferential process.

Since images on the retina ought to bear some similarity to artists' pictures then the way we perceive pictures should be similar to the way we perceive solid objects. However, whereas we benefit from binocular vision when we observe a real three-dimensional object, we only see the

Figure A4 *An ambiguous photograph: gravestone or archway in the wall?*

single projection of the object chosen by the artist or camera when we look at a picture. Thus, observers of a picture will have a much more limited set of cues at their disposal. If the artist has used a technique familiar to us then this will ease our interpretation of the picture; if, on the other hand, we look at a picture from an unfamiliar artistic tradition then our interpretation of it might be more difficult. According to a constructivist position, then, our perception of pictures is very much dependent on our familiarity with the techniques the artist has used (what the art historian Gombrich, 1954, has called 'schemata'). Both Gombrich and the philosopher Goodman (1968) claimed that pictures succeed as representations because the artist and the observer have a shared understanding of the pictorial conventions being used. To a large extent this is true. In western societies we are very familiar with pictures executed in linear convergence perspective and have no difficulty in interpreting them. Equally, we are familiar with some other projection systems such as oblique perspective, as these are commonly used in mathematical and scientific textbooks. But people in modern western societies may be less comfortable with the divergent perspective common in some African cultures, the 'folding out' pictures of Haida artists in north-western Canada and the aerial perspective of some of the imagery used in Warlpiri paintings of central Australia. For Gregory, then, picture recognition is learned and will differ depending on our familiarity with the cultural conventions of depiction.

Marr's computational theory of visual perception

Marr's (1982) approach to visual perception is similar to the constructivist approach in that it attempts to explain how we construct meaning out of the static two-dimensional images on the retina and, like the constructivist approach, it is also a 'picture' theory (Costall 1985). Marr suggested some operations that the visual system first applies to the two-dimensional retinal image, which is a 'viewer-centred' description (i.e., a kind of snapshot from a particular angle of view). He argued that the system generates,

Figure A5 *We can easily recognise these pipe-cleaner figures from their linear axes (Marr & Nishihara 1978).*

through a set of subprocesses, a three-dimensional 'object-centred' description of an object that includes depth, volume and spatial context; this description is independent of any particular viewpoint and enables us to recognise the object even if we and the object are moving. It does this by setting up co-ordinate systems using the principal axes of the shapes being represented. It creates a kind of 'pipe-cleaner' or line-based model (see figure A5), which is easily recognised despite the lack of information about the surfaces of the object (Marr & Nishihara 1978).

Marr (1982) was inspired by the ability of line drawings to represent the visual world so powerfully and economically. Since it is unlikely that the visual system has developed separate processes for the interpretation of line drawings as well as real objects, then we might suppose that the same basic processes underscore both (see Hayes & Ross 1995). The artist's use of lines corresponds with the natural symbols that the brain computes out of the image during the normal course of its interpretation. That we do recognise representations of objects based on their principal axes is evident from the matchstick figures in paintings by L. S. Lowry and the spindly figures sculpted by Giacometti. Many of the human figures in prehistoric art are also similarly stylised. So, Marr's computational theory proposes that representations of the retinal image are matched against a stored catalogue of internal models, enabling us to recognise objects.

Gibson's ecological theory

When Gibson (1950) first developed his ideas about visual perception and the perception of pictures in the late 1940s his view was very much in line with the picture theory of perception. However, as various criticisms and problems emerged he reformulated it (e.g., Gibson 1979). In contrast to the constructivist account, Gibson argued that our normal perception does not depend upon ambiguous 'pictorial' depth cues. We do not normally look at the world with our eyes in a fixed position. Normal perception, for Gibson, does not work like a camera, taking brief and fixed snapshots of the environment. In our everyday lives we are surrounded by the 'optic array', which changes as we (and other objects) move around. The optic array contains information that allows us to specify what objects are and where they are, as well as our relation to them. From the ever-changing stimulus in the light to the eye we extract the permanent or unchanging properties of the environment – its *invariant* structure. In this 'ecological' theory the retinal image is not interpreted by the observer through some kind of secondary processing such as hypothesis testing; rather, the meaning is in the environment itself – in the light reflected from objects to the eye – and we simply 'pick up' that information directly. The perceptual process is said to be *direct*. It does not rely on any successive *static* appearance of objects but, rather, takes place as the environment changes and as our viewpoint changes in relation to our own movement. That visual perception in human infants seems already primed to respond to movement – the movement of objects, the movement of the perceiver or an interaction of both of these – seems to support Gibson's theory.

Under normal viewing conditions we can always tell if we are looking at a real scene or at a picture. Pictures, Gibson claimed, are less informative than real-world scenes, the reason being that they present the observer with a 'frozen' sample of the invariant information for the real objects they depict. A picture will be a successful representation to the extent that it captures *some* of the invariant information about the objects depicted; an unsuccessful representation will contain no invariant information.

The point of a picture is to convey information and the artist makes a deliberate choice as to the method of depiction best suited for this purpose. These methods of depiction are, to some extent, conventional in that some will be preferred by certain cultures or for certain purposes. But pictures are not like language, in which the relationship between words and their meaning is largely arbitrary (Goodman 1976); rather, pictures are based on an intrinsic, structural relation between the pictorial image and the object it represents. Unlike the constructivists, who see the lines and colours of pictures as sensations that the eye and brain must process, Gibson argued that the meaning of a representational picture is to be found in the picture itself and not within the observer. The process of recognising objects in pictures is essentially the same as recognition of the real environment, requiring no special skill, and should therefore be the same for everyone.

References

Abell, S. C., Briesen, P. D. von, & Watz, L. S. (1996) 'Intellectual evaluations of children using human figure drawings: an empirical investigation of two methods', *Journal of Clinical Psychology* 52, 67–74.

Abell, S. C., Wood, W., & Liebman, S. J. (2001) 'Children's human figure drawings as measures of intelligence: the comparative validity of three scoring systems', *Journal of Psychoeducational Assessment* 19, 204–15.

Acosta, M. L. (1990) 'The kinetic family drawing: a developmental and validity study', unpublished doctoral dissertation, University of Washington.

Adi-Japha, E., Levin, I., & Solomon, S. (1998) 'Emergence of representation in drawing: the relation between kinetic and referential aspects', *Cognitive Development* 13, 25–51.

Aikman, K. G., Belter, R. W., & Finch, A. J. (1992) 'Human figure drawings: validity in assessing intellectual level and academic achievement', *Journal of Clinical Psychology* 48, 114–20.

Alland, A. (1983) *Playing with Form: children draw in six cultures*, New York: Columbia University Press.

Alschuler, R. H., & Hattwick, L. B. W. (1947) *Painting and Personality: a study of young children*, Chicago: University of Chicago Press.

American Art Therapy Association (1996) *Art Therapy: definition of the profession*, Mundelein, IL: American Art Therapy Association.

Ames, L. B., & Ilg, F. L. (1963) 'The Gesell incomplete man test as a measure of developmental status', *Genetic Psychology Monographs* 68, 247–307.

Anastasi, A. (1976) *Psychological Testing*, New York: Collier-Macmillan.

Anastasi, A., & Foley, J. P. (1936) 'An analysis of spontaneous drawings by children of different cultures', *Journal of Applied Psychology* 20, 689–726.

Andersson, S. (2003) 'Local conventions in children's drawings in the Namibian region', unpublished manuscript, University of Linköping.

Anwar, F., & Hermelin, B. (1982) 'An analysis of drawing skills in mental handicap', *Australia and New Zealand Journal of Developmental Disabilities* 8, 147–55.

Archer, R. P., Maruish, M., Imhof, E. A., & Piotrowski, C. (1991) 'Psychological test usage with adolescent clients: 1990 survey findings', *Professional Psychology Research and Practice* 22, 247–52.

Arkell, R. N. (1976) 'Naïve prediction of pathology from human figure drawings', *Journal of School Psychology* 14, 114–17.

Arnheim, R. (1974) *Art and Visual Perception: a psychology of the creative eye. The New Version*. Berkeley and Los Angeles: University of California Press.

(1978) 'Expressions', *Art Education* 31, 37–8.

(1997) 'A look at a century of growth', in *Child Development in Art*, Reston, VA: National Art Education Association, pp. 9–15.

Aronsson, K., & Andersson, S. (1996) 'Social scaling in children's drawings of classroom life: a cultural comparative analysis of social scaling in Africa and Sweden, *British Journal of Developmental Psychology* 14, 301–14.

Arrowsmith, C. J., Cox, M. V., & Eames, K. (1994) 'Eliciting partial occlusion in the drawings of 4- and 5-year-olds', *British Journal of Developmental Psychology* 12, 577–84.

Asaad, G., & Shapiro, B. (1986) 'Hallucinations: theoretical and clinical overview', *American Journal of Psychiatry* 143, 1088–97.P

Asperger, H. (1944) 'Die "Autistischen Psychopathen" im Kindesalter', *Archiv für Psychiatrie und Nervenkrankheiten* 117, 76–136.

Attneave, F. (1954) 'Some informational aspects of visual perception', *Psychological Review* 61, 183–93.

Audouin, F., & Plisson, H. (1982) 'Les ocres et leurs témoins au Paléolithique en France: enquête et expériences sur leur validité archéologique', *Cahiers du Centre de Recherches Préhistoriques* 8, 33–80.

Baars, B. J. (1986) *The Cognitive Revolution in Psychology*, New York: Guilford Press.

Baddeley, A. D., & Hitch, G. J. (1974) 'Working memory', in *The Psychology of Learning and Motivation*, vol. VIII, ed. G. Bower, New York: Academic Press, pp. 47–90.

Bahn, P. (1995) 'Cave art without the caves', *Antiquity* 69, 231–7.

(1997) *Journey through the Ice Age*, 2nd edition, London: Weidenfeld & Nicolson.

Baker-Ward, L., Gordon, B. N., Ornstein, P. A., Larus, D. N., & Clubb, P. A. (1993) 'Young children's retention of a pediatric examination', *Child Development* 64, 1519–33.

Barham, L. S. (2002) 'Systematic pigment use in the Middle Pleistocene of South Central Africa', *Current Anthropology* 43, 181–90.

Barlow, C. M. (2003) 'Rigidity in children's drawings and its relationship with representational change', unpublished D.Phil. thesis, Staffordshire University.

Barnes, E. (1893) 'A study of children's drawings', *Pedagogical Seminary* 2, 451–63.

Barnhart, E. N. (1942) 'Developmental stages in compositional construction in children's drawings', *Journal of Experimental Education* 11, 156–84.

Baron-Cohen, S. (2003) *The Essential Difference: men, women and the extreme male brain*, London: Allen Lane.

Baron-Cohen, S., Ring, H. A., Bullmore, E. T., Wheelwright, S., Ashwin, C., & Williams, S. C. R. (2000) 'The amygdala theory of autism', *Neuroscience and Biobehavioural Reviews* 24, 355–64.

Baron-Cohen, S., Spitz, A., & Cross, P. (1993) 'Do children with autism recognise surprise? A research note', *Cognition and Emotion* 7, 507–16.

Barrett, M. D., & Bridson, A. (1983) 'The effect of instructions upon children's drawings', *British Journal of Developmental Psychology* 1, 175–8.

Bassett, E. M. (1977) 'Production strategies in children's drawings', in *The Child's Representation of the World*, ed. G. Butterworth, New York: Plenum Press, pp. 49–59.

Bates, J. L., Ricciardelli, L. A., & Clarke, V. A. (1999) 'The effects of participation and presentation media on the eyewitness memory of children', *Australian Journal of Psychology* 15, 71–6.

Baxandall, M. (1972) *Painting and Experience in Fifteenth-Century Italy*, Oxford: Oxford University Press.

Bayraktar, R. (1985) 'Cross-cultural analysis of drawing errors', in *Visual Order: the nature and development of pictorial representation*, ed. N. H. Freeman & M. V. Cox, Cambridge: Cambridge University Press, pp. 333–55.

Beach, H. P. (1901) *Geography and Atlas for Protestant Missions*, New York: Student Volunteer Movement for Foreign Missions.

Beilin, H., & Pearlman, E. G. (1991) 'Children's iconic realism: object versus property realism', in *Advances in Child Development and Behavior*, vol. XXIII, ed. H. W. Reese, New York: Academic Press, pp. 73–111.

Bekhit, N. S., Thomas, G. V., Lalonde, S., & Jolley, R. (2002) 'Psychological assessment in clinical practice in Britain', *Clinical Psychology and Psychotherapy* 9, 285–91.

Bell, R., & Bell, G. (1979) 'Individual differences in children's preferences among recent paintings', *British Journal of Educational Psychology* 49, 182–7.

Bender, L. (1938) 'A visual motor *Gestalt* test and its clinical use', *American Orthopsychiatric Association Research Monograph* 3.

Berti, A. E., & Freeman, N. H. (1997) 'Representational change in resources for pictorial innovation: a three component analysis', *Cognitive Development* 12, 405–26.

Biederman, I., & Ju, G. (1988) 'Surface versus edge-based determinants of visual recognition', *Cognitive Psychology* 20, 115–47.

Blank, P., Massey, C., Gardner, H., & Winner, E. (1984) 'Perceiving what paintings express', in *Cognitive Processes in the Perception of Art*, ed. W. R. Crozier & A. J. Chapman, Amsterdam: Elsevier Science, pp. 127–43.

Blatt, S. J. (1994) 'Concurrent conceptual revolutions in art and science', in *Development in the Arts*, ed. M. B. Franklin & B. Kaplan, Hillsdale, NJ: Lawrence Erlbaum, pp. 195–226.

Bourguignon, E. (1989) 'Trance and shamanism: what's in a name?', *Journal of Psychoactive Drugs* 21, 9–15.

Bower, T. G. R. (1966) 'The visual world of infants', *Scientific American* 215, 80–92.

  (2002) 'Space and objects', in *Introduction to Infant Development*, ed. A. Slater & M. Lewis, Oxford: Oxford University Press, pp. 131–46.

Boyatzis, C. J. (2000) 'The artistic evolution of Mommy: a longitudinal case study of symbolic and social processes', in *Symbolic and Social Constraints on the Development of Children's Artistic Style*, ed. C. J. Boyatzis & M. W. Watson, San Franscisco: Jossey-Bass, pp. 5–29.

Boyatzis, C. J., & Albertini, G. (2000) 'A naturalistic observation of children drawing: peer collaboration processes and influences in children's art', in *Symbolic and Social Constraints on the Development of Children's Artistic Style*, ed. C. J. Boyatzis & M. W. Watson, San Franscisco: Jossey-Bass, pp. 31–48.

Boyatzis, C. J., & Varghese, R. (1993) 'Children's emotional associations with colours', *Journal of Genetic Psychology* 155, 77–85.

Brainerd, C. J. (1978) 'The stage question in cognitive-developmental theory', *Behavioral and Brain Sciences* 2, 173–213.

Braswell, G. S. (2001) 'Collaborative drawing during early mother–child interactions', *Visual Arts Research* 27, 27–39.

Bremner, J. G. (1985) 'Figural biases and young children's drawings', in *Visual Order: the nature and development of pictorial representation*, ed. N. H. Freeman & M. V. Cox, Cambridge: Cambridge University Press, pp. 310–32.

(1996) 'Children's drawings and the evolution of art', in *Handbook of Human Symbolic Evolution*, ed. A. Lock & C. R. Peters, Oxford: Clarendon Press, pp. 501–19.

Bremner, J. G., & Moore, S. (1984) 'Prior visual inspection and object naming: two factors that enhance hidden feature inclusion in young children's drawings', *British Journal of Developmental Psychology* 2, 371–6.

Brennan, K. H., & Fisher, R. P. (1998) *'Drawing as a technique to facilitate children's recall'*, cited in *Investigative Interviews of Children: a guide for helping professionals*, ed. D. A. Poole & M. E. Lamb, Washington, DC: American Psychological Society, p. 184.

Breuil, H. (1952) *Quatre cents siècles d'art pariétal*, Montignac, France: Centre d'Etudes et de Documentation Préhistoriques.

Bridges, K. M. B. (1932) 'Emotional development in early infancy', *Child Development* 3, 324–41.

Briggs, F., & Lehmann, K. (1989) 'Significance of children's drawings in cases of sexual abuse', *Early Child Development and Care* 47, 131–47.

Brimble, A. R. (1962) 'The construction of a non-verbal intelligence test in Northern Rhodesia', *Rhodes-Livingstone Journal* 34, 23–35.

Brittain, W. L., & Chien, Y-C. (1983) 'Relationship between preschool children's ability to name boy parts and their ability to construct a man', *Perceptual and Motor Skills* 57, 19–24.

Brooks, L. R. (1968) 'Spatial and verbal aspects of the act of recall', *Canadian Journal of Psychology* 22, 349–50.

Brooks, M. R., Glenn, S. M., & Crozier, W. R. (1988) 'Pre-school children's preferences for drawings of a similar complexity to their own', *British Journal of Educational Psychology* 58, 165–71.

Brown, G., & Desforges, C. (1977) 'Piagetian theory and education: time for revision', *British Journal of Educational Psychology*, 47, 7–17.

Browne, C. A., & Woolley, J. D. (2001) 'Theory of mind in children's naming of drawings', *Journal of Cognition and Development* 2, 389–412.

Bruce, V., & Green, P. R. (1990) *Visual Perception: physiology, psychology and ecology*, 2nd edition, London: Lawrence Erlbaum.

Bruner, J. S. (1964) 'The course of cognitive growth', *American Psychologist* 19, 1–15.

Brunswick, E. (1956) *Perception and the Representative Design of Psychological Experiments*, 2nd edition, Berkeley: University of California Press.

Buck, J. N. (1948) 'The HPT test', *Journal of Clinical Psychology* 4, 151–9.

Buck, L. (2003) 'Pop art and after', *Independent Review*, Tuesday 21 January, 12–13.

Bühler, K. (1930) *The Mental Development of the Child*, London: Routledge & Kegan Paul.

Burgess, A. W., & Hartman, C. R. (1993) 'Children's drawings', *Child Abuse and Neglect* 17, 161–8.

Burgess, A. W., McCausland, M. P., & Wolbert, W. A. (1981) 'Children's drawings as indicators of sexual trauma', *Perspectives in Psychiatric Care* 19, 50–9.

Burkitt, E., Barrett, M., & Davis, A. (2003a) 'Children's colour choices for completing drawings of affectively characterised topics', *Journal of Child Psychology and Psychiatry* 44, 445–55.

(2003b) 'The effect of emotional characterisation on the size of children's drawings', *British Journal of Developmental Psychology* 21, 565–84.

(2004) 'The effect of affective characteristics on the use of size and colour in drawings produced by children in the absence of a model', *Educational Psychology* 24, 315–43.

Burns, R., & Kaufman, S. H. (1970) *Kinetic Family Drawings (K-F-D)*, New York: Brunner/Mazel.

Burt, C. (1933) *Mental and Scholastic Tests*, 4th edition, London: King & Son.

Bushnell, I. W. R. (2001) 'Mother's face recognition in newborn infants: learning and memory', *Infant and Child Development* 10, 67–74.

Butler, S., Gross, J., & Hayne, H. (1995) 'The effect of drawing on memory performance in young children', *Developmental Psychology* 31, 597–608.

Butterworth, G. (1989) 'Events and encounters in infant perception', in *Infant Development*, ed. A. Slater & G. Bremner, Hove, East Sussex: Lawrence Erlbaum, pp. 73–83.

Cabe, P. A. (1980) 'Picture perception in nonhuman subjects', in *The Perception of Pictures*, vol. II, ed. M. A. Hagen, New York: Academic Press, pp. 305–43.

Calder, A. J., Young, A. W., Rowland, D., Perrett, D. I., Hodges, J. R., & Etcoff, N. L. (1996) 'Facial emotion recognition after bilateral amygdala damage: differentially severe impairment of fear', *Cognitive Neuropsychology* 13, 699–745.

Callaghan, T. C. (1994) 'Drawing from perceptual, emotional and motor resources', paper presented at the Thirteenth International Congress of the Association for Empirical Aesthetics, Montreal, August.

(1995) 'Developmental trends in the judgements of emotion in visual art', poster presented at the British Psychological Society Developmental Section conference, University of Warwick, September.

(1997) 'Children's judgments of emotions portrayed in museum art', *British Journal of Developmental Psychology* 15, 515–29.

(1999) 'Early understanding and production of graphic symbols', *Child Development* 70, 1314–24.

(2000a) 'Factors affecting graphic symbol understanding in the third year: language, similarity and iconicity', *Cognitive Development* 15, 207–36.

(2000b) 'The role of context in preschoolers' judgments of emotion in art', *British Journal of Developmental Psychology* 18, 465–74.

Callaghan, T. C., & MacFarlane, J. M. (1998) 'An attentional analysis of children's sensitivity to artistic style in paintings', *Developmental Science* 1, 307–13.

Callaghan, T. C., & MacGregor, L. (1997) 'Children drawing emotion and experiencing emotion', unpublished manuscript, St Francis Xavier University, Nova Scotia.

Callaghan, T. C., & Rochat, P. (2003) 'Traces of the artist: sensitivity to the role of the artist in children's pictorial reasoning', *British Journal of Developmental Psychology* 21, 415–46.

Callaghan, T. C., Rochat, P., MacGillivray, T., & MacLellan, C. (2004) 'Grasping at depicted objects in 6- to 18-month-olds: stimulus and task influences', unpublished manuscript, St Francis Xavier University, Nova Scotia.

Capitan, L. (1923) 'Les manifestations ethnographiques et magiques sur les parois de la grotte de Montespan', *Revue Anthropologique* 33, 545–50.

Capitan, L., & Peyrony, D. (1921) 'Les origines de l'art à l'aurignacien moyen', *Revue Anthropologique* 31, 92–112.

Caron-Pargue, J. (1985) *Le dessin du cube chez l'enfant*, New York: Peter Lang.

Carothers, T., & Gardner, H. (1979) 'When children's drawings become art: the emergence of aesthetic production and perception', *Developmental Psychology* 15, 570–80.

Cartailhac, E., & Breuil, H. (1910) 'Les peintures et gravures murales des cavernes pyrénéennes. IV. Gargas', *L'Anthropologie* 21, 129–50.

Case, R. (1985) *Intellectual Development: birth to adulthood*, New York: Academic Press.

(1992) *The Mind's New Staircase: exploring the conceptual underpinnings of children's thought and knowledge*, Hillsdale, NJ: Lawrence Erlbaum.

Catte, M. (1998) 'Emotional indicators in children's human figure drawings: an evaluation of the Draw-a-Person test', unpublished D.Phil. thesis, University of York.

Ceci, S. J., & Bruck, M. (1993) 'Suggestibility of the child witness: a historical review and synthesis', *Psychological Bulletin* 113, 403–39.

Chan, J., Eysenck, H., & Götz, K. (1980) 'A new visual aesthetic sensitivity test: cross-cultural comparisons between Hong Kong children and adults, and English and Japanese samples', *Perceptual and Motor Skills* 50, 1385–6.

Chandler, M. J. (1988) 'Doubts and developing theories of mind', in *Developing Theories of Mind*, ed. J. W. Astington, P. L. Harris & D. R. Olson, Cambridge: Cambridge University Press, pp. 387–413.

Chandler, M. J., & Helm, D. (1984) 'Developmental changes in the contributions of shared experience to social role-taking competence', *International Journal of Behavioral Development* 7, 145–56.

Charman, T., & Baron-Cohen, S. (1993) 'Drawing development in autism: the intellectual to visual realism shift', *British Journal of Developmental Psychology* 11, 171–85.

Chauvet, J.-M., Deschamps, E. B., & Hillaire, C. (1995) *La grotte Chauvet, à Vallon-Pont-d'Arc*, Paris: Editions du Seuil.

Chen, M. J. (1985) 'Young children's representational drawings of solid objects: a comparison of drawing and copying', in *Visual Order: the nature and development of pictorial representation*, ed. N. H. Freeman & M. V. Cox, Cambridge: Cambridge University Press, pp. 157–75.

Chen, M. J., & Cook, M. L. (1984) 'Representational drawings of solid objects by young children', *Perception* 13, 377–85.

Child, I. L. (1965) 'Personality correlates of aesthetic judgement in college students', *Journal of Personality* 33, 476–511.

Church, J. (1961) *Language and the Discovery of Reality*, New York: Random House.

Claparède, E. (1907) 'Plan d'expériences collectives sur le dessin des enfants', *Archives de Psychologie* 6, 276–8.

Clark, A. B. (1896–1897) 'The child's attitude towards perspective problems', in *Studies in Education*, vol. i, ed. E. Barnes, Stanford, CA: Stanford University Press, pp. 283–94.

Clement, R. (1992) 'The classroom reality of drawing', in *Drawing Research and Development*, ed. D. Thistlewood, Harlow: Longman/NSEAD, pp. 121–9.

(1993) *The Art Teacher's Handbook*, Cheltenham: Stanley Thornes.

(1994) 'The readiness of primary schools to teach the National Curriculum in Art and Design', *Journal of Art and Design Education* 13, 9–19.

(1997) 'A survey of teachers' use of the works of artists, craftsworkers and designers in teaching the National Curriculum in Art, 1996 to 1997', unpublished report, University of Plymouth.

Clements, W., & Barrett, M. (1994) 'The drawings of children and young people with Down's syndrome: a case of delay or difference?', *British Journal of Educational Psychology* 64, 441–52.

Clottes, J. (1996) 'Epilogue' (pp. 89–128), in *Dawn of Art: the Chauvet cave*, ed. J. M. Chauvet, E. B. Deschamps & C. Hillaire, New York: Abrams.

Cocking, R. R., & Copple, C. E. (1987) 'Social influences on representational awareness: plans for representing and plans as representation', in *Blueprints for Thinking: the role of planning in cognitive development*, ed. S. L. Friedman, E. F. Scholnick & R. R. Cocking, Cambridge: Cambridge University Press, pp. 428–65.

Coffey, A. (1968) 'A developmental study of aesthetic preferences for realistic and nonobjective paintings', *Dissertation Abstracts International* 29, 4328B.

Cohen, F. W., & Phelps, R. E. (1985) 'Incest markers in children's artwork', *Arts in Psychotherapy* 12, 265–83.

Collingwood, R. (1938) *The Principles of Art*, Oxford: Clarendon Press.

Connolly, B. H., Morgan, S. B., Russell, F. F., & Fulliton, W. L. (1993) 'A longitudinal study of children with Down syndrome who experienced early intervention programming', *Physical Therapy* 73, 170–81.

Cook, M., Field, J., & Griffiths, K. (1978) 'The perception of solid form in early infancy', *Child Development* 49, 866–9.

Cooke, E. (1886) 'Our art teaching and child nature', *London Journal of Education*, January, 12–15.

Cooke, G. (1986) *Drawing and Talking with Infants*, Royal Borough of Kingston: Brycbox.

Cooke, G., Griffin, D., & Cox, M. (1998) *Teaching Young Children to Draw: imaginative approaches to representational drawing*, London: Falmer Press.

Coppen, H. (1970) *Visual Perception: a review of the literature relating to studies relevant to the development of teaching materials in the Commonwealth*, London: Commonwealth Secretariat.

Corcoran, A. (1954) 'Color usage in nursery school painting', *Child Development* 25, 107–13.

Costall, A. (1985) 'How meaning covers the traces', in *Visual Order: the nature and development of pictorial representation*, ed. N. H. Freeman & M. V. Cox, Cambridge: Cambridge University Press, pp. 17–30.

Cotterill, A., & Thomas, G. V. (1990) 'Children's production and perception of drawings of emotionally significant topics', poster presented at the Fourth European Conference on Developmental Psychology, University of Stirling, August.

Courage, M. L., & Adams, R. J. (1990) 'Visual acuity assessment from birth to three years using the acuity card procedures: cross-sectional and longitudinal samples', *Optometry and Vision Science* 67, 713–18.

Court, E. (1981) 'The dual vision: factors affecting Kenyan children's drawing behaviour', paper presented at the INSEA World Congress, Rotterdam, August.

   (1989) 'Drawing on culture: the influence of culture on children's drawing performance in rural Kenya', *Journal of Art and Design Education* 8, 65–88.

   (1992) 'Researching social influences in the drawings of rural Kenyan children', in *Drawing Research and Development*, ed. D. Thistlewood, Harlow: Longman/NSEAD, pp. 51–67.

   (1994) 'How culture influences children's drawing performance in rural Kenya', in *International Perspectives on Culture and Schooling*, ed. E. Thomas, London: Institute of Education, pp. 219–60.

Cox, M. V. (1978) 'Spatial depth relationships in young children's drawings', *Journal of Experimental Child Psychology* 26, 551–4.

   (1980) 'Visual perspective-taking in children', in *Are Young Children Egocentric?*, ed. M. V. Cox, London: Batsford, pp. 61–79.

   (1981) 'One thing behind another: problems of representation in children's drawings', *Educational Psychology* 1, 275–87.

   (1985) 'One object behind another: young children's use of array-specific or view-specific representations', in *Visual Order: the nature and development of pictorial representation*, ed. N. H. Freeman & M. V. Cox, Cambridge: Cambridge University Press, pp. 188–201.

   (1986) 'Cubes are difficult things to draw', *British Journal of Developmental Psychology* 4, 341–5.

(1989) 'Knowledge and appearance in children's pictorial representation', *Educational Psychology* 9, 15–25.

(1991) *The Child's Point of View*, 2nd edition, Hemel Hempstead: Harvester/ Wheatsheaf.

(1992) *Children's Drawings*, Harmondsworth: Penguin.

(1993) *Children's Drawings of the Human Figure*, Hove, East Sussex: Lawrence Erlbaum.

(1997) *Drawings of People by the Under-5s*, London: Falmer Press.

(1998) 'Drawings of people by Australian Aboriginal Children: the intermixing of cultural styles', *Journal of Art and Design Education* 17, 71–9.

Cox, M. V., & Bayraktar, R. (1989) 'A cross-cultural study of children's human figure drawings', paper presented at the Tenth Biennial Conference of the International Society for the Study of Behavioural Development, University of Jyväskylä, Finland, July.

Cox, M. V., & Braga, C. (1985) 'The representation of spatial relationships in the drawings of ESN(M) and normal children', *Educational Psychology* 5, 279–86.

Cox, M. V., & Catte, M. (2000) 'Severely disturbed children's human figure drawings: are they unusual or just poor drawings?', *European Child and Adolescent Psychiatry* 9, 301–6.

Cox, M. V., & Chapman, L. (1995) 'The air-gap phenomenon in young children's pictures', *Educational Psychology* 15, 313–22.

Cox, M. V., Cooke, G., & Griffin, D. (1995) 'Teaching children to draw in the Infants schools', *Journal of Art and Design Education* 14, 153–63.

Cox, M. V., & Cotgreave, S. (1996) 'The human figure drawings of normal children and those with mild learning difficulties', *Educational Psychology* 16, 433–8.

Cox, M. V., & Eames, K. (1999) 'Contrasting styles of drawing in gifted individuals with autism', *Autism* 3, 397–409.

Cox, M. V., Eames, K., & Cooke, G. (1994) 'The teaching of drawing in the infants school: an evaluation of the "negotiated drawing" approach', *International Journal of Early Years Education* 2, 68–83.

Cox, M. V., & Hill, R. (1996) 'Different strokes', *Times Higher Educational Supplement*, 9 August, 18.

Cox, M. V., & Hodsoll, J. (2000) 'Children's diachronic thinking in relation to developmental changes in their drawings of the human figure', *British Journal of Developmental Psychology* 18, 13–24.

Cox, M. V., & Howarth, C. (1989) 'The human figure drawings of normal children and those with severe learning difficulties', *British Journal of Developmental Psychology* 7, 333–9.

Cox, M. V., Koyasu, M., Hiranuma, H., & Perara, J. (2001) 'Children's human figure drawings in the UK and Japan: the effects of age, sex and culture', *British Journal of Developmental Psychology* 19, 275–92.

Cox, M. V., & Lambon Ralph, M. (1996) 'Young children's ability to adapt their drawings of the human figure', *Educational Psychology* 16, 245–5.

Cox, M. V., & Littleton, K. (1995) 'Children's use of converging obliques in their perspective drawings', *Educational Psychology* 15, 127–39.

Cox, M. V., & Martin, A. (1988) 'Young children's viewer-centred representations: drawings of a cube placed inside or behind a transparent or opaque beaker', *International Journal of Behavioral Development* 11, 233–45.

Cox, M. V., & Mason, S. (1998) 'The young child's pictorial representation of the human figure', *International Journal of Early Years Education* 6, 31–8.

Cox, M. V., & Maynard, S. (1998) 'The human figure drawings of children with Down's syndrome', *British Journal of Developmental Psychology* 16, 133–7.

Cox, M. V., & Moore, R. (1994) 'Children's depictions of different views of the human figure', *Educational Psychology* 14, 427–36.

Cox, M. V., & Parkin, C. E. (1986) 'Young children's human figure drawing: cross-sectional and longitudinal studies', *Educational Psychology* 6, 353–68.

Cox, M. V., & Perara, J. (1998) 'Children's observational drawings: a nine-point scale for scoring drawings of a cube', *Educational Psychology* 18, 309–17.
    (2001) 'Children's use of the height and size cues to depict a projective depth relationship in their pictures', *Psychologia* 44, 99–110.

Cox, M. V., Perara, J., & Xu, F. (1998) 'Children's drawing ability in the UK and China', *Psychologia* 41, 171–82.
    (1999) 'Children's drawings in the UK and China', *Journal of Arts and Design Education* 18, 173–81.

Cox, M. V., & Rowlands, A. (2000) 'The effect of three different educational approaches on children's drawing ability: Steiner, Montessori and traditional', *British Journal of Educational Psychology* 70, 485–503.

Craddick, R. A. (1963) 'Size of Hallowe'en witch drawings prior to, on and after Hallowe'en', *Perceptual and Motor Skills* 16, 235–8.

Critchley, H. D., Daly, E. M., Bullmore, E. T., Williams, S. C. R., van Amelsvoort, T., Robertson, D. M., Rowe, A., Phillips, M., McAlonan, G., Howlin, P., & Murphy, D. G. M. (2000) 'The functional neuroanatomy of social behaviour: changes in cerebral blood flow when people with autistic disorder process facial expressions', *Brain* 123, 2203–12.

Crook, C. (1985) 'Knowledge and appearance', in *Visual Order: the nature and development of pictorial representation*, ed. N. H. Freeman & M. V. Cox, Cambridge: Cambridge University Press, pp. 248–65.

Cunningham, J., & Odom, R. (1986) 'Differential salience of facial features in children's perception of affective expression', *Child Development* 57, 136–42.

Dale, P. S. (1976) *Language Development: structure and function*, 2nd edition, New York: Holt, Rinehart & Winston.

Dalley, T. (1980) 'Assessing the therapeutic effect of art: an illustrated case study', *Arts in Psychotherapy* 7, 11–17.
    (1984) 'Introduction', in *Art as Therapy*, ed. T. Dalley, London and New York: Routledge & Kegan Paul, pp. xi–xxviii.

Damerow, P. (1998) 'Prehistory and cognitive development', in *Piaget, Evolution, and Development*, ed. J. Langer & M. Killen, Mahwah, NJ: Lawrence Erlbaum, pp. 247–69.

D'Angiulli, A., & Kennedy, J. M. (2000) 'Guided exploration enhances tactual picture recognition in blindfolded sighted children: implications for blind children', *International Journal of Rehabilitation Research* 23, 319–20.

D'Angiulli, A., Kennedy, J. M., & Heller, M. A. (1998) 'Blind children recognizing tactile pictures respond like sighted children given guidance in exploration', *Scandinavian Journal of Psychology* 39, 187–90.

Darwin, C. (1872) *The Expression of the Emotions in Man and Animals*, London: Murray.

(1877) 'A biographical sketch of an infant', *Mind* 11, 286–94.

Davis, A. M. (1983) 'Contextual sensitivity in young children's drawings', *Journal of Experimental Child Psychology* 35, 478–86.

Davis, A. M., & Bentley, M. (1984) 'Young children's interpretation of the task demands in a simple experimental situation: an example from drawings', *Educational Psychology* 4, 249–54.

Davis, J. H. (1997) 'The what and the whether of the U: cultural implications of understanding development in graphic symbolization', *Human Development* 40, 145–54.

Davis, W. (1986) 'The origins of image making', *Current Anthropology* 27, 193–202.

Davison, L. E., & Thomas, G. V. (2001) 'Effects of drawing on children's item recall', *Journal of Experimental Child Psychology* 78, 155–77.

Dayton, G. O., Jones, M. H., Giu, P., Rawson, R. H., Steele, B., & Rose, M. (1964) 'Developmental study of coordinated eye movements in the human infant: 1 – visual activity in the newborn: a study based on induced autokinetic nystagmus recorded by electrooculography, *Archives of Ophthalmology* 71, 865–70.

DeLoache, J. S. (1989) 'The development of representation in young children', in *Advances in Child Development and Behavior*, vol. xxii, ed. H. W. Reese, New York: Academic Press, pp. 1–39.

(1991) 'Symbolic functioning in very young children: understanding of pictures and models', *Child Development* 62, 737–52.

(1995a) 'Early symbol understanding and use', *Psychology of Learning and Motivation* 33, 65–114.

(1995b) 'Early understanding and the use of symbols: the model model', *Current Directions in Cognitive Science* 4, 109–13.

(2002) 'Early development of the understanding and use of symbolic artifacts', in *Handbook of Childhood Cognitive Development*, ed. U. Goswami, Oxford: Basil Blackwell, pp. 206–26.

DeLoache, J. S., & Burns, N. M. (1994) 'Early understanding of the representational function of pictures', *Cognition* 52, 83–110.

DeLoache, J. S., Pierroutsakos, S. L., & Troseth, G. L. (1997) 'The three Rs of pictorial competence', in *Annals of Child Development*, vol. xii, ed. R. A. Vasta, London: Jessica Kingsley, pp. 1–48.

DeLoache, J. S., Pierroutsakos, S. L., Uttal, D. H., Rosengren, K. S., & Gottlieb, A. (1998) 'Grasping the nature of pictures', *Psychological Science* 9, 205–10.

DeLoache, J.S., Strauss, M.S., & Maynard, J. (1979) 'Picture perception in infancy', *Infant Behavior and Development* 2, 77–89.

De Meredieu, F. (1974) *Le dessin d'enfant*, Paris: Editions Universitaires Jean-Pierre de Large.

Dennis, W. (1957) 'Performance of Near-Eastern children on the Draw-a-Man test', *Child Development* 28, 427–30.

(1966) *Group Values through Children's Drawings*, New York: John Wiley.

De Piles, R. (1708) *Cours de peinture par principes*, Paris: Jacques Estienne.

Derȩgowski, J.B. (1962) 'Preference for chain-type drawings in Zambian domestic servants and primary school children', *Psychologia Africana* 12, 172–80.

(1971) 'Responses mediating pictorial recognition', *Journal of Social Psychology* 84, 27–33.

(1977) 'Pictures, symbols and frames of reference', in *The Child's Representation of the World*, ed. G. Butterworth, New York: Plenum Press, pp. 219–36.

(1980) *Illusions, Patterns and Pictures: a cross-cultural perspective*, London: Academic Press.

(1998) 'A man is a difficult beast to draw: the neglected determinant in rock art', in *Rock Art Research moving into the Twenty-First Century*, ed. S.A. Pager, Occasional SARARA Publications 4.

(2000) 'Pictorial perception: individual and group differences within the human species', in *Picture Perception in Animals*, ed. J. Fagot, Hove, East Sussex: Psychology Press, pp. 395–429.

Derȩgowski, J.B., Ellis, H., & Shepherd, J. (1973) 'A cross-cultural study of recognition of pictures of faces and cups', *International Journal of Psychology* 8, 269–73.

Derȩgowski, J.B., Muldrow, E.S., & Muldrow, W.F. (1972) 'Pictorial recognition in a remote Ethiopian population', *Perception* 1, 417–25.

Derȩgowski, J.B., & Serpell, R. (1971) 'Performance on a sorting task: a cross-cultural experiment', *International Journal of Psychology* 6, 273–81.

DFE (Department for Education) (1995) *Art in the National Curriculum*, London: HMSO.

DFE&E (Department for Education & Employment) (1999a) *The National Curriculum: handbook for primary teachers in England, key stages 1 and 2*, London: Department of Education & Employment/Qualifications and Curriculum Authority.

(1999b) *The National Curriculum: handbook for secondary teachers in England, key stages 3 and 4*, London: Department of Education & Employment/ Qualifications and Curriculum Authority.

Dieffenbach, E.W. (1977) 'Koppitz HFD test: the reliability and clinical validity of its emotional indicators', *Dissertation Abstracts International* 38 (10-A), 6053.

Di Leo, J. (1970) *Young Children and their Drawings*, New York: Brunner/Mazel.

(1973) *Children's Drawings as Diagnostic Aids*, New York: Brunner/Mazel.

Dirks, J., & Gibson, E. (1977) 'Infants' perception of similarity between live people and their photographs', *Child Development* 48, 124–30.

Dobkin de Rios, M., & Winkelman, M. (1989) 'Shamanism and altered states of consciousness: an introduction', *Journal of Psychoactive Drugs* 21, 1–7.

D'Onofrio, A., & Nodin, C. F. (1990) 'Parson's model painted realistically', *Journal of Aesthetic Education* 14, 103–6.

Dubery, F., & Willats, J. (1972) *Perspective and Other Drawing Systems*, London: Herbert Press.

Du Bois, C. (1944) *The People of Alor: a social-psychological study of an East Indian island*, Minneapolis: University of Minnesota Press.

Duncum, P. (1993) '"I need to do Sophie . . . !" When scribbling is representational', *Australian Journal of Early Childhood* 18, 29–35.

Dye, L., & Dowker, A. (1996) 'Children's concepts of age differences in human figure drawing style', poster presented at the Growing Mind Conference, Geneva, September.

Eames, K., & Cox, M. V. (1994) 'Visual realism in the drawings of autistic, Down's syndrome and normal children', *British Journal of Developmental Psychology* 12, 235–9.

Earl, C. J. C. (1933) 'The human figure drawing of feeble-minded adults', *Proceedings of the American Association of Mental Deficiency* 38, 107–20.

Edgerton, S. Y. (1975) *The Renaissance Rediscovery of Linear Perspective*, New York: Basic Books.

(1980) 'The Renaissance artist as quantifier', in *The Perception of Pictures*, vol. I, ed. M. A. Hagen, New York: Academic Press, pp. 179–212.

Edmunds, F. (1975) *Rudolf Steiner's Gift to Education: the Waldorf Schools*, London: Rudolf Steiner Press.

Edwards, B. (1986) *Drawing on the Artist Within*, Glasgow: Fontana/Collins.

(1992) *Drawing on the Right Side of the Brain*, London: Souvenir Press.

Edwards, C. A., & Forman, B. D. (1989) 'Effects of child interview method on accuracy and completeness of sexual abuse information recall', *Social Behavior & Personality* 17, 237–47.

Eisner, E. (1972) *Educating Artistic Vision*, New York: Macmillan.

(1976) 'What we know about children's art – and what we need to know', in *The Arts, Human Development, and Education*, ed. E. Eisner, Berkeley: McCutchan, pp. 5–18.

(1989) 'Structure and magic in discipline-based art education', in *Critical Studies in Art and Design Education*, ed. D. Thistlewood, Portsmouth, NH: Heinemann, pp. 14–26.

Ekman, P. (1982) *Emotion in the Human Face*, Cambridge: Cambridge University Press.

Ekman, P., & Friesen, W. V. (1975) *Unmasking the Face*, Englewood Cliffs, NJ: Prentice-Hall.

(1986) 'A new pan-cultural facial expression of emotion', *Motivation and Emotion* 10, 159–68.

Elatta, T. (1992) 'Sudanese graphic imagery: a survey for art education', in *Drawing Research and Development*, ed. D. Thistlewood, Harlow: Longman/NSEAD, pp. 68–74.

Ellis, H., Deregowski, J., & Shepherd, J. (1975) 'Descriptions of white and black faces by white and black subjects', *International Journal of Psychology* 10, 119–23.

Ellis, W. D. (1969) *A Source Book for Gestalt Psychology*, London: Routledge & Kegan Paul.

Eng, H. (1954) *The Psychology of Children's Drawings*, 2nd edition, London: Routledge & Kegan Paul.

English, M. R. (1987) 'The effects of using computer graphics with preschool children', unpublished Master's thesis, University of British Columbia, Vancouver, Canada.

Ericsson, K. A., Krampe, R. T., & Tesch-Romer, C. (1993) 'The role of deliberate practice in the acquisition of expert performance', *Psychological Review* 100, 363–406.

Fagot, J., Martin-Malivel, J., & Dépy, D. (2000) 'What is the evidence for an equivalence between objects and pictures in birds and nonhuman primates?', in *Picture Perception in Animals*, ed. J. Fagot, Hove, East Sussex: Psychology Press, pp. 295–320.

Fantz, R. L. (1961) 'A method for studying depth perception in infants under six months of age', *Psychological Record* 11, 27–32.

  (1963) 'Pattern vision in newborn infants', *Science* 140, 296–7.

Fayol, M., Barrouillet, P., & Chevrot, C. (1995) 'Judgement and production of drawings by 3- and 10-year-olds: comparison of declarative and procedural drawing knowledge', *European Journal of Psychology of Education* 10, 303–13.

Fein, D., Lucci, D., & Waterhouse, L. (1990) 'Brief report: fragmental drawings in autistic children', *Journal of Autism and Developmental Disorders* 20, 263–9.

Fein, G. G. (1981) 'Pretend play in childhood: an integrative review', *Child Development* 52, 1095–118.

Feldman, D. H., with Goldsmith, L. (1986) *Nature's Gambit*, New York: Basic Books.

Feldman, G. (1987) 'Developmental psychology and art education: two fields at the crossroads', *Journal of Aesthetic Education* 21, 243–59.

Fineberg, J. (1997) *The Innocent Eye: children's art and the modern artist*, Princeton, NJ: Princeton University Press.

Fivush, R., Haden, C., & Adam, S. (1995) 'Structure and coherence of preschoolers' personal narrative over time: implications for childhood amnesia', *Journal of Experimental Child Psychology* 60, 32–56.

Flavell, J. H. (1971) 'Stage related properties of cognitive development, *Cognitive Psychology* 2, 421–53.

Ford, C. S., Prothro, E. T., & Child, I. L. (1966) 'Some transcultural comparisons of esthetic judgment', *Journal of Social Psychology* 68, 19–26.

Forrest, M., & Thomas, G. V. (1991) 'An exploratory study of drawings by bereaved children', *British Journal of Clinical Psychology* 30, 373–4.

Fortes, M. (1940) 'Children's drawings among the Tallensi', *Africa* 13, 239–95.

  (1981) 'Tallensi children's drawings', in *Universals of Human Thought: some African evidence*, ed. B. Lloyd & J. Gay, Cambridge: Cambridge University Press, pp. 46–70.

Fox, T., & Thomas, G. V. (1990) 'Children's drawings of an anxiety-eliciting topic effect on size of the drawing', *British Journal of Clinical Psychology* 29, 71–81.

Fraser, A. K. (1923) *Teaching Healthcraft to African Women*, London: Longmans.

Freeman, N. H. (1976) 'Children's drawings: cognitive aspects', *Journal of Child Psychology and Psychiatry* 17, 345–50.

   (1980) *Strategies of Representation in Young Children: analysis of spatial skills and drawing processes*, London: Academic Press.

   (1990) 'Innovation in children's art', *European Journal for High Ability* 1, 52–63.

   (1995) 'The emergence of a framework theory of pictorial reasoning', in *Drawing and Looking*, ed. C. Lange-Küttner & G. V. Thomas, Hemel Hempstead: Harvester/Wheatsheaf, pp. 135–46.

   (1996) 'Art learning in developmental perspective', *Journal of Art and Design Education* 15, 125–31.

Freeman, N. H., Eiser, C., & Sayers, J. (1977) 'Children's strategies in producing 3-D relationships on a 2-D surface', *Journal of Experimental Child Psychology* 23, 305–14.

Freeman, N. H., & Janikoun, R. (1972) 'Intellectual realism in children's drawings of a familiar object with distinctive features', *Child Development* 43, 1116–21.

Freeman, N. H., & Parsons, M. J. (2001) 'Children's intuitive understandings of pictures', in *Understanding and Teaching the Intuitive Mind: student and teacher learning*, ed. B. Tordoff & R. J. Sternberg, Mahwah, NJ: Lawrence Erlbaum, pp. 73–91.

Freund, L. S. (1990) 'Maternal regulation of children's problem-solving behavior and its impact on children's performance', *Child Development* 61, 113–26.

Fridlund, A. J. (1994) *Human Facial Expression: an Evolutionary View*, San Diego, CA: Academic Press.

Frijda, N. H. (1969) 'Recognition of emotion', in *Advances in Experimental Social Psychology*, vol. IV, ed. L. Berkowitz, New York: Academic Press, pp. 167–223.

Frisch, R. G., & Handler, L. (1967) 'Differences in negro and white drawings: a cultural interpretation', *Perceptual and Motor Skills* 24, 667–70.

Frith, U. (1989) *Autism: exploring the enigma*, Oxford: Basil Blackwell.

   (1994) *Autism and Asperger Syndrome*, Cambridge: Cambridge University Press.

Fujimoto, K. (1979) 'Developmental study on the drawings of the human figure in motion', *Japanese Journal of Educational Psychology* 27, 245–52.

Furman, L. (1991) 'Human figure drawings and sexual abuse', *Journal of Pediatrics* 118, 164.

Gablik, S. (1976) *Progress in Art*, London: Thames & Hudson.

Ganchrow, J. R., Steiner, J. E., & Daher, M. (1983) 'Neonatal facial expressions in response to different qualities and intensities of gustatory stimuli', *Infant Behavior and Development* 6, 473–84.

Gardner, H. (1972) 'The development of sensitivity to figural and stylistic aspects of paintings', *British Journal of Psychology* 63, 605–15.

   (1980) *Artful Scribbles*, London: Jill Norman.

(1993) *Multiple Intelligences: the theory in practice*, New York: Basic Books.

Gardner, H., & Winner, E. (1982) 'First intimations of artistry', in *U-shaped Behavioral Growth*, ed. S. Strauss, New York: Academic Press, pp. 147–68.

Gardner, H., Winner, E., & Kircher, M. (1975) 'Children's conception of the arts', *Journal of Aesthetic Education* 9, 60–77.

Gathercole, S. E. (1998) 'The development of memory', *Journal of Child Psychology and Psychiatry* 39, 3–27.

Gautier, T. (1856) *L'art moderne*, Paris: Michel Lévy Frères.

Gazzaniga, M. S. (1988) 'The dynamics of cerebral specialization and modular interactions', in *Thought without Language*, ed. L. Weiskrantz, Oxford: Clarendon Press, pp. 430–50.

Gee, S., Gregory, M., & Pipe, M-E. (1999) '"What colour is your pet dinosaur?" The impact of pre-interview training and question type on children's answers', *Legal and Criminological Psychology* 4, 111–28.

Geiger, S. (1977) 'The role of peer imitation and its significance toward change of spatial features', unpublished graduate project, Massachusetts College of Art.

Gentle, K. (1993) *Teaching Painting in the Primary School*, London: Cassell.

Geschwind, N., & Galaburda, A. M. (1987) *Cerebral Lateralization*, Cambridge, MA: MIT Press.

Gibson, E. J. (1969) *Principles of Perceptual Learning and Development*, New York: Appleton-Century Crofts.

(1987) 'What does infant perception tell us about theories of perception?', *Journal of Experimental Psychology: Human Perception and Performance* 13, 515–23.

Gibson, J. J. (1950) *The Perception of the Visual World*, Boston, MA: Houghton Mifflin.

(1979) *The Ecological Approach to Visual Perception*, Boston, MA: Houghton Mifflin.

(1980) 'Foreword', in *The Perception of Pictures*, vol. I, ed. M. A. Hagen, New York: Academic Press, pp. xi–xviii.

Gillings, F. (2003) 'The influence of a groundline as an external orientation cue in children's human figure drawing', unpublished undergraduate project, University of York.

Gillison, F. (1995) 'An experimental approach to aesthetic development', unpublished project, University of Southampton.

Ginsburg, I. H. (1982) 'Jean Piaget and Rudolf Steiner: stages of child development and implications for pedagogy', *Teachers College Record* 84, 327–37.

Glaser, B. (1968) 'Questions to Stella and Judd', in *Minimal Art: a critical anthology*, ed. G. Battcock, New York: Dutton, pp. 148–64.

Golomb, C. (1973) 'Children's representation of the human figure: the effects of models, media and instruction', *Genetic Psychology Monographs* 95, 36–48.

(1974) *Young Children's Sculpture and Drawing*, Cambridge, MA: Harvard University Press.

(1981) 'Representation and reality: the origins and determinants of young children's drawings', *Review of Research in Visual Art Education* 14, 36–48.

(1988) 'Symbolic inventions and transformation in child art', in *Imagination and Education*, ed. K. Egan & D. Nadaner, New York: Teachers College Press, pp. 222–36.

(1992) *The Child's Creation of a Pictorial World*, Berkeley, CA: University of California Press.

(1993) 'Art and the young child: another look at the developmental question', *Visual Arts Research* 19, 1–15.

(1995) 'Eitan: the artistic development of a child prodigy', in *The Development of Artistically Gifted Children*, ed. C. Golomb, Hillsdale, NJ: Lawrence Erlbaum, pp. 171–96.

(2002) *Child Art in Context*, Washington, DC: American Psychological Association.

Golomb, C., & Barr-Grossman, T. (1977) 'Representational development of the human figure in familial retardates', *Genetic Psychology Monographs* 95, 247–66.

Gombrich, E. H. (1954) *The Story of Art*, 6th edition, London: Phaidon.

(1960) *Art and Illusion: a study in the psychology of pictorial representation*, London: Phaidon.

(1972) 'The mask and the face', in *Art, Perception, and Reality*, ed. M. Mandelbaum, Baltimore: Johns Hopkins University Press, pp. 1–46.

(2002) *The Preference for the Primitive*, London: Phaidon.

Goodenough, F. L. (1926) *Measurement of Intelligence by Drawings*, New York: Harcourt, Brace & World.

Goodenough, F. L., & Harris, D. B. (1950) 'Studies in the psychology of children's drawings: II. 1928–1949', *Psychological Bulletin* 47, 369–433.

Goodman, G. S., & Reed, R. S. (1986) 'Age differences in eyewitness testimony', *Law and Human Behavior* 10, 317–32.

Goodman, N. (1968) *Languages of Art*, New York: Bobbs-Merrill.

(1976) *Languages of Art*, 2nd edition, Indianapolis: Hackett.

Goodnow, J. (1977) *Children's Drawing*, London: Fontana/Open Books.

(1978) 'Visible thinking: cognitive aspects of change in drawings', *Child Development* 49, 637–41.

Goodnow, J., & Friedman, S. (1972) 'Orientation in children's human figure drawings', *Developmental Psychology* 7, 10–16.

Goodnow, J. J., Wilkins, P., & Dawes, L. (1986) 'Acquiring cultural forms: cognitive aspects of socialization illustrated by children's drawings and judgments of drawings', *International Journal of Behavioural Development* 9, 485–505.

Goodwin, J. (1982) 'Use of drawings in evaluating children who may be incest victims', *Children and Youth Services Review* 4, 269–78.

Goren, C. C., Sarty, M., & Wu, P. Y. K. (1975) 'Visual following and pattern discrimination of face-like stimuli of newborn infants', *Pediatrics* 56, 544–9.

Goude, G. (1972) 'A multidimensional scaling approach to the perception of art II', *Scandinavian Journal of Psychology* 13, 272–84.

Gowans, A. (1979) 'Child art as an instrument for studying history', *Art History* 2, 247–74.

Gray, R., & Thomas, G. (1986) 'Children's drawings of topics differing in significance: effects on placement relative to self-drawings', unpublished paper, University of Birmingham.

Grayson, C. (1972) *Leon Battista Alberti: On Painting and On Sculpture*, London: Phaidon.

Greenhoot, A. F., Ornstein, P. A., Gordon, B. N., & Baker-Ward, L. (1999) 'Acting out the details of a pediatric check-up: the impact of interview condition and behavioral style on children's memory report', *Child Development* 70, 363–80.

Gregory, R. L. (1970) *The Intelligent Eye*, London: Weidenfeld & Nicolson.

(1972) *Eye and Brain*, London: World University Library.

(1974) *Concepts and Mechanisms of Perception*, London: Duckworth.

Gross, J., & Hayne, H. (1998) 'Drawing facilitates children's verbal reports of emotionally laden events', *Journal of Experimental Psychology: Applied* 4, 163–79.

(1999) 'Drawing facilitates children's verbal reports after long delays', *Journal of Experimental Psychology: Applied 5*, 265–83.

Guilford, J. P. (1940) 'There is a system in color preferences', *Journal of the Optical Society of America* 30, 455–9.

Haas, M. (1978) *Children Drawing*, Oranim: Institute for Science Education and the Improvement of Teaching, School of Education of the Kibbutz Movement.

Haber, R. N. (1979) 'Perceiving the lay-out of space in pictures: a perspective theory based upon Leonardo da Vinci', in *Perception and Pictorial Representation*, ed. C. Nodine & D. Fisher, New York: Praeger, pp. 84–99.

(1980) 'Perceiving space from pictures: a theoretical analysis', in *The Perception of Pictures*, vol. I, ed. M. A. Hagen, New York: Academic Press, pp. 3–31.

Haeckel, E. (1906) *The Evolution of Man*, London: Watts & Co. (original work published 1874).

Hagen, M. A. (1976) 'Development of ability to perceive and produce pictorial depth cue of overlapping', *Perceptual and Motor Skills* 42, 1007–14.

(1980) 'Generative theory: a perceptual theory of pictorial representation', in *The Perception of Pictures*, vol. II, ed. M. A. Hagen, New York: Academic Press, pp. 3–46.

(1985) 'There is no development in art', in *Visual Order: the nature and development of pictorial representation*, ed. N. H. Freeman & M. V. Cox, Cambridge: Cambridge University Press, pp. 59–77.

Hagen, M. A., & Elliott, H. B. (1976) 'An investigation of the relationship between viewing condition and preference for true and modified linear perspective with adults', *Journal of Experimental Psychology: Human Perception and Performance* 2, 479–90.

Hagen, M. A., & Jones, R. K. (1978) 'Differential patterns of preference for modified linear perspective in children and adults', *Journal of Experimental Psychology* 26, 205–15.

Hagen, M. A., & Johnson, M. M. (1977) 'Hudson pictorial depth perception test: cultural content and question with a western sample', *Journal of Social Psychology* 101, 3–11.

Hahn, J. (1972) 'Aurignacian signs, pendants, and art objects in central and eastern Europe', *World Archaeology* 3, 253–66.

Halford, G. S. (1989) 'Reflections on 25 years of Piagetian cognitive developmental psychology, 1963–1988', *Human Development* 32, 325–57.

Hall, J. (2002) 'Older and wiser', a review of E. H. Gombrich's *The Preference for the Primitive*, *Times Literary Supplement* 5194 (18 October), 3–5.

Halverson, J. (1992) 'The first pictures: perceptual foundations of Paleolithic art', *Perception* 21, 389–404.

Hamburger, V., & Oppenheim, R. W. (1982) 'Naturally occurring neuronal death in vertebrates', *Neuroscience Commentaries* 1, 39–55.

Happé, F. (1995) *Autism*, Cambridge, MA: Harvard University Press.

  (1999) 'Why success is more interesting than failure', *Psychologist* 12, 540–6.

Hargreaves, D. J., & Galton, M. J. (1992) 'Aesthetic learning: psychological theory and educational practice', in *The Arts, Education, and Aesthetic Knowing* (91st yearbook of the National Society for the Study of Education, part 2), ed. B. Reimer & R. A. Smith, Chicago: NSSE, pp. 124–50.

Hargreaves, D. J., Jones, P. M., & Martin, D. (1981) 'The air gap phenomenon in children's landscape drawings', *Journal of Experimental Child Psychology* 32, 11–20.

Harris, D. B. (1963) *Children's Drawings as Measures of Intellectual Maturity: a revision and extension of the Goodenough Draw-a-Man Test*, New York: Harcourt, Brace & World.

  (1971) 'The case method in art education', in *A Report on Preconference Education Research Training Program for Descriptive Research in Art Education*, ed. G. Kensler, Reston, VA: National Art Education Association, pp. 29–49.

Harris, M., & Butterworth, G. (2002) *Developmental Psychology*, Hove, East Sussex: Psychology Press.

Harrison, E. R. (1990) 'The emergence of children's ability to classify paintings: a developmental study using computer-manipulated images', *Visual Arts Research* 16, 48–57.

Hart, L. M. (1993) 'The role of cultural context in multicultural aesthetics', *Journal of Multi-cultural and Cross-cultural Research in Art Education* 11, 5–19.

Harvey, W. (1962) *On the Movement of the Heart and Blood in Animals* (translated by K. J. Franklin), London and New York: Dent Dutton, Everyman's Library (original work published 1628).

Hauser, S. L., Delong, G. R., & Rosman, N. P. (1975) 'Pneumographic findings in the infantile autism syndrome', *Brain* 98, 667–88.

Havighurst, R. J., Gunther, M. K., & Pratt, I. E. (1946) 'Environment and the Draw-a-Man test: the performance of Indian children', *Journal of Abnormal and Social Psychology* 41, 50–63.

Hayes, A., & Ross, J. (1995) 'Lines of sight', in *The Artful Eye*, ed. R. Gregory, J. Harris, P. Heard & D. Rose, Oxford: Oxford University Press, pp. 337–52.

Hedges, K. (1983) Review of 'The shamanic origins of rock art', in *Ancient Images on Stone: rock art in the Californias*, ed. J. A. van Tilburg, Los Angeles, CA: Cotsen Institute of Archaeology, UCLA, pp. 46–59.

Heller, M. A., & Kennedy, J. M. (1990) 'Perspective taking, pictures, and the blind', *Perception and Psychophysics* 48, 459–66.

Heller, M. A., Kennedy, J. M., & Joyner, T. D. (1995) 'Production and interpretation of pictures of houses by blind people', *Perception* 24, 1049–58.

Henderson, J. A., & Thomas, G. V. (1990) 'Looking ahead: planning for the inclusion of detail affects relative sizes of head and trunk in children's human figure drawings', *British Journal of Developmental Psychology* 8, 383–91.

Henderson, S. E., Morris, J., & Frith, U. (1981) 'The motor deficit in Down's syndrome children: a problem of timing?', *Journal of Child Psychology and Psychiatry* 22, 233–45.

Henshilwood, C. S., Sealy, J. C., Yates, R., Cruz-Uribe, K., Goldberg, P., Grine, F. E., Klein, R. G., Poggenpoel, C., van Niekerk, K., & Watts, I. (2001) 'Blombos Cave, Southern Cape, South Africa: preliminary report on the 1992–1999 excavations of the Middle Stone Age levels', *Journal of Archaeological Science* 28, 421–48.

Hermelin, B., & O'Connor, N. (1986) 'Spatial representations in mathematically and in artistically gifted children', *British Journal of Educational Psychology* 56, 150–7.

Herne, S. (1996) 'The place of abstract and non-figurative art practice in the primary art curriculum', *Chreods* 6, 39–47.

Hibbard, R. A., Roghmann, K., & Hoekelman, R. A. (1987) 'Genitalia in children's drawings: an association with sexual abuse', *Pediatrics* 79, 129–36.

Hiler, E. W., & Nesvig, D. (1965) 'An evaluation of criteria used by clinicians to infer pathology from figure drawings', *Journal of Consulting Psychology* 29, 523–9.

Hiller, P. E. (1993) 'How should we teach art and why we should', *Australian Art Education* 16, 29–37.

Ho, W. C. (1989) *Yani: the brush of innocence*, New York: Hudson Hills Press.

Hochberg, J., & Brooks, V. (1962) 'Pictorial recognition as an unlearned ability in a study of one child's performance', *American Journal of Psychology* 75, 624–8.

Hockney, D., & Joyce, P. (1999) *Hockney on 'Art'*, London: Little, Brown.

Hodgson, D. (2002) 'Canonical perspective and typical features in children's drawings: a neuroscientific appraisal', *British Journal of Developmental Psychology* 20, 565–79.

Horowitz, M. J. (1964) 'The imagery of visual hallucinations', *Journal of Nervous and Mental Disease* 138, 513–23.

   (1975) 'Hallucinations: an information-processing aproach', in *Hallucinations: behaviour, experience and theory*, ed. R. K. Siegel & L. J. West, New York: John Wiley, pp. 163–95.

Howe, M. J. A. (1989) *Fragments of Genius: the strange feats of idiots savants*, London: Routledge & Kegan Paul.

   (1990) *The Origins of Exceptional Abilities*, Oxford: Basil Blackwell.

Hudson, W. (1960) 'Pictorial depth perception in subcultural groups in Africa', *Journal of Social Psychology* 52, 183–208.

   (1962) 'Pictorial perception and educational adaptation in Africa', *Psychologia Africana* 9, 226–39.

Huttenlocher, P. R. (1994) 'Synaptogenesis, synapse elimination, and neural plasticity in human cerebral cortex: threats to optimal development' (pp. 35–54), in *The Minnesota Symposia on Child Psychology*, ed. C. A. Nelson, Hillsdale, NJ: Lawrence Erlbaum.

Ibbotson, A., & Bryant, P. E. (1976) 'The perpendicular error and the vertical effect in children's drawing', *Perception* 5, 319–26.

Ingram, N. A. (1983) 'Representation of three-dimensional spatial relationships on a two-dimensional picture surface', unpublished Ph.D. thesis, University of Southampton.

Israelite, J. (1936) 'A comparison of the difficulty of items for intellectually normal children and mental defectives on the Goodenough drawing test', *American Journal of Ortho-psychiatry* 6, 494–503.

Ivanoff, E. (1909) 'Recherches expérimentales sur le dessin des écoliers de la Suisse Romande: correlation entre l'aptitude au dessin et les autres aptitudes', *Archives de Psychologie* 8, 97–156.

Ives, W. (1980) 'Preschool children's ability to coordinate spatial perspectives through language and pictures', *Child Development* 51, 1303–6.

(1983) 'The development of strategies for coordinating spatial perspectives of an array', in *Spatial Cognition: the structure and development of mental representations of spatial relations*, ed. D. R. Olson & E. Bialystock, Hillsdale, NJ: Lawrence Erlbaum, pp. 127–44.

(1984) 'The development of expressivity in drawing', *British Journal of Educational Psychology* 54, 152–9.

Ives, W., & Rovet, J. (1982) 'Elementary school children's use of construction rules in drawings of familiar and novel objects: a cross-cultural replication', *Journal of Genetic Psychology* 140, 315–16.

Izard, C. E. (1971) *The Face of Emotion*, New York: Appleton-Century Crofts.

(1977) *Human Emotions*, New York: Plenum Press.

(1991) *The Psychology of Emotions*, New York: Plenum Press.

Izard, C. E., Fantauzzo, C. A., Castle, J. M., Haynes, O. M., Rayias, M. F., & Putnam, P. H. (1995) 'The ontogeny and significance of infants' facial expressions in the first 9 months of life', *Developmental Psychology* 31, 997–1013.

Jahoda, G., & McGurk, H. (1974) 'Pictorial depth perception in Scottish and Ghanaian children: a critique of some findings with the Hudson test', *International Journal of Psychology* 9, 255–67.

Jahoda, G., Cheyne, W., Derȩgowski, J., Sinha, D., & Collingbourne, R. (1976) 'Utilisation of pictorial information in classroom learning: a cross-cultural study', *Audio-Visual Communication Review* 24, 295–315.

James, W. (1890) *The Principles of Psychology*, vol. I, New York: Henry Holt.

Jobling, A. (1998) 'Motor development in school-aged children with Down's syndrome: a longitudinal perspective', *International Journal of Disability, Development and Education* 45, 283–93.

Jobling, A., & Gunn, P. (1995) 'The motor proficiency of children and adolescents with Down's syndrome', in *Physical and Motor Development in Mental Retardation*, ed. W. E. Davis & A. Vermeer, New York: Karger, pp. 181–90.

Johnson, M. H., Dziurawiec, S., Ellis, H., & Morton, J. (1991) 'Newborns' preferential tracking of face-like stimuli and its subsequent decline', *Cognition* 40, 1–19.

Joiner, T. E., Schmidt, K. L., & Barnett, J. (1996) 'Size, detail, and line heaviness in children's drawings as correlates of emotional distress: (more) negative evidence', *Journal of Personality Assessment* 67, 127–41.

Jolley, R. P. (1991) 'Children's ability to draw two partial occlusion scenes in perspective', unpublished undergraduate project, University of York.

  (1995) 'Children's production and perception of visual metaphors for mood and emotion in line drawings and in art', unpublished Ph.D. thesis, University of Birmingham.

Jolley, R. P., Apperley, A., & Bokhari, S. (2002) 'Drawing improves young children's recall of video information', paper presented at the British Psychological Society Developmental Section conference, University of Sussex, September.

Jolley, R. P., Cox, M. V., & Barlow, C. (2003) 'What develops and why in British children's expressive drawings', paper presented at the British Psychological Society Developmental Section Annual Conference, Coventry, September.

Jolley, R. P., Fenn, K., & Jones, L. (2004) 'The development of children's expressive drawing', *British Journal of Developmental Psychology* 22, 545–67.

Jolley, R. P., Knox, E. L., & Foster, S. G. (2000) 'The relationship between children's production and comprehension of realism in drawing', *British Journal of Developmental Psychology* 18, 557–82.

Jolley, R. P., & Thomas, G. V. (1994) 'The development of sensitivity to metaphorical expression of moods in abstract art', *Educational Psychology* 14, 437–50.

  (1995) 'Children's sensitivity to metaphorical expression of mood in line drawings', *British Journal of Developmental Psychology* 13, 335–46.

Jolley, R. P., & Vulic-Prtoric, A. (2001) 'Croatian children's experience of war is not reflected in the size and placement of emotive topics in their drawings', *British Journal of Clinical Psychology* 40, 107–10.

Jolley, R. P., Zhi, Z., & Thomas, G. V. (1998) 'The development of understanding moods metaphorically expressed in pictures', *Journal of Cross-Cultural Psychology* 29, 358–76.

Jones, R. K., & Hagen, M. A. (1980) 'A perspective on cross-cultural picture perception', in *The Perception of Pictures*, vol. II, ed. M. A. Hagen, New York: Academic Press, pp. 193–226.

Jung, C. (1964) *Man and his Symbols*, London: Picador.

Kahill, S. (1984) 'Human figure drawing in adults: an update of the empirical evidence, 1967–1982', *Canadian Psychology* 25, 269–92.

Kamphaus, R. W., & Pleiss, K. L. (1991) 'Draw-a-person techniques: tests in search of a construct', *Journal of School Psychology* 29, 395–401.

Kaneda, T. (1994) 'Children's art activities in non-/less industrialised societies: a case study in Nepal', *Art Education* 47, 20–4.

Karmiloff-Smith, A. (1990) 'Constraints on representational change: evidence from children's drawing', *Cognition* 34, 57–83.

(1992) *Beyond Modularity: a developmental perspective on cognitive science*, Cambridge, MA: MIT Press.

(1999) 'Taking development seriously', *Human Development* 42, 325–7.

Keane, L. (2003) 'The perpendicular bias: gender differences and the effect of different response methods', unpublished undergraduate project, University of York.

Keeley, L. (1980) *Experimental Determination of Stone Tool Use: a microwear analysis*, Chicago: University of Chicago Press.

Kelley, S. J. (1984) 'The use of art therapy with the sexually-abused child', *Journal of Psychosocial Nursing and Mental Health Services* 22, 12–18.

Kellogg, R. (1969) *Analysing Children's Art*, Palo Alto, CA: Mayfield.

Kellogg, R., & O'Dell, S. (1967) *The Psychology of Children's Art*, New York: CRM Random House.

Kennedy, J. M. (1974) *A Psychology of Picture Perception*, San Francisco: Jossey-Bass.

(1980) 'Blind people recognising and making pictures', in *The Perception of Pictures*, vol. II, ed. M. A. Hagen, New York: Academic Press, pp. 263–303.

(1983) 'What can we learn about pictures from the blind?', *American Scientist* 71, 19–21.

(1997) 'How the blind draw', *Scientific American* 276, 60–5.

(2000) 'Recognising outline pictures via touch: alignment theory', in *Touch, Representation and Blindness*, ed. M. A. Heller, Oxford: Oxford University Press, pp. 67–98.

(2003) 'Drawings from Gaia, a blind girl', *Perception* 32, 321–40.

Kennedy, J. M., & Campbell, J. (1982) 'Convergence principle in blind people's pointing', unpublished paper, University of Toronto.

Kennedy, J. M., & Ross, A. S. (1975) 'Outline picture perception by the Songe of Papua', *Perception* 4, 391–406.

Kerschensteiner, G. (1905) *Die Entwicklung der zeichnerischen Begabung*, Munich: Karl Gerber.

Kidd, D. (1905) *The Essential Kaffir*, London: Black.

Killcross, S. (2000) 'The amygdala, emotion and learning', *Psychologist* 13, 502–7.

Kinard, E. M. (1994) 'Methodological issues and practical problems in conducting research on maltreated children', *Child Abuse and Neglect* 18, 645–56.

Kindler, A. M. (1992) 'Worship of creativity and artistic development of young children', *Canadian Society for Education through Art Journal* 23, 12–17.

(1993) 'Preference for realism in art among First Nation Children', paper presented at the International Society for Education through Art World Congress, Montreal, August.

(1994a) 'Artistic learning in early childhood: a study of social interaction', *Canadian Review of Art Education* 21, 91–106.

(1994b) 'Children and the culture of a multicultural society', *Art Education* July, 54–60.

(1995) 'Significance of adult input in early childhood artistic development', in *The Visual Arts and Early Childhood Learning*, ed. C. M. Thompson, Reston, VA: National Art Education Association, pp. 10–14.

(2000) 'From the U-curve to dragons: culture and understanding of artistic development', *Visual Arts Research* 26, 15–28.

Kindler, A. M., & Darras, B. (1994) 'Artistic development in context: emergence and development of pictorial imagery in early childhood years', *Visual Arts Research* 20, 1–13.

(1997) 'Map of artistic development', in *Child Development in Art*, ed. A. M. Kindler, Reston, VA: National Art Education Association, pp. 17–44.

(1998) 'Culture and development of pictorial repertoires', *Studies in Art Education* 39, 147–67.

Kindler, A. M., Darras, B., & Kuo, A. C. S. (2000) 'When culture takes a trip: evidence of heritage and enculturation in early conceptions of art', *Journal of Art and Design Education* 19, 44–53.

Kindler, A. M., Pariser, D., van den Berg, A., & Liu, W. C. (2001) 'Visions of Eden: the differential effects of skill on adults' judgements of children's drawings: two cross-cultural studies', *Canadian Review of Art Education* 28, 35–63.

Kindler, A. M., Pariser, D. A., van den Berg, A., Liu, W. C., & Dias, B. (2002) 'Aesthetic modernism, the first among equals? A look at aesthetic value systems in cross-cultural, age and visual arts educated and non-visual arts educated judging cohorts', *International Journal of Cultural Policy* 8, 135–52.

King, M. A., & Yuille, J. C. (1987) 'Suggestibility and the child witness', in *Children's Eyewitness Memory*, ed. S. J. Ceci, M. P. Toglia & D. F. Ross, Heidelberg and New York: Springer-Verlag, pp. 24–35.

Klaue, K. (1992) 'The development in depth representation in children's drawings: effects of graphic surface and visibility of the model', *British Journal of Developmental Psychology* 10, 71–83.

Klinnert, M. (1984) 'The regulation of infant behaviour by maternal facial expression', *Infant Behaviour and Development* 7, 447–65.

Klopfer, W. G., & Taulbee, E. S. (1976) 'Projective tests', *Annual Review of Psychology* 27, 543–67.

Knight, C. D., Power, C., & Watts, I. (1995) 'The human symbolic revolution: a Darwinian account', *Cambridge Archaeological Journal* 5, 75–114.

Koffka, K. (1935) *Principles of Gestalt Psychology*, New York: Harcourt Brace & World.

Köhler, W. (1925) *The Mentality of Apes*, New York: Harcourt Brace & World.

Koppitz, E. M. (1968) *Psychological Evaluation of Children's Human Figure Drawings*, New York: Grune & Stratton.

Korzenik, D. (1995) 'The changing concept of artistic giftedness', in *The Development of Artistically Gifted Children*, ed. C. Golomb, Hillsdale, NJ: Lawrence Erlbaum, pp. 1–29.

Kuo, A. C. (1993) 'Theory and practice in art-education appreciation achievement among students in Taiwan and America: a cross-cultural study', paper presented at the International Society for Education through Art World Congress, Montreal, August.

Langer, S. K. (1953) *Feeling and Form: a theory of art developed from philosophy in a new key*, London: Routledge & Kegan Paul.

Lark-Horovitz, B. (1937) 'On art appreciation of children: I. Preferences of picture subjects in general', *Journal of Educational Research* 31, 118–37.

Lark-Horovitz, B., Lewis, H., & Luca, M. (1973) *Understanding Children's Art for Better Teaching*, Columbus, OH: Merrill.

Larkin, R. (2001) 'Children's ability to communicate emotions through their drawings: are there age and gender effects?', unpublished undergraduate project, University of York.

Laszlo, J. I., & Broderick, P. A. (1985) 'The perceptual-motor skill of drawing', in *Visual Order: the nature and development of pictorial representation*, ed. N. H. Freeman & M. V. Cox, Cambridge: Cambridge University Press, pp. 356–73.

Latto, R. (1995) 'The brain of the beholder', in *The Artful Eye*, ed. R. Gregory, J. Harris, P. Heard & D. Rose, Oxford: Oxford University Press, pp. 66–94.

Lawler, C. O., & Lawler, E. E. (1965) 'Color-mood associations in young children', *Journal of Genetic Psychology* 107, 29–32.

Laws, G., & Lawrence, L. (2001) 'Spatial representation in the drawings of children with Down's syndrome and its relationship to language and motor development: a preliminary investigation', *British Journal of Developmental Psychology* 19, 453–73.

Leach, M. L. (1975) 'The effect of training on the pictorial depth perception of Shona children', *Journal of Cross-Cultural Psychology* 6, 457–70.

Lee, M. (1989) 'When is an object not an object? The effect of "meaning" upon the copying of line drawings', *British Journal of Psychology* 80, 15–37.

Leichtman, M. D., Ceci, S. J., & Morse, M. B. (1997) 'The nature and development of children's event memory', in *Trauma and Memory: clinical and legal controversies*, ed. P. S. Appelbaum, L. A. Uyehara & M. R. Elin, Oxford: Oxford University Press, pp. 158–87.

Leroi-Gourhan, A., & Allain, J. (1979) *Lascaux inconnu*, Paris: Centre National de la Recherche Scientifique.

Lewis, C., Russell, C., & Berridge, D. (1993) 'When is a mug not a mug? Effects of content, naming, and instructions on children's drawings', *Journal of Experimental Child Psychology* 56, 291–302.

Lewis, M. (1969) 'Infants' response to facial stimuli during the first year of life', *Developmental Psychology* 1, 75–86.

Lewis, V. (1990) 'Young children's painting of the sky and the ground', *International Journal of Behavioral Development* 13, 49–65.

Lewis, V., & Boucher, J. (1991) 'Skill, content and generative strategies in autistic children's drawings', *British Journal of Developmental Psychology* 9, 393–416.

Lewis-Williams, J. D. (1981) *Believing and Seeing: symbolic meanings in southern San rock paintings*, London: Academic Press.

   (2002) *A Cosmos in Stone: interpreting religion and society through rock art*, Walnut Creek, CA: AltaMira Press.

Liben, L. (1978) 'Perspective taking skills in young children: seeing the world through rose-coloured glasses', *Developmental Psychology* 14, 87–92.

(1999) 'Developing an understanding of external spatial representations', in *Development of Mental Representation*, ed. I. E. Sigel, Mahwah, NJ: Lawrence Erlbaum, pp. 297–321.

Liben, L., & Belknap, B. (1981) 'Intellectual realism: implications for investigations of perceptual perspective-taking in young children', *Child Development* 52, 921–4.

Liben, L. S., & Szechter, L. E. (2000) 'Developing an understanding of representational surfaces', poster presented at the Children's Knowledge and Judgements about Drawings and Drawing Processes workshop at the Meeting of the Jean Piaget Society, Montreal, June.

Light, P. H., & Foot, T. (1985) 'Partial occlusion in young children's drawings', *Journal of Experimental Child Psychology* 41, 38–48.

Light, P. H., & MacIntosh, E. (1980) 'Depth relationships in young children's drawings', *Journal of Experimental Child Psychology* 30, 79–87.

Light, P. H., & Nix, C. (1983) '"Own view" versus "good view" in a perspective-taking task', *Child Development* 54, 480–3.

Lindström, L. (1997) 'Integration, creativity or communication? Paradigm shifts and continuity in Swedish art education', *Arts Education Policy Review* 99, 17–24.

(2000) 'Introduction', in *The Cultural Context: comparative studies of art education and children's drawings*, ed. L. Lindström, Stockholm: Stockholm Institute of Education Press, pp. 9–18.

Littleton, K. S. (1991) 'The representation of depth in children's drawings', unpublished D.Phil. thesis, University of York.

Livingstone, D. (1857) *Missionary Travels and Researches in South Africa*, London: Murray.

Lloyd, A. B. (1904) 'Acholi country: Part II', *Uganda Notes* 5, 18.

Lobsien, M. (1905) 'Kinderzeichnung und Kunstkanon', *Zeitschrift für Pedagogische Psychologie* 7, 393–404.

Lock, A., Service, V., Brito, A., & Chandler, P. (1989) 'The social structuring of infant cognition', in *Infant Development*, ed. A. Slater & G. Bremner, Hove, East Sussex: Lawrence Erlbaum, pp. 243–71.

Lommel, A. (1967) *Shamanism: the beginnings of art*, New York: McGraw-Hill.

Lorblanchet, M. (1977) 'From naturalism to abstraction in European prehistoric rock art', in *Form in Indigenous Art*, ed. P. J. Ucko, London: Duckworth, pp. 44–56.

Lourenço, O., & Machado, A. (1996) 'In defense of Piaget's theory: a reply to 10 common criticisms', *Psychological Review* 103, 143–64.

Löwenfeld, V. (1939) *The Nature of Creative Activity*, New York: Macmillan.

Löwenfeld, V., & Brittain, W. L. (1970) *Creative and Mental Growth*, 5th edition, New York: Macmillan.

Lowry, K., & Wolf, C. (1988) 'Arts education in the People's Republic of China: results of interviews with Chinese musicians and visual artists', *Journal of Aesthetic Education* 22, 89–98.

Lubin, B., Larsen, R. M., Matarazzo, J. D., & Seever, M. (1985) 'Psychological test usage patterns in five professional settings', *American Psychologist* 40, 857–61.

Luquet, G. -H. (1910) 'Sur les caractères des figures humaines dans l'art paléo-
    lithique', *L'Anthropologie* 21, 409–23.
    (1913) *Les dessins d'un enfant*, Paris: Alcan.
    (1923) 'Le réalisme dans l'art paléolithique', *L'Anthropologie* 33, 17–48.
    (1927) *Le dessin enfantin*, Paris: Alcan.
    (2001) *Children's Drawings* (translated and with an introduction by A. Costall),
    London: Free Association Books (original work published 1927).
MacDonald, P. M., Kirkpatrick, S. W., & Sullivan, L. A. (1996) 'Schematic draw-
    ings of facial expressions for emotion recognition and interpretation
    by preschool-aged children', *Genetic, Social, and General Psychology
    Monographs* 122, 373–88.
Machotka, P. (1966) 'Aesthetic criteria in childhood: justifications of preference',
    Child Development 37, 877–85.
Machover, K. (1949) *Personality Projection in the Drawings of the Human Figure*,
    Springfield, IL: C. C. Thomas.
    (1951) 'Drawings of the human figure: a method of personality investigation',
    in *An Introduction to Projective Techniques*, ed. H. H. Anderson &
    G. L. Anderson, Englewood Cliffs, NJ: Prentice-Hall, pp. 341–69.
Magwaza, A. S., Killian, B. J., Petersen, I., & Pillay, Y. (1993) 'The effects of
    chronic violence on preschool children living in South African
    Townships', *Child Abuse and Neglect* 17, 795–803.
Major, D. R. (1906) *First Steps in Mental Growth*, New York: Macmillan.
Malchiodi, C. (1998) *Understanding Children's Drawings*, London: Jessica Kingsley.
Males, J. (1990) 'Are art activities therapeutic?', in *Creative Arts and Mental
    Disability*, ed. S. S. Segal, Bicester, Oxfordshire: A. B. Academic
    Publishers, pp. 79–86.
Manale, P. (1982) 'The relative effects of color, detail, perspective and proportion
    on children's preference: an exploration of child aesthetics', Honors
    thesis, University of Massachusetts, Boston.
Mann, B. S., & Lehman, E. B. (1976) 'Transparencies in children's human figure
    drawings: a developmental approach', *Studies in Art Education* 18, 41–8.
Marfleet, R. (2002) 'Recognition and understanding of facial expressions of
    emotion by children with autism', unpublished undergraduate project,
    University of York.
Marr, D. (1982) *Vision: a computational investigation into the human representa-
    tion and processing of visual information*, San Francisco: W. H. Freeman.
Marr, D., & Nishihara, H. K. (1978) 'Representation and recognition of the
    spatial organisation of three-dimensional shapes', *Proceedings of the
    Royal Society*, London, series B 200, 269–94.
Marshack, A. (1976) 'Some implications of the Paleolithic symbolic evidence for
    the origin of language', *Current Anthropology* 17, 274–81.
Martlew, M., & Connolly, K. J. (1996) 'Human figure drawings by schooled and
    unschooled children in Papua New Guinea', *Child Development* 67,
    2743–62.
Matthews, J. (1983) 'Children drawing: are young children really scribbling?',
    paper presented at the British Psychological Society International
    Conference on Psychology and the Arts, Cardiff.

(1984) 'Children drawing: are young children really scribbling?', *Early Child Development and Care* 18, 1–39.

(1994) 'Deep structures in children's art: development and culture', *Visual Arts Research* 20, 10–25.

(1997) 'Liang ge dong xi bu yi yang (Mandarin for: "Two objects not the same")', *Visual Arts Research* 23, 73–96.

(1999) *The Art of Childhood and Adolescence*, London: Falmer Press.

(2003) *Drawing and Painting: children and visual representation*, London: Paul Chapman.

Matthews, J., & Jessel, J. (1993) 'Very young children's use of electronic paint: a study of the beginnings of drawing with traditional media and computer paintbox', *Visual Arts Research* 19, 47–62.

McCarthy, D. (1944) 'A study of the reliability of the Goodenough Drawing Test of Intelligence', *Journal of Psychology* 18, 201–16.

McElwee, E. W. (1934) 'Profile drawings of normal and subnormal children', *Journal of Applied Psychology* 18, 599–603.

McFee, J. K. (1978) 'Cultural influences on aesthetic experience', in *Arts in Cultural Diversity*, ed. J. Condous, J. Howlett & J. Skull, New York: Holt, Rinehart & Winston, pp. 42–52.

McGhee, K., & Dziuban, C. D. (1993) 'Visual preferences of preschool children for abstract and realistic paintings', *Perceptual and Motor Skills* 76, 155–8.

McInally, M. (2003) *Children's Art: the development in imaginative drawing and painting, ages 3 to 11*, Crediton, Deron: Southgate.

Mebert, C. J., & Michel, G. F. (1980) 'Handedness in artists', in *Neuropsychology of Left-Handedness*, ed. J. Herron, New York: Academic Press, pp. 273–9.

Mehta, Z., & Newcombe, F. (1991) 'A role for the left hemisphere in spatial processing', *Cortex* 27, 153–67.

Meighand, R. (1995) *The Freethinker's Pocket Guide to the Educational Universe*, Nottingham: Educational Heretic Press.

Melendez, P., Bales, D., & Pick, A. (1995) 'Direct and indirect perception: four-year-olds' grouping of toys', paper presented at the biennial meeting of the Society for Research in Child Development, Indianapolis, April.

Meltzoff, A. N., & Moore, M. K. (1983) 'Newborn infants imitate adult facial gestures', *Child Development* 54, 702–9.

Merz, T. (1996) 'Begin simply, simply begin: sustaining an art area in the elementary classroom', *Montessori Life* 8, 27–8.

Michotte, A. (1962) *Causalité, permanence et réalité phénoménales*, Louvain: Publications Universitaires Belgium.

Miesel, V. H. (1970) *Voices of German Expressionism*, Englewood Cliffs, NJ: Prentice-Hall.

Milbrath, C. (1995) 'Germinal motifs in the work of a gifted child artist', in *The Development of Artistically Gifted Children*, ed. C. Golomb, Hillsdale, NJ: Lawrence Erlbaum, pp. 101–34.

(1998) *Patterns of Artistic Development in Children*, Cambridge: Cambridge University Press.

Millar, S. (1975) 'Visual experience or a translation of rules? Drawing the human figure by blind and sighted children', *Perception* 4, 363–71.

—— (1994) *Understanding and Representing Space: theory and evidence from studies with blind and sighted children*, Oxford: Oxford University Press.

Miller, R. J. (1973) 'Cross cultural research in the perception of pictorial materials', *Psychological Bulletin* 80, 135–50.

Missaghi-Lakshman, M., & Whissell, C. (1991) 'Children's understanding of facial expression of emotion: II. Drawing of emotion-faces', *Perceptual and Motor Skills* 72, 1228–30.

Mitchelmore, M. C. (1978) 'Developmental stages in children's representation of regular solid figures', *Journal of Genetic Psychology* 133, 229–39.

Montessori, M. (1912) *The Montessori Method*, London: Heinemann.

—— (1918) *The Advanced Montessori Method*. London: Heinemann.

—— (1965) *Spontaneous Activity in Education*, New York: Schocken Books.

Moore, D. M., & Bedient, D. (1986) 'Effects of presentation mode and visual characteristics on cognitive style', *Journal of Instructional Psychology* 13, 19–24.

Moore, V. (1986) 'The use of a colouring task to elucidate children's drawings of a solid cube', *British Journal of Developmental Psychology* 4, 335–40.

Morra, S. (1995) 'A neo-Piagetian approach to children's drawings', in *Drawing and Looking*, ed. C. Lange-Küttner & G. V. Thomas, Hemel Hempstead: Harvester/Wheatsheaf, pp. 93–106.

Morra, S., Caloni, B., & d'Amico, M. R. (1994) 'Working memory and the intentional depiction of emotions', *Archives de Psychologie* 62, 71–87.

Morra, S., Moizo, C., & Scopesi, A. (1988) 'Working memory (or the M operator) and the planning of children's drawings', *Journal of Experimental Child Psychology* 46, 41–73.

Morra, S., & Perchinenna, R. (1993) 'Thinkable images: cognitive accounts of change in drawings', poster presented at the Sixth European Conference on Developmental Psychology, Bonn, 28 August–1 September.

Morse, R., & Bremner, G. J. (1998) 'Representational flexibility in young children's drawings', poster presented at the British Psychological Society Developmental Section Annual Conference, Lancaster, September.

Morss, J. R. (1985) 'Early cognitive development: differences or delay?', in *Current Approaches to Down's Syndrome*, ed. D. Lane & B. Stratford, New York: Holt, Rinehart & Winston, pp. 242–59.

Motta, R. W., Little, S. G., & Tobin, M. I. (1993) 'The use and abuse of human figure drawings', *School Psychology Quarterly* 8, 162–9.

Munn, N. (1973) *Walbiri Iconography: graphic representation and cultural symbolism in a central Australian society*, New York: Cornell University Press.

Munro, T., Lark-Horowitz, B., & Barnhart, E. N. (1942) 'Children's art abilities: studies at the Cleveland Museum of Art', *Journal of Experimental Education* 11, 97–155.

Murphy, C. M. (1978) 'Pointing in the context of a shared activity', *Child Development* 49, 371–80.

Naglieri, J. A. (1988) *Draw a Person: a quantitative scoring system*, San Antonio, TX: Psychological Corporation.

Nicholls, A. L. (1995) 'Influence of visual projection on young children's depictions of object proportions', *Journal of Experimental Child Psychology* 60, 304–26.

Nicholls, A. L., & Kennedy, J. M. (1992) 'Drawing development: from similarity of features to direction', *Child Development* 63, 227–41.

Ninio, A., & Bruner, J. (1978) 'The achievement and antecedents of labeling', *Journal of Child Language* 5, 1–15.

Nye, R., Thomas, G. V., & Robinson, E. (1995) 'Children's understanding about pictures', in *Drawing and Looking*, ed. C. Lange-Küttner & G. V. Thomas, Hemel Hempstead: Harvester/Wheatsheaf, pp. 123–34.

O' Connor, N., & Hermelin, B. (1983) 'The role of general ability and specific talents in information processing', *British Journal of Developmental Psychology* 1, 389–403.

(1988) 'Low intelligence and special abilities', *Journal of Child Psychology and Psychiatry* 29, 391–6.

Odbert, H. S., Karwoski, T. F., & Eckerson, A. B. (1942) 'Studies in synesthetic thinking: I. Musical and verbal associates of color and mood', *Journal of Genetic Psychology* 26, 153–73.

O'Hare, D., & Cook, D. (1983) 'Children's sensitivity to different modes of colour use in art', *British Journal of Educational Psychology* 53, 267–77.

O'Hare, D., & Westwood, H. (1984) 'Features of style classification: a multivariate experimental analysis of children's responses to drawings', *Developmental Psychology* 20, 150–8.

Olsen, J. (1992) 'Evaluating young children's cognitive capacities through computer versus hand drawings', *Scandinavian Journal of Psychology* 33, 193–211.

Omari, I. M., & MacGintie, W. H. (1974) 'Some pictorial artefacts in studies of African children's pictorial depth perception', *Child Development* 45, 535–9.

O'Neill, K. (1997) 'The child's use of colour as an affective tool', unpublished undergraduate project, University of York.

Opie, I., & Opie, P. (1969) *Children's Games in Street and Playground*, Oxford: Oxford University Press.

Opolot, J. (1976) 'Differential cognitive cues in pictorial depth perception among Ugandan children', *International Journal of Psychology* 11, 81–8.

Page, H. (1970) 'Pictorial depth perception: a note', *South African Journal of Psychology* 1, 45–8.

(1972) *Ndedema*, Portland: International Scholarly Book Services.

Paget, G. W. (1932) 'Some drawings of men and women made by children of certain non-European races', *Journal of the Royal Anthropological Institute* 62, 127–44.

Pariser, D. (1979) 'Two methods of teaching drawing skills', *Studies in Art Education* 20, 30–42.

(1987) 'The juvenile drawings of Klee, Toulouse Lautrec and Picasso', *Visual Arts Research* 13, 53–67.

(1991) 'What does giftedness mean in the context of Chinese visual art? Chinese artists look at drawings by a prolific Chinese child-artist, Wang Yani', paper presented at the Twelfth Annual Ethnography in Education Research Forum, University of Pennsylvania.

(1995a) 'A cross-cultural examination of the U-curve in aesthetic development', Spencer Foundation Small Grant Final Report, May.

(1995b) 'Lautrec – gifted child artist and artistic monument: connections between juvenile and mature work', in *The Development of Artistically Gifted Children*, ed. C. Golomb, Hillsdale, NJ: Lawrence Erlbaum, pp. 31–70.

(1997) 'Graphic development in artistically exceptional children', in *Child Development in Art*, ed. A. M. Kindler, Reston, VA: National Art Education Association, pp. 115–30.

Parker, F. W. (1894) *Talks on Pedagogies: an outline of the theory of concentration*, New York: E. L. Kellogg.

Parsons, M. J. (1987) *How We Understand Art: a cognitive developmental account of aesthetic experience*, Cambridge: Cambridge University Press.

(1996) 'Visual and verbal learning in art: the consequences and developments in aesthetics for art education and the psychology of art', in *Art and Fact: learning effects of arts education (a collection of lectures given during the international conference in Rotterdam, March 1995)*, Utrecht: LOKV, Netherlands Institute for Arts Education, pp. 12–20.

Partridge, L. (1902) 'Children's drawings of men and women', *Studies in Education* 2, 163–79.

Pascual-Leone, J. (1970) 'A mathematical model for the transition rule in Piaget's developmental stages', *Acta Psychologica* 63, 301–45.

Pemberton, E. F., & Nelson, K. E. (1987) 'Using interactive graphic challenges to foster young children's drawing ability', *Visual Arts Research* 13, 29–41.

Perara, J., & Cox, M. V. (2000) 'The effect of background context on children's understanding of the spatial depth arrangement of objects in a drawing', *Psychologia* 43, 144–53.

Perner, J. (1991) *Understanding the Representational Mind*, Cambridge, MA: MIT Press.

Pettitt, P., & Bahn, P. (2003) 'Current problems in dating Palaeolithic cave art: Candamo and Chauvet', *Antiquity* 77, 134–41.

Pfeffer, K. (1984) 'Interpretation of studies of ethnic identity: Draw-a-person as a measure of ethnic identity', *Perceptual and Motor Skills* 59, 835–8.

Phillips, W. A., Hobbs, S. B., & Pratt, F. R. (1978) 'Intellectual realism in children's drawings of cubes', *Cognition* 6, 15–33.

Piaget, J. (1929) *The Child's Conception of the World*, Totowa, NJ: Littlefield, Adams.

(1952) *The Origins of Intelligence in Children*, New York: Harcourt Brace.

(1954) *The Construction of Reality in the Child*, New York: Basic Books.

(1969) *The Child's Conception of Time*, London: Routledge & Kegan Paul.

(1970) 'Piaget's theory', in *Carmichael's Manual of Child Psychology*, vol. I, 3rd edition, ed. P. H. Mussen, New York: John Wiley, pp. 703–32.

Piaget, J., & Inhelder, B. (1956) *The Child's Conception of Space*, London: Routledge & Kegan Paul.

(1969) *The Psychology of the Child*, London: Routledge & Kegan Paul.

(1971) *Mental Imagery in the Child*, London: Routledge & Kegan Paul.

Picard, D., & Vinter, A. (1999) 'Representational flexibility in children's drawings: effects of age and verbal instructions', *British Journal of Developmental Psychology* 17, 605–22.

Pierroutsakos, S. L., & DeLoache, J. S. (1997) 'Infants' manual investigation of pictures as a function of picture type and referent', paper presented at the biennial meeting of the Society for Research in Child Development, Washington, DC.

Pillow, B. H., & Flavell, J. H. (1985) 'Intellectual realism: the role of children's interpretations of pictures and perceptual verbs', *Child Development* 56, 664–70.

(1986) 'Young children's knowledge about visual perception: projective size and shape', *Child Development* 57, 125–35.

Pillow, B .H., & Henrichon, A. J. (1996) 'There's more to the picture than meets the eye: young children's difficulty understanding biased interpretations', *Child Development* 67, 803–19.

Pipp, S. L., & Haith, M. M. (1977) 'Infant visual scanning of two- and three-dimensional forms', *Child Development* 48, 1640–4.

Piven, J., Arndt, S., Bailey, J., Havercamp, S., Andreasen, N. C., & Palmer, P. (1991) 'An MRI study of brain size in autism', *American Journal of Psychiatry* 152, 1145–9.

Plant, B. T. W. (1995) 'Children's perception and production of pictorial depth cues', unpublished D.Phil. thesis, University of York.

Platten, M. (2003) 'Can children use colour expressively? Specific colour associations with happiness, sadness and anger', unpublished undergraduate project, University of York.

Prentice, R. (1999) 'Art: visual thinking', in *The Curriculum for 7–11 year olds*, ed. J. Riley & R. Prentice, London: Paul Chapman, pp. 146–64.

Pring, L., & Hermelin, B. (1997) 'Native savant talent and acquired skill', *Autism* 1, 199–214.

Pring, L., Hermelin, B., & Heavey, L. (1995) 'Savants, segments, art and autism', *Journal of Child Psychology and Psychiatry* 36, 1065–76.

Profyt, L., & Whissell, C. M. (1991) 'Children's understanding of facial expressions of emotion: I. Voluntary creation of emotion – faces', *Perceptual and Motor Skills* 73, 199–202.

Prout, H. (1983) 'School psychologists and social-emotional assessment techniques: patterns in training and use', *School Psychology Review* 12, 377–83.

Pynoos, R. S., & Eth, S. (1986) 'Witness to violence: the child interview', *Journal of the American Academy of Child Psychiatry* 25, 306–19.

Pynoos, R. S., & Nader, K. (1989) 'Children's memory and proximity to violence', *Journal of the American Academy of Child and Adolescent Psychiatry* 28, 473–90.

Qin, J., Quas, J. A., Redlich, A. D., & Goodman, G. S. (1997) 'Children's eyewitness testimony: memory development in the legal context', in *The*

Development of Memory in Childhood, ed. N. Cowan & C. Hulme, Hove, East Sussex: Psychology Press, pp. 301–41.

Raven, J. C., Court, J. H., & Raven, J. (1990) *Coloured Progressive Matrices*, Oxford: Oxford Psychologists Press.

Read, H. (1956) *Education through Art*, 3rd edition, New York: Pantheon.

Reinach, S. (1903) 'L'art et la magie: à propos des peintures et des gravures de l'Age du Renne', *L'Anthropologie* 14, 257–66.

Reissland, N. (1988) 'Neonatal imitation in the first hour of life: observations in rural Nepal', *Developmental Psychology* 24, 464–9.

Reuning, H., & Wortley, W. (1973) 'Psychological studies of the bushmen', *Psychologia Africana Monograph Supplement* 7.

Ricci, C. (1887) *L'arte dei bambini*, Bologna: N. Zanichelli.

Riding, R. J., & Douglas, G. (1993) 'The effect of cognitive style and mode of presentation on learning performance', *British Journal of Educational Psychology* 63, 297–307.

Rimland, B. (1978) 'Inside the mind of the autistic savant', *Psychology Today* 12, 68–80.

Roback, H. B. (1968) 'Human figure drawings: their utility in the psychologist's armamentarium for personality assessment', *Psychological Bulletin* 70, 1–19.

Robertson, J. (1962) *Practical Problems of the Portrait Painter*, London: Darton, Longman & Todd.

Robinson, A. (1995) *The Story of Writing*, London: Thames & Hudson.

Robinson, S. (2002) 'An investigation into the effectiveness of the National Curriculum's "observational approach" to art education', unpublished undergraduate project, University of York.

Rogoff, B. (1990) *Apprenticeship in Thinking: cognitive development in social context*, Oxford: Oxford University Press.

  (1998) 'Cognition as a collaborative process', in *Handbook of Child Psychology*, vol. II, *Cognition, language, and perceptual development*, ed. D. Kuhn & R. S. Siegler, New York: John Wiley, pp. 679–744.

Rogoff, B., Mistry, J., Goncu, A., & Mosier, C. (1993) 'Guided participation in cultural activity by toddlers and caregivers', *Monographs of the Society for Research in Child Development* 58, 236.

Rosand, D. (2002) *Drawing Acts: studies in graphic expression and representation*, Cambridge: Cambridge University Press.

Rosen, A., & Boe, E. (1968) 'Frequency of nude figure drawings', *Journal of Projective Technique and Personality Assessment* 32, 483–5.

Rosenblatt, E., & Winner, E. (1988) 'Is superior visual memory a component of superior drawing ability?', in *The Exceptional Brain: neuropsychology of talent and special abilities*, ed. L. K. Obler & D. A. Fein, New York: Guilford Press, pp. 341–63.

Rosenblum, R. (1960) *Cubism and Twentieth-Century Art*, New York: Abrams.

Ross, D. F., Dunning, D., Toglia, M. P., & Ceci, S. J. (1990) 'The child in the eyes of the jury: assessing mock jurors' perceptions of the child witness', *Law and Behavior* 14, 2–23.

Ross, D. F., Miller, B. S., & Moran, P. B. (1987) 'The child in the eyes of the jury: assessing mock jurors' perceptions of the child witness', in *Children's Eyewitness Memory*, ed. S. J. Ceci, M. P. Toglia & D. F. Ross, Heidelberg and New York: Springer Verlag, pp. 142–54.

Rothschild, H. (2003) 'My day with Hockney', *Independent Review*, Tuesday 14 January, 12–13.

Rouma, G. (1913) *Le langage graphique de l'enfant*, Brussels: Mish & Thron.

Rousseau, J. J. (1964) *Emile*, New York: Barrons Educational Series (original work published 1762).

Rowlands, A. (2003) 'The use of drawing to facilitate children's event memory recall', unpublished Ph.D. thesis, University of York.

Ruffman, T. K., Olson, D. R., & Astington, J. W. (1991) 'Children's understanding of visual ambiguity', *British Journal of Developmental Psychology* 9, 89–102.

Rump, E. E., & Southgate, V. (1967) 'Variables affecting aesthetic appreciation in relation to age', *British Journal of Educational Psychology* 37, 58–72.

Ruskin, J. (1857) *The Elements of Drawing*, London: George Allen.

Russell, J. A., & Bullock, M. (1985) 'Multidimensional scaling of emotional facial expressions: similarity from preschoolers to adults', *Journal of Personality & Social Psychology* 48, 1290–8.

(1986) 'On the dimensions preschoolers use to interpret facial expressions of emotion', *Developmental Psychology* 22, 97–102.

Russell, J. A., & Fernández-Dols, J. M. (eds.) (1997) *The Psychology of Facial Expression*, Cambridge: Cambridge University Press.

Ruurs, R. (1987) *Saenredam: the art of perspective*, Amsterdam: Benjamins.

Saenger, E. A. (1981) 'Drawing systems: a developmental study of representation', unpublished Ph.D. thesis, Harvard University.

Salmon, K., & Pipe, M-E. (2000) 'Recalling an event one year later: the impact of props, drawing and a prior interview', *Applied Cognitive Psychology* 2, 99–120.

Salmon, K., Roncolato, W., & Gleitzman, M. (2003) 'Children's reports of emotionally laden events: adapting the interview to the child', *Applied Cognitive Psychology* 17, 65–79.

Saloviita, T., Ruusila, L., & Ruusila, U. (2000) 'Incidence of savant syndrome in Finland', *Perceptual and Motor Skills* 91, 120–2.

Sayil, M. (1996) 'Okulöncesi dönemdeki çocuklarin duygusal yüz ifadelerini tanima ve çizme becerileri', *Türk Psikoloji Dergisi* 11, 61–71.

(1997a) 'Children's drawings of emotional facial expressions', poster presented at the Eighth European Conference on Developmental Psychology, Rennes, 3–7 September.

(1997b) 'Ilkokul çocuklarinda duygusal yüz ifadesi çizimlerinin gelisimi', *Çocuk ve Gençlik Ruh Sagligi Dergisi* 4, 129–34.

Saywitz, K. J. (2002) 'Developmental underpinnings of children's testimony', in *Children's Testimony: a handbook of psychological research and forensic practice*, ed. H. L. Westcott, G. M. Davies & R. H. C. Bull, Chichester: John Wiley, pp. 3–19.

Saywitz, K. J., Goodman, G. S., Nicholas, E., & Moan, S. F. (1991) 'Children's memories of a physical examination involving genital touch: implications for reports of child sexual abuse', *Journal of Consulting and Clinical Psychology* 59, 682–91.

Schapiro, M. (1978) 'Courbet and popular imagery: an essay on realism and naïveté', in *Modern Art: 19th and 20th centuries*, ed. M. Schapiro, London: Chatto & Windus, pp. 47–85.

Schodt, F. L. (1983) '*Manga, Manga!: the world of Japanese comics*', San Francisco: Kodansha International.

Schneider, M. (1996) 'Art is elementary: is there enough?', *Montessori Life* 8, 20–1 & 26.

Schulenburg, D. (1999) 'Young children's perception of the face and facial expression', unpublished undergraduate project, University of York.

Schuyten, M. (1904) 'De oorspronkelijke "Ventjes" der Antwerpsch Schoolkindern', *Paedologisch Jaarboek* 5, 1–87.

Sechrest, L., & Wallace, J. (1964) 'Figure drawings and naturally occurring events: elimination of the expansive euphoria hypothesis', *Journal of Educational Psychology* 53, 42–4.

Selfe, L. (1977) *Nadia: a case of extraordinary drawing ability in an autistic child*, London: Academic Press.

(1983) *Normal and Anomalous Representational Drawing Ability in Children*, London: Academic Press.

(1995) 'Nadia reconsidered', in *The Development of Gifted Child Artists: selected case studies*, ed. C. Golomb, Hillsdale, NJ: Lawrence Erlbaum, pp. 197–236.

Shepherd, J., Deręgowski, J., & Ellis, H. (1974) 'A cross-cultural study of recognition memory for faces', *International Journal of Psychology* 9, 205–11.

Siegel, R. K. (1977) 'Hallucinations', *Scientific American* 237, 132–40.

Siegel, R. K., & Jarvik, M. E. (1975) 'Drug-induced hallucinations in animals and man', in *Hallucinations: behaviour, experience and theory*, ed. R. K. Siegel & L. J. West, New York: John Wiley, pp. 81–161.

Sigman, M., & Capps, L. (1997) *Children with Autism*, Cambridge, MA: Harvard University Press.

Skipper, D. (2001) 'Age and sex differences in the ability to recognise and depict facial expressions of emotion', unpublished undergraduate project, University of York.

Slater, A. M. (1989) 'Visual memory and perception in early infancy', in *Infant Development*, ed. A. Slater & G. Bremner, Hove, East Sussex: Lawrence Erlbaum, pp. 43–71.

Slater, A. M., & Morison, V. (1985) 'Shape constancy and slant perception at birth', *Perception* 14, 337–44.

Slater, A. M., Mattock, A., & Brown, E. (1990) 'Size constancy at birth: newborn infants' responses to retinal and real size', *Journal of Experimental Child Psychology* 49, 314–22.

Slater, A. M., Rose, D., & Morison, V. (1984) 'New-born infants' perception of similarities and differences between two- and three-dimensional stimuli', *British Journal of Developmental Psychology* 2, 287–94.

Smith, L. (2001) 'Piaget's model', in *Blackwell Handbook of Childhood Cognitive Development*, ed. U. Goswami, Oxford: Basil Blackwell, pp. 515–37.

Smith, N. R. (1983) *Experience and Art: teaching children to paint*, New York: Columbia University, Teachers College Press.

Smith, N. R., & Drawing Study Group (1998) *Observation Drawing with Children: a framework for teachers*, New York: Columbia University, Teachers College Press.

Smith, P. M. (1993) 'Young children's depiction of contrast in human figure drawing: standing and walking', *Educational Psychology* 13, 107–18.

Spelke, E. (1991) 'Physical knowledge in infancy: reflections on Piaget's theory', in *The Epigenesis of Mind*, ed. S. Carey & R. Gelman, New York: Revnal & Hitchcock, pp. 133–69.

Spencer, J. R. (1966) *Leon Battista Alberti on Painting*, New Haven: Yale University Press.

Spensley, F., & Taylor, J. (1999) 'The development of cognitive flexibility: evidence from children's drawings', *Human Development* 42, 300–24.

Spiegel, J., & Machotka, P. (1974) *Messages of the Body*, New York: Free Press.

Spoerl, D. T. (1940) 'The drawing ability of mentally retarded children', *Journal of Genetic Psychology* 57, 259–77.

Springer, S. P., & Deutsch, G. (1989) *Left Brain, Right Brain*, 3rd edition, New York: W. H. Freeman.

Steinberg, D., & DeLoache, J. S. (1986) 'Preschool children's sensitivity to artistic style in paintings', *Visual Arts Research* 12, 1–10.

Steiner, R. (1965) *The Education of the Child*, London: Rudolf Steiner Press.

Stone, J. G. (1989) 'Young children's mental image of the human figure: a study of its graphic representation', unpublished undergraduate project, University of York.

Stratford, B. (1985) 'Learning and knowing: the education of Down's syndrome children', in *Current Approaches to Down's Syndrome*, ed. D. Lane & B. Stratford, London: Cassell, pp. 149–66.

Strauss, S. (1982) *U-shaped Behavioral Growth*, New York: Academic Press.

Stricker, G. (1967) 'Actuarial, naïve clinical and sophisticated clinical prediction of pathology from figure drawings', *Journal of Consulting Psychology* 31, 492–4.

Stringer, C., & Gamble, C. (1993) *In Search of Neanderthals*, London: Thames & Hudson.

Su, C-M. (1991) 'One object behind another: problems of partial occlusion in children's drawings', *Visual Arts Research* 17, 52–64.

Sully, J. (1895) *Studies of Childhood*, London: Longman's, Green & Co.

Sundberg, N. (1961) 'The practice of psychological testing in clinical services in the United States', *American Psychologist* 16, 79–83.

Sundberg, N., & Ballinger, T. (1968) 'Nepalese children's cognitive development as revealed by drawings of man, woman, and self', *Child Development* 39, 969–85.

Sutton, P. (1991) *Dreamings*, London: Viking.

Sutton, P. J., & Rose, D. H. (1998) 'The role of strategic visual attention in children's drawing development', *Journal of Experimental Child Psychology* 68, 87–107.

Swensen, C. H. (1957) 'Empirical evaluations of human figure drawings', *Psychological Bulletin* 54, 431–66.

(1968) 'Empirical evaluations of human figure drawings: 1957–1966', *Psychological Bulletin* 70, 20–44.

Tan, L. (1993) 'A case study of an artistically gifted Chinese girl: Wang Yani', unpublished master's thesis, Concordia University, Montreal.

Tarr, M. J., & Bülthoff, H. H. (1995) 'Is human object recognition better described by geon structural descriptions or by multiple views? Comment on Biederman and Gerhardstein (1993)', *Journal of Experimental Psychology: Human Perception and Performance* 21, 1494–505.

Taunton, M. (1980) 'The influence of age on preferences for subject matter, realism, and spatial depth in painting reproductions', *Studies in Art Education* 21, 40–52.

Taylor, B. (1989) 'Art history in the classroom: a plea for caution', in *Critical Studies in Art and Design Education*, ed. D. Thistlewood, Harlow: Longman/NSEAD, pp. 100–12.

Taylor, M. (1988) 'Conceptual perspective taking: children's ability to distinguish what they know from what they see', *Child Development* 59, 703–11.

Taylor, M., & Bacharach, V. R. (1981) 'The development of drawing rules: metaknowledge about drawing influences performance on nondrawing tasks', *Child Development* 52, 373–5.

Terman, L. M., & Merrill, M. A. (1960) *Stanford-Binet Intelligence Scale*, Boston, MA: Houghton Mifflin.

Thistlewood, D. (1992) 'Observational drawing and the National Curriculum', in *Drawing Research and Development*, ed. D. Thistlewood, Harlow: Longman/NSEAD, pp. 153–64.

Thomas, G. V., Chaigne, E., & Fox, T. J. (1989) 'Children's drawings of topics differing in significance: effects on size of drawing', *British Journal of Developmental Psychology* 7, 321–31.

Thomas, G. V., & Gray, R. (1992) 'Children's drawings of topics differing in emotional significance – effects on placement relative to self-drawing: a research note', *Journal of Child Psychology and Psychiatry* 33, 1097–104.

Thomas, G. V., & Jolley, R. P. (1998) 'Drawing conclusions: a re-examination of empirical and conceptual bases for psychological evaluation of children from their drawings', *British Journal of Clinical Psychology* 37, 127–39.

Thomas, G. V., Nye, R., & Robinson, E. J. (1994) 'How children view pictures: children's responses to pictures and things in themselves and as representations of something else', *Cognitive Development* 9, 141–64.

Thomas, G. V., Nye, R., Rowley, M., & Robinson, E. J. (2001) 'What is a picture? Children's conceptions of pictures', *British Journal of Developmental Psychology* 19, 475–91.

Thomas, G. V., & Tsalimi, A. (1988) 'Effects of order of drawing head and trunk on their relative sizes in children's human figure drawings', *British Journal of Developmental Psychology* 6, 191–203.

Thompson, J. (1885) *Through Masailand – a Journey of Exploration*, London: Sampson Low, Marston Searle & Rivington.

Thompson, T. M. (1999) 'Drawing together: peer influence in preschool-kindergarten art classes', *Visual Arts Research* 25, 61–8.

Toku, M. (2002) 'Cross-cultural analysis of artistic development: drawing by Japanese and US children', *Visual Arts Research* 27, 46–59.

Tomkins, S. S. (ed.) (1995) *Exploring Affect: the Selected Writings of Sylvan S. Tomkins*, Cambridge: Cambridge University Press.

Töpffer, R. (1848) *Réflexions et menus à propos d'un peintre génevois: ou essai sur le beau dans les arts*, 2 vols., Paris: J. J. Dubochet, Lechevalier et cie.

Trautner, H. M., Lohaus, A., Sahm, W. B., & Helbing, N. (1989) 'Age-graded judgments of children's drawings by children and adults', *International Journal of Behavioural Development* 12, 421–31.

Treffert, D. A. (1989) *Extraordinary People*, New York: Bantam Press.

Trowbridge, M. M. (1995) 'Graphic indicators of sexual abuse in children's drawings: a review of the literature', *Arts in Psychotherapy* 22, 485–93.

Tryphon, A., & Montangero, J. (1992) 'The development of diachronic thinking in children: children's ideas about changes in drawing skills', *International Journal of Behavioural Development* 15, 411–24.

Tsoi, M. M., & Sundberg, N. D. (1989) 'Patterns of psychological test use in Hong Kong', *Professional Psychology: Research and Practice* 20, 248–50.

Tyldesley, J. A., & Bahn, P. G. (1983) 'Use of plants in the European Palaeolithic: a review of the evidence', *Quaternary Science Reviews* 2, 53–81.

Tyler, C. W. (1978) 'Some new entoptic phenomena', *Vision Research* 18, 1633–9.

Tyrrell, D. J., Anderson, J. T., Clubb, M., & Bradbury, A. (1987) 'Infants' recognition of the correspondence between photographs and caricature of the human face', *Bulletin of the Psychonomic Society* 25, 41–3.

Ulman, E., & Levy, B. I. (1973) 'Art therapists as diagnosticians', paper presented at the annual meeting of the American Art Therapy Association, Columbus, Ohio.

Van Sommers, P. (1984) *Drawing and Cognition*, Cambridge: Cambridge University Press.

(1995) 'Observational, experimental and neuropsychological studies of drawing', in *Drawing and Looking*, ed. C. Lange-Küttner & G. V. Thomas, Hemel Hempstead: Harvester/Wheatsheaf, pp. 44–61.

Vasari, G. (1885–7) *Lives of the Most Eminent Painters, Sculptors and Architects*, translated by Mrs J. Foster, London: Bell.

Velo, J. (1984) 'Ochre as medicine: a suggestion from the interpretation of the archaeological record', *Current Anthropology* 25, 674.

Viola, W. (1936) *Child Art and Franz Cizek*, Vienna: Austrian Junior Red Cross.

Vitebsky, P. (1995) *The Shaman*, London: Macmillan.

Vygotsky, L. (1962) *Thought and Language*, Cambridge, MA: MIT Press.

(1978) *Mind in Society: the development of higher psychological processes*, Cambridge, MA: Harvard University Press.

Wales, R. (1990) 'Children's pictures', in *Understanding Children*, ed. R. Grieve & M. Hughes, Oxford: Basil Blackwell, pp. 140–55.

Wall, J. (1959) 'The base line in children's drawings of self and its relationship to aspects of overt behavior', Ph.D. dissertation, Florida State University.

Walton, G. E., Armstrong, E., & Bower, T. G. R. (1998) 'Newborns learn to identify a face in eight-tenths of a second', *Developmental Science* 1, 79–84.

Walton, G. E., Bower, N. J. A., & Bower, T. G. R. (1992) 'Recognition of familiar faces by newborns', *Infant Behavior and Development* 15, 265–9.

Wartofsky, M. W. (1972) 'Pictures, representation and the understanding', in *Logic and Art: essays in honor of Nelson Goodman*, ed. R. Rudner & I. Scheffler, Indianapolis: Bobbs-Merrill, pp. 150–62.

Watkins, C. E., Campbell, V. L., Nieberding, R., & Hallmark, R. (1995) 'Contemporary practice of psychological assessment by clinical psychologists', *Professional Psychology: Research and Practice* 26, 54–60.

Wechsler, D. (1974) *Manual for the Wechsler Intelligence Scale for Children*, revised edition, New York: Psychological Corporation.

Wellman, H. (1990) *Children's Theories of Mind*, Cambridge, MA: MIT Press/Bradford Books.

Werner, H. (1948) *Comparative Psychology of Mental Development*, Chicago, IL: Follett.

Werner, H., & Kaplan, B. (1963) *Symbol Formation*, New York: John Wiley.

Wertheimer, M. (1923) 'Untersuchungen zur Lehre von der Gestalt, II', *Psychologische Forschung* 4, 301–50.

Wesson, M., & Salmon, K. (2001) 'Drawing and showing: helping children to report emotionally laden events', *Applied Cognitive Psychology* 15, 301–20.

Wexner, L. B. (1954) 'The degree to which colors' hues are associated with mood-toners', *Journal of Applied Psychology* 38, 432–5.

Whitley, D. S. (1988) 'Comment on J. D. Lewis-Williams & T. A. Dowson, "The signs of all times: entoptic phenomena in Upper Palaeolithic art"', *Current Anthropology* 29, 238.

Wilkinson, R. (1993) *Rudolf Steiner on Education: a compendium*, Gloucester: Hawthorn Press.

Willats, J. (1977) 'How children learn to draw realistic pictures', *Quarterly Journal of Experimental Psychology* 29, 367–82.

(1981) 'What do the marks in the picture stand for?', *Review of Research in Visual Art Education* 13, 18–33.

(1985) 'Drawing systems revisited: the role of denotation systems in children's figure drawings', in *Visual Order: the nature and development of pictorial representation*, ed. N. H. Freeman & M. V. Cox, Cambridge: Cambridge University Press, pp. 78–100.

(1987) 'Marr and pictures: an information processing account of children's drawings', *Archives de Psychologie* 55, 105–25.

(1992a) 'Seeing lumps, sticks, and slabs in silhouettes', *Perception* 21, 481–96.

(1992b) 'The representation of extendedness in children's drawings of sticks and discs', *Child Development* 63, 692–710.

(1992c) 'What *is* the matter with Mary Jane's drawing?', in *Drawing Research and Development*, ed. D. Thistlewood, Harlow: Longman/NSEAD, pp. 141–52.

(1995) 'An information-processing approach to drawing development', in *Drawing and Looking*, ed. C. Lange-Küttner & G. V. Thomas, Hemel Hempstead: Harvester/Wheatsheaf, pp. 27–43.

(1997) *Art and Representation: new principles in the analysis of pictures*, Princeton, NJ: Princeton University Press.

Wilson, A. (1993) 'Children's drawings: more than just pretty pictures?', *Top Santé Health and Beauty*, September, 36–9.

Wilson, B. (1985) 'The artistic tower of Babel: inextricable links between culture and graphic development', *Visual Arts Research* 11, 90–104.

(1992) 'Primitivism, the avant-garde and the art of little children', in *Drawing Research and Development*, ed. D. Thistlewood, Harlow: Longman/NSEAD, pp. 14–25.

(1997a) 'Child art, multiple interpretations, and conflicts of interest', in *Child Development in Art*, ed. A. M. Kindler, Reston, VA: National Art Education Association, pp. 81–94.

(1997b) 'Types of child art and alternative developmental accounts: interpreting the interpreters', *Human Development* 40, 155–68.

(2000) 'Empire of signs revisited: children's manga and the changing face of Japan', in *The Cultural Context: comparative studies of art education and children's drawings*, ed. L. Lindström, Stockholm: Stockholm University Press, pp. 160–78.

Wilson, B., & Ligtvoet, J. (1992) 'Across time and cultures: stylistic changes in the drawings of Dutch children', in *Drawing Research and Development*, ed. D. Thistlewood, Harlow: Longman/NSEAD, pp. 75–88.

Wilson, B., & Wilson, M. (1977) 'An iconoclastic view of the imagery sources in the drawings of young people', *Art Education* 30, 4–12.

(1982) 'The case of the disappearing two-eyed profile: or how little children influence the drawings of little children', *Review of Research in Visual Arts Education* 15, 19–32.

(1984) 'Children's drawings in Egypt: cultural style acquisition as graphic development', *Visual Arts Research* 10, 13–26.

(1987) 'Pictorial composition and narrative structure: themes and the creation of meaning in the drawings of Egyptian and Japanese children', *Visual Arts Research* 10, 10–21.

Wilson, I. D. (1995) 'Children's experience of war as expressed through their drawing', unpublished undergraduate thesis, University of Birmingham.

Wiltshire, S. (1987) *Drawings*, London: J. M. Dent.

(1991) *Floating Cities: Venice, Amsterdam, Moscow, Leningrad*, London: Michael Joseph.

Winner, E. (1982) 'Children's conceptions (and misconceptions) of the arts', in *Art, Mind and Brain: a cognitive approach to creativity*, ed. H. Gardner, New York: Basic Books, pp. 103–9.

(1989) 'How can Chinese children draw so well?', *Journal of Aesthetic Education* 22, 17–34.

(1996) *Gifted Children: myths and realities*, New York: Basic Books.

Winner, E., Blank, P., Massey, C., & Gardner, H. (1983) 'Children's sensitivity to aesthetic properties of line drawings', in *The Acquisition of Symbolic Skills*, ed. D. Rogers & J. A. Sloboda, New York: Plenum Press, pp. 97–104.

Winner, E., & Gardner, H. (1981) 'The art in children's drawings', *Review of Research in Visual Arts Education* 14, 18–31.

(1988) Book review of Parsons' *How We Understand Art: a cognitive developmental account of aesthetic experience*, *Human Development* 31, 256–60.

Winner, E., & Martino, G. (1993) 'Giftedness in the visual arts and music', in *International Handbook of Research and Development of Giftedness and Talent*, New York: Pergamon Press, pp. 253–81.

Winner, E., Rosenblatt, E., Windmueller, G., Davidson, L., & Gardner, H. (1986) 'Children's perception of "aesthetic" properties of the arts: domain-specific or pan-artistic?', *British Journal of Developmental Psychology* 4, 149–60.

Winston, A. S., Kenyon, B., Stewardson, J., & Lepine, T. (1995) 'Children's sensitivity to expression of emotion in drawings', *Visual Arts Research* 21, 1–14.

Winter, W. (1963) 'The perception of safety posters by Bantu industrial workers', *Psychologia Africana* 10, 127–35.

Wishart, J. G. (1993) 'The development of learning difficulties in children with DS', *Journal of Intellectual Disability Research* 37, 389–403.

Wohl, A., & Kaufman, B. (1985) *Silent Screams and Hidden Cries: an interpretation of artwork by children from violent homes*, New York: Brunner/Mazel.

Wolf, D., & Perry, D. (1988) 'From endpoints to repertoires: some new conclusions about drawing development', *Journal of Aesthetic Education* 22, 17–34.

Wollheim, R. (1993) *The Mind and its Depth*, Cambridge, MA: Harvard University Press.

Wood, D. J., Bruner, J. S., & Ross, G. (1976) 'The role of tutoring in problem-solving', *Journal of Child Psychology & Psychiatry* 17, 89–100.

Wood, D., & Middleton, D. (1975) 'A study of assisted problem-solving', *British Journal of Psychology* 66, 181–91.

Woodhouse, M. J. (1998) 'Investigating and managing the child with special needs', *Ophthalmic and Physiological Optics* 18, 147–52.

Woolley, J. D., & Wellman, H. M. (1990) 'Young children's understanding of realities, nonrealities, and appearances', *Child Development* 61, 946–61.

Yamagata, K. (1997) 'Representational activity during mother–child interaction: the scribbling stage of drawing', *British Journal of Developmental Psychology* 15, 355–66.

(2001) 'Emergence of representational activity during the early drawing stage: process analysis', *Japanese Psychological Research* 43, 130–40.

Yates, A., Bentler, L. E., & Crago, M. (1985) 'Drawings by child victims of incest', *Child Abuse and Neglect* 9, 183–9.

Yonas, A., Arterberry, M., & Granrud, C. E. (1987) 'Space perception in infancy', in *Annals of Child Development*, vol. 4, ed. R. A. Vasta, Greenwich, CT: JAI Press, pp. 1–34.

Yonas, A., Cleaves, W., & Pettersen, L. (1978) 'Development of sensitivity to pictorial depth', *Science* 200, 77–9.

Young, A. W., Newcombe, F., de Haan, E. H. F., Small, M., & Hay, D. C. (1993) 'Face perception after brain injury: selective impairments affecting identity and expression', *Brain* 116, 941–59.

Zagòrska, W. (1996) 'Pictorial expression of emotions', *Polish Quarterly of Developmental Psychology* 2, 63–8.

Zentner, M. R. (2001) 'Preferences for colours and colour-emotion combinations in early childhood', *Developmental Science* 4, 389–98.

Zhi, Z., Thomas, G. V., & Robinson, E. J. (1997) 'Constraints on representational change: drawing a man with two heads', *British Journal of Developmental Psychology* 15, 275–90.

Zigler, E. (1969) 'Developmental versus difference theories of mental retardation and the problem of motivation', *American Journal of Mental Deficiency* 73, 536–56.

Index

Happy   Sad   Angry

Melissa, aged 5 years

Happy   Excited

Sad   Angry

Tracy, aged 7 years

Plate 1 *Drawings of different emotions by a 5-year-old and a 7-year-old.*

Happy

Excited

Calm

Sad

Sara, aged 10 years

Plate 2 *A 10-year-old's drawings of different emotions.*

Sebastian, aged 12 years

Plate 3 *A 12-year-old's drawings of different emotions.*

a. The art teacher demonstrates some swimming strokes.

b. A few children are selected to draw on the blackboard.

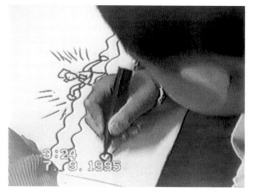

c. The children begin to draw their own pictures.

d. The children have their own sets of felt-pens.

e. The teacher discusses the drawings on the blackboard.

f. The teacher shows the children some pictures drawn by another class.

Plate 4 *An art lesson in Beijing with a class of 7-year-olds.*

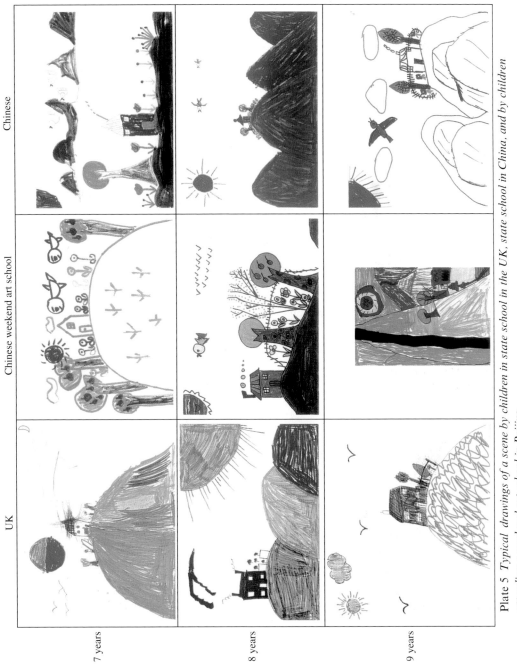

Plate 5 *Typical drawings of a scene by children in state school in the UK, state school in China, and by children attending a weekend art school in Beijing.*

Plate 6 *Typical drawings of a scene by children in state school in the UK, state school in China, and by children attending a weekend art school in Beijing.*

Steiner

Fairies in a cave with crystals (girl, 7y 6m)

A sailing boat and man (boy, 6y 5m)

A sunset (girl, 6y 7m)

Montessori

A necklace (girl, 6y 4m)

A flag (boy, 7y)

Girl with a balloon (girl, 5y 10m)

Traditional

A man on a horse (boy, 6y)

The hills (girl, 7y 11m)

An alien (boy, 7y 2m)

Plate 7 *Examples of children's free drawings in Steiner, Montessori and traditional classrooms.*

Steiner

Girl, 7y 6m   Boy, 6y 5m   Girl, 7y 4m

Montessori

Girl, 5y 11m   Boy, 7y   Girl, 6y 10m

Traditional

Boy, 7y 9m   Girl, 6y 10m   Boy, 6y

Plate 8 *Examples of drawings of a scene by children in Steiner, Montessori and traditional classrooms.*